THE OXFORD AUTHORS

GEORGE HERBERT

AND

HENRY VAUGHAN

EDITED BY

LOUIS L. MARTZ

D0206591

Oxford   New York

OXFORD UNIVERSITY PRESS

Oxford University Press, Walton Street, Oxford OX2 6DP

Oxford New York Toronto
Delhi Bombay Calcutta Madras Karachi
Petaling Jaya Singapore Hong Kong Tokyo
Nairobi Dar es Salaam Cape Town
Melbourne Auckland
and associated companies in
Berlin Ibadan

Oxford is a trade mark of Oxford University Press

First published 1986
Paperback reprinted 1992

British Library Cataloguing in Publication Data
Herbert, George, 1593–1633
George Herbert and Henry Vaughan.—
(The Oxford authors)
1. English poetry—Early modern, 1500–1700
I. Title.   II. Vaughan, Henry, 1621–1695
III. Martz, Louis L.
821'.3'08   PR1205
ISBN 0–19–281342–0

Library of Congress Cataloging in Publication Data
Herbert, George, 1593–1633.
George Herbert and Henry Vaughan.
(The Oxford authors)
Bibliography: p.   Includes index.
1. English literature—Early modern, 1500–1700.
I. Vaughan, Henry, 1621–1695.
II. Martz, Louis Lohr.   III. Series.
PR1127.H4 1985   821'.3   85–7184
ISBN 0–19–281342–0

Printed in Great Britain by
Biddles Ltd.,
Guildford and King's Lynn

THE OXFORD AUTHORS

General Editor: Frank Kermode

GEORGE HERBERT (1593–1633), descendant of two eminent families on the border of Wales, began his career as Fellow and Public Orator at Cambridge. 'Setting foot into Divinity' as early as 1618, he gradually made his way, despite ill health, toward his ordination as priest of the Church of England, in 1630, when he became rector of the parish of Fuggleston-cum-Bemerton, near Salisbury. His book of poems, *The Temple*, was published in 1633, some months after his death. His prose treatise, *The Country Parson*, did not appear until 1652. His poems met with immediate favour, and their popularity has continued up to the present day, when his reputation as poet is higher than at any time since the seventeenth century.

HENRY VAUGHAN (1621–95) was born of Welsh parents at Newton-by-Usk, in Breconshire, and may, like his twin brother Thomas, have spoken Welsh as his earliest language. After attending Oxford he went to London for the study of law, but this plan was broken off by the outbreak of civil war in 1642. Returning to his home in Wales, he seems to have joined the King's army there in 1645, and may have participated in the battle of Rowton Heath. He deeply resented the overthrow of the monarchy and the established Church in the late 1640s, years which also saw the death of a much-loved younger brother. These events coincided with the development of Vaughan's intense admiration for the poetry of George Herbert, demonstrated in *Silex Scintillans* (1650), where Vaughan transcends his earlier secular poems by creating religious poetry in a manner strongly influenced by Herbert. After the second edition of *Silex Scintillans* (1655) he wrote little poetry, but pursued for his remaining forty years a successful career as a country physician in Breconshire. His poems received little attention until the nineteenth century; today it is generally recognized that his poems at their best can 'match' Herbert's, as he hoped.

Louis L. Martz is Sterling Professor Emeritus of English at Yale University. He is the author of four books on seventeenth-century poetry: *The Poetry of Meditation, The Paradise Within, The Wit of Love,* and *Poet of Exile* (on Milton). He is co-editor of Thomas More's *Dialogue of Comfort* in the Yale edition of More's works. He has also written extensively on twentieth-century poetry, and has recently edited the *Collected Poems* of 'H.D.'.

Frank Kermode, retired King Edward VII Professor of English Literature at Cambridge, the General Editor of the Oxford Authors Series, is the author of many books, including *Romantic Image, The Sense of an Ending, The Classic, Genesis of Secrecy, Forms of Attention,* and *History and Value.*

CONTENTS

INTRODUCTION

THE appearance of the poems of Herbert and Vaughan in one volume might have pleased both poets, although Vaughan would surely have disclaimed any thought of equality with the earlier poet whom he called a 'true saint and a seer', a writer of 'incomparable prophetic poems', and 'the first that with any effectual success attempted a diversion of this foul and overflowing stream' of secular poetry in England.[1] Vaughan treated Herbert's poetry as virtually a continuation of sacred scripture, and he echoed Herbert's words almost as much as he echoed the Bible. These manifold echoes of Herbert—frequent beyond the signs of influence found in any other important English poet—are a tribute to a guide both in poetry and in personal life; they serve as a constant reminder of the example that helped to transform Henry Vaughan from a writer of competent social and memorial verse (in the manner of the Sons of Ben Jonson) into a powerful religious poet.

The tribute is announced and implied throughout the first edition of *Silex Scintillans* (1650), where Vaughan's subtitle echoes the sub-title of *The Temple* (1633), and the poems themselves gradually reveal their debt to Herbert, until, in the middle of the volume, the debt is openly and gratefully acknowledged, as Vaughan in *The Match* thrusts his 'stubborn heart' into the 'Deed' that Herbert had signed over to God in his poem *Obedience*, with the closing wish: 'How happy were my part, / If some kind man would thrust his heart / Into these lines.' Vaughan is that kindred man, and he proves it in poems that immediately precede and follow *The Match*, poems where Herbertian echoes are concentrated, especially in *The Resolve, Unprofitableness*, and *Rules and Lessons*, with its twenty-four epigrammatic stanzas in the very mode of Herbert's *Church-porch*. The titles throughout remind us of Herbert, and the final poem, *Begging*, utters its prayer of hope in the cadences of Herbert's *L'Envoy*:

> King of Mercy, King of Love,
> In whom I live, in whom I move,
> Perfect what thou hast begun,
> Let no night put out this Sun;

[1] *Mount of Olives*, Vaughan's *Works*, ed. L. C. Martin (2nd edn., Oxford, 1957), p. 186; and the 1655 Preface, below, p. 346.

> Grant I may, my chief desire!
> Long for thee, to thee aspire,
> Let my youth, my bloom of days
> Be my comfort and thy praise . . .

Such is the dominant tone of *Silex 1650*, despite its sombre view of the world at large. The volume takes its basic motive from the experience symbolized by the engraved title-page, which shows a stony heart changed into living flesh by the hand of God, striking from a cloud. *Regeneration*, the opening poem, tells the full story: the speaker has been born again. Answering the mysterious call, he is led into 'a fair, fresh field' reserved for 'Prophets, and friends of God'. From here he sees a grove

> Of stately height, whose branches met
> And mixed on every side;
> I entered, and once in
> (Amazed to see't)
> Found all was changed, and a new spring
> Did all my senses greet . . .

What actually happened we shall never know: only what the poems tell us. We do know that some time during the early 1640s, at the outbreak of civil war, Vaughan gave up his study of law in London and returned to his native Wales, in the valley of the Usk; there at some point he took up or resumed his studies in that occult 'Hermetic philosophy' in which his twin brother Thomas was immersed;[2] and these studies, it seems, led him toward his later, forty-year career as a country physician in Breconshire. He renounced his earlier secular verse, in *Mount of Olives* (I) and *Idle Verse*, and delayed the publication of his secular volume *Olor Iscanus*, issued belatedly (and evidently with some pruning) in 1651, with a dedication by the author dated 17 December 1647. The death of his brother William, the destruction of his beloved 'British Church', the defeat and execution of his King—all these events no doubt played their part. His identification of himself as 'Henry Vaughan, Silurist' on the title-page of *Silex 1650* shows his determined loyalty to his native Wales, for *Silures* was the name given by Tacitus to the Welsh tribe of Vaughan's region which fiercely opposed the Roman conquest[3] (does

---

[2] See the long note on *Resurrection and Immortality*, below, pp. 486–8, the studies by Elizabeth Holmes and Ross Garner (Further Reading), and the numerous articles on this topic listed in Rudrum's edition of Vaughan's poems.

[3] See Tacitus, *Annals*, xii. 32–3, 39–40, and *Agricola*, 11, 17.

this imply an equal opposition to the powers now victorious in England?).

Whatever the causes, in 1650 Vaughan emerges as a different poet, in theme, in style, in quality. He has learned from Herbert the use of easy colloquial language in poetical colloquy with God and with the self; and he uses that language flexibly in variant stanza-forms, as Herbert did. But he does not give up his earlier training in the School of Ben, which also practised a colloquial mode: many of his best poems here are cast in pentameter or octosyllabic couplets—forms not often used by Herbert in *The Church*. Vaughan is his own man; if he echoes a Herbertian title or phrase, the context is usually quite different; it is as though Herbert's words had become part of Vaughan's own vocabulary, and so he uses them as he will.

The differences between the two poets are great. Herbert, born in 1593, is writing in the era when the Church of England is still attempting to hold many branches of belief within its fold. The Calvinist clergy are dominant, but they are not all-powerful. They cannot change or remove the Book of Common Prayer, and they cannot alter the Thirty-Nine Articles toward a firmer Calvinism, as they attempted to do in 1595, in the days of the Lambeth Articles, when their efforts were brusquely averted by the intervention of Cecil on the Queen's behalf. Richard Hooker has written his temperate, inclusive, reasonable treatises on ecclesiastical polity—not yet nearly as influential as they were later to become. Still, the residue of traditionalism ('popery', some would call it) was large enough, and the reaction against Calvinism represented by Arminius in Holland was strong enough, to encourage Laud and Charles I, after his accession in 1625, to attempt a massive movement of the Church to the right—thus leaving the firm Calvinists to feel that, somehow, after years of acceptance, they were no longer regarded as members in good standing.

Herbert grew to maturity amid these rising tensions. As a student and fellow at Cambridge, stronghold of Calvinism in his day, he may well have been attracted toward the stricter aspects of that creed; evidence may be found throughout *The Temple*, as recent studies of Herbert have shown.[4] The problem is to ascertain the role these doctrines play in the whole body of Herbert's work, as he moved toward his ordination in the Church, first as deacon in 1624, and

[4] See the studies by Barbara Lewalski, A. D. Nuttall, and Richard Strier, listed in Further Reading.

then as priest in 1630, only three years before his death. The problem may be illustrated by looking closely at *The Holdfast*, a poem that certainly lends itself to a Calvinist interpretation.

The title is especially characteristic of Herbert, since a 'holdfast' in his day meant any common device for holding things together, such as a clamp or bolt; but the term also holds fast three biblical echoes (see notes). The poem dramatizes a situation of acute significance in this era: the human being feels that there must be *something*, however small, that he can do in striving toward his own salvation; but the strict doctrine of the Calvinist says that one can do nothing: only faith can save, faith granted by God to some, through the imputed merits of Christ. We have nothing to do with the process; to the strict Calvinist the recipients of faith have been predestined by the will of God before the beginning of time. But the persistent human urge to believe that there must be *some* part a person can play was the constant enemy of Calvinism.

Thus the speaker in Herbert's sonnet begins by saying, 'I threatened to observe the strict decree / Of my dear God with all my power and might.' (This is a peculiar and perhaps colloquial use of the word 'threatened'; it means something like, 'I vowed earnestly'.) 'But', the poem continues, 'I was told by one, it could not be; / Yet I might trust in God to be my light.' All right, says the speaker, 'Then will I trust . . . in him alone.' I will have Faith. 'Nay,' says the other voice, 'ev'n to trust in him, was also his: / We must confess that nothing is our own.' All right, says the speaker, 'Then I confess that he my succour is'; only to receive the stern reply: 'But to have nought is ours, not to confess / That we have nought.' This crucial point of Reformation teaching brings the speaker to a state of astonishment, puzzlement, and deep anxiety: 'I stood amazed at this, / Much troubled, till I heard a friend express, / That all things were more ours by being his.' Is the 'friend' the same as the 'one' who has brought the speaker into such trouble? Possibly so, and yet the tones of voice are quite different, and we know from other poems who the 'friend' is. It is the inward voice of Christ explaining that all things, including all human powers, all human faculties, are now 'more ours by being his'. The Incarnation redeemed humanity, so that our human powers are restored: we *can* do something now, as the final couplet may be taken to explain: 'What Adam had, and forfeited for all, / Christ keepeth now, who cannot fail or fall.' To the strict Calvinist, these lines might indicate no more than the doctrine of imputed righteousness. To others, they might indicate the restoration of free will; 'What Adam had' is now 'more ours'. Whichever view we take, salvation is ours, since the 'holdfast' is the Christ of Hebrews 4: 14: 'Seeing then that we have a great high priest, that is passed into the heavens, Jesus the Son of God, let us hold fast our profession.' The ambiguity seems deliberate; as Herbert says in *Divinity*, he would avoid those 'curious questions and divisions' that have 'jagged' the 'seamless coat' of Christ.

In line with this pacific aim, his poem *The Priesthood* shows Herbert to be a sturdy Protestant of the middle way: the office of the priest is twofold: to convey the Word of God in sermons and to convey God himself in the sacrament of Communion. His 'Parson's Church' shows a discreet love of ceremonies; Herbert urges that the church should, for example, be 'at great festivals strawed, and stuck with boughs, and perfumed with incense', and 'that there be a fitting and sightly Communion cloth of fine linen, with an handsome and seemly carpet of good and costly stuff'. 'And all this he doth, not as out of necessity, or as putting a holiness in the things, but as desiring to keep the middle way between superstition and slovenliness.'[5] Herbert's treatment of the bitter controversies over the question of the efficacy of the Communion sacrament is equally judicious. In his poem *The H. Communion* which appears in *The Temple* (unlike the laboured and brashly witty poem by that title that he discarded) Herbert tactfully and subtly grants a measure of truth to both sides. He grants the elements of bread and wine a limited efficacy: they do work to subdue sin in the flesh: they 'spread their forces into every part / Meeting sin's force and art.' But the major work of participation is spiritual, performed by 'thy grace, which with these elements comes'. Still, the sacrament is more than a 'token', more than a mere commemoration. Elsewhere, as in *Love Unknown*, the poem may suggest that all is done by solely spiritual means, directed toward the chosen individual participant: the speaker bathes his heart 'with holy blood, / Which at a board, while many drunk bare wine, / A friend did steal into my cup for good'. But this is the utterance of a naïve speaker who does not understand what is happening to him. In *The Invitation* the speaker invites 'All' to the Communion, saying that 'it seems but just and right / In my sight / Where is All, there All should be.' He is not speaking as one of the chosen to the chosen. In any case, the theology implicit in any given poem arises from that poem's individual dramatic situation.

[5] *The Country Parson*, chapter 13.

Herbert's ideal, then, is represented in his poem *The British Church*: going neither to the extreme of elaborate ceremony fostered by Rome, nor to the extreme of naked worship advocated by Geneva: 'The mean, thy praise and glory is, / And long may be.' This is his ideal of Christianity, founded among the ancient Britons, legend says, by Joseph of Arimathea, and thus independent of Rome from the first: hence, the *British* Church, the true, primeval Church. But this is, as Herbert well knows, an ideal hardly to be found on earth. His poem *Church-rents and Schisms* shows his full awareness of how 'debates and fretting jealousies' did 'worm and work within' the lovely Rose of Sharon until its 'ruddy' hue has turned to 'pale and bleak'. And in *The Priesthood* he feels how the Church seems to shake 'Through th' old sins and new doctrines of our land'.

The poems dramatize the self in the act of confronting almost every sort of problem met by a devout Christian in his day, problems of sin and salvation, faith, grace, predestination, conscience, assurance, confession, Communion, Baptism—every issue finds its echo here within the soul of the speaker as he attempts, in the presence of God, to quell the quarrels of sense with spirit, of doctrine with doctrine, and to find a way in which his ideal of *The Family* may in some measure work within the self: 'What doth this noise of thoughts within my heart, / As if they had a part? . . . Turn out these wranglers, which defile thy seat: / For where thou dwellest all is neat.'

> Joys oft are there, and griefs as oft as joys;
> But griefs without a noise:
> Yet speak they louder than distempered fears.
> What is so shrill as silent tears?

But again, it is a goal not to be reached on earth; the 'noise' breaks out in the next poem: 'Content thee, greedy heart.'

Other issues are at work here too, for Herbert is a man who loves the arts of the Renaissance in poetry, music, and oratory. He was himself official Orator at Cambridge: a man who had trained himself to use all the flowers of rhetoric. He frequently speaks of his lute and his 'ditties', his kindred arts of music and poetry. Unlike Vaughan, Herbert is highly sophisticated in these arts; his problem is, how to subdue these acquirements to the service of God, how to display his craft and wit without self-interest, how to praise God with his 'versing'. The problem and the solution are both presented in *Jordan* (II), a poem that might be said to work in the shape of a Yeatsian gyre, or two Poundian vortices set end to end. Most of the poem is given over to showing how much art he has learned, how much craft he knows, until at the close the divine 'friend' of all his poems tells him, smiling, we may suppose, as in *Love* (III): 'There is in love a sweetness ready penned: / Copy out only that, and save expense.' Here, as everyone has noted, Herbert echoes the ending of Sidney's opening sonnet to Stella; but beyond this, the whole poem evokes the ironic Sidneyan posture that appears frequently in *Astrophil and Stella*, the guise of one who seeks only 'simplicity.' This poet knows all the arts of secular love-poetry. But how, how does one proceed to 'copy out' the 'sweetness' of the love of God? True, the story of that love is 'ready penned' in the Bible, but how does one 'copy out' the story of a universal, immortal, sacrificial love, told by one who says, in the gospel of John, 'all things that I have heard of my Father I have made known unto you'? Copy out *only* that? The friend, it seems, has given the poet an inexhaustible, unfathomable subject, but not the way of copying. The way is human and must be found in human art, which, after all, is the work of the creative faculties implanted in man as the Image of God. The problem is to find the proper restrained, 'decent', moderate, 'neat' use of those faculties in poetry.

The result is the peculiar achievement of intense compression found in Herbert's best poems: a powerful wit condensed and concentrated; immense skill and art held under firm control, the craft revealing itself in a crafty management of the reader, who often, like the naïve speaker in the poem, finds the ending a witty surprise.

It was a mode of writing from which Vaughan could learn much, but he could not re-create the essence of Herbert's concentrated art; and he did not often try to do so. Vaughan's best manner is diffuse, expansive, earnest, groping, seeking to express an inner conviction, seeking to maintain the memory of an inner light—not to engage in sharp interior debate, contesting with the noise of thoughts within the heart. His poem *Mount of Olives* (II) is a companion-piece to Herbert's *Jordan* (II) and *The Glance*; it is replete with Herbertian echoes, but its floating, associative, incremental movement, done in fluent pentameter couplets, is all Vaughan's own, as its sense of actual landscape is his own:

> So have I known some beauteous *paisage* rise
> In sudden flowers and arbours to my eyes,
> And in the depth and dead of winter bring
> To my cold thoughts a lively sense of spring.

As this whole poem implies, the centre of Vaughan's poetical inspiration lies in such memories of moments of 'light', moments of a felt, experienced unity with the Creation and with the divine power working through this Creation. The basic drama that runs throughout his poetry has little to do with theological issues or with internal debates: his best poems either enact a search for a light that has disappeared, or break forth in praise of a moment when the vision of a possible unity of all being has been glimpsed, as in *The Morning-watch*:

> O joys! Infinite sweetness! with what flowers,
> And shoots of glory, my soul breaks and buds!
> > All the long hours
> > Of night and rest
> > Through the still shrouds
> > Of sleep and clouds,
> This dew fell on my breast;
> > O how it *bloods*,
> And *spirits* all my earth! hark! In what rings,
> And *hymning circulations* the quick world
> > Awakes and sings . . .

The outer world of *Man* is a sombre scene:

> He knows he hath a home, but scarce knows where,
> > He says it is so far
> That he hath quite forgot how to go there . . .
> Man is the shuttle, to whose winding quest
> > And passage through these looms
> God ordered motion, but ordained no rest.

But in nature, in herbs and stars, in vivid and sustained reading of the Bible, and sometimes in the depths of the self, Vaughan can find the sense of unity with the divine that he is seeking. In *Religion*, where he walks in the 'groves' of the Bible, in *Vanity of Spirit*, where he briefly, very briefly, seems to have a glimpse of the shattered Image of God within the self, in 'And do they so', where he communes with the other creatures, in *Corruption*, where he lingers in the afterglow of the Bible's 'early days', in *The Retreat*, where he imagines the 'early days' of the soul's new birth, in *The World*, where all the dark follies and evils of man are enclosed within that 'great *Ring* of pure and endless light'—in such poems Vaughan seems to move beyond the reach of art into regions of experience that Herbert does not enter. In his quest Vaughan calls upon many traditions of thought to help: the three 'Books' of the old Augustinians, a triad still current in Vaughan's day, the Bible, the Book of the Creatures, and the Book of the Soul; the contemporary renaissance of platonism in England; the occult philosophy attributed to the mythical Hermes Trismegistus; and the principles of 'regeneration' according to the Reformed theology of the Church of England. But mainly he proceeds by the sort of interior search of the memory represented in the next-to-last poem of *Silex 1650*, 'I walked the other day (to spend my hour)'. Here the fluent, associative movement of thought begins with the 'gallant flower'—a phrase borrowed from Herbert—but this flower is remembered growing from the 'soil' of a certain 'field'. He recalls how in winter he 'digged about' and finally found 'the warm Recluse'—'Where fresh and green / He lived of us unseen.' This personification of the root, with religious overtones, leads toward a sudden shift into a memory of the deathbed or grave of the dead brother ('I threw the clothes quite o'er his head'), and from here by an easy transition into a prayer that the speaker may 'track' the 'steps' of God in the Creation, 'And by those hid ascents climb to that day / Which breaks from thee / Who art in all things, though invisibly . . .'

> There, hid in thee, show me his life again
> At whose dumb urn
> Thus all the year I mourn.

The quiet conclusion returns the poem to earth and to the memory of the beloved brother, drawing the whole poem together. It is a poem well placed at the close of *Silex 1650*, for it seems, in Vaughan's associative way, to draw the whole volume together with an action of the whole man in meditation. The contrast between the 'day' that breaks from God and the mourner at the 'dumb urn' completes the imagery of light against darkness that runs in many patterns throughout the book: the beams, flames, fires, rays, sunshine, the 'fiery thread' of stars, the 'train of lights' remembered sadly from 'those sunshine days' of Eden, the 'fiery-liquid light' that 'some say' makes up the heavens—all these and many other flashes of light play off against the imagery of cloud, mist, shadow, veil, dust, and grave[6] that constitute the 'thick darkness' of this life. *Silex Scintillans*: the flashing flint: the search to remember, maintain, or recover the 'ray' thus provides the volume's unifying imagery and central theme.

The large body of new poems added in 1655 creates a subtle shift in the dominant tone and meaning of the book, a change in which

---

[6] See Frank Kermode, 'The Private Imagery of Henry Vaughan', *Review of English Studies*, New Series, i (1950), pp. 206–25.

some of the causes may perhaps be glimpsed in the second poem
Begging:

> My sins long since have made thee strange,
> A very stranger unto me;
> No morning-meetings since this change,
> Nor evening-walks have I with thee.
>
> Why is my God thus slow and cold,
> When I am most, most sick and sad?
> Well fare those blessèd days of old
> When thou didst hear the *weeping lad*!

Something has happened between 1650 and 1655 to change the
dominant tone, as Vaughan suggests in the enigmatic words of the
prose preface that he added for the 1655 edition (in which the unsold sheets of 1650 were bound up with new matter): 'By the last
poems in the book (were not that mistake here prevented) you would
judge all to be fatherless, and the edition posthume; for (indeed) *I
was nigh unto death*, and am still at no great distance from it; which
was the necessary reason for that solemn and accomplished dress,
you will now find this impression in.' What does he mean by the
'solemn and accomplished dress' of this second edition? First of all,
perhaps, he refers to the removal of the dramatic title-page of 1650,
with its engraved emblem, and its replacement by a sober, even
sombre, printed title-page bearing the motto from Job that begins
'Where is God my Maker, who giveth Songs in the night?' The
earlier title-page had no need to ask that question. Following the
prose preface we have now the solemn series of biblical texts, a chain
of verses woven into a personal psalm of prayer and thanksgiving for
deliverance from death. And then we have the extended verses of
dedication, where the new portion begins by saying 'Dear Lord, 'tis
finished.' That is, the book of poems (and perhaps the life that wrote
them) is finished: the book is truly 'accomplished', done, and the
poems of the second part, with all their frequent laments, move
toward a faith consolidated, stable, and affirmed—ready for death.
Stable and affirmed, yes, but except for eight or nine poems that
show the poet at his best, the new poems do not work at the level
generally though not always achieved in 1650. They rely more overtly
on the Bible than the poems of 1650, and many seem to struggle
for utterance, as in *Childhood* (a poem that one might compare with
The Retreat of 1650). The 1655 volume has a completeness of its
own, but it is not the vital unity of 1650, where, as one looks back,
everything seems to radiate outward from the face within the blazing,

bleeding, weeping heart on the title-page, and also from the *Rules and Lessons* and *The Match* manifested at the volume's literal centre.

Herbert's *Temple* has its unity too, chiefly in its major, central portion, *The Church*, rather than in the side-wings, *The Church-porch* and *The Church Militant*, long poems that seem rather imposed on either side than organically related to the whole. The first of course serves as preparation for entering the heart's sanctuary, and the latter shows the results in the outer world; but these relations seem more theoretical than poetically proven. *The Church*, however, has a sustained dramatic unity that has been the subject of many critical essays—and justly so, for the means of unity are manifold and subtle. After the first fifteen poems have set forth the basic principles of Christianity in sacramental and liturgical terms, the book plunges with *Nature* into the long body of conflicts that constitute the major drama of the inward 'Church'. These conflicts reveal, with all their veerings and reversals, a progress toward a region of greater assurance and joy, a region attained and realized in *The Flower*:

> And now in age I bud again,
> After so many deaths I live and write;
> I once more smell the dew and rain,
> And relish versing: O my only light,
>   It cannot be
>   That I am he
> On whom thy tempests fell all night.

The struggle of course is not over; in *The Answer*, four poems later, 'My comforts drop and melt away like snow.' But the comforts soon return and they are frequent: the dominant mood of the book after *The Flower* is set by his version of *The 23d Psalm*:

> The God of love my shepherd is,
>   And he that doth me feed:
> While he is mine, and I am his,
>   What can I want or need?

He feels unworthy, but at the close he chooses to accept the generous and urgent invitation of his smiling host: 'You must sit down, says Love, and taste my meat: / So I did sit and eat.'

Along with this larger movement the poems offer many other modes of affiliation. Sometimes, as with *Longing* and *The Bag*, poems are explicitly paired; at other times the pairing is done at a distance: *Sin* (I) and its antidote *Prayer* (I) are separated by three sizeable poems, but they are closely affiliated, not only by their sonnet-form, but also by their identical mode of development, through a rapid series of brief analogies and definitions. At the same time, the two sonnets are held together by the sequence of poems between them: *Sin, Affliction, Repentance, Faith, Prayer*: the sequence contains the essence of Reformation theology! Similar sequences occur throughout. (Vaughan seems to have been aware of these sequences; similar patterns appear in *Silex*.)

Another poetical action working for unity is Herbert's way of repeating certain key, thematic words, sometimes dozens of times, from beginning to end of *The Church*: 'grief', 'love', 'blood', 'tears', 'sweet' or 'sweetness', 'groans', 'wine', 'affliction', 'friend'—these and other words, running throughout the volume, tend to tie the poems together as the work of one controlling mind. And finally, there is the dominant voice of the poems, a wise and trusting voice that sometimes includes within its reach a naïve and rebellious voice, along with the voice of the divine 'friend'. It is the voice that we hear plainly in *The Country Parson*, down to earth, colloquial, practical, willing to use the concrete things and words of this life as ways toward a higher reality, as in *Conscience*:

> Peace prattler, do not lour:
> Not a fair look, but thou dost call it foul:
> Not a sweet dish, but thou dost call it sour:
> Music to thee doth howl.
> By list'ning to thy chatting fears
> I have both lost mine eyes and ears.
>
> Prattler, no more, I say:
> My thoughts must work, but like a noiseless sphere;
> Harmonious peace must rock them all the day:
> No room for prattlers there.
> If thou persistest, I will tell thee,
> That I have physic to expel thee.

Thus the major voice can quell the rebel voice, with patience, with humour, and with the help of the ever-present friend.

LOUIS L. MARTZ

London, October 1984

ACKNOWLEDGEMENTS

I wish to thank the general editor, Frank Kermode, for his careful scrutiny of the introduction and notes, and for a number of helpful suggestions. I am indebted to frequent discussions with my former colleague, Conrad Russell, for a better understanding of the religious situation in seventeenth-century England. For assistance in the preparation of the modernized text and the notes I am grateful to JoLynn Bennett, Kevin Dunn, Cheryl German, and Claire Preston; it has been a pleasure to work with this gifted young generation of scholars. The notes are frequently indebted to the annotation provided in earlier editions of these poets by Hutchinson, Martin, Fogle, Rudrum, Patrides, and Lewalski, as listed in the 'Further Reading'. The extensive annotation by Hutchinson and Rudrum has been of particular help. I also wish to thank the staff of several libraries whose courtesies have helped to advance the work: Dr Williams's Library, London, the Bodleian Library, the Beinecke Rare Book and Manuscript Library, and the Sterling Memorial Library of Yale University. The Bodleian Library has supplied photographs for the reproductions of title pages: *The Temple* (Mason CC 87); *Herbert's Remains* (Mar. 376); *Silex Scintillans*, 1650 (Don. f. 208); *Silex Scintillans*, 1655 (Arch A f. 106). I am grateful to Martha Achilles for her careful preparation of the typescript. Finally, I wish to thank Hilary Feldman for her valuable advice and encouragement throughout the process of publication, and Richard Jeffery for his scrupulous reading of the notes.

L. L. M.

CHRONOLOGY

GEORGE HERBERT

1593	3 April, Herbert born in Montgomery, Wales, the fifth son of Richard and Magdalen (Newport) Herbert.
1596	Herbert's father dies, leaving his wife with seven sons and three daughters.
1596–9	Magdalen Herbert and her children living with her mother at Eyton-upon-Severn.
1599–1601	Magdalen Herbert and family move to Oxford.
1601	Magdalen Herbert establishes her household in London at Charing Cross.
1603	Queen Elizabeth dies; James VI of Scotland becomes James I of England.
1604–5	Herbert enters Westminster School.
1608	John Milton born.
1609	Magdalen Herbert marries Sir John Danvers.
	Herbert enters Trinity College, Cambridge.
1610	Near 1 January or 25 March writes letter to his mother, with two sonnets, declaring his resolution to write only religious poetry; reference to 'my late ague' suggests the bad health from which he suffered throughout his life.
1613	Bachelor of Arts degree.
1614	Minor Fellow at Trinity.
1615	John Donne ordained priest at age 43; Donne has been a friend of Herbert's mother for at least a decade.
1616	Major Fellow at Trinity.
	Shakespeare dies.
1617	Sublector at Trinity.
1618	18 March, letter to Sir John Danvers: 'You know, Sir, how I am now setting foot into Divinity, to lay the platform of my future life.'
	Praelector in Rhetoric, Cambridge.
1620	Public Orator, Cambridge (held this position until 1628).
1624	Represents Montgomery in Parliament.
	November or December (?), ordained deacon.
1625	Death of James I; accession of Charles I.
	Nicholas Ferrar establishes his community at Little Gidding, Huntingdonshire.
1626	Herbert installed by proxy in the prebend of Leighton Ecclesia, with church at Leighton Bromswold, Huntingdonshire (his presence not required for this office).
1627	Herbert's mother dies; her memorial sermon delivered by John Donne: published along with Herbert's tribute in Latin and Greek verse, *Memoriae Matris Sacrum*.

1629   Marries Jane Danvers.
1630   26 April, installed as rector of the parish of Fuggleston-cum-
            Bemerton, Wiltshire, near Salisbury.
            19 September, ordained priest in Salisbury Cathedral.
1631   John Donne dies.
1633   1 March, Herbert dies; burial in Bemerton church.
            The Temple published at Cambridge, under the supervision of
            Nicholas Ferrar.
            First edition of Donne's *Poems* published.
1652   *Herbert's Remains* published, including *The Country Parson*.

                           HENRY VAUGHAN

1621   Henry and his twin brother Thomas born at Newton-by-Usk,
            in the parish of Llansantffraed, Breconshire, Wales.
1632–8   Henry and Thomas taught by Matthew Herbert, a school-
            master and clergyman at Llangattock.
1637   Death of Ben Jonson.
1638   Thomas Vaughan admitted to Jesus College, Oxford, 4 May.
            No records for Henry, but the assumption is that he also
            attended Oxford at this time.
1640   Leaves Oxford to study law in London. Here comes under the
            influence of the poetical sons of Ben Jonson.
1642   Returns to his home in Breconshire at outbreak of civil war.
1643–5?   Serves as secretary to Judge Marmaduke Lloyd, of Brecon.
1645   Appears to have joined the armed forces being raised for King
            Charles in Wales; evidently took part in battle of Rowton
            Heath, near Chester (24 September), a disastrous defeat for
            the King. Archbishop Laud executed (10 January). Book of
            Common Prayer disestablished (4 January).
1646   *Poems, with the Tenth Satire of Juvenal Englished.* Married to
            Catherine Wise, perhaps about this time.
1647   Prepares a second volume of secular poetry, with dedication
            dated 17 December 1647; later issued with changes as *Olor
            Iscanus*, 1651.
1648   14 July, Vaughan's younger brother William dies.
            Second Civil War; the King's forces defeated.
1649   30 January. King Charles executed.
1650   *Silex Scintillans*, first edition.
            Thomas Vaughan publishes four treatises on 'Hermetic phil-
            osophy': *Anthroposophia Theomagica*, *Anima Magica Abscondita*,
            Magia Adamica, and *The Man-Mouse*, the last an answer to an
            attack by Henry More on the first two treatises.
1651   *Olor Iscanus*. Containing occasional and memorial poems, verse
            translations from Ovid (poems in exile), Ausonius, Boethius,
            and Casimir, with translations of four short prose pieces, two
            by Plutarch, one by Maximus of Tyre, and one by Antonio de
            Guevara.

Thomas Vaughan publishes another 'Hermetic' treatise, *Lumen de Lumine: or A New Magical Light Discovered*; and *The Second Wash*, another answer to his opponent Henry More.

1652   *The Mount of Olives: or, Solitary Devotions*, a prose handbook for private meditations, followed by an original prose work, *Man in Darkness, or, A Discourse of Death*, and a translation of a treatise attributed to Anselm, *Man in Glory*.

Thomas Vaughan publishes two more 'Hermetic' treatises, *Aula Lucis, or, The House of Light*, and *The Fame and Confession of the Fraternity . . . of the Rosy Cross*.

1653–4 Suffers serious illness.

1654   *Flores Solitudinis. Certain Rare and Elegant Pieces . . . Collected in his Sickness and Retirement*. Contains the following translations: *Of Temperance and Patience* and *Of Life and Death*, by Johannes Eusebius Nierembergius (a Jesuit); *The World Contemned*, by Eucherius, Bishop of Lyons (5th century); and the *Life of Blessed Paulinus . . . Bishop of Nola* (d.431), largely a translation of a Latin life by the Jesuit Francesco Sacchini.

1655   *Silex Scintillans*, second edition, enlarged.

Translation of *Hermetical Physic*, by Henry Nollius.

About this time (?) begins the practice of medicine. His first wife has died, and he marries, perhaps in this year, her sister Elizabeth. Thomas Vaughan publishes his last 'Hermetic' treatise, *Euphrates, or The Waters of the East; Being a short Discourse of that Secret Fountain, whose Water flows from Fire; and carries in it the Beams of the Sun and Moon*.

1657   Translation of *The Chymist's Key*, by Henry Nollius.

1660   Restoration of Charles II.

1666   Thomas Vaughan dies.

1678   *Thalia Rediviva*. A collection of early and late poems hitherto unpublished.

1695   23 April. Henry Vaughan dies; burial in Llansantffraed churchyard.

NOTE ON THE TEXT

THE modernized texts here presented are based upon the old-spelling texts provided by the edition of Herbert's *Works* edited by F. E. Hutchinson, and the edition of Vaughan's *Works* edited by L. C. Martin, in the Oxford English Texts (see Further Reading at end of this volume). Here and there old forms and spellings have been retained for special reasons of meaning and sound, and a few readings for Herbert have been adopted from the complete Bodleian manuscript of Herbert's poems (Tanner MS 307), and from the early manuscript of his poems now in Dr Williams's Library, London (Jones MS B 62). The latter contains only sixty-nine of the 164 poems in *The Temple*, plus six poems that were not included in the final version; I am grateful to Dr Williams's Library for permission to include these additional poems. For a full account of the Herbert manuscripts see Hutchinson's edition, pp. l–lvi, and the introductions to the facsimile editions of both manuscripts, listed in Further Reading. I would like to thank Ted-Larry Pebworth and the editors of *English Literary Renaissance* for permission to base my text of Herbert's verses to the Queen of Bohemia on the edition of those verses published in *ELR* (see Appendix I). The punctuation, in accord with the practice of Hutchinson and Martin, generally follows that of the first editions, with alterations made in cases of obscurity or excessive use of commas. A few emendations, specially noted, have also been made. In Vaughan's poems the use of italic has been retained, except for proper names, since Vaughan uses the italic to indicate special meanings: biblical echoes, technical terms, multiple meanings, and the like; the typography serves rather as the words 'pray mark' in stanza 8 of *Regeneration*.

The degree sign (°) indicates a note at the end of the book.

GEORGE HERBERT

THE
TEMPLE.
SACRED POEMS
AND
PRIVATE EJA-
CULATIONS.

By Mr. GEORGE HERBERT,
late Oratour of the Universitie
of *Cambridge*.

PSAL. 29.

*In his Temple doth every
man speak of his honour.*

CAMBRIDGE:
Printed by *Thomas Buck*
and *Roger Daniel*:

¶ And are to be sold by *Francis
Green*, stationer in
Cambridge.

The Printers to the Reader°

The dedication of this work having been made by the author to the Divine Majesty only, how should we now presume to interest any mortal man in the patronage of it? Much less think we it meet to seek the recommendation of the Muses for that which himself was confident to have been inspired by a diviner breath than flows from Helicon. The world therefore shall receive it in that naked simplicity with which he left it, without any addition either of support or ornament more than is included in itself. We leave it free and unforestalled to every man's judgement and to the benefit that he shall find by perusal. Only for the clearing of some passages, we have thought it not unfit to make the common reader privy to some few particularities of the condition and disposition of the person.

Being nobly born, and as eminently endued with gifts of the mind, and having by industry and happy education perfected them to that great height of excellency, whereof his fellowship of Trinity College in Cambridge and his Oratorship in the University, together with that knowledge which the King's court had taken of him, could make relation far above ordinary. Quitting both his deserts and all the opportunities that he had for worldly preferment, he betook himself to the sanctuary and temple of God, choosing rather to serve at God's altar than to seek the honour of State-employments. As for those inward enforcements to this course (for outward there was none) which many of these ensuing verses bear witness of, they detract not from the freedom, but add to the honour of this resolution in him. As God had enabled him, so he accounted him meet not only to be called, but to be compelled to this service, wherein his faithful discharge was such as may make him justly a companion to the primitive Saints, and a pattern or more for the age he lived in.

To testify his independency upon all others and to quicken his diligence in this kind, he used in his ordinary speech, when he made mention of the blessed name of our Lord and Saviour Jesus Christ, to add, *My Master*.

Next God, he loved that which God himself hath magnified above all things, that is, his Word, so as he hath been heard to make solemn protestation that he would not part with one leaf thereof for the whole world, if it were offered him in exchange.

His obedience and conformity to the Church and the discipline thereof was singularly remarkable. Though he abounded in private devotions, yet went he every morning and evening with his family to the church, and by his example, exhortations, and encouragements drew the greater part of his parishioners to accompany him daily in the public celebration of divine service.

As for worldly matters, his love and esteem to them was so little, as no man can more ambitiously seek, than he did earnestly endeavour the resignation of an ecclesiastical dignity° which he was possessor of. But God permitted not the accomplishment of this desire, having ordained him his instrument for reedifying of the church belonging thereunto, that had lain ruinated almost twenty years. The reparation whereof, having been uneffectually attempted by public collections, was in the end by his own and some few others' private free-will offerings successfully effected. With the remembrance whereof, as of an especial good work, when a friend went about to comfort him on his death-bed, he made answer, *It is a good work, if it be sprinkled with the blood of Christ.* Otherwise than in this respect he could find nothing to glory or comfort himself with, neither in this nor in any other thing.

And these are but a few of many that might be said, which we have chosen to premise as a glance to some parts of the ensuing book and for an example to the reader. We conclude all with his own motto, with which he used to conclude all things that might seem to tend any way to his own honour:

Less than the least of God's mercies.

The Dedication

Lord, my first fruits present themselves to thee;
Yet not mine neither: for from thee they came,
And must return. Accept of them and me,
And make us strive, who shall sing best thy name.
    Turn their eyes hither, who shall make a gain:
    Theirs, who shall hurt themselves or me, refrain.°

THE CHURCH-PORCH

Perirrhanterium°

1

Thou, whose sweet youth and early hopes enhance
Thy rate and price, and mark thee for a treasure;
Hearken unto a verser, who may chance
Rhyme thee to good, and make a bait of pleasure.
    A verse may find him, who a sermon flies,
      And turn delight into a sacrifice.

2

Beware of lust: it doth pollute and foul
Whom God in Baptism washed with his own blood.
It blots thy lesson written in thy soul;
The holy lines cannot be understood.   10
    How dare those eyes upon a Bible look,
      Much less towards God, whose lust is all their book?

3

Abstain wholly, or wed. Thy bounteous Lord
Allows thee choice of paths: take no by-ways;
But gladly welcome what he doth afford;°
Not grudging, that thy lust hath bounds and stays.°
    Continence hath his joy: weigh both; and so
      If rottenness have more, let Heaven go.

4

If God had laid all common, certainly
Man would have been th' incloser: but since now°   20
God hath impaled us, on the contrary°
Man breaks the fence, and every ground will plough.
    O what were man, might he himself misplace!
      Sure to be cross he would shift feet and face.°

5

Drink not the third glass, which thou canst not tame,
When once it is within thee, but before
Mayst rule it, as thou list; and pour the shame,°
Which it would pour on thee, upon the floor.
  It is most just to throw that on the ground,
    Which would throw me there, if I keep the round.°   30

6

He that is drunken, may his mother kill
Big with his sister: he hath lost the reins,
Is outlawed by himself: all kind of ill
Did with his liquor slide into his veins.
  The drunkard forfeits Man, and doth devest°
    All worldly right, save what he hath by beast.

7

Shall I, to please another's wine-sprung mind,°
Lose all mine own? God hath giv'n me a measure
Short of his can and body; must I find°
A pain in that, wherein he finds a pleasure?   40
  Stay at the third glass: if thou lose thy hold,
    Then thou art modest, and the wine grows bold.

8

If reason move not gallants, quit the room,
(All in a shipwrack shift their several way)°
Let not a common ruin thee intomb:
Be not a beast in courtesy; but stay,
  Stay at the third cup, or forgo the place.
    Wine above all things doth God's stamp deface.

9

Yet, if thou sin in wine or wantonness,
Boast not thereof; nor make thy shame thy glory.°   50
Frailty gets pardon by submissiveness;
But he that boasts, shuts that out of his story.
  He makes flat war with God, and doth defy°
    With his poor clod of earth the spacious sky.

10

Take not his name, who made thy mouth, in vain:
It gets thee nothing, and hath no excuse.
Lust and wine plead a pleasure, avarice gain:
But the cheap swearer through his open sluice
    Lets his soul run for nought, as little fearing.
    Were I an Epicure, I could bate swearing.°   60

11

When thou dost tell another's jest, therein
Omit the oaths, which true wit cannot need:
Pick out of tales the mirth, but not the sin.
He pares his apple, that will cleanly feed.
    Play not away the virtue of that name,
    Which is thy best stake, when griefs make thee tame.

12

The cheapest sins most dearly punished are;
Because to shun them also is so cheap:
For we have wit to mark them, and to spare.
O crumble not away thy soul's fair heap.   70
    If thou wilt die, the gates of hell are broad:
    Pride and full sins have made the way a road.

13

Lie not; but let thy heart be true to God,
Thy mouth to it, thy actions to them both:
Cowards tell lies, and those that fear the rod;
The stormy working soul spits lies and froth.
    Dare to be true. Nothing can need a lie:
    A fault, which needs it most, grows two thereby.

14

Fly idleness, which yet thou canst not fly
By dressing, mistressing, and compliment.°   80
If those take up thy day, the sun will cry
Against thee: for his light was only lent.
    God gave thy soul brave wings; put not those feathers°
    Into a bed, to sleep out all ill weathers.

15

Art thou a magistrate? then be severe:
If studious, copy fair what time hath blurred;
Redeem truth from his jaws: if soldier,
Chase brave employments with a naked sword°
   Throughout the world. Fool not: for all may have,
   If they dare try, a glorious life, or grave.   90

16

O England! full of sin, but most of sloth;
Spit out thy phlegm, and fill thy breast with glory:°
Thy gentry bleats, as if thy native cloth
Transfused a sheepishness into thy story:
   Not that they all are so; but that the most
   Are gone to grass, and in the pasture lost.

17

This loss springs chiefly from our education.
Some till their ground, but let weeds choke their son:
Some mark a partridge, never their child's fashion:°
Some ship them over, and the thing is done.°   100
   Study this art, make it thy great design;
   And if God's image move thee not, let thine.°

18

Some great estates provide, but do not breed
A mast'ring mind; so both are lost thereby:
Or else they breed them tender, make them need
All that they leave: this is flat poverty.
   For he, that needs five thousand pound to live,
   Is full as poor as he, that needs but five.

19

The way to make thy son rich is to fill
His mind with rest, before his trunk with riches: 110
For wealth without contentment climbs a hill
To feel those tempests, which fly over ditches.
   But if thy son can make ten pound his measure,
   Then all thou addest may be called his treasure.

20

When thou dost purpose aught within thy power,
Be sure to do it, though it be but small:
Constancy knits the bones, and makes us stour,°
When wanton pleasures beckon us to thrall.°
  Who breaks his own bond, forfeiteth himself:
  What nature made a ship, he makes a shelf.°   120

21

Do all things like a man, not sneakingly:
Think the king sees thee still; for his King does.
Simp'ring is but a lay-hypocrisy:°
Give it a corner, and the clue undoes.°
  Who fears to do ill, sets himself to task:
  Who fears to do well, sure should wear a mask.

22

Look to thy mouth; diseases enter there.
Thou hast two sconces, if thy stomach call;°
Carve, or discourse; do not a famine fear.
Who carves, is kind to two; who talks, to all.   130
  Look on meat, think it dirt, then eat a bit;
  And say withal, Earth to earth I commit.°

23

Slight those who say amidst their sickly healths,
Thou liv'st by rule. What doth not so, but man?
Houses are built by rule, and commonwealths.
Entice the trusty sun, if that thou can,
  From his ecliptic line: beckon the sky.°
  Who lives by rule then, keeps good company.

24

Who keeps no guard upon himself, is slack,
And rots to nothing at the next great thaw.   140
Man is a shop of rules, a well trussed pack,
Whose every parcel underwrites a law.°
  Lose not thyself, nor give thy humours way:
  God gave them to thee under lock and key.

25

By all means use sometimes to be alone.°
Salute thyself: see what thy soul doth wear.°
Dare to look in thy chest, for 'tis thine own:
And tumble up and down what thou find'st there.
 Who cannot rest till he good fellows find,
  He breaks up house, turns out of doors his mind.   150

26

Be thrifty, but not covetous: therefore give
Thy need, thine honour, and thy friend his due.
Never was scraper brave man. Get to live;
Then live, and use it: else, it is not true
 That thou hast gotten. Surely use alone
 Makes money not a contemptible stone.

27

Never exceed thy income. Youth may make°
Ev'n with the year: but age, if it will hit,
Shoots a bow short, and lessens still his stake,
As the day lessens, and his life with it.   160
 Thy children, kindred, friends upon thee call;
 Before thy journey fairly part with all.

28

Yet in thy thriving still misdoubt some evil;
Lest gaining gain on thee, and make thee dim
To all things else. Wealth is the conjurer's devil;
Whom when he thinks he hath, the devil hath him.
 Gold thou mayst safely touch; but if it stick
 Unto thy hands, it woundeth to the quick.

29

What skills it, if a bag of stones or gold°
About thy neck do drown thee? raise thy head;   170
Take stars for money; stars not to be told°
By any art, yet to be purchased.
 None is so wasteful as the scraping dame.
 She loseth three for one; her soul, rest, fame.

30

By no means run in debt: take thine own measure.
Who cannot live on twenty pound a year,
Cannot on forty: he's a man of pleasure,
A kind of thing that's for itself too dear.
   The curious unthrift makes his clothes too wide,°
   And spares himself, but would his tailor chide.   180

31

Spend not on hopes. They that by pleading clothes
Do fortunes seek, when worth and service fail,
Would have their tale believèd for their oaths,
And are like empty vessels under sail.
   Old courtiers know this; therefore set out so,
   As all the day thou mayst hold out to go.

32

In clothes, cheap handsomeness doth bear the bell.°
Wisdom's a trimmer thing than shop e'er gave.
Say not then, This with that lace will do well;
But, This with my discretion will be brave.°   190
   Much curiousness is a perpetual wooing,°
   Nothing with labour, folly long a-doing.

33

Play not for gain, but sport. Who plays for more
Than he can lose with pleasure, stakes his heart;
Perhaps his wife's too, and whom she hath bore:
Servants and churches also play their part.
   Only a herald, who that way doth pass,°
   Finds his cracked name at length in the church glass.

34

If yet thou love game at so dear a rate,
Learn this, that hath old gamesters dearly cost: 200
Dost lose? rise up: dost win? rise in that state.
Who strive to sit out losing hands, are lost.
   Game is a civil gunpowder, in peace
   Blowing up houses with their whole increase.°

35

In conversation boldness now bears sway.°
But know, that nothing can so foolish be,
As empty boldness: therefore first assay°
To stuff thy mind with solid bravery;°
   Then march on gallant: get substantial worth.
   Boldness gilds finely, and will set it forth.   210

36

Be sweet to all. Is thy complexion sour?°
Then keep such company; make them thy allay:°
Get a sharp wife, a servant that will lour.
A stumbler stumbles least in rugged way.
   Command thyself in chief. He life's war knows,
   Whom all his passions follow, as he goes.

37

Catch not at quarrels. He that dares not speak°
Plainly and home, is coward of the two.°
Think not thy fame at ev'ry twitch will break:
By great deeds show, that thou canst little do;   220
   And do them not: that shall thy wisdom be;
   And change thy temperance into bravery.

38

If that thy fame with ev'ry toy be posed,°
'Tis a thin web, which poisonous fancies make:
But the great soldier's honour was composed
Of thicker stuff, which would endure a shake.
   Wisdom picks friends; civility plays the rest.°
   A toy shunned cleanly passeth with the best.°

39

Laugh not too much: the witty man laughs least:
For wit is news only to ignorance.   230
Less at thine own things laugh; lest in the jest
Thy person share, and the conceit advance.°
   Make not thy sport, abuses: for the fly
   That feeds on dung, is colourèd thereby.

40

Pick out of mirth, like stones out of thy ground,
Profaneness, filthiness, abusiveness.
These are the scum, with which coarse wits abound:
The fine may spare these well, yet not go less.
    All things are big with jest: nothing that's plain,
    But may be witty, if thou hast the vein.°   240

41

Wit's an unruly engine, wildly striking
Sometimes a friend, sometimes the engineer.
Hast thou the knack? pamper it not with liking:
But if thou want it, buy it not too dear.°
    Many, affecting wit beyond their power,
    Have got to be a dear fool for an hour.

42

A sad wise valour is the brave complexion,°
That leads the van, and swallows up the cities.°
The giggler is a milk-maid, whom infection
Or a fired beacon frighteth from his ditties.°   250
    Then he's the sport: the mirth then in him rests,
    And the sad man is cock of all his jests.°

43

Towards great persons use respective boldness:°
That temper gives them theirs, and yet doth take°
Nothing from thine: in service, care or coldness
Doth rateably thy fortunes mar or make.°
    Feed no man in his sins: for adulation
    Doth make thee parcel-devil in damnation.°

44

Envy not greatness: for thou mak'st thereby
Thyself the worse, and so the distance greater.   260
Be not thine own worm: yet such jealousy,
As hurts not others, but may make thee better,
    Is a good spur. Correct thy passions' spite;
    Then may the beasts draw thee to happy light.

45

When baseness is exalted, do not bate°
The place its honour, for the person's sake.
The shrine is that which thou dost venerate,
And not the beast, that bears it on his back.
  I care not though the cloth of state should be
  Not of rich arras, but mean tapestry.   270

46

Thy friend put in thy bosom: wear his eyes
Still in thy heart, that he may see what's there.°
If cause require, thou art his sacrifice;
Thy drops of blood must pay down all his fear:
  But love is lost, the way of friendship's gone,
  Though David had his Jonathan, Christ his John.°

47

Yet be not surety, if thou be a father.
Love is a personal debt. I cannot give
My children's right, nor ought he take it: rather
Both friends should die, than hinder them to live.   280
  Fathers first enter bonds to nature's ends;
  And are her sureties, ere they are a friend's.

48

If thou be single, all thy goods and ground
Submit to love; but yet not more than all.
Give one estate, as one life. None is bound
To work for two, who brought himself to thrall.
  God made me one man; love makes me no more,°
  Till labour come, and make my weakness score.

49

In thy discourse, if thou desire to please,
All such is courteous, useful, new, or witty.   290
Usefulness comes by labour, wit by ease;
Courtesy grows in court; news in the city.
  Get a good stock of these, then draw the card
  That suits him best, of whom thy speech is heard.

50

Entice all neatly to what they know best;
For so thou dost thyself and him a pleasure:
(But a proud ignorance will lose his rest,°
Rather than show his cards.) Steal from his treasure
    What to ask further. Doubts well raised do lock
    The speaker to thee, and preserve thy stock.   300

51

If thou be master-gunner, spend not all
That thou canst speak, at once; but husband it,
And give men turns of speech: do not forestall
By lavishness thine own, and others' wit,
    As if thou mad'st thy will. A civil guest
    Will no more talk all, than eat all the feast.

52

Be calm in arguing: for fierceness makes
Error a fault, and truth discourtesy.
Why should I feel another man's mistakes
More than his sicknesses or poverty?   310
    In love I should: but anger is not love,
    Nor wisdom neither: therefore gently move.

53

Calmness is great advantage: he that lets
Another chafe, may warm him at his fire,
Mark all his wand'rings, and enjoy his frets;
As cunning fencers suffer heat to tire.
    Truth dwells not in the clouds: the bow that's there
    Doth often aim at, never hit the sphere.

54

Mark what another says: for many are
Full of themselves, and answer their own notion.   320
Take all into thee; then with equal care
Balance each dram of reason, like a potion.
    If truth be with thy friend, be with them both:
    Share in the conquest, and confess a troth.

55

Be useful where thou livest, that they may
Both want and wish thy pleasing presence still.
Kindness, good parts, great places are the way°
To compass this. Find out men's wants and will,
   And meet them there. All worldly joys go less°
    To the one joy of doing kindnesses.   330

56

Pitch thy behaviour low, thy projects high;
So shalt thou humble and magnanimous be:
Sink not in spirit: who aimeth at the sky,
Shoots higher much than he that means a tree.°
   A grain of glory mixed with humbleness
    Cures both a fever and lethargicness.

57

Let thy mind still be bent, still plotting where,
And when, and how the business may be done.
Slackness breeds worms; but the sure traveller,
Though he alight sometimes, still goeth on.   340
   Active and stirring spirits live alone.°
    Write on the others, Here lies such a one.

58

Slight not the smallest loss, whether it be
In love or honour: take account of all;
Shine like the sun in every corner: see
Whether thy stock of credit swell, or fall.
   Who say, I care not, those I give for lost;
    And to instruct them, will not quit the cost.°

59

Scorn no man's love, though of a mean degree;
Love is a present for a mighty king.   350
Much less make anyone thy enemy.
As guns destroy, so may a little sling.°
   The cunning workman never doth refuse
    The meanest tool, that he may chance to use.

60

All foreign wisdom doth amount to this,
To take all that is given; whether wealth,
Or love, or language; nothing comes amiss:
A good digestion turneth all to health:
 And then as far as fair behaviour may,
 Strike off all scores; none are so clear as they. 360

61

Keep all thy native good, and naturalize
All foreign of that name; but scorn their ill:
Embrace their activeness, not vanities.
Who follows all things, forfeiteth his will.
 If thou observest strangers in each fit,°
 In time they'll run thee out of all thy wit.

62

Affect in things about thee cleanliness,°
That all may gladly board thee, as a flower.°
Slovens take up their stock of noisomeness
Beforehand, and anticipate their last hour. 370
 Let thy mind's sweetness have his operation
 Upon thy body, clothes, and habitation.

63

In alms regard thy means, and others' merit.
Think heav'n a better bargain, than to give
Only thy single market-money for it.
Join hands with God to make a man to live.
 Give to all something; to a good poor man,
 Till thou change names, and be where he began.

64

Man is God's image; but a poor man is
Christ's stamp to boot: both images regard. 380
God reckons for him, counts the favour his:
Write, So much giv'n to God; thou shalt be heard.
 Let thy alms go before, and keep heav'ns gate
 Open for thee; or both may come too late.

65

Restore to God his due in tithe and time:
A tithe purloined cankers the whole estate.
Sundays observe: think when the bells do chime,
'Tis angels' music; therefore come not late.
   God then deals blessings: if a king did so,
    Who would not haste, nay give, to see the show?   390

66

Twice on the day his due is understood;°
For all the week thy food so oft he gave thee.
Thy cheer is mended; bate not of the food,°
Because 'tis better, and perhaps may save thee.
   Thwart not the Mighty God: O be not cross.°
    Fast when thou wilt but then, 'tis gain not loss.°

67

Though private prayer be a brave design,°
Yet public hath more promises, more love:
And love's a weight to hearts, to eyes a sign.
We all are but cold suitors; let us move   400
   Where it is warmest. Leave thy six and seven;°
    Pray with the most: for where most pray, is heaven.

68

When once thy foot enters the church, be bare.°
God is more there, than thou: for thou art there
Only by his permission. Then beware,
And make thyself all reverence and fear.
   Kneeling ne'er spoiled silk stocking: quit thy state.°
    All equal are within the church's gate.

69

Resort to sermons, but to prayers most:°
Praying's the end of preaching. O be dressed;   410
Stay not for th' other pin: why, thou hast lost
A joy for it worth worlds. Thus hell doth jest
   Away thy blessings, and extremely flout thee,
    Thy clothes being fast, but thy soul loose about thee.

70

In time of service seal up both thine eyes,
And send them to thine heart; that spying sin,
They may weep out the stains by them did rise:
Those doors being shut, all by the ear comes in.
    Who marks in church-time others' symmetry,
    Makes all their beauty his deformity.   420

71

Let vain or busy thoughts have there no part:
Bring not thy plough, thy plots, thy pleasures thither.°
Christ purged his temple; so must thou thy heart.
All worldly thoughts are but thieves met together
    To cozen thee. Look to thy actions well:
    For churches are either our heav'n or hell.

72

Judge not the preacher; for he is thy judge:
If thou mislike him, thou conceiv'st him not.°
God calleth preaching folly. Do not grudge°
To pick out treasures from an earthen pot.°   430
    The worst speak something good: if all want sense,
    God takes a text, and preacheth patience.

73

He that gets patience, and the blessing which
Preachers conclude with, hath not lost his pains.
He that by being at church escapes the ditch,
Which he might fall in by companions, gains.
    He that loves God's abode, and to combine
    With saints on earth, shall one day with them shine.

74

Jest not at preachers' language, or expression:
How know'st thou, but thy sins made him miscarry?   440
Then turn thy faults and his into confession:
God sent him, whatsoe'er he be: O tarry,
    And love him for his Master: his condition,°
    Though it be ill, makes him no ill physician.

75

None shall in hell such bitter pangs endure,
As those, who mock at God's way of salvation.
Whom oil and balsams kill, what salve can cure?
They drink with greediness a full damnation.
   The Jews refusèd thunder; and we, folly.°
   Though God do hedge us in, yet who is holy?°   450

76

Sum up at night, what thou hast done by day;
And in the morning, what thou hast to do.
Dress and undress thy soul: mark the decay
And growth of it: if with thy watch, that too
   Be down, then wind up both; since we shall be
   Most surely judged, make thy accounts agree.

77

In brief, acquit thee bravely; play the man.
Look not on pleasures as they come, but go.
Defer not the least virtue: life's poor span
Make not an ell, by trifling in thy woe.°   460
   If thou do ill; the joy fades, not the pains:
   If well; the pain doth fade, the joy remains.

Superliminare°

   Thou, whom the former precepts have
   Sprinkled and taught, how to behave
   Thyself in church; approach, and taste
   The church's mystical repast.°

———————

   Avoid, profaneness; come not here:°
   Nothing but holy, pure, and clear,
   Or that which groaneth to be so,
   May at his peril further go.

THE CHURCH

The Altar°

A broken ALTAR, Lord, thy servant rears,°
Made of a heart, and cemented with tears:
  Whose parts are as thy hand did frame;°
  No workman's tool hath touched the same.°
          A   HEART   alone°
          Is   such   a   stone,
          As   nothing   but
          Thy pow'r doth cut.
          Wherefore each part
          Of my hard heart   10
          Meets in this frame,°
          To praise thy Name:
  That, if I chance to hold my peace,°
  These stones to praise thee may not cease.
O let thy blessed SACRIFICE be mine,
And   sanctify   this   ALTAR   to   be   thine.

The Sacrifice°

Oh all ye, who pass by, whose eyes and mind°
To worldly things are sharp, but to me blind;
To me, who took eyes that I might you find:
                Was ever grief like mine?°

The princes of my people make a head°
Against their Maker: they do wish me dead,
Who cannot wish, except I give them bread:°
                Was ever grief like mine?

Without me each one, who doth now me brave,°
Had to this day been an Egyptian slave.   10
They use that power against me, which I gave:
                Was ever grief like mine?

Mine own apostle, who the bag did bear,°
Though he had all I had, did not forbear
To sell me also, and to put me there:
                    Was ever grief like mine?

For thirty pence he did my death devise,
Who at three hundred did the ointment prize,°
Not half so sweet as my sweet sacrifice:
                    Was ever grief like mine?   20

Therefore my soul melts, and my heart's dear treasure
Drops blood (the only beads) my words to measure:°
O let this cup pass, if it be thy pleasure:°
                    Was ever grief like mine?

These drops being tempered with a sinner's tears°
A balsam are for both the hemispheres:
Curing all wounds, but mine; all, but my fears:
                    Was ever grief like mine?

Yet my disciples sleep: I cannot gain
One hour of watching; but their drowsy brain   30
Comforts not me, and doth my doctrine stain:
                    Was ever grief like mine?

Arise, arise, they come. Look how they run!
Alas! what haste they make to be undone!
How with their lanterns do they seek the sun!
                    Was ever grief like mine?

With clubs and staves they seek me, as a thief,
Who am the Way and Truth, the true relief;°
Most true to those, who are my greatest grief:
                    Was ever grief like mine?   40

Judas, dost thou betray me with a kiss?
Canst thou find hell about my lips? and miss
Of life, just at the gates of life and bliss?
                    Was ever grief like mine?

See, they lay hold on me, not with the hands
Of faith, but fury: yet at their commands
I suffer binding, who have loosed their bands:°
                    Was ever grief like mine?

All my disciples fly; fear puts a bar
Betwixt my friends and me. They leave the star,   50
That brought the wise men of the East from far.
                    Was ever grief like mine?

Then from one ruler to another bound
They lead me; urging, that it was not sound
What I taught: comments would the text confound.
                    Was ever grief like mine?

The priest and rulers all false witness seek
'Gainst him, who seeks not life, but is the meek
And ready Paschal Lamb of this great week:°
                    Was ever grief like mine?   60

Then they accuse me of great blasphemy,
That I did thrust into the Deity,
Who never thought that any robbery:°
                    Was ever grief like mine?

Some said, that I the Temple to the floor°
In three days razed, and raisèd as before.
Why, he that built the world can do much more:
                    Was ever grief like mine?

Then they condemn me all with that same breath,
Which I do give them daily, unto death.   70
Thus Adam my first breathing rendereth:°
                    Was ever grief like mine?

They bind, and lead me unto Herod: he
Sends me to Pilate. This makes them agree;
But yet their friendship is my enmity:
                    Was ever grief like mine?

Herod and all his bands do set me light,°
Who teach all hands to war, fingers to fight,
And only am the Lord of Hosts and might:
                            Was ever grief like mine?   80

Herod in judgement sits, while I do stand;
Examines me with a censorious hand:
I him obey, who all things else command:
                            Was ever grief like mine?

The Jews accuse me with despitefulness;°
And vying malice with my gentleness,
Pick quarrels with their only happiness:
                            Was ever grief like mine?

I answer nothing, but with patience prove°
If stony hearts will melt with gentle love.   90
But who does hawk at eagles with a dove?
                            Was ever grief like mine?

My silence rather doth augment their cry;
My dove doth back into my bosom fly,°
Because the raging waters still are high:
                            Was ever grief like mine?

Heark how they cry aloud still, *Crucify:*
It is not fit he live a day, they cry,
Who cannot live less than eternally:
                            Was ever grief like mine?   100

Pilate, a stranger, holdeth off; but they,
Mine own dear people, cry, *Away, away*,
With noises confusèd frighting the day:
                            Was ever grief like mine?

Yet still they shout, and cry, and stop their ears,
Putting my life among their sins and fears,
And therefore wish *my blood on them and theirs*:°
                            Was ever grief like mine?

See how spite cankers things. These words aright
Usèd, and wishèd, are the whole world's light: 110
But honey is their gall, brightness their night:
                              Was ever grief like mine?

They choose a murderer, and all agree°
In him to do themselves a courtesy:
For it was their own case who killèd me:
                              Was ever grief like mine?

And a seditious murderer he was:
But I the Prince of peace; peace that doth pass°
All understanding, more than heav'n doth glass:°
                              Was ever grief like mine?   120

Why, Caesar is their only king, not I:
He clave the stony rock, when they were dry;°
But surely not their hearts, as I well try:
                              Was ever grief like mine?

Ah! how they scourge me! yet my tenderness
Doubles each lash: and yet their bitterness
Winds up my grief to a mysteriousness:°
                              Was ever grief like mine?

They buffet him, and box him as they list,°
Who grasps the earth and heaven with his fist,   130
And never yet, whom he would punish, missed:
                              Was ever grief like mine?

Behold, they spit on me in scornful wise,
Who by my spittle gave the blind man eyes,°
Leaving his blindness to my enemies:
                              Was ever grief like mine?

My face they cover, though it be divine.
As Moses' face was veilèd, so is mine,°
Lest on their double-dark souls either shine:
                              Was ever grief like mine?   140

Servants and abjects flout me; they are witty:°
Now prophesy who strikes thee, is their ditty.°
So they in me deny themselves all pity:
                    Was ever grief like mine?

And now I am delivered unto death,
Which each one calls for so with utmost breath,
That he before me well nigh suffereth:
                    Was ever grief like mine?

Weep not, dear friends, since I for both have wept°
When all my tears were blood, the while you slept: 150
Your tears for your own fortunes should be kept:
                    Was ever grief like mine?

The soldiers lead me to the common hall;
There they deride me, they abuse me all:
Yet for twelve heav'nly legions I could call:
                    Was ever grief like mine?

Then with a scarlet robe they me array;
Which shows my blood to be the only way
And cordial left to repair man's decay:
                    Was ever grief like mine?   160

Then on my head a crown of thorns I wear:°
For these are all the grapes Sion doth bear,
Though I my vine planted and watered there:
                    Was ever grief like mine?

So sits the earth's great curse in Adam's fall°
Upon my head: so I remove it all
From th' earth unto my brows, and bear the thrall:°
                    Was ever grief like mine?

Then with the reed they gave to me before,
They strike my head, the rock from whence all store°   170
Of heav'nly blessings issue evermore:
                    Was ever grief like mine?

They bow their knees to me, and cry, *Hail king*:
Whatever scoffs and scornfulness can bring,
I am the floor, the sink, where they it fling:°
                    Was ever grief like mine?

Yet since man's sceptres are as frail as reeds,
And thorny all their crowns, bloody their weeds;°
I, who am Truth, turn into truth their deeds:
                    Was ever grief like mine?   180

The soldiers also spit upon that face,
Which angels did desire to have the grace,
And prophets, once to see, but found no place:
                    Was ever grief like mine?

Thus trimmèd, forth they bring me to the rout,°
Who *Crucify him*, cry with one strong shout.
God holds his peace at man, and man cries out:
                    Was ever grief like mine?

They lead me in once more, and putting then
Mine own clothes on, they lead me out again.   190
Whom devils fly, thus is he tossed of men:
                    Was ever grief like mine?

And now weary of sport, glad to engross°
All spite in one, counting my life their loss,
They carry me to my most bitter cross:
                    Was ever grief like mine?

My cross I bear myself, until I faint:
Then Simon bears it for me by constraint,
The decreed burden of each mortal Saint:°
                    Was ever grief like mine?   200

O all ye who pass by, behold and see;
Man stole the fruit, but I must climb the tree;
The tree of life to all, but only me:°
                    Was ever grief like mine?

Lo, here I hang, charged with a world of sin,°
The greater world o' th' two; for that came in
By words, but this by sorrow I must win:
                         Was ever grief like mine?

Such sorrow as, if sinful man could feel,
Or feel his part, he would not cease to kneel,   210
Till all were melted, though he were all steel:
                         Was ever grief like mine?

But, *O my God, my God!* why leav'st thou me,°
The son, in whom thou dost delight to be?
My God, my God——
                         Never was grief like mine.

Shame tears my soul, my body many a wound;
Sharp nails pierce this, but sharper that confound;
Reproaches, which are free, while I am bound.
                         Was ever grief like mine?   220

Now heal thyself, physician; *now come down.*°
Alas! I did so, when I left my crown
And father's smile for you, to feel his frown:
                         Was ever grief like mine?

In healing not myself, there doth consist
All that salvation, which ye now resist;
Your safety in my sickness doth subsist:
                         Was ever grief like mine?

Betwixt two thieves I spend my utmost breath,
As he that for some robbery suffereth.   230
Alas! what have I stolen from you?   Death.
                         Was ever grief like mine?

A king my title is, prefixed on high;°
Yet by my subjects am condemned to die
A servile death in servile company:
                         Was ever grief like mine?

They give me vinegar mingled with gall,
But more with malice: yet, when they did call,
With manna, angels' food, I fed them all:°
                Was ever grief like mine?   240

They part my garments, and by lot dispose
My coat, the type of love, which once cured those°
Who sought for help, never malicious foes:
                Was ever grief like mine?

Nay, after death their spite shall further go;
For they will pierce my side, I full well know;
That as sin came, so Sacraments might flow:
                Was ever grief like mine?

But now I die; now all is finishèd.
My woe, man's weal: and now I bow my head.°   250
Only let others say, when I am dead,
                Never was grief like mine.

The Thanksgiving

Oh King of grief! (a title strange, yet true,°
    To thee of all kings only due)
Oh King of wounds! how shall I grieve for thee,
    Who in all grief preventest me?°
Shall I weep blood? why, thou hast wept such store°
    That all thy body was one door.
Shall I be scourgèd, flouted, boxèd, sold?
    'Tis but to tell the tale is told.
My God, my God, why dost thou part from me?°
    Was such a grief as cannot be.   10
Shall I then sing, skipping thy doleful story,
    And side with thy triumphant glory?
Shall thy strokes be my stroking? thorns, my flower?
    Thy rod, my posy? cross, my bower?°
But how then shall I imitate thee, and
    Copy thy fair, though bloody hand?°
Surely I will revenge me on thy love,

And try who shall victorious prove.
If thou dost give me wealth, I will restore
    All back unto thee by the poor.   20
If thou dost give me honour, men shall see,
    The honour doth belong to thee.
I will not marry; or, if she be mine,
    She and her children shall be thine.
My bosom friend, if he blaspheme thy Name,
    I will tear thence his love and fame.
One half of me being gone, the rest I give
    Unto some chapel, die or live.
As for thy passion—But of that anon,
    When with the other I have done.   30
For thy predestination I'll contrive,
    That three years hence, if I survive,
I'll build a spittle, or mend common ways,°
    But mend mine own without delays.
Then I will use the works of thy creation,
    As if I used them but for fashion.
The world and I will quarrel; and the year
    Shall not perceive, that I am here.
My music shall find thee, and ev'ry string
    Shall have his attribute to sing;   40
That all together may accord in thee,
    And prove one God, one harmony.
If thou shalt give me wit, it shall appear,°
    If thou hast giv'n it me, 'tis here.
Nay, I will read thy book, and never move
    Till I have found therein thy love,
Thy art of love, which I'll turn back on thee:°
    O my dear Saviour, Victory!
Then for thy passion—I will do for that—
    Alas, my God, I know not what.   50

The Reprisal°

    I have considered it, and find
There is no dealing with thy mighty passion:
For though I die for thee, I am behind;
    My sins deserve the condemnation.

O make me innocent, that I
May give a disentangled state and free:°
And yet thy wounds still my attempts defy,
    For by thy death I die for thee.°

Ah! was it not enough that thou
By thy eternal glory didst outgo me?
Couldst thou not grief's sad conquests me allow,
    But in all vict'ries overthrow me?

Yet by confession will I come
Into thy conquest: though I can do nought
Against thee, in thee I will overcome
    The man, who once against thee fought.

The Agony°

Philosophers have measured mountains,°
Fathomed the depths of seas, of states, and kings,
Walked with a staff to heav'n, and tracèd fountains:°
    But there are two vast, spacious things,
The which to measure it doth more behove:°
Yet few there are that sound them; Sin and Love.

Who would know Sin, let him repair°
Unto Mount Olivet; there shall he see
A man so wrung with pains, that all his hair,
    His skin, his garments bloody be.
Sin is that press and vice, which forceth pain°
To hunt his cruel food through ev'ry vein.

Who knows not Love, let him assay°
And taste that juice, which on the cross a pike
Did set again abroach; then let him say
    If ever he did taste the like.
Love is that liquor sweet and most divine,
Which my God feels as blood; but I, as wine.

The Sinner

Lord, how I am all ague, when I seek°
What I have treasured in my memory!
    Since, if my soul make even with the week,
Each seventh note by right is due to thee.
I find there quarries of piled vanities,
    But shreds of holiness that dare not venture
    To show their face, since cross to thy decrees:°
There the circumference earth is, heav'n the centre.
In so much dregs the quintessence is small:°
    The spirit and good extract of my heart
    Comes to about the many hundred part.°
Yet Lord restore thine image, hear my call:
    And though my hard heart scarce to thee can groan,
    Remember that thou once didst write in stone.°

Good Friday°

    O my chief good,
How shall I measure out thy blood?
How shall I count what thee befell,
    And each grief tell?°

    Shall I thy woes
Number according to thy foes?
Or, since one star showed thy first breath,
    Shall all thy death?

    Or shall each leaf,
Which falls in Autumn, score a grief?
Or can not leaves, but fruit, be sign°
    Of the true vine?

    Then let each hour
Of my whole life one grief devour;
That thy distress through all may run,
    And be my sun.

          Or rather let
My several sins their sorrows get;°
That as each beast his cure doth know,
          Each sin may so.   20

Since blood is fittest, Lord, to write
Thy sorrows in, and bloody fight;
My heart hath store, write there, where in
One box doth lie both ink and sin:

That when sin spies so many foes,
Thy whips, thy nails, thy wounds, thy woes,
All come to lodge there, sin may say,
No room for me, and fly away.

Sin being gone, oh fill the place,
And keep possession with thy grace;   30
Lest sin take courage and return,
And all the writings blot or burn.

Redemption°

Having been tenant long to a rich Lord,
      Not thriving, I resolvèd to be bold,
      And make a suit unto him, to afford
A new small-rented lease, and cancel th' old.
In heaven at his manor I him sought:
      They told me there, that he was lately gone
      About some land, which he had dearly bought
Long since on earth, to take possession.
I straight returned, and knowing his great birth,°
      Sought him accordingly in great resorts;°   10
      In cities, theatres, gardens, parks, and courts:
At length I heard a ragged noise and mirth
      Of thieves and murderers: there I him espied,
      Who straight, *Your suit is granted*, said, and died.

Sepulchre

O blessed body! Whither art thou thrown?
No lodging for thee, but a cold hard stone?
So many hearts on earth, and yet not one
        Receive thee?
Sure there is room within our hearts good store;°
For they can lodge transgressions by the score:
Thousands of toys dwell there, yet out of door°
        They leave thee.

But that which shows them large, shows them unfit.
What ever sin did this pure rock commit,   10
Which holds thee now? Who hath indicted it
        Of murder?
Where our hard hearts have took up stones to brain thee,°
And missing this, most falsely did arraign thee;
Only these stones in quiet entertain thee,
        And order.

And as of old the Law by heav'nly art
Was writ in stone; so thou, which also art°
The letter of the word, find'st no fit heart°
        To hold thee.   20
Yet do we still persist as we began,
And so should perish, but that nothing can,
Though it be cold, hard, foul, from loving man
        Withhold thee.

Easter

Rise heart; thy Lord is risen. Sing his praise
        Without delays,
Who takes thee by the hand, that thou likewise
        With him mayst rise:
That, as his death calcinèd thee to dust,
His life may make thee gold, and much more, just.

Awake, my lute, and struggle for thy part
        With all thy art.

The cross taught all wood to resound his name,
                   Who bore the same.   10
His stretched sinews taught all strings, what key
Is best to celebrate this most high day.

Consort both heart and lute, and twist a song°
                   Pleasant and long:
Or, since all music is but three parts vied°
                   And multiplied,
O let thy blessed Spirit bear a part,
And make up our defects with his sweet art.

     I got me flowers to straw thy way;°
     I got me boughs off many a tree: 20
     But thou wast up by break of day,
     And brought'st thy sweets along with thee.°

     The sun arising in the East,
     Though he give light, and th' East perfume;
     If they should offer to contest
     With thy arising, they presume.

     Can there be any day but this,
     Though many suns to shine endeavour?
     We count three hundred, but we miss:°
     There is but one, and that one ever.   30

Easter-wings

     Lord, who createdst man in wealth and store,°
         Though foolishly he lost the same,
             Decaying more and more,
                Till he became
                  Most poor:
                  With thee
               O let me rise
            As larks, harmoniously,
         And sing this day thy victories:
     Then shall the fall further the flight in me.°   10

My tender age in sorrow did begin:
 And still with sicknesses and shame
  Thou didst so punish sin,
   That I became
    Most thin.
   With thee
  Let me combine
 And feel this day thy victory:
For, if I imp my wing on thine,°
Affliction shall advance the flight in me.   20

H. Baptism (I)

As he that sees a dark and shady grove,
 Stays not, but looks beyond it on the sky;
 So when I view my sins, mine eyes remove
More backward still, and to that water fly,
Which is above the heav'ns, whose spring and vent
 Is in my dear Redeemer's piercèd side.
 O blessed streams! either ye do prevent°
And stop our sins from growing thick and wide,
Or else give tears to drown them, as they grow.
 In you Redemption measures all my time,   10
 And spreads the plaster equal to the crime.
You taught the Book of Life my name, that so
 What ever future sins should me miscall,°
 Your first acquaintance might discredit all.

H. Baptism (II)

   Since, Lord, to thee
  A narrow way and little gate°
Is all the passage, on my infancy
   Thou didst lay hold, and antedate
    My faith in me.

O let me still
Write thee great God, and me a child:
Let me be soft and supple to thy will,
Small to myself, to others mild,
Behither ill.°   10

Although by stealth
My flesh get on, yet let her sister
My soul bid nothing, but preserve her wealth:
The growth of flesh is but a blister;
Childhood is health.

Nature

Full of rebellion, I would die,
Or fight, or travel, or deny
That thou hast ought to do with me.
O tame my heart;
It is thy highest art°
To captivate strongholds to thee.

If thou shalt let this venom lurk,
And in suggestions fume and work,
My soul will turn to bubbles straight,°
And thence by kind°   10
Vanish into a wind,
Making thy workmanship deceit.

O smooth my rugged heart, and there°
Engrave thy rev'rend Law and fear;
Or make a new one, since the old
Is sapless grown,
And a much fitter stone
To hide my dust, than thee to hold.

Sin (I)

Lord, with what care hast thou begirt us round!
 Parents first season us: then schoolmasters
 Deliver us to laws; they send us bound
To rules of reason, holy messengers,
Pulpits and Sundays, sorrow dogging sin,
 Afflictions sorted, anguish of all sizes,°
 Fine nets and stratagems to catch us in,
Bibles laid open, millions of surprises,
Blessings beforehand, ties of gratefulness,
 The sound of glory ringing in our ears: 10
 Without, our shame; within, our consciences;
Angels and grace, eternal hopes and fears.
 Yet all these fences and their whole array
 One cunning bosom-sin blows quite away.°

Affliction (I)

When first thou didst entice to thee my heart,
  I thought the service brave:°
So many joys I writ down for my part,
  Besides what I might have
Out of my stock of natural delights,
Augmented with thy gracious benefits.

I lookèd on thy furniture so fine,°
  And made it fine to me:
Thy glorious household-stuff did me entwine,
  And 'tice me unto thee.
Such stars I counted mine: both heav'n and earth
Paid me my wages in a world of mirth.°   10

What pleasures could I want, whose King I served,
  Where joys my fellows were?
Thus argued into hopes, my thoughts reserved
  No place for grief or fear.
Therefore my sudden soul caught at the place,
And made her youth and fierceness seek thy face.

At first thou gav'st me milk and sweetnesses;
   filled I had my wish and way: 20
My days were strawed with flow'rs and happiness;°
    There was no month but May.
But with my years sorrow did twist and grow,
And made a party unawares for woe.°

My flesh began unto my soul in pain,° *rheumatism*
    Sicknesses cleave my bones;
Consuming agues dwell in ev'ry vein,
    And tune my breath to groans.
Sorrow was all my soul; I scarce believed,
Till grief did tell me roundly, that I lived.   30

When I got health, thou took'st away my life,
    And more; for my friends die:
My mirth and edge was lost; a blunted knife
    Was of more use than I.
Thus thin and lean without a fence or friend,
I was blown through with ev'ry storm and wind.

Whereas my birth and spirit rather took
    The way that takes the town;
Thou didst betray me to a ling'ring book,
    And wrap me in a gown.   40
I was entangled in the world of strife,
Before I had the power to change my life.

Yet, for I threatened oft the siege to raise,
    Not simp'ring all mine age,
Thou often didst with academic praise
    Melt and dissolve my rage.
I took thy sweetened pill, till I came where°
I could not go away, nor persevere.

Yet lest perchance I should too happy be
    In my unhappiness,   50
Turning my purge to food, thou throwest me
    Into more sicknesses.
Thus doth thy power cross-bias me, not making°
Thine own gift good, yet me from my ways taking.

Now I am here, what thou wilt do with me
              None of my books will show:
I read, and sigh, and wish I were a tree;
              For sure then I should grow
To fruit or shade: at least some bird would trust
Her household to me, and I should be just.°   60

Yet, though thou troublest me, I must be meek;
              In weakness must be stout.
Well, I will change the service, and go seek
              Some other master out.
Ah my dear God! though I am clean forgot,°
Let me not love thee, if I love thee not.

Repentance

Lord, I confess my sin is great;
  Great is my sin. Oh! gently treat
With thy quick flow'r, thy momentary bloom;°
            Whose life still pressing
            Is one undressing,
  A steady aiming at a tomb.

Man's age is two hours' work, or three:
  Each day doth round about us see.
Thus are we to delights: but we are all
            To sorrows old,   10
            If life be told
From what life feeleth, Adam's fall.

O let thy height of mercy then
  Compassionate short-breathèd men.°
Cut me not off for my most foul transgression:
            I do confess
            My foolishness;
  My God, accept of my confession.

Sweeten at length this bitter bowl,
Which thou hast poured into my soul;   20
Thy wormwood turn to health, winds to fair weather:°
    For if thou stay,°
    I and this day,
As we did rise, we die together.

When thou for sin rebukest man,°
Forthwith he waxeth woe and wan:°
Bitterness fills our bowels; all our hearts
    Pine, and decay,
    And drop away,
And carry with them th' other parts.   30

But thou wilt sin and grief destroy;
That so the broken bones may joy,°
And tune together in a well-set song,
    Full of his praises,
    Who dead men raises.
Fractures well cured make us more strong.

Faith

Lord, how couldst thou so much appease
Thy wrath for sin as, when man's sight was dim,
And could see little, to regard his ease,
    And bring by Faith all things to him?

Hungry I was, and had no meat:
I did conceit a most delicious feast;°
I had it straight, and did as truly eat,
    As ever did a welcome guest.

There is a rare outlandish root,°
Which when I could not get, I thought it here: 10
That apprehension cured so well my foot,°
    That I can walk to heav'n well near.

I owèd thousands and much more:
I did believe that I did nothing owe,
And lived accordingly; my creditor
 Believes so too, and lets me go.

 Faith makes me anything, or all
That I believe is in the sacred story:
And where sin placeth me in Adam's fall,
 Faith sets me higher in his glory.   20

 If I go lower in the book,
What can be lower than the common manger?
Faith puts me there with him, who sweetly took
 Our flesh and frailty, death and danger.

 If bliss had lien in art or strength,
None but the wise or strong had gainèd it:
Where now by Faith all arms are of a length;
 One size doth all conditions fit.

 A peasant may believe as much
As a great clerk, and reach the highest stature.° 30
Thus dost thou make proud knowledge bend and crouch,
 While grace fills up uneven nature.

 When creatures had no real light
Inherent in them, thou didst make the sun
Impute a lustre, and allow them bright;°
 And in this show, what Christ hath done.

 That which before was darkened clean°
With bushy groves, pricking the lookers eye,
Vanished away, when Faith did change the scene:
 And then appeared a glorious sky.   40

 What though my body run to dust?
Faith cleaves unto it, counting ev'ry grain
With an exact and most particular trust,
 Reserving all for flesh again.

Handwritten margin notes: "closest to atonal music destroys logic & grammatical rules; ever inventing", "No verb Rhythmic Explanation cf. Marley & Eliot", "SONNET, Extra: Diction"

Prayer (I)

Prayer the Church's banquet, angels' age,°
    God's breath in man returning to his birth,°
    The soul in paraphrase, heart in pilgrimage,°
The Christian plummet sounding heav'n and earth;
Engine against th' Almighty, sinners' tower,°
    Reversèd thunder, Christ-side-piercing spear,
    The six-days' world transposing in an hour,°
A kind of tune, which all things hear and fear;
Softness, and peace, and joy, and love, and bliss,
    Exalted manna, gladness of the best,°   10
    Heaven in ordinary, man well dressed,°
The milky way, the bird of Paradise,°
    Church-bells beyond the stars heard, the soul's blood,
    The land of spices; something understood.

Handwritten margin notes: "Depicting Human Cond. in a poem", "in a series of anti rhyme - rhyme word clusters"

The H. Communion°

Not in rich furniture, or fine array,°
    Nor in a wedge of gold,
    Thou, who for me wast sold,°
    To me dost now thyself convey;
For so thou should'st without me still have been,°
    Leaving within me sin:

But by the way of nourishment and strength
    Thou creep'st into my breast;
    Making thy way my rest,
    And thy small quantities my length;   10
Which spread their forces into every part,
    Meeting sin's force and art.

Yet can these not get over to my soul,°
    Leaping the wall that parts
    Our souls and fleshy hearts;
    But as th' outworks, they may control°
My rebel-flesh, and carrying thy name,
    Affright both sin and shame.

Only thy grace, which with these elements comes,
    Knoweth the ready way,   20
    And hath the privy key,°
    Op'ning the soul's most subtle rooms;
While those to spirits refined, at door attend°
    Dispatches from their friend.°

Give me my captive soul, or take
    My body also thither.
Another lift like this will make
    Them both to be together.

Before that sin turned flesh to stone,
    And all our lump to leaven;   30
A fervent sigh might well have blown
    Our innocent earth to heaven.

For sure when Adam did not know
    To sin, or sin to smother;
He might to heav'n from Paradise go,
    As from one room t' another.

Thou hast restored us to this ease
    By this thy heav'nly blood;
Which I can go to, when I please,
    And leave th' earth to their food.   40

Antiphon (I)°

Cho. Let all the world in ev'ry corner sing,
    My God and King.

  Vers. The heav'ns are not too high,
    His praise may thither fly:
    The earth is not too low,
    His praises there may grow.

Cho. Let all the world in ev'ry corner sing,
    My God and King.

Vers. The church with psalms must shout,
 No door can keep them out:
 But above all, the heart
 Must bear the longest part.   10

Cho. Let all the world in ev'ry corner sing,
  My God and King.

Love I

Immortal Love, author of this great frame,°
 Sprung from that beauty which can never fade;
 How hath man parcelled out thy glorious name,
And thrown it on that dust which thou hast made,
While mortal love doth all the title gain!
 Which siding with invention, they together°
 Bear all the sway, possessing heart and brain,
(Thy workmanship) and give thee share in neither.
Wit fancies beauty, beauty raiseth wit:
 The world is theirs; they two play out the game, 10
 Thou standing by: and though thy glorious name
Wrought our deliverance from th' infernal pit,
 Who sings thy praise? only a scarf or glove
 Doth warm our hands, and make them write of love.

II

Immortal Heat, O let thy greater flame
 Attract the lesser to it: let those fires,
 Which shall consume the world, first make it tame;
And kindle in our hearts such true desires,
As may consume our lusts, and make thee way.
 Then shall our hearts pant thee; then shall our brain°
 All her invention on thine Altar lay,
And there in hymns send back thy fire again:
Our eyes shall see thee, which before saw dust;
 Dust blown by wit, till that they both were blind: 10

Thou shalt recover all thy goods in kind,
Who wert disseizèd by usurping lust:°
　All knees shall bow to thee; all wits shall rise,°
　And praise him who did make and mend our eyes.

The Temper (I)°

How should I praise thee, Lord! how should my rhymes
　　Gladly engrave thy love in steel,
　If what my soul doth feel sometimes,
　　My soul might ever feel!

Although there were some forty heav'ns, or more,°
　　Sometimes I peer above them all;
　Sometimes I hardly reach a score,
　　Sometimes to hell I fall.

O rack me not to such a vast extent;
　　Those distances belong to thee: 10
　The world's too little for thy tent,
　　A grave too big for me.

Wilt thou meet arms with man, that thou dost stretch°
　　A crumb of dust from heav'n to hell?
　Will great God measure with a wretch?
　　Shall he thy stature spell?°

O let me, when thy roof my soul hath hid,
　　O let me roost and nestle there:
　Then of a sinner thou art rid,
　　And I of hope and fear.   20

Yet take thy way; for sure thy way is best:
　　Stretch or contract me, thy poor debtor:
　This is but tuning of my breast,
　　To make the music better.

Whether I fly with angels, fall with dust,
   Thy hands made both, and I am there:
   Thy power and love, my love and trust
Make one place ev'rywhere.

The Temper (II)

It cannot be. Where is that mighty joy,
   Which just now took up all my heart?
   Lord, if thou must needs use thy dart,
Save that, and me; or sin for both destroy.°

The grosser world stands to thy word and art;
   But thy diviner world of grace
   Thou suddenly dost raise and race,°
And ev'ry day a new Creator art.

O fix thy chair of grace, that all my powers°
   May also fix their reverence:
   For when thou dost depart from hence,
They grow unruly, and sit in thy bowers.

Scatter, or bind them all to bend to thee:
   Though elements change, and heaven move,
   Let not thy higher Court remove,
But keep a standing Majesty in me.

about
Writing Poems & Its

Jordan (I)°

Who says that fictions only and false hair
Become a verse? Is there in truth no beauty?
Is all good structure in a winding stair?
May no lines pass, except they do their duty
   Not to a true, but painted chair?°

fellow
courtiers
social
climbers

Is it no verse, except enchanted groves
And sudden arbours shadow coarse-spun lines?°
Must purling streams refresh a lover's loves?
Must all be veiled, while he that reads, divines,
    Catching the sense at two removes?   10

Shepherds are honest people; let them sing:
Riddle who list, for me, and pull for prime:°
I envy no man's nightingale or spring;
Nor let them punish me with loss of rhyme,
    Who plainly say, *My God, My King*.

Employment (I)

    If as a flower doth spread and die,
        Thou wouldst extend me to some good,
    Before I were by frost's extremity
                        Nipped in the bud;

    The sweetness and the praise were thine;
        But the extension and the room,
    Which in thy garland I should fill, were mine
                        At thy great doom.°

    For as thou dost impart thy grace,
        The greater shall our glory be.   10
    The measure of our joys is in this place,
                        The stuff with thee.

    Let me not languish then, and spend
        A life as barren to thy praise,
    As is the dust, to which that life doth tend,
                        But with delays.

    All things are busy; only I
        Neither bring honey with the bees,
    Nor flowers to make that, nor the husbandry
                        To water these.   20

I am no link of thy great chain,
But all my company is a weed.
Lord place me in thy consort; give one strain°
To my poor reed.°

The H. Scriptures. I

Oh Book! infinite sweetness! let my heart°
Suck ev'ry letter, and a honey gain,
Precious for any grief in any part;
To clear the breast, to mollify all pain.
Thou art all health, health thriving till it make
A full eternity: thou art a mass
Of strange delights, where we may wish and take.
Ladies, look here; this is the thankful glass°
That mends the looker's eyes: this is the well
That washes what it shows. Who can endear   10
Thy praise too much? thou art heav'n's lidger here,°
Working against the states of death and hell.
Thou art joy's handsel: heav'n lies flat in thee,°
Subject to ev'ry mounter's bended knee.

II

Oh that I knew how all thy lights combine,
And the configurations of their glory!°
Seeing not only how each verse doth shine,
But all the constellations of the story.
This verse marks that, and both do make a motion
Unto a third, that ten leaves off doth lie:
Then as dispersèd herbs do watch a potion,°
These three make up some Christian's destiny:
Such are thy secrets, which my life makes good,
And comments on thee: for in ev'rything   10
Thy words do find me out, and parallels bring,
And in another make me understood.
Stars are poor books, and oftentimes do miss:
This book of stars lights to eternal bliss.

Whitsunday°

Listen sweet Dove unto my song,
 And spread thy golden wings in me;
 Hatching my tender heart so long,
Till it get wing, and fly away with thee.

Where is that fire which once descended
 On thy Apostles? thou didst then
 Keep open house, richly attended,
Feasting all comers by twelve chosen men.

Such glorious gifts thou didst bestow,
 That th' earth did like a heav'n appear;   10
 The stars were coming down to know
If they might mend their wages, and serve here.

The sun, which once did shine alone,
 Hung down his head, and wished for night,
 When he beheld twelve suns for one
Going about the world, and giving light.

But since those pipes of gold, which brought°
 That cordial water to our ground,
 Were cut and martyred by the fault
Of those, who did themselves through their side wound,   20

Thou shutt'st the door and keep'st within;
 Scarce a good joy creeps through the chink:
 And if the braves of conqu'ring sin°
Did not excite thee, we should wholly sink.

Lord, though we change, thou art the same;
 The same sweet God of love and light:
 Restore this day, for thy great name,
Unto his ancient and miraculous right.

Grace

My stock lies dead, and no increase°
Doth my dull husbandry improve:
O let thy graces without cease
   Drop from above!

If still the sun should hide his face,
Thy house would but a dungeon prove,
Thy works night's captives: O let grace
   Drop from above!

The dew doth ev'ry morning fall;
And shall the dew outstrip thy Dove? 10
The dew, for which grass cannot call,
   Drop from above.

Death is still working like a mole,
And digs my grave at each remove:
Let grace work too, and on my soul
   Drop from above.

Sin is still hammering my heart
Unto a hardness void of love:
Let suppling grace, to cross his art,
   Drop from above. 20

O come! for thou dost know the way:
Or if to me thou wilt not move,
Remove me, where I need not say,
   Drop from above.

Praise (I)

To write a verse or two is all the praise,
    That I can raise:
  Mend my estate in any ways,
    Thou shalt have more.

I go to Church; help me to wings, and I
              Will thither fly;
      Or, if I mount unto the sky,
            I will do more.

Man is all weakness; there is no such thing
             As Prince or King: 10
      His arm is short; yet with a sling°
            He may do more.

An herb distilled, and drunk, may dwell next door,°
             On the same floor,
      To a brave soul: exalt the poor,
            They can do more.

O raise me then! Poor bees, that work all day,
             Sting my delay,
      Who have a work, as well as they,
            And much, much more.   20

Affliction (II)

        Kill me not ev'ry day,
Thou Lord of life; since thy one death for me
Is more than all my deaths can be,
       Though I in broken pay°
Die over each hour of Methusalem's stay.°

        If all men's tears were let
Into one common sewer, sea, and brine;
    What were they all, compared to thine?
       Wherein if they were set,
They would discolour thy most bloody sweat.°   10

        Thou art my grief alone,
Thou Lord conceal it not: and as thou art
    All my delight, so all my smart:
       Thy cross took up in one,
By way of imprest, all my future moan.°

Mattens°

I cannot ope mine eyes,
But thou art ready there to catch
My morning-soul and sacrifice:
Then we must needs for that day make a match.

My God, what is a heart?
Silver, or gold, or precious stone,
Or star, or rainbow, or a part
Of all these things, or all of them in one?

My God, what is a heart,
That thou shouldst it so eye, and woo,   10
Pouring upon it all thy art,
As if that thou hadst nothing else to do?

Indeed man's whole estate
Amounts (and richly) to serve thee:
He did not heav'n and earth create,
Yet studies them, not him by whom they be.

Teach me thy love to know;
That this new light, which now I see,
May both the work and workman show:
Then by a sun-beam I will climb to thee.   20

Sin (II)

O that I could a sin once see!
We paint the devil foul, yet he
Hath some good in him, all agree.
Sin is flat opposite to th' Almighty, seeing°
It wants the good of *virtue*, and of *being*.

But God more care of us hath had:
If apparitions make us sad,
By sight of sin we should grow mad.
Yet as in sleep we see foul death, and live:
So devils are our sins in perspective.°   10

Evensong

Blest be the God of love,
Who gave me eyes, and light, and power this day,
Both to be busy, and to play.
But much more blest be God above,
Who gave me sight alone,
Which to himself he did deny:
For when he sees my ways, I die:
But I have got his son, and he hath none.

What have I brought thee home
For this thy love? have I discharged the debt,   10
Which this day's favour did beget?
I ran; but all I brought, was foam.
Thy diet, care, and cost
Do end in bubbles, balls of wind;
Of wind to thee whom I have crossed,
But balls of wild-fire to my troubled mind.

Yet still thou goest on,
And now with darkness closest weary eyes,
Saying to man, *It doth suffice:*
Henceforth repose; your work is done.   20
Thus in thy ebony box
Thou dost inclose us, till the day
Put our amendment in our way,
And give new wheels to our disordered clocks.

I muse, which shows more love,
The day or night: that is the gale, this th' harbour;
That is the walk, and this the arbour;
Or that the garden, this the grove.
My God, thou art all love.
Not one poor minute scapes thy breast,   30
But brings a favour from above;
And in this love, more than in bed, I rest.

Church-monuments°

While that my soul repairs to her devotion,
Here I intomb my flesh, that it betimes
May take acquaintance of this heap of dust;
To which the blast of death's incessant motion,
Fed with the exhalation of our crimes,
Drives all at last. Therefore I gladly trust
My body to this school, that it may learn
To spell his elements, and find his birth°
Written in dusty heraldry and lines;
Which dissolution sure doth best discern,   10
Comparing dust with dust, and earth with earth.
These laugh at jet and marble put for signs,
To sever the good fellowship of dust,
And spoil the meeting. What shall point out them,
When they shall bow, and kneel, and fall down flat
To kiss those heaps, which now they have in trust?
         Dear flesh, while I do pray, learn here thy stem
And true descent; that when thou shalt grow fat,
And wanton in thy cravings, thou mayst know,
That flesh is but the glass, which holds the dust   20
That measures all our time; which also shall
Be crumbled into dust. Mark here below
How tame these ashes are, how free from lust,
That thou mayst fit thyself against thy fall.°

Church-music

Sweetest of sweets, I thank you: when displeasure°
     Did through my body wound my mind,
You took me thence, and in your house of pleasure
     A dainty lodging me assigned.

Now I in you without a body move,
     Rising and falling with your wings:
We both together sweetly live and love,
     Yet say sometimes, *God help poor Kings.*

Comfort, I'll die; for if you post from me,°
           Sure I shall do so, and much more: 10
But if I travel in your company,
           You know the way to heaven's door.

Church-lock and Key

I know it is my sin, which locks thine ears,
           And binds thy hands,
Out-crying my requests, drowning my tears;
Or else the chillness of my faint demands.

But as cold hands are angry with the fire,
           And mend it still;
So I do lay the want of my desire,
Not on my sins, or coldness, but thy will.

Yet hear, O God, only for his blood's sake
           Which pleads for me: 10
For though sins plead too, yet like stones they make
His blood's sweet current much more loud to be.

The Church-floor

Mark you the floor? that square and speckled stone,
           Which looks so firm and strong,
              Is *Patience*:

And th' other black and grave, wherewith each one
           Is checkered all along,
              Humility:

The gentle rising, which on either hand
           Leads to the Choir above,
              Is *Confidence*:

But the sweet cement, which in one sure band°   10
            Ties the whole frame, is *Love*
                And *Charity*.

Hither sometimes Sin steals, and stains
    The marble's neat and curious veins:°
But all is cleansèd when the marble weeps.
    Sometimes Death, puffing at the door,
    Blows all the dust about the floor:
But while he thinks to spoil the room, he sweeps.
    Blest be the *Architect*, whose art
    Could build so strong in a weak heart.   20

The Windows

Lord, how can man preach thy eternal word?
        He is a brittle crazy glass:°
Yet in thy temple thou dost him afford
            This glorious and transcendent place,
            To be a window, through thy grace.

But when thou dost anneal in glass thy story,°
        Making thy life to shine within
The holy preacher's; then the light and glory
            More rev'rend grows, and more doth win:
            Which else shows wat'rish, bleak, and thin.   10

Doctrine and life, colours and light, in one
        When they combine and mingle, bring
A strong regard and awe: but speech alone
            Doth vanish like a flaring thing,
            And in the ear, not conscience ring.

Trinity Sunday

Lord, who hast formed me out of mud,
    And hast redeemed me through thy blood,
    And sanctified me to do good;

Purge all my sins done heretofore:
    For I confess my heavy score,
    And I will strive to sin no more.

Enrich my heart, mouth, hands in me,
    With faith, with hope, with charity;
    That I may run, rise, rest with thee.

Content

Peace mutt'ring thoughts, and do not grudge to keep
        Within the walls of your own breast:
Who cannot on his own bed sweetly sleep,
        Can on another's hardly rest.

Gad not abroad at ev'ry quest and call
        Of an untrainèd hope or passion.
To court each place or fortune that doth fall,
        Is wantonness in contemplation.

Mark how the fire in flints doth quiet lie,
        Content and warm t' itself alone: 10
But when it would appear to other's eye,
        Without a knock it never shone.

Give me the pliant mind, whose gentle measure
        Complies and suits with all estates;
Which can let loose to a crown, and yet with pleasure°
        Take up within a cloister's gates.

This soul doth span the world, and hang content
        From either pole unto the centre:
Where in each room of the well-furnished tent
        He lies warm, and without adventure.   20

The brags of life are but a nine-days' wonder;
        And after death the fumes that spring
From private bodies make as big a thunder,
        As those which rise from a huge King.

Only thy Chronicle is lost; and yet
       Better by worms be all once spent,
Than to have hellish moths still gnaw and fret
       Thy name in books, which may not rent:°

When all thy deeds, whose brunt thou feel'st alone,
       Are chawed by others' pens and tongue;   30
And as their wit is, their digestion,
       Thy nourished fame is weak or strong.

Then cease discoursing soul, till thine own ground,°
       Do not thyself or friends importune.
He that by seeking hath himself once found,
       Hath ever found a happy fortune.

The Quiddity°

My God, a verse is not a crown,
No point of honour, or gay suit,
No hawk, or banquet, or renown,
Nor a good sword, nor yet a lute:

It cannot vault, or dance, or play;
It never was in France or Spain,
Nor can it entertain the day
With my great stable or demesne:°

It is no office, art, or news,
Nor the Exchange, or busy Hall;°   10
But it is that which while I use
I am with thee, and *most take all.*°

Humility

I saw the Virtues sitting hand in hand
In sev'ral ranks upon an azure throne,
Where all the beasts and fowl by their command
Presented tokens of submission.

Humility, who sat the lowest there
    To execute their call,
When by the beasts the presents tendered were,
    Gave them about to all.

The angry Lion did present his paw,
Which by consent was giv'n to Mansuetude.°   10
The fearful Hare her ears, which by their law
Humility did reach to Fortitude.
The jealous Turkey brought his coral-chain;°
    That went to Temperance.
On Justice was bestowed the Fox's brain,
    Killed in the way by chance.

At length the Crow bringing the Peacock's plume,
(For he would not) as they beheld the grace
Of that brave gift, each one began to fume,
And challenge it, as proper to his place,   20
Till they fell out: which when the beasts espied,
    They leapt upon the throne;
And if the Fox had lived to rule their side,
    They had deposed each one.

Humility, who held the plume, at this
Did weep so fast, that the tears trickling down
Spoiled all the train: then saying, *Here it is*°
For which ye wrangle, made them turn their frown
Against the beasts: so jointly bandying,°
    They drive them soon away;   30
And then amerced them, double gifts to bring°
    At the next Session-day.°

Frailty

  Lord, in my silence how do I despise
    What upon trust
  Is stylèd *honour*, *riches*, or *fair eyes*;
    But is *fair dust*!

I surname them *gilded clay*,
    Dear earth, fine grass or *hay*;
In all, I think my foot doth ever tread
    Upon their head.

But when I view abroad both Regiments;°
    The world's, and thine: 10
Thine clad with simpleness, and sad events;°
    The other fine,
Full of glory and gay weeds,°
    Brave language, braver deeds:°
That which was dust before, doth quickly rise,
    And prick mine eyes.°

O brook not this, lest if what even now
    My foot did tread,
Affront those joys, wherewith thou didst endow°
    And long since wed   20
My poor soul, ev'n sick of love:
    It may a Babel prove
Commodious to conquer heav'n and thee
    Planted in me.

Constancy

    Who is the honest man?
He that doth still and strongly good pursue,°
To God, his neighbour, and himself most true:
    Whom neither force nor fawning can
Unpin, or wrench from giving all their due.

    Whose honesty is not
So loose or easy, that a ruffling wind
Can blow away, or glittering look it blind:
    Who rides his sure and even trot,
While the world now rides by, now lags behind.   10

Who, when great trials come,
Nor seeks, nor shuns them; but doth calmly stay,
Till he the thing and the example weigh:
    All being brought into a sum,
What place or person calls for, he doth pay.

    Whom none can work or woo
To use in anything a trick or sleight;
For above all things he abhors deceit:
    His words and works and fashion too
All of a piece, and all are clear and straight.   20

    Who never melts or thaws
At close tentations: when the day is done,°
His goodness sets not, but in dark can run:
    The sun to others writeth laws,
And is their virtue; Virtue is his Sun.

    Who, when he is to treat
With sick folks, women, those whom passions sway,
Allows for that, and keeps his constant way:
    Whom others' faults do not defeat;
But though men fail him, yet his part doth play.   30

    Whom nothing can procure,
When the wide world runs bias from his will,
To writhe his limbs, and share, not mend the ill.°
    This is the mark-man, safe and sure,°
Who still is right, and prays to be so still.

Affliction (III)

My heart did heave, and there came forth, *O God!*
By that I knew that thou wast in the grief,
To guide and govern it to my relief,
    Making a scepter of the rod:
      Hadst thou not had thy part,
Sure the unruly sigh had broke my heart.

But since thy breath gave me both life and shape,
Thou know'st my tallies; and when there's assigned°
So much breath to a sigh, what's then behind?
    Or if some years with it escape,°   10
    The sigh then only is
A gale to bring me sooner to my bliss.

Thy life on earth was grief, and thou art still
Constant unto it, making it to be
A point of honour, now to grieve in me,
    And in thy members suffer ill.
    They who lament one cross,
Thou dying daily, praise thee to thy loss.

The Star

Bright spark, shot from a brighter place,
    Where beams surround my Saviour's face,
        Canst thou be anywhere
        So well as there?

Yet, if thou wilt from thence depart,
    Take a bad lodging in my heart;
        For thou canst make a debtor,
        And make it better.

First with thy fire-work burn to dust
    Folly, and worse than folly, lust: 10
        Then with thy light refine,
        And make it shine:

So disengaged from sin and sickness,
    Touch it with thy celestial quickness,°
        That it may hang and move
        After thy love.

Then with our trinity of light,
    Motion, and heat, let's take our flight
        Unto the place where thou
        Before didst bow.   20

Get me a standing there, and place
  Among the beams, which crown the face
    Of him, who died to part
      Sin and my heart:

That so among the rest I may
  Glitter, and curl, and wind as they:
    That winding is their fashion
      Of adoration.

Sure thou wilt joy, by gaining me
  To fly home like a laden bee   30
    Unto that hive of beams
      And garland-streams.

Sunday

    O day most calm, most bright,
The fruit of this, the next world's bud,
Th' endorsement of supreme delight,
Writ by a friend, and with his blood;
The couch of time; care's balm and bay:
The week were dark, but for thy light:
    Thy torch doth show the way.

    The other days and thou
Make up one man; whose face thou art,
Knocking at heaven with thy brow: 10
The worky-days are the back-part;°
The burden of the week lies there,
Making the whole to stoop and bow,
    Till thy release appear.

    Man had straight forward gone
To endless death: but thou dost pull
And turn us round to look on one,
Whom, if we were not very dull,
We could not choose but look on still;°
Since there is no place so alone,   20
    The which he doth not fill.

Sundays the pillars are,
On which heav'n's palace archèd lies:
The other days fill up the spare
And hollow room with vanities.
They are the fruitful beds and borders°
In God's rich garden: that is bare,
       Which parts their ranks and orders.

    The Sundays of man's life,
Threaded together on time's string,   30
Make bracelets to adorn the wife
Of the eternal glorious King.
On Sunday heaven's gate stands ope;
Blessings are plentiful and rife,
       More plentiful than hope.

    This day my Saviour rose,
And did inclose this light for his:
That, as each beast his manger knows,
Man might not of his fodder miss.
Christ hath took in this piece of ground,°   40
And made a garden there for those
       Who want herbs for their wound.

    The rest of our Creation°
Our great Redeemer did remove
With the same shake, which at his passion
Did th' earth and all things with it move.
As Sampson bore the doors away,°
Christ's hands, though nailed, wrought our salvation,
       And did unhinge that day.°

    The brightness of that day   50
We sullied by our foul offence:
Wherefore that robe we cast away,°
Having a new at his expense,
Whose drops of blood paid the full price,
That was required to make us gay,
       And fit for Paradise.

Thou art a day of mirth:
And where the week-days trail on ground,
Thy flight is higher, as thy birth.
O let me take thee at the bound,　　　　　　　　　60
Leaping with thee from sev'n to sev'n,
Till that we both, being tossed from earth,
　　　Fly hand in hand to heav'n!

Avarice

Money, thou bane of bliss, and source of woe,
　　Whence com'st thou, that thou art so fresh and fine?
　　I know thy parentage is base and low:
Man found thee poor and dirty in a mine.
Surely thou didst so little contribute
　　To this great kingdom, which thou now hast got,
　　That he was fain, when thou wert destitute,°
To dig thee out of thy dark cave and grot:
Then forcing thee by fire he made thee bright:
　　Nay, thou hast got the face of man; for we　　　　10
　　Have with our stamp and seal transferred our right:
Thou art the man, and man but dross to thee.
　　Man calleth thee his wealth, who made thee rich;
　　And while he digs out thee, falls in the ditch.

Ana- ${\begin{Bmatrix} \text{MARY} \\ \text{ARMY} \end{Bmatrix}}$ gram

How well her name an *Army* doth present,
In whom the *Lord of Hosts* did pitch his tent!

To All Angels and Saints

Oh glorious spirits, who after all your bands°
See the smooth face of God without a frown
　　　　　　　Or strict commands;
Where ev'ry one is king, and hath his crown,
If not upon his head, yet in his hands:°

Not out of envy or maliciousness
Do I forbear to crave your special aid:
                 I would address
My vows to thee most gladly, Blessed Maid,
And Mother of my God, in my distress.   10

Thou art the holy mine, whence came the gold,
The great restorative for all decay°
                 In young and old;
Thou art the cabinet where the jewel lay:
Chiefly to thee would I my soul unfold:

But now, alas, I dare not; for our King,°
Whom we do all jointly adore and praise,
                 Bids no such thing:
And where his pleasure no injunction lays,
('Tis your own case) ye never move a wing.   20

All worship is prerogative, and a flower
Of his rich crown, from whom lies no appeal
                 At the last hour:
Therefore we dare not from his garland steal,
To make a posy for inferior power.°

Although then others court you, if ye know
What's done on earth, we shall not fare the worse,
                 Who do not so;
Since we are ever ready to disburse,
If anyone our Master's hand can show.   30

Employment (II)

He that is weary, let him sit.
                 My soul would stir
And trade in courtesies and wit,
                 Quitting the fur
To cold complexions needing it.°

Man is no star, but a quick coal°
       Of mortal fire:
Who blows it not, nor doth control
       A faint desire,
Lets his own ashes choke his soul.   10

When th' elements did for place contest°
       With him, whose will
Ordained the highest to be best,
       The earth sat still,
And by the others is oppressed.

Life is a business, not good cheer;
       Ever in wars.
The sun still shineth there or here,
       Whereas the stars
Watch an advantage to appear.°   20

Oh that I were an orange-tree,
       That busy plant!°
Then should I ever laden be,
       And never want
Some fruit for him that dressèd me.°

But we are still too young or old;°
       The Man is gone,°
Before we do our wars unfold:
       So we freeze on,
Until the grave increase our cold.   30

Denial

When my devotions could not pierce
       Thy silent ears;
Then was my heart broken, as was my verse:
       My breast was full of fears
          And disorder:

sense of failure in creative artist

My bent thoughts, like a brittle bow,
      Did fly asunder:
Each took his way; some would to pleasures go,
      Some to the wars and thunder
           Of alarms.°   10

As good go anywhere, they say,
      As to benumb
Both knees and heart, in crying night and day,
      Come, come, my God, O come,
           But no hearing.

O that thou shouldst give dust a tongue
      To cry to thee,
And then not hear it crying! all day long
      My heart was in my knee,
           But no hearing.   20

Therefore my soul lay out of sight,
      Untuned, unstrung:
My feeble spirit, unable to look right,
      Like a nipped blossom, hung
           Discontented.

O cheer and tune my heartless breast,
      Defer no time;
That so thy favours granting my request,
      They and my mind may chime,
           And mend my rhyme.   30

Christmas

All after pleasures as I rid one day,
    My horse and I, both tired, body and mind,
    With full cry of affections, quite astray,°
I took up in the next inn I could find.
There when I came, whom found I but my dear,
    My dearest Lord, expecting till the grief°
    Of pleasures brought me to him, ready there

To be all passengers' most sweet relief?°
O Thou, whose glorious, yet contracted light,
   Wrapped in night's mantle, stole into a manger;   10
   Since my dark soul and brutish is thy right,
To man of all beasts be not thou a stranger:
   Furnish and deck my soul, that thou mayst have
   A better lodging than a rack or grave.

The shepherds sing; and shall I silent be?
          My God, no hymn for thee?
My soul's a shepherd too; a flock it feeds
          Of thoughts, and words, and deeds.
The pasture is thy word: the streams, thy grace
          Enriching all the place.   20
Shepherd and flock shall sing, and all my powers
          Out-sing the daylight hours.
Then we will chide the sun for letting night
          Take up his place and right:
We sing one common Lord; wherefore he should
          Himself the candle hold.°
I will go searching, till I find a sun
          Shall stay, till we have done;
A willing shiner, that shall shine as gladly,
          As frost-nipped suns look sadly.   30
Then we will sing, and shine all our own day,
          And one another pay:
His beams shall cheer my breast, and both so twine,
Till ev'n his beams sing, and my music shine.

Ungratefulness

Lord, with what bounty and rare clemency
     Hast thou redeemed us from the grave!
       If thou hadst let us run,
     Gladly had man adored the sun,
       And thought his god most brave;°
Where now we shall be better gods than he.°

Thou hast but two rare cabinets full of treasure,
   The *Trinity*, and *Incarnation*:
      Thou hast unlocked them both,
      And made them jewels to betroth   10
      The work of thy creation
Unto thyself in everlasting pleasure.

The statelier cabinet is the *Trinity*,
      Whose sparkling light access denies:
      Therefore thou dost not show
      This fully to us, till death blow
      The dust into our eyes:
For by that powder thou wilt make us see.

But all thy sweets are packed up in the other;°
      Thy mercies thither flock and flow: 20
      That as the first affrights,
      This may allure us with delights;
      Because this box we know;
For we have all of us just such another.

But man is close, reserved, and dark to thee:
      When thou demandest but a heart,
      He cavils instantly.
      In his poor cabinet of bone
      Sins have their box apart,
Defrauding thee, who gavest two for one.   30

Sighs and Groans

      O do not use me
After my sins! look not on my desert,°
But on thy glory! then thou wilt reform
And not refuse me: for thou only art
The mighty God, but I a silly worm;°
      O do not bruise me!

O do not urge me!
For what account can thy ill steward make?
I have abused thy stock, destroyed thy woods,
Sucked all thy magazines: my head did ache,°   10
Till it found out how to consume thy goods:
             O do not scourge me!

             O do not blind me!
I have deserved that an Egyptian night°
Should thicken all my powers; because my lust
Hath still sewed fig-leaves to exclude thy light:°
But I am frailty, and already dust;
             O do not grind me!

             O do not fill me
With the turned vial of thy bitter wrath!°   20
For thou hast other vessels full of blood,
A part whereof my Saviour emptied hath,
Ev'n unto death: since he died for my good,
             O do not kill me!

             But O reprieve me!
For thou hast life and death at thy command;
Thou art both *Judge* and *Saviour*, *feast* and *rod*,
Cordial and *Corrosive*: put not thy hand°
Into the bitter box; but O my God,
             My God, relieve me!   30

The World

Love built a stately house; where Fortune came,
And spinning fancies, she was heard to say,
That her fine cobwebs did support the frame,
Whereas they were supported by the same:
But Wisdom quickly swept them all away.

Then Pleasure came, who, liking not the fashion,
Began to make Balconies, Terraces,°
Till she had weakened all by alteration:
But rev'rend laws, and many a proclamation
Reformèd all at length with menaces.   10

Then entered Sin, and with that Sycamore,°
Whose leaves first sheltered man from drought and dew,
Working and winding slyly evermore,
The inward walls and sommers cleft and tore:°
But Grace shored these, and cut that as it grew.

Then Sin combined with Death in a firm band
To raze the building to the very floor:
Which they effected, none could them withstand.
But Love and Grace took Glory by the hand,
And built a braver palace than before.   20

Coloss. 3. 3
Our life is hid with Christ in God°

My words and thoughts do both express this notion,
That *Life* hath with the sun a double motion.°
The first *Is* straight, and our diurnal friend,
The other *Hid* and doth obliquely bend.
One life is wrapped *In* flesh, and tends to earth:
The other winds towards *Him*, whose happy birth
Taught me to live here so, *That* still one eye°
Should aim and shoot at that which *Is* on high:
Quitting with daily labour all *My* pleasure,°
To gain at harvest an eternal *Treasure*.   10

Vanity (I)

The fleet astronomer can bore,
And thread the spheres with his quick-piercing mind:°
He views their stations, walks from door to door,°
Surveys, as if he had designed
To make a purchase there: he sees their dances,
And knoweth long before
Both their full-eyed aspects, and secret glances.°

The nimble diver with his side
Cuts through the working waves, that he may fetch
His dearly-earnèd pearl, which God did hide   10
      On purpose from the vent'rous wretch:
That he might save his life, and also hers,
      Who with excessive pride
Her own destruction and his danger wears.

      The subtle chymick can devest°
And strip the creature naked, till he find
The callow principles within their nest:
      There he imparts to them his mind,
Admitted to their bed-chamber, before
      They appear trim and dressed   20
To ordinary suitors at the door.

      What hath not man sought out and found,
But his dear God? who yet his glorious law
Embosoms in us, mellowing the ground
      With showers and frosts, with love and awe,
So that we need not say, Where's this command?
      Poor man, thou searchest round
To find out *death*, but missest *life* at hand.

Lent°

Welcome dear feast of Lent: who loves not thee,
He loves not temperance, or authority,
      But is composed of passion.
The Scriptures bid us *fast*; the Church says, *now*:
Give to thy Mother, what thou wouldst allow
      To ev'ry Corporation.°

The humble soul composed of love and fear
Begins at home, and lays the burden there,
      When doctrines disagree.
He says, in things which use hath justly got,   10
I am a scandal to the Church, and not
      The Church is so to me.

True Christians should be glad of an occasion
To use their temperance, seeking no evasion,
        When good is seasonable;
Unless authority, which should increase
The obligation in us, make it less,
        And power itself disable.

Besides the cleanness of sweet abstinence,
Quick thoughts and motions at a small expense,   20
        A face not fearing light:
Whereas in fullness there are sluttish fumes,
Sour exhalations, and dishonest rheums,°
        Revenging the delight.

Then those same pendant profits, which the spring
And Easter intimate, enlarge the thing,
        And goodness of the deed.
Neither ought other men's abuse of Lent
Spoil the good use; lest by that argument
        We forfeit all our Creed.   30

It's true, we cannot reach Christ's fortieth day;°
Yet to go part of that religious way,
        Is better than to rest:
We cannot reach our Saviour's purity;
Yet are we bid, *Be holy ev'n as he.*°
        In both let's do our best.

Who goeth in the way which Christ hath gone,
Is much more sure to meet with him, than one
        That travelleth by-ways:
Perhaps my God, though he be far before,   40
May turn, and take me by the hand, and more
        May strengthen my decays.

Yet Lord instruct us to improve our fast
By starving sin and taking such repast
        As may our faults control:
That ev'ry man may revel at his door,
Not in his parlour; banqueting the poor,
        And among those his soul.

Virtue

Sweet day, so cool, so calm, so bright,°
The bridal of the earth and sky:°
The dew shall weep thy fall tonight;
        For thou must die.

Sweet rose, whose hue angry and brave°
Bids the rash gazer wipe his eye:
Thy root is ever in its grave,
        And thou must die.

Sweet spring, full of sweet days and roses,
A box where sweets compacted lie;   10
My music shows ye have your closes,°
        And all must die.

Only a sweet and virtuous soul,
Like seasoned timber, never gives;
But though the whole world turn to coal,°
        Then chiefly lives.

The Pearl. Matth. 13. 45°

I know the ways of Learning; both the head°
And pipes that feed the press, and make it run;
What reason hath from nature borrowèd,
Or of itself, like a good huswife, spun°
In laws and policy; what the stars conspire,°
What willing nature speaks, what forced by fire;°
Both th' old discoveries, and the new-found seas,
The stock and surplus, cause and history:
All these stand open, or I have the keys:
        Yet I love thee.   10

I know the ways of Honour, what maintains
The quick returns of courtesy and wit:°
In vies of favours whether party gains,°

When glory swells the heart, and mouldeth it
To all expressions both of hand and eye,
Which on the world a true-love-knot may tie,
And bear the bundle, wheresoe'er it goes:
How many drams of spirit there must be°
To sell my life unto my friends or foes:
                Yet I love thee.   20

I know the ways of Pleasure, the sweet strains,
The lullings and the relishes of it;°
The propositions of hot blood and brains;
What mirth and music mean; what love and wit
Have done these twenty hundred years, and more:
I know the projects of unbridled store:°
My stuff is flesh, not brass; my senses live,
And grumble oft, that they have more in me
Than he that curbs them, being but one to five:
                Yet I love thee.   30

I know all these, and have them in my hand:
Therefore not sealèd, but with open eyes°
I fly to thee, and fully understand
Both the main sale, and the commodities;°
And at what rate and price I have thy love;
With all the circumstances that may move:
Yet through these labyrinths, not my grovelling wit,°
But thy silk twist let down from heav'n to me,°
Did both conduct and teach me, how by it
                To climb to thee.   40

Affliction (IV)

Broken in pieces all asunder,
        Lord, hunt me not,
        A thing forgot,
Once a poor creature, now a wonder,°
        A wonder tortured in the space
        Betwixt this world and that of grace.

My thoughts are all a case of knives,
      Wounding my heart
      With scattered smart,
As wat'ring pots give flowers their lives.   10
      Nothing their fury can control,
      While they do wound and pink my soul.°

All my attendants are at strife,
      Quitting their place
      Unto my face:
Nothing performs the task of life:
      The elements are let loose to fight,
      And while I live, try out their right.

Oh help, my God! let not their plot
      Kill them and me,   20
      And also thee,
Who art my life: dissolve the knot,
      As the sun scatters by his light
      All the rebellions of the night.

Then shall those powers, which work for grief,
      Enter thy pay,
      And day by day
Labour thy praise, and my relief;
      With care and courage building me,
      Till I reach heav'n, and much more, thee.   30

Man

colloquial

      My God, I heard this day,
That none doth build a stately habitation,
      But he that means to dwell therein.
      What house more stately hath there been,
Or can be, than is Man? to whose creation°
      All things are in decay.

For Man is ev'ry thing,
And more: he is a tree, yet bears more fruit;°
    A beast, yet is, or should be more:
    Reason and speech we only bring.
Parrots may thank us, if they are not mute,
    They go upon the score.°　*MUSICAL*　　　10

    Man is all symmetry,
Full of proportions, one limb to another,
    And all to all the world besides:
    Each part may call the furthest, brother:
For head with foot hath private amity,
    And both with moons and tides.

    Nothing hath got so far,
But Man hath caught and kept it, as his prey.　　　20
    His eyes dismount the highest star:°
    He is in little all the sphere.°　*MICRO-MACRO*
Herbs gladly cure our flesh; because that they
    Find their acquaintance there.

    For us the winds do blow,
The earth doth rest, heav'n move, and fountains flow.
    Nothing we see, but means our good,
    As our delight, or as our treasure:
The whole is, either our cupboard of food,　*met. CONCEIT*
    Or cabinet of pleasure.　*ANTITHESIS* 30

    The stars have us to bed;
Night draws the curtain, which the sun withdraws;
    Music and light attend our head.
    All things unto our flesh are kind°
In their descent and being; to our mind
    In their ascent and cause.

    Each thing is full of duty:
Waters united are our navigation;
    Distinguishèd, our habitation;°
    Below, our drink; above, our meat;°　*food OF*
Both are our cleanliness. Hath one such beauty?　　40
    Then how are all things neat?°

More servants wait on Man, *RECApitulation*
Than he'll take notice of: in ev'ry path
    He treads down that which doth befriend him,
    When sickness makes him pale and wan.
Oh mighty love! Man is one world, and hath
      Another to attend him.
       MACRO

      Since then, my God, thou hast *Epigram*
1st So brave a palace built; O dwell in it,°   50
STANZA   That it may dwell with thee at last!
    Till then, afford us so much wit,°
That, as the world serves us, we may serve thee,
      And both thy servants be.

Antiphon (II)°

Chor. Praisèd be the God of love,
      Men. Here below,
      Angels. And here above:
Cho. Who hath dealt his mercies so,
      Ang. To his friend,
      Men. And to his foe;

Cho. That both grace and glory tend
      Ang. Us of old,
      Men. And us in th' end.
Cho. The great shepherd of the fold   10
      Ang. Us did make,
      Men. For us was sold.

Cho. He our foes in pieces brake;
      Ang. Him we touch;
      Men. And him we take.°
Cho. Wherefore since that he is such,
      Ang. We adore,
      Men. And we do crouch.°

   Cho.   Lord, thy praises should be more.
             Men. We have none,   20
             Ang. And we no store.
   Cho.   Praisèd be the God alone,
           Who hath made of two folds one.

Unkindness°

Lord, make me coy and tender to offend:°
In friendship, first I think, if that agree,
            Which I intend,
      Unto my friend's intent and end.
I would not use a friend, as I use Thee.

If any touch my friend, or his good name,
It is my honour and my love to free
            His blasted fame
      From the least spot or thought of blame.
I could not use a friend, as I use Thee.   10

My friend may spit upon my curious floor:°
Would he have gold? I lend it instantly;
            But let the poor,
      And thou within them, starve at door.°
I cannot use a friend, as I use Thee.

When that my friend pretendeth to a place,°
I quit my interest, and leave it free:
            But when thy grace
      Sues for my heart, I thee displace,
Nor would I use a friend, as I use Thee.   20

Yet can a friend what thou hast done fulfil?
O write in brass, *My God upon a tree*
            His blood did spill
     Only to purchase my good-will.
Yet use I not my foes, as I use Thee.

Life

I made a posy, while the day ran by:°
Here will I smell my remnant out, and tie
             My life within this band.°
But Time did beckon to the flowers, and they
By noon most cunningly did steal away,
             And withered in my hand.

My hand was next to them, and then my heart:
I took, without more thinking, in good part
             Time's gentle admonition:
Who did so sweetly death's sad taste convey,   10
Making my mind to smell my fatal day;
             Yet sug'ring the suspicion.

Farewell dear flowers, sweetly your time ye spent,
Fit, while ye lived, for smell or ornament,
             And after death for cures.
I follow straight without complaints or grief,
Since if my scent be good, I care not if
             It be as short as yours.

Submission

But that thou art my wisdom, Lord,
    And both mine eyes are thine,
My mind would be extremely stirred
    For missing my design.°

Were it not better to bestow
    Some place and power on me?
Then should thy praises with me grow,
    And share in my degree.°

But when I thus dispute and grieve,
    I do resume my sight,°   10
And pilf'ring what I once did give,
    Disseize thee of thy right.°

How know I, if thou shouldst me raise,
    That I should then raise thee?
Perhaps great places and thy praise
    Do not so well agree.

Wherefore unto my gift I stand;
    I will no more advise:
Only do thou lend me a hand,
    Since thou hast both mine eyes.   20

Justice (I)

    I cannot skill of these thy ways.°
Lord, thou didst make me, yet thou woundest me;
Lord, thou dost wound me, yet thou dost relieve me:
Lord, thou relievest, yet I die by thee:
Lord, thou dost kill me, yet thou dost reprieve me.
    But when I mark my life and praise,
    Thy justice me most fitly pays:
For, I do praise thee, yet I praise thee not:
My prayers mean thee, yet my prayers stray:°
I would do well, yet sin the hand hath got:°   10
My soul doth love thee, yet it loves delay.
    I cannot skill of these my ways.

Charms and Knots°

Who read a chapter when they rise,
Shall ne'er be troubled with ill eyes.

A poor man's rod, when thou dost ride,
Is both a weapon and a guide.

Who shuts his hand, hath lost his gold:
Who opens it, hath it twice told.°

Who goes to bed and does not pray,
Maketh two nights to ev'ry day.

Who by aspersions throw a stone
At th' head of others, hit their own.   10

Who looks on ground with humble eyes,
Finds himself there, and seeks to rise.

When th' hair is sweet through pride or lust,
The powder doth forget the dust.

Take one from ten, and what remains?°
Ten still, if sermons go for gains.

In shallow waters heav'n doth show;
But who drinks on, to hell may go.

Affliction (V)

My God, I read this day,
That planted Paradise was not so firm,°
As was and is thy floating Ark; whose stay°
And anchor thou art only, to confirm
        And strengthen it in ev'ry age,
        When waves do rise, and tempests rage.

At first we lived in pleasure;
Thine own delights thou didst to us impart:
When we grew wanton, thou didst use displeasure
To make us thine: yet that we might not part,   10
        As we at first did board with thee,
        Now thou wouldst taste our misery.

There is but joy and grief;
If either will convert us, we are thine:
Some angels used the first; if our relief°
Take up the second, then thy double line
        And sev'ral baits in either kind°
        Furnish thy table to thy mind.

Affliction then is ours;
We are the trees, whom shaking fastens more,   20
While blust'ring winds destroy the wanton bowers,
And ruffle all their curious knots and store.°
     My God, so temper joy and woe,
     That thy bright beams may tame thy bow.°

Mortification°

     How soon doth man decay!
When clothes are taken from a chest of sweets°
     To swaddle infants, whose young breath
         Scarce knows the way;
     Those clouts are little winding sheets,°
Which do consign and send them unto death.

     When boys go first to bed,
They step into their voluntary graves,
     Sleep binds them fast; only their breath
         Makes them not dead: 10
     Successive nights, like rolling waves,
Convey them quickly, who are bound for death.

     When youth is frank and free,°
And calls for music, while his veins do swell,
     All day exchanging mirth and breath
         In company;
     That music summons to the knell,°
Which shall befriend him at the hour of death.°

     When man grows staid and wise,
Getting a house and home, where he may move   20
     Within the circle of his breath,
         Schooling his eyes;
     That dumb inclosure maketh love
Unto the coffin, that attends his death.°

When age grows low and weak,
Marking his grave, and thawing ev'ry year,
Till all do melt, and drown his breath
When he would speak;
A chair or litter shows the bier,
Which shall convey him to the house of death.   30

Man, ere he is aware,
Hath put together a solemnity,°
And dressed his hearse, while he has breath°
As yet to spare:
Yet Lord, instruct us so to die,
That all these dyings may be life in death.

How sees Renais-
Creation

contrast God's
presence in Bib.
times & absence
in present (17c.)

— *Decay*

Sweet were the days, when thou didst lodge with Lot,°
Struggle with Jacob, sit with Gideon,°
Advise with Abraham, when thy power could not°
Encounter Moses' strong complaints and moan:°   *murmuring*
Thy words were then, *Let me alone.*

One might have sought and found thee presently°
At some fair oak, or bush, or cave, or well:°
Is my God this way? No, they would reply:
He is to Sinai gone, as we heard tell:
List, ye may hear great Aaron's bell.°   10

But now thou dost thyself immure and close
In some one corner of a feeble heart:
Where yet both Sin and Satan, thy old foes,
Do pinch and straiten thee, and use much art°
To gain thy thirds and little part.°

science, wars, religion

I see the world grows old, whenas the heat°
Of thy great love, once spread, as in an urn
Doth closet up itself, and still retreat,
Cold Sin still forcing it, till it return,
And calling *Justice*, all things burn.   20

Misery

Lord, let the angels praise thy name.
Man is a foolish thing, a foolish thing,
   Folly and Sin play all his game.
His house still burns, and yet he still doth sing,
      Man is but grass,°
      He knows it, fill the glass.

How canst thou brook his foolishness?
Why, he'll not lose a cup of drink for thee:
   Bid him but temper his excess;
Not he: he knows where he can better be,   10
      As he will swear,
      Than to serve thee in fear.

What strange pollutions doth he wed,
And make his own? as if none knew but he.
   No man shall beat into his head,
That thou within his curtains drawn canst see:°
      They are of cloth,
      Where never yet came moth.°

The best of men, turn but thy hand
For one poor minute, stumble at a pin: 20
   They would not have their actions scanned,
Nor any sorrow tell them that they sin,
      Though it be small,
      And measure not their fall.

      find fault with
They quarrel thee, and would give over°
The bargain made to serve thee: but thy love
   Holds them unto it, and doth cover
Their follies with the wing of thy mild Dove,
      Not suff'ring those
      Who would, to be thy foes.   30

My God, Man cannot praise thy name:
Thou art all brightness, perfect purity;
    The sun holds down his head for shame,
Dead with eclipses, when we speak of thee:
        How shall infection
        Presume on thy perfection?

As dirty hands foul all they touch,
And those things most, which are most pure and fine:
    So our clay hearts, ev'n when we crouch°
To sing thy praises, make them less divine.   40
        Yet either this,
        Or none, thy portion is.

Man cannot serve thee; let him go,
And serve the swine: there, there is his delight:
    He doth not like this virtue, no;
Give him his dirt to wallow in all night:
        These Preachers make
        His head to shoot and ache.

Oh foolish man! where are thine eyes?
How hast thou lost them in a crowd of cares?   50
    Thou pull'st the rug, and wilt not rise,°
No, not to purchase the whole pack of stars:
        There let them shine,
        Thou must go sleep, or dine.

The bird that sees a dainty bower
Made in the tree, where she was wont to sit,
    Wonders and sings, but not his power
Who made the arbour: this exceeds her wit.
        But Man doth know
        The spring, whence all things flow: 60

And yet, as though he knew it not,
His knowledge winks, and lets his humours reign;°
    They make his life a constant blot,
And all the blood of God to run in vain.
        Ah wretch! what verse
        Can thy strange ways rehearse?

Indeed at first Man was a treasure,
A box of jewels, shop of rarities,
    A ring, whose posy was, *My pleasure*:°
He was a garden in a Paradise: 70
        Glory and grace
        Did crown his heart and face.

But sin hath fooled him. Now he is°
A lump of flesh, without a foot or wing
    To raise him to a glimpse of bliss:
A sick tossed vessel, dashing on each thing;
        Nay, his own shelf:°
        My God, I mean myself.

Jordan (II)°

When first my lines of heav'nly joys made mention,
Such was their lustre, they did so excel,
That I sought out quaint words, and trim invention;°
My thoughts began to burnish, sprout, and swell,°
Curling with metaphors a plain intention,
Decking the sense, as if it were to sell.

Thousands of notions in my brain did run,
Off'ring their service, if I were not sped:°
I often blotted what I had begun;
This was not quick enough, and that was dead.°   10
Nothing could seem too rich to clothe the sun,
Much less those joys which trample on his head.

As flames do work and wind, when they ascend,
So did I weave myself into the sense.
But while I bustled, I might hear a friend°
Whisper, *How wide is all this long pretence!*°
There is in love a sweetness ready penned:°
Copy out only that, and save expense.

Prayer (II)

Of what an easy quick access,
My blessed Lord, art thou! how suddenly
    May our requests thine ear invade!
To show that state dislikes not easiness,°
If I but lift mine eyes, my suit is made:
Thou canst no more not hear, than thou canst die.

Of what supreme almighty power
Is thy great arm, which spans the east and west,
    And tacks the centre to the sphere!°
By it do all things live their measured hour: 10
We cannot ask the thing, which is not there,
Blaming the shallowness of our request.

Of what unmeasurable love
Art thou possessed, who, when thou couldst not die,
    Wert fain to take our flesh and curse,°
And for our sakes in person sin reprove,
That by destroying that which tied thy purse,
Thou mightst make way for liberality!

Since then these three wait on thy throne,
Ease, *Power*, and *Love*; I value prayer so,   20
    That were I to leave all but one,
Wealth, fame, endowments, virtues, all should go;
I and dear prayer would together dwell,
And quickly gain, for each inch lost, an ell.°

Obedience

My God, if writings may
Convey a Lordship any way°
Whither the buyer and the seller please;
    Let it not thee displease,
If this poor paper do as much as they.

On it my heart doth bleed
As many lines, as there doth need
To pass itself and all it hath to thee.°
To which I do agree,
And here present it as my special Deed.   10

If that hereafter Pleasure
Cavil, and claim her part and measure,
As if this passèd with a reservation,°
Or some such words in fashion;
I here exclude the wrangler from thy treasure.

O let thy sacred will
All thy delight in me fulfil!
Let me not think an action mine own way,
But as thy love shall sway,
Resigning up the rudder to thy skill.   20

Lord, what is man to thee,°
That thou shouldst mind a rotten tree?°
Yet since thou canst not choose but see my actions;
So great are thy perfections,
Thou mayst as well my actions guide, as see.

Besides, thy death and blood
Showed a strange love to all our good:
Thy sorrows were in earnest; no faint proffer,°
Or superficial offer
Of what we might not take, or be withstood.   30

Wherefore I all forgo:
To one word only I say, No:
Where in the Deed there was an intimation
Of a gift or donation,
Lord, let it now by way of purchase go.

He that will pass his land,
As I have mine, may set his hand
And heart unto this Deed, when he hath read;
And make the purchase spread
To both our goods, if he to it will stand.   40

How happy were my part,
If some kind man would thrust his heart°
Into these lines; till in heav'n's Court of Rolls°
They were by wingèd souls
Entered for both, far above their desert!

Conscience

Peace prattler, do not lour:
Not a fair look, but thou dost call it foul:
Not a sweet dish, but thou dost call it sour:
Music to thee doth howl.
By list'ning to thy chatting fears
I have both lost mine eyes and ears.

Prattler, no more, I say:
My thoughts must work, but like a noiseless sphere;
Harmonious peace must rock them all the day:
No room for prattlers there.   10
If thou persistest, I will tell thee,
That I have physic to expel thee.°

And the receipt shall be°
My Saviour's blood: whenever at his board°
I do but taste it, straight it cleanseth me,
And leaves thee not a word;
No, not a tooth or nail to scratch,
And at my actions carp, or catch.

Yet if thou talkest still,
Besides my physic, know there's some for thee: 20
Some wood and nails to make a staff or bill°
For those that trouble me:
The bloody cross of my dear Lord
Is both my physic and my sword.

Sion

Lord, with what glory wast thou served of old,
When Solomon's temple stood and flourishèd!°
 Where most things were of purest gold;
 The wood was all embellishèd
With flowers and carvings, mystical and rare:°
All showed the builder's, craved the seer's care.

Yet all this glory, all this pomp and state
Did not affect thee much, was not thy aim;
 Something there was, that sowed debate:
 Wherefore thou quitt'st thy ancient claim: 10
And now thy Architecture meets with sin;°
For all thy frame and fabric is within.

There thou art struggling with a peevish heart,
Which sometimes crosseth thee, thou sometimes it:
 The fight is hard on either part.
 Great God doth fight, he doth submit.
All Solomon's sea of brass and world of stone
Is not so dear to thee as one good groan.

And truly brass and stones are heavy things,
Tombs for the dead, not temples fit for thee: 20
 But groans are quick, and full of wings,°
 And all their motions upward be;
And ever as they mount, like larks they sing;
The note is sad, yet music for a King.

Home

Come Lord, my head doth burn, my heart is sick,
 While thou dost ever, ever stay:°
Thy long deferrings wound me to the quick,
 My spirit gaspeth night and day.
  O show thyself to me,
  Or take me up to thee!

How canst thou stay, considering the pace
    The blood did make, which thou didst waste?
When I behold it trickling down thy face,
    I never saw thing make such haste.   10
        O show thyself to me,
        Or take me up to thee!

When man was lost, thy pity looked about
    To see what help in th' earth or sky:
But there was none; at least no help without:°
    The help did in thy bosom lie.
        O show thyself to me,
        Or take me up to thee!

There lay thy son: and must he leave that nest,
    That hive of sweetness to remove   20
Thraldom from those, who would not at a feast
    Leave one poor apple for thy love?
        O show thyself to me,
        Or take me up to thee!

He did, he came: O my Redeemer dear,
    After all this canst thou be strange?
So many years baptized, and not appear?
    As if thy love could fail or change.
        O show thyself to me,
        Or take me up to thee!   30

Yet if thou stayest still, why must I stay?
    My God, what is this world to me,
This world of woe? hence all ye clouds, away,
    Away; I must get up and see.
        O show thyself to me,
        Or take me up to thee!

What is this weary world; this meat and drink,°
    That chains us by the teeth so fast?
What is this womankind, which I can wink°
    Into a blackness and distaste?   40
        O show thyself to me,
        Or take me up to thee!

With one small sigh thou gav'st me th' other day
    I blasted all the joys about me:
And scowling on them as they pined away,
    Now come again, said I, and flout me.
        O show thyself to me,
        Or take me up to thee!

Nothing but drought and dearth, but bush and brake,
    Which way soe'er I look, I see.
Some may dream merrily, but when they wake,   50
    They dress themselves and come to thee.
        O show thyself to me,
        Or take me up to thee!

We talk of harvests; there are no such things,
    But when we leave our corn and hay:°
There is no fruitful year, but that which brings
    The last and loved, though dreadful day.
        O show thyself to me,
        Or take me up to thee!   60

Oh loose this frame, this knot of man untie!
    That my free soul may use her wing,
Which now is pinioned with mortality,
    As an entangled, hampered thing.
        O show thyself to me,
        Or take me up to thee!

What have I left, that I should stay and groan?
    The most of me to heav'n is fled:
My thoughts and joys are all packed up and gone,
    And for their old acquaintance plead.
        O show thyself to me,   70
        Or take me up to thee!

Come dearest Lord, pass not this holy season,°
    My flesh and bones and joints do pray:
And ev'n my verse, when by the rhyme and reason
    The word is, *Stay*, says ever, *Come*.°
        O show thyself to me,
        Or take me up to thee!

The British Church

I joy, dear Mother, when I view
Thy perfect lineaments and hue
             Both sweet and bright.
Beauty in thee takes up her place,
And dates her letters from thy face,°
             When she doth write.

A fine aspect in fit array,
Neither too mean, nor yet too gay,°
             Shows who is best.
Outlandish looks may not compare:°
For all they either painted are,
             Or else undressed.

She on the hills, which wantonly°
Allureth all in hope to be
             By her preferred,°
Hath kissed so long her painted shrines,
That ev'n her face by kissing shines,
             For her reward.

She in the valley is so shy
Of dressing, that her hair doth lie
             About her ears:
While she avoids her neighbour's pride,
She wholly goes on th' other side,
             And nothing wears.

But, dearest Mother, what those miss,
The mean, thy praise and glory is,°
             And long may be.
Blessed be God, whose love it was
To double-moat thee with his grace,
             And none but thee.

The Quip

The merry world did on a day
With his train-bands and mates agree°
To meet together, where I lay,
And all in sport to jeer at me.

First, Beauty crept into a rose,
Which when I plucked not, Sir, said she,
Tell me, I pray, Whose hands are those?
But thou shalt answer, Lord, for me.°

Then Money came, and chinking still,
What tune is this, poor man? said he: 10
I heard in music you had skill.°
But thou shalt answer, Lord, for me.

Then came brave Glory puffing by
In silks that whistled, who but he?
He scarce allowed me half an eye.°
But thou shalt answer, Lord, for me.

Then came quick Wit and Conversation,
And he would needs a comfort be,
And, to be short, make an Oration.°
But thou shalt answer, Lord, for me.   20

Yet when the hour of thy design
To answer these fine things shall come;
Speak not at large; say, I am thine:°
And then they have their answer home.°

Vanity (II)

Poor silly soul, whose hope and head lies low;°
Whose flat delights on earth do creep and grow;
To whom the stars shine not so fair, as eyes;
Nor solid work, as false embroideries;
Hark and beware, lest what you now do measure
And write for sweet, prove a most sour displeasure.

O hear betimes, lest thy relenting°
     May come too late!
To purchase heaven for repenting
     Is no hard rate.   10
If souls be made of earthly mould,°
     Let them love gold;
     If born on high,
Let them unto their kindred fly:
For they can never be at rest,
Till they regain their ancient nest.
Then silly soul take heed; for earthly joy
Is but a bubble, and makes thee a boy.

The Dawning°

Awake sad heart, whom sorrow ever drowns;
  Take up thine eyes, which feed on earth;
Unfold thy forehead gathered into frowns:
  Thy Saviour comes, and with him mirth:
          Awake, awake;
And with a thankful heart his comforts take.
  But thou dost still lament, and pine, and cry;
  And feel his death, but not his victory.

Arise sad heart; if thou do not withstand,
  Christ's resurrection thine may be: 10
Do not by hanging down break from the hand,
  Which as it riseth, raiseth thee:
          Arise, arise;
And with his burial-linen dry thine eyes:°
  Christ left his grave-clothes, that we might, when grief
  Draws tears, or blood, not want a handkerchief.

JESU

JESU is in my heart, his sacred name
Is deeply carvèd there: but th'other week
A great affliction broke the little frame,

Ev'n all to pieces: which I went to seek:
And first I found the corner, where was *J*,
After, where *ES*, and next where *U* was graved.
When I had got these parcels, instantly°
I sat me down to spell them, and perceived
That to my broken heart he was *I ease you*,°
　　　　　And to my whole is *JESU*.　　　　10

Business°

　　　Canst be idle? canst thou play,
　　　Foolish soul who sinned today?

Rivers run, and springs each one
Know their home, and get them gone:
Hast thou tears, or hast thou none?

If, poor soul, thou hast no tears,
Would thou hadst no faults or fears!
Who hath these, those ill forbears.

Winds still work: it is their plot,
Be the season cold, or hot:　　　　　　　　10
Hast thou sighs, or hast thou not?

If thou hast no sighs or groans,
Would thou hadst no flesh and bones!
Lesser pains 'scape greater ones.

　　　But if yet thou idle be,
　　　Foolish soul, Who died for thee?

Who did leave his Father's throne,
To assume thy flesh and bone;
Had he life, or had he none?

If he had not lived for thee,　　　　　　　　20
Thou hadst died most wretchedly;
And two deaths had been thy fee.°

He so far thy good did plot,
That his own self he forgot.
Did he die, or did he not?

If he had not died for thee,
Thou hadst lived in misery.
Two lives worse than ten deaths be.°

    And hath any space of breath
      'Twixt his sins and Saviour's death? 30

He that loseth gold, though dross,
Tells to all he meets, his cross:°
He that sins, hath he no loss?

He that finds a silver vein,
Thinks on it, and thinks again:
Brings thy Saviour's death no gain?

    Who in heart not ever kneels,
    Neither sin nor Saviour feels.

Dialogue

    Sweetest Saviour, if my soul
      Were but worth the having,
    Quickly should I then control
      Any thought of waving.°
    But when all my care and pains
    Cannot give the name of gains
    To thy wretch so full of stains,
    What delight or hope remains?

    What, Child, is the balance thine,°
      Thine the poise and measure?° 10
    If I say, Thou shalt be mine;
      Finger not my treasure.
    What the gains in having thee
    Do amount to, only he,
    Who for man was sold, can see;
    That transferred th' accounts to me.

But as I can see no merit,
    Leading to this favour:
So the way to fit me for it
    Is beyond my savour.°   20
As the reason then is thine;
So the way is none of mine:
I disclaim the whole design:
Sin disclaims and I resign.

That is all, if that I could
    Get without repining;
And my clay, my creature, would
    Follow my resigning:
That as I did freely part
With my glory and desert,°   30
Left all joys to feel all smart——
    Ah! no more: thou break'st my heart.

Dullness

Why do I languish thus, drooping and dull,
    As if I were all earth?
O give me quickness, that I may with mirth°
        Praise thee brim-full!

The wanton lover in a curious strain°
        Can praise his fairest fair;
And with quaint metaphors her curlèd hair°
        Curl o'er again.

Thou art my loveliness, my life, my light,
        Beauty alone to me: 10
Thy bloody death and undeserved, makes thee
        Pure red and white.°

When all perfections as but one appear,
        That those thy form doth show,
The very dust, where thou dost tread and go,
        Makes beauties here.

Where are my lines then? my approaches? views?
     Where are my window-songs?°
Lovers are still pretending, and ev'n wrongs°
     Sharpen their Muse: 20

But I am lost in flesh, whose sugared lies
     Still mock me, and grow bold:
Sure thou didst put a mind there, if I could
     Find where it lies.

Lord, clear thy gift, that with a constant wit
     I may but look towards thee:
Look only; for to *love* thee, who can be,
     What angel fit?

Love-joy

As on a window late I cast mine eye,
I saw a vine drop grapes with *J* and *C*
Annealed on every bunch. One standing by°
Asked what it meant. I, who am never loth
To spend my judgement, said, It seemed to me
To be the body and the letters both
Of *Joy* and *Charity*. Sir, you have not missed,
The man replied; it figures *JESUS CHRIST*.°

Providence°

O sacred Providence, who from end to end°
Strongly and sweetly movest, shall I write,
And not of thee, through whom my fingers bend
To hold my quill? shall they not do thee right?

Of all the creatures both in sea and land
Only to Man thou hast made known thy ways,
And put the pen alone into his hand,
And made him Secretary of thy praise.

Beasts fain would sing; birds ditty to their notes;°
Trees would be tuning on their native lute　　　　　　　　10
To thy renown: but all their hands and throats
Are brought to Man, while they are lame and mute.

Man is the world's high priest: he doth present
The sacrifice for all; while they below
Unto the service mutter an assent,
Such as springs use that fall, and winds that blow.

He that to praise and laud thee doth refrain,
Doth not refrain unto himself alone,
But robs a thousand who would praise thee fain,
And doth commit a world of sin in one.　　　　　　　　20

The beasts say, Eat me: but, if beasts must teach,
The tongue is yours to eat, but mine to praise.
The trees say, Pull me: but the hand you stretch,
Is mine to write, as it is yours to raise.

Wherefore, most sacred Spirit, I here present
For me and all my fellows praise to thee:
And just it is that I should pay the rent,
Because the benefit accrues to me.

We all acknowledge both thy power and love
To be exact, transcendent, and divine;　　　　　　　　30
Who dost so strongly and so sweetly move,
While all things have their will, yet none but thine.

For either thy command or thy permission
Lay hands on all: they are thy right and left.
The first puts on with speed and expedition;
The other curbs sin's stealing pace and theft.

Nothing escapes them both; all must appear,
And be disposed, and dressed, and tuned by thee,
Who sweetly temper'st all. If we could hear°
Thy skill and art, what music would it be!　　　　　　　　40

Thou art in small things great, not small in any:
Thy even praise can neither rise, nor fall.
Thou art in all things one, in each thing many:
For thou art infinite in one and all.

Tempests are calm to thee; they know thy hand,°
And hold it fast, as children do their fathers,
Which cry and follow. Thou hast made poor sand°
Check the proud sea, ev'n when it swells and gathers.°

Thy cupboard serves the world: the meat is set,°
Where all may reach: no beast but knows his feed.   50
Birds teach us hawking; fishes have their net:°
The great prey on the less, they on some weed.

Nothing engendered doth prevent his meat:°
Flies have their table spread, ere they appear.
Some creatures have in winter what to eat;
Others do sleep, and envy not their cheer.°

How finely dost thou times and seasons spin,
And make a twist checkered with night and day!
Which as it lengthens winds, and winds us in,
As bowls go on, but turning all the way.°   60

Each creature hath a wisdom for his good.
The pigeons feed their tender offspring, crying,
When they are callow; but withdraw their food
When they are fledge, that need may teach them flying.°

Bees work for man; and yet they never bruise
Their master's flower, but leave it, having done,
As fair as ever, and as fit to use;
So both the flower doth stay, and honey run.

Sheep eat the grass, and dung the ground for more:
Trees after bearing drop their leaves for soil: 70
Springs vent their streams, and by expense get store:
Clouds cool by heat, and baths by cooling boil.

Who hath the virtue to express the rare°
And curious virtues both of herbs and stones?°
Is there an herb for that? O that thy care
Would show a root, that gives expressions!

And if an herb hath power, what have the stars?
A rose, besides his beauty, is a cure.
Doubtless our plagues and plenty, peace and wars
Are there much surer than our art is sure.   80

Thou hast hid metals: man may take them thence;
But at his peril: when he digs the place,
He makes a grave; as if the thing had sense,
And threatened man, that he should fill the space.

Ev'n poisons praise thee. Should a thing be lost?°
Should creatures want for want of heed their due?
Since where are poisons, antidotes are most:
The help stands close, and keeps the fear in view.

The sea, which seems to stop the traveller,
Is by a ship the speedier passage made.   90
The winds, who think they rule the mariner,
Are ruled by him, and taught to serve his trade.

And as thy house is full, so I adore
Thy curious art in marshalling thy goods.°
The hills with health abound; the vales with store;
The South with marble; North with furs and woods.

Hard things are glorious; easy things good cheap.°
The common all men have; that which is rare
Men therefore seek to have, and care to keep.
The healthy frosts with summer-fruits compare.   100

Light without wind is glass: warm without weight
Is wool and fur: cool without closeness, shade:
Speed without pains, a horse: tall without height,
A servile hawk: low without loss, a spade.

All countries have enough to serve their need:
If they seek fine things, thou dost make them run
For their offence; and then dost turn their speed
To be commerce and trade from sun to sun.

Nothing wears clothes, but Man; nothing doth need
But he to wear them. Nothing useth fire,   110
But Man alone, to show his heav'nly breed:
And only he hath fuel in desire.

When th' earth was dry, thou mad'st a sea of wet:
When that lay gathered, thou didst broach the mountains:
When yet some places could no moisture get,
The winds grew gard'ners, and the clouds good fountains.

Rain, do not hurt my flowers; but gently spend
Your honey drops: press not to smell them here:
When they are ripe, their odour will ascend,
And at your lodging with their thanks appear.   120

How harsh are thorns to pears! and yet they make
A better hedge, and need less reparation.
How smooth are silks compared with a stake,
Or with a stone! yet make no good foundation.

Sometimes thou dost divide thy gifts to man,
Sometimes unite. The Indian nut alone°
Is clothing, meat and trencher, drink and can,
Boat, cable, sail and needle, all in one.

Most herbs that grow in brooks, are hot and dry.
Cold fruits warm kernels help against the wind.°   130
The lemon's juice and rind cure mutually.
The whey of milk doth loose, the milk doth bind.

Thy creatures leap not, but express a feast,°
Where all the guests sit close, and nothing wants.
Frogs marry fish and flesh; bats, bird and beast;
Sponges, nonsense and sense; mines, th' earth and plants.

To show thou art not bound, as if thy lot
Were worse than ours, sometimes thou shiftest hands.
Most things move th' under-jaw; the crocodile not.
Most things sleep lying; th' elephant leans or stands.   140

But who hath praise enough? nay, who hath any?
None can express thy works, but he that knows them:
And none can know thy works, which are so many,
And so complete, but only he that owes them.°

All things that are, though they have sev'ral ways,°
Yet in their being join with one advice°
To honour thee: and so I give thee praise
In all my other hymns, but in this twice.°

Each thing that is, although in use and name
It go for one, hath many ways in store   150
To honour thee; and so each hymn thy fame
Extolleth many ways, yet this one more.

Hope°

    I gave to Hope a watch of mine: but he
                An anchor gave to me.
    Then an old prayer-book I did present:
                And he an optic sent.
    With that I gave a vial full of tears:
                But he a few green ears.
    Ah Loiterer! I'll no more, no more I'll bring:
                I did expect a ring.

Sin's Round

Sorry I am, my God, sorry I am,
That my offences course it in a ring.° RUN ABOUT
My thoughts are working like a busy flame,
Until their cockatrice they hatch and bring:°
And when they once have perfected their draughts,
My words take fire from my inflamèd thoughts.

My words take fire from my inflamèd thoughts,
Which spit it forth like the Sicilian Hill.°   *Mt. Etna*
They vent the wares, and pass them with their faults,°   *expel, sell*
And by their breathing ventilate the ill.°   *increase & make public*   10
But words suffice not, where are lewd intentions:°   *evil, bad*
My hands do join to finish the inventions.

My hands do join to finish the inventions:
And so my sins ascend three stories high,
As Babel grew, before there were dissensions.°
Yet ill deeds loiter not: for they supply
New thoughts of sinning: wherefore, to my shame,
Sorry I am, my God, sorry I am.

Time

Meeting with Time, Slack thing, said I,
Thy scythe is dull; whet it for shame.
No marvel Sir, he did reply,
If it at length deserve some blame:
   But where one man would have me grind it,
   Twenty for one too sharp do find it.

Perhaps some such of old did pass,
Who above all things loved this life;
To whom thy scythe a hatchet was,
Which now is but a pruning-knife.   10
   Christ's coming hath made man thy debtor,
   Since by thy cutting he grows better.

And in his blessing thou art blest:
For where thou only wert before
An executioner at best;
Thou art a gard'ner now, and more,
   An usher to convey our souls
   Beyond the utmost stars and poles.

And this is that makes life so long,
While it detains us from our God.   20
Ev'n pleasures here increase the wrong,
And length of days lengthen the rod.
  Who wants the place, where God doth dwell,°
  Partakes already half of hell.

Of what strange length must that needs be,
Which ev'n eternity excludes!
Thus far Time heard me patiently:
Then chafing said, This man deludes:
  What do I here before his door?
  He doth not crave less time, but more.   30

Gratefulness

Thou that hast giv'n so much to me,
Give one thing more, a grateful heart.
See how thy beggar works on thee
    By art.

He makes thy gifts occasion more,
And says, If he in this be crossed,
All thou hast giv'n him heretofore
    Is lost.

But thou didst reckon, when at first
Thy word our hearts and hands did crave,   10
What it would come to at the worst
    To save.

Perpetual knockings at thy door,
Tears sullying thy transparent rooms,
Gift upon gift, much would have more,
    And comes.

This notwithstanding, thou wentst on,
And didst allow us all our noise:
Nay, thou hast made a sigh and groan
    Thy joys.   20

Not that thou hast not still above
Much better tunes, than groans can make;
But that these country-airs thy love°
        Did take.

Wherefore I cry, and cry again;
And in no quiet canst thou be,
Till I a thankful heart obtain
        Of thee:

Not thankful, when it pleaseth me;
As if thy blessings had spare days: 30
But such a heart, whose pulse may be
        Thy praise.

Peace

Sweet Peace, where dost thou dwell? I humbly crave,
        Let me once know.
    I sought thee in a secret cave,
        And asked, if Peace were there.
A hollow wind did seem to answer, No:
        Go seek elsewhere.

I did; and going did a rainbow note:
        Surely, thought I,
    This is the lace of Peace's coat:
        I will search out the matter.   10
But while I looked, the clouds immediately
        Did break and scatter.

Then went I to a garden, and did spy
        A gallant flower,
    The Crown Imperial: Sure, said I,
        Peace at the root must dwell.
But when I digged, I saw a worm devour
        What showed so well.

At length I met a rev'rend good old man,
          Whom when for Peace   20
I did demand, he thus began:
          There was a Prince of old°
At Salem dwelt, who lived with good increase
          Of flock and fold.

He sweetly lived; yet sweetness did not save
          His life from foes.
But after death out of his grave
          There sprang twelve stalks of wheat:°
Which many wond'ring at, got some of those
          To plant and set.   30

It prospered strangely, and did soon disperse
          Through all the earth:
For they that taste it do rehearse,°
          That virtue lies therein,°
A secret virtue bringing peace and mirth
          By flight of sin.

Take of this grain, which in my garden grows,
          And grows for you;
Make bread of it: and that repose
          And peace, which ev'rywhere   40
With so much earnestness you do pursue,
          Is only there.

Confession

O what a cunning guest
Is this same grief! within my heart I made
    Closets; and in them many a chest;
    And, like a master in my trade,
In those chests, boxes; in each box, a till:
Yet grief knows all, and enters when he will.

No screw, no piercer can
Into a piece of timber work and wind,
    As God's afflictions into man,
      When he a torture hath designed.   10
They are too subtle for the subtlest hearts;
And fall, like rheums, upon the tend'rest parts.°

     We are the earth; and they,
Like moles within us, heave, and cast about:
    And till they foot and clutch their prey,
      They never cool, much less give out.
No smith can make such locks but they have keys:
Closets are halls to them; and hearts, highways.

     Only an open breast
Doth shut them out, so that they cannot enter;   20
    Or, if they enter, cannot rest,
      But quickly seek some new adventure.
Smooth open hearts no fast'ning have; but fiction
Doth give a hold and handle to affliction.

     Wherefore my faults and sins,
Lord, I acknowledge; take thy plagues away:
    For since confession pardon wins,
      I challenge here the brightest day,
The clearest diamond: let them do their best,
They shall be thick and cloudy to my breast.°   30

Giddiness

Oh, what a thing is man! how far from power,
      From settled peace and rest!
He is some twenty sev'ral men at least°
      Each sev'ral hour.

One while he counts of heav'n, as of his treasure:
      But then a thought creeps in,
And calls him coward, who for fear of sin
      Will lose a pleasure.

Now he will fight it out, and to the wars;
      Now eat his bread in peace,   10
And snudge in quiet: now he scorns increase;°
      Now all day spares.

He builds a house, which quickly down must go,
      As if a whirlwind blew
And crushed the building: and it's partly true,
      His mind is so.

O what a sight were Man, if his attires
      Did alter with his mind;
And like a dolphin's skin, his clothes combined°
      With his desires!   20

Surely if each one saw another's heart,
      There would be no commerce,
No sale or bargain pass: all would disperse,
      And live apart.

Lord, mend or rather make us: one creation
      Will not suffice our turn:
Except thou make us daily, we shall spurn
      Our own salvation.

The Bunch of Grapes°

Joy, I did lock thee up: but some bad man
      Hath let thee out again:
And now, methinks, I am where I began
      Sev'n years ago: one vogue and vein,°
      One air of thoughts usurps my brain.°
I did towards Canaan draw; but now I am
Brought back to the Red Sea, the sea of shame.

For as the Jews of old by God's command
      Travelled, and saw no town;
So now each Christian hath his journeys spanned:°   10
      Their story pens and sets us down.

A single deed is small renown.
God's works are wide, and let in future times;
His ancient justice overflows our crimes.

Then have we too our guardian fires and clouds;°
        Our Scripture-dew drops fast:°
We have our sands and serpents, tents and shrouds;°
        Alas! our murmurings come not last.°
        But where's the cluster? where's the taste
Of mine inheritance? Lord, if I must borrow,   20
Let me as well take up their joy, as sorrow.

But can he want the grape, who hath the wine?
        I have their fruit and more.°
Blessed be God, who prospered Noah's vine,°
        And made it bring forth grapes good store.°
        But much more him I must adore,
Who of the Law's sour juice sweet wine did make,°
Ev'n God himself being pressèd for my sake.

Love Unknown

Dear Friend, sit down, the tale is long and sad:
And in my faintings I presume your love
Will more comply than help. A Lord I had,
And have, of whom some grounds, which may improve,
I hold for two lives, and both lives in me.°
To him I brought a dish of fruit one day,
And in the middle placed my heart. But he
            (I sigh to say)
Looked on a servant, who did know his eye
Better than you know me, or (which is one)   10
Than I myself. The servant instantly
Quitting the fruit, seized on my heart alone,°
And threw it in a font, wherein did fall
A stream of blood, which issued from the side
Of a great rock: I well remember all,
And have good cause: there it was dipped and dyed,
And washed, and wrung: the very wringing yet

Enforceth tears. *Your heart was foul, I fear.*
Indeed 'tis true. I did and do commit
Many a fault more than my lease will bear;　　　　20
Yet still asked pardon, and was not denied.
But you shall hear. After my heart was well,
And clean and fair, as I one even-tide
　　　　　　(I sigh to tell)
Walked by myself abroad, I saw a large
And spacious furnace flaming, and thereon°
A boiling cauldron, round about whose verge
Was in great letters set *AFFLICTION.*
The greatness showed the owner. So I went
To fetch a sacrifice out of my fold,　　　　30
Thinking with that, which I did thus present,
To warm his love, which I did fear grew cold.
But as my heart did tender it, the man,
Who was to take it from me, slipped his hand,
And threw my heart into the scalding pan;
My heart, that brought it (do you understand?)
The offerer's heart. *Your heart was hard, I fear.*
Indeed it's true. I found a callous matter
Began to spread and to expatiate there:
But with a richer drug than scalding water　　　　40
I bathed it often, ev'n with holy blood,
Which at a board, while many drunk bare wine,°
A friend did steal into my cup for good,
Ev'n taken inwardly, and most divine
To supple hardnesses. But at the length
Out of the cauldron getting, soon I fled
Unto my house, where to repair the strength
Which I had lost, I hasted to my bed.
But when I thought to sleep out all these faults
　　　　　　(I sigh to speak)　　　　50
I found that some had stuffed the bed with thoughts,
I would say *thorns.* Dear, could my heart not break,
When with my pleasures ev'n my rest was gone?
Full well I understood, who had been there:
For I had giv'n the key to none, but one:
It must be he. *Your heart was dull, I fear.*
Indeed a slack and sleepy state of mind
Did oft possess me, so that when I prayed,

Though my lips went, my heart did stay behind.
But all my scores were by another paid,   60
Who took the debt upon him. *Truly, Friend,*
For ought I hear, your Master shows to you
More favour than you wot of. Mark the end.°
The Font did only, what was old, renew:
The Cauldron suppled, what was grown too hard:
The Thorns did quicken, what was grown too dull:°
All did but strive to mend, what you had marred.
Wherefore be cheered, and praise him to the full
Each day, each hour, each moment of the week,
Who fain would have you be new, tender, quick.   70

Man's Medley°

Hark, how the birds do sing,
            And woods do ring.
All creatures have their joy: and man hath his.
            Yet if we rightly measure,
                        Man's joy and pleasure
Rather hereafter, than in present, is.

            To this life things of sense
                        Make their pretence:°
In th' other angels have a right by birth:
            Man ties them both alone,
                        And makes them one,   10
With th' one hand touching heav'n, with th' other earth.

            In soul he mounts and flies,
                        In flesh he dies.
He wears a stuff whose thread is coarse and round,°
            But trimmed with curious lace,
                        And should take place°
After the trimming, not the stuff and ground.°

            Not that he may not here
                        Taste of the cheer,   20
But as birds drink, and straight lift up their head,

So he must sip and think
Of better drink
He may attain to, after he is dead.

But as his joys are double;
So is his trouble.
He hath two winters, other things but one:
Both frosts and thoughts do nip,
And bite his lip;
And he of all things fears two deaths alone.   30

Yet ev'n the greatest griefs
May be reliefs,
Could he but take them right, and in their ways.
Happy is he, whose heart
Hath found the art
To turn his double pains to double praise.

The Storm

If as the winds and waters here below
Do fly and flow,
My sighs and tears as busy were above;
Sure they would move
And much affect thee, as tempestuous times
Amuse poor mortals, and object their crimes.°

Stars have their storms, ev'n in a high degree,°
As well as we.
A throbbing conscience spurrèd by remorse
Hath a strange force: 10
It quits the earth, and mounting more and more
Dares to assault thee, and besiege thy door.

There it stands knocking, to thy music's wrong,
And drowns the song.
Glory and honour are set by, till it
An answer get.
Poets have wronged poor storms: such days are best;
They purge the air without, within the breast.

Paradise

I bless thee, Lord, because I GROW
Among thy trees, which in a ROW
To thee both fruit and order OW.

What open force, or hidden CHARM
Can blast my fruit, or bring me HARM,
While the inclosure is thine ARM?

Inclose me still for fear I START.
Be to me rather sharp and TART,
Than let me want thy hand and ART.

When thou dost greater judgements SPARE,   10
And with thy knife but prune and PARE,
Ev'n fruitful trees more fruitful ARE.

Such sharpness shows the sweetest FREND:
Such cuttings rather heal than REND:
And such beginnings touch their END.

The Method

Poor heart, lament.
For since thy God refuseth still,
There is some rub, some discontent,°
Which cools his will.

Thy Father could
Quickly effect, what thou dost move;°
For he is *Power*: and sure he would;
For he is *Love*.°

Go search this thing,
Tumble thy breast, and turn thy book.   10
If thou hadst lost a glove or ring,
Wouldst thou not look?

What do I see
Written above there? *Yesterday*
I did behave me carelessly,
    When I did pray.

    And should God's ear
To such indifferents chainèd be,
Who do not their own motions hear?°
    Is God less free?   20

    But stay! what's there?
Late when I would have something done,
I had a motion to forbear,°
    Yet I went on.

    And should God's ear,
Which needs not man, be tied to those
Who hear not him, but quickly hear
    His utter foes?

    Then once more pray:
Down with thy knees, up with thy voice.   30
Seek pardon first, and God will say,
    Glad heart rejoice.

Divinity

As men, for fear the stars should sleep and nod,
    And trip at night, have spheres supplied;°
As if a star were duller than a clod,°
    Which knows his way without a guide:

Just so the other heav'n they also serve,
    Divinity's transcendent sky:
Which with the edge of wit they cut and carve.
    Reason triumphs, and faith lies by.

Could not that Wisdom, which first broached the wine,
    Have thickened it with definitions?   10
And jagged his seamless coat, had that been fine,°
    With curious questions and divisions?

But all the doctrine, which he taught and gave,
    Was clear as heav'n, from whence it came.
At least those beams of truth, which only save,
    Surpass in brightness any flame.

Love God, and love your neighbour. Watch and pray.°
    Do as ye would be done unto.
O dark instructions; ev'n as dark as day!
    Who can these Gordian knots undo?   20

But he doth bid us take his blood for wine.
    Bid what he please; yet I am sure,
To take and taste what he doth there design,
    Is all that saves, and not obscure.

Then burn thy Epicycles, foolish man;°
    Break all thy spheres, and save thy head.
Faith needs no staff of flesh, but stoutly can
    To heav'n alone both go, and lead.

Ephes. 4. 30°
Grieve not the Holy Spirit, etc.

And art thou grievèd, sweet and sacred Dove,
        When I am sour,
        And cross thy love?
Grievèd for me? the God of strength and power
        Grieved for a worm, which when I tread,
    I pass away and leave it dead?

Then weep mine eyes, the God of love doth grieve:
        Weep foolish heart,
        And weeping live:

For death is dry as dust. Yet if ye part,   10
　　　End as the night, whose sable hue
　　　Your sins express; melt into dew.

When saucy mirth shall knock or call at door,
　　　Cry out, Get hence,
　　　Or cry no more.
Almighty God doth grieve, he puts on sense:°
　　　I sin not to my grief alone,
　　　But to my God's too; he doth groan:

Oh take thy lute, and tune it to a strain,
　　　Which may with thee   20
　　　All day complain.
There can no discord but in ceasing be.
　　　Marbles can weep; and surely strings
　　　More bowels have, than such hard things.°

Lord, I adjudge myself to tears and grief,
　　　Ev'n endless tears
　　　Without relief.
If a clear spring for me no time forbears,
　　　But runs, although I be not dry;
　　　I am no crystal, what shall I?   30

Yet if I wail not still, since still to wail°
　　　Nature denies;
　　　And flesh would fail,
If my deserts were masters of mine eyes:
　　　Lord, pardon, for thy Son makes good
　　　My want of tears with store of blood.°

The Family

What doth this noise of thoughts within my heart,
　　　As if they had a part?
What do these loud complaints and puling fears,
　　　As if there were no rule or ears?

But, Lord, the house and family are thine,
    Though some of them repine.
Turn out these wranglers, which defile thy seat:
    For where thou dwellest all is neat.

First Peace and Silence all disputes control,
    Then Order plays the soul;   10
And giving all things their set forms and hours,
    Makes of wild woods sweet walks and bowers.

Humble Obedience near the door doth stand,
    Expecting a command:°
Than whom in waiting nothing seems more slow,
    Nothing more quick when she doth go.

Joys oft are there, and griefs as oft as joys;
    But griefs without a noise:
Yet speak they louder than distempered fears.
    What is so shrill as silent tears?   20

This is thy house, with these it doth abound:
    And where these are not found,
Perhaps thou com'st sometimes, and for a day;
    But not to make a constant stay.

The Size°

    Content thee, greedy heart.
Modest and moderate joys to those, that have
Title to more hereafter when they part,
    Are passing brave.°
    Let th' upper springs into the low
    Descend and fall, and thou dost flow.

    What though some have a fraught°
Of cloves and nutmegs, and in cinnamon sail;
If thou hast wherewithal to spice a draught,
    When griefs prevail;   10
    And for the future time art heir
    To th' Isle of spices, is't not fair?

To be in both worlds full
Is more than God was, who was hungry here.
Wouldst thou his laws of fasting disannul?
        Exact good cheer?°
    Lay out thy joy, yet hope to save it?
    Wouldst thou both eat thy cake, and have it?

    Great joys are all at once;
But little do reserve themselves for more: 20
Those have their hopes; these what they have renounce,
        And live on score:°
    Those are at home; these journey still,
    And meet the rest on Sion's hill.

    Thy Saviour sentenced joy,
And in the flesh condemned it as unfit,
At least in lump: for such doth oft destroy;
        Whereas a bit
    Doth 'tice us on to hopes of more,
    And for the present health restore.   30

    A Christian's state and case°
Is not a corpulent, but a thin and spare,
Yet active strength: whose long and bony face
        Content and care
    Do seem to equally divide,
    Like a pretender, not a bride.°

    Wherefore sit down, good heart;
Grasp not at much, for fear thou losest all.
If comforts fell according to desert,°
        They would great frosts and snows destroy: 40
    For we should count, Since the last joy.

    Then close again the seam,
Which thou hast opened: do not spread thy robe
In hope of great things. Call to mind thy dream,
        An earthly globe,
    On whose meridian was engraven,°
    These seas are tears, and heav'n the haven.

Artillery

As I one ev'ning sat before my cell,
Me thoughts a star did shoot into my lap.°
I rose, and shook my clothes, as knowing well,
That from small fires comes oft no small mishap.
    When suddenly I heard one say,
    Do as thou usest, disobey,°
    Expel good motions from thy breast,°
Which have the face of fire, but end in rest.

I, who had heard of music in the spheres,
But not of speech in stars, began to muse: 10
But turning to my God, whose ministers°
The stars and all things are; If I refuse,
    Dread Lord, said I, so oft my good;
    Then I refuse not ev'n with blood
    To wash away my stubborn thought:
For I will do or suffer what I ought.

But I have also stars and shooters too,°
Born where thy servants both artilleries use.
My tears and prayers night and day do woo,
And work up to thee; yet thou dost refuse.   20
    Not but I am (I must say still)
    Much more obliged to do thy will,
    Than thou to grant mine: but because
Thy promise now hath ev'n set thee thy laws.

Then we are shooters both, and thou dost deign
To enter combat with us, and contest
With thine own clay. But I would parley fain:
Shun not my arrows, and behold my breast.
    Yet if thou shunnest, I am thine:
    I must be so, if I am mine.   30
    There is no articling with thee:°
I am but finite, yet thine infinitely.

Church-rents and Schisms

Brave rose, (alas!) where art thou? in the chair°
Where thou didst lately so triumph and shine
A worm doth sit, whose many feet and hair
Are the more foul, the more thou wert divine.
This, this hath done it, this did bite the root
And bottom of the leaves: which when the wind
Did once perceive, it blew them under foot,
Where rude unhallowed steps do crush and grind
    Their beauteous glories. Only shreds of thee,
    And those all bitten, in thy chair I see.   10

Why doth my Mother blush? is she the rose,
And shows it so? Indeed Christ's precious blood
Gave you a colour once; which when your foes
Thought to let out, the bleeding did you good,
And made you look much fresher than before.
But when debates and fretting jealousies
Did worm and work within you more and more,
Your colour faded, and calamities
    Turnèd your ruddy into pale and bleak:
    Your health and beauty both began to break.   20

Then did your sev'ral parts unloose and start:°
Which when your neighbours saw, like a north wind
They rushèd in, and cast them in the dirt
Where Pagans tread. O Mother dear and kind,
Where shall I get me eyes enough to weep,
As many eyes as stars? since it is night,
And much of Asia and Europe fast asleep,
And ev'n all Afric'; would at least I might
    With these two poor ones lick up all the dew,
    Which falls by night, and pour it out for you!   30

Justice (II)

O dreadful Justice, what a fright and terror
        Wast thou of old,
        When sin and error
    Did show and shape thy looks to me,
    And through their glass discolour thee!
He that did but look up, was proud and bold.

The dishes of thy balance seemed to gape,
        Like two great pits;
        The beam and scape°
    Did like some torturing engine show;°   10
    Thy hand above did burn and glow,
Daunting the stoutest hearts, the proudest wits.

But now that Christ's pure veil presents the sight,°
        I see no fears:
        Thy hand is white,
    Thy scales like buckets, which attend
    And interchangeably descend,
Lifting to heaven from this well of tears.

For where before thou still didst call on me,
        Now I still touch   20
        And harp on thee.
    God's promises have made thee mine;
    Why should I justice now decline?
Against me there is none, but for me much.

The Pilgrimage

I travelled on, seeing the hill, where lay
           My expectation.
    A long it was and weary way.
    The gloomy cave of Desperation
I left on th' one, and on the other side
           The rock of Pride.

And so I came to Fancy's meadow strowed°
                    With many a flower:
             Fain would I here have made abode,
             But I was quickened by my hour.°   10
So to Care's copse I came, and there got through
                    With much ado.

That led me to the wild of Passion, which°
                    Some call the wold;
             A wasted place, but sometimes rich.
             Here I was robbed of all my gold,
Save one good Angel, which a friend had tied°
                    Close to my side.

At length I got unto the gladsome hill,
                    Where lay my hope,   20
             Where lay my heart; and climbing still,
             When I had gained the brow and top,
A lake of brackish waters on the ground
                    Was all I found.

With that abashed and struck with many a sting
                    Of swarming fears,
             I fell, and cried, Alas my King!
             Can both the way and end be tears?
Yet taking heart I rose, and then perceived
                    I was deceived: 30

My hill was further: so I flung away,
                    Yet heard a cry,
             Just as I went, *None goes that way*
             And lives: If that be all, said I,
After so foul a journey death is fair,
                    And but a chair.°

The Holdfast°

I threatened to observe the strict decree
    Of my dear God with all my power and might.
    But I was told by one, it could not be;°
Yet I might trust in God to be my light.
Then will I trust, said I, in him alone.
    Nay, ev'n to trust in him, was also his:
    We must confess that nothing is our own.
Then I confess that he my succour is:
But to have nought is ours, not to confess
    That we have nought. I stood amazed at this,   10
    Much troubled, till I heard a friend express,
That all things were more ours by being his.
    What Adam had, and forfeited for all,
    Christ keepeth now, who cannot fail or fall.

Complaining

Do not beguile my heart,
    Because thou art
My power and wisdom. Put me not to shame,
    Because I am
Thy clay that weeps, thy dust that calls.

Thou art the Lord of glory;
    The deed and story
Are both thy due: but I a silly fly,
    That live or die
According as the weather falls.   10

Art thou all justice, Lord?
    Shows not thy word
More attributes? Am I all throat or eye,
    To weep or cry?
Have I no parts but those of grief?

Let not thy wrathful power
Afflict my hour,
My inch of life: or let thy gracious power
Contract my hour,
That I may climb and find relief.   20

The Discharge°

Busy enquiring heart, what wouldst thou know?
Why dost thou pry,
And turn, and leer, and with a lickerous eye°
Look high and low;
And in thy lookings stretch and grow?

Hast thou not made thy counts, and summed up all?
Did not thy heart
Give up the whole, and with the whole depart?°
Let what will fall:
That which is past who can recall?   10

Thy life is God's, thy time to come is gone,
And is his right.
He is thy night at noon: he is at night
Thy noon alone.
The crop is his, for he hath sown.

And well it was for thee, when this befell,
That God did make
Thy business his, and in thy life partake:
For thou canst tell,
If it be his once, all is well.   20

Only the present is thy part and fee.°
And happy thou,
If, though thou didst not beat thy future brow,
Thou couldst well see
What present things required of thee.

They ask enough; why shouldst thou further go?
        Raise not the mud
Of future depths, but drink the clear and good.
        Dig not for woe
    In times to come; for it will grow.   30

Man and the present fit: if he provide,°
        He breaks the square.°
This hour is mine: if for the next I care,
        I grow too wide,
    And do encroach upon death's side.

For death each hour environs and surrounds.
        He that would know
And care for future chances, cannot go
        Unto those grounds,
    But through a church-yard which them bounds.   40

Things present shrink and die: but they that spend
        Their thoughts and sense
On future grief, do not remove it thence,
        But it extend,
    And draw the bottom out an end.°

God chains the dog till night: wilt loose the chain,°
        And wake thy sorrow?
Wilt thou forestall it, and now grieve tomorrow,
        And then again
    Grieve over freshly all thy pain?   50

Either grief will not come: or if it must,
        Do not forecast.
And while it cometh, it is almost past.
        Away distrust:
    My God hath promised; he is just.

Praise (II)

King of Glory, King of Peace,
       I will love thee:
And that love may never cease,
       I will move thee.

Thou hast granted my request,
       Thou hast heard me:
Thou didst note my working breast,
       Thou hast spared me.

Wherefore with my utmost art
       I will sing thee,   10
And the cream of all my heart
       I will bring thee.

Though my sins against me cried,
       Thou didst clear me;
And alone, when they replied,
       Thou didst hear me.

Sev'n whole days, not one in seven,
       I will praise thee.
In my heart, though not in heaven,
       I can raise thee.   20

Thou grew'st soft and moist with tears,
       Thou relentedst:
And when Justice called for fears,
       Thou dissentedst.

Small it is, in this poor sort
       To enrol thee:
Ev'n eternity is too short
       To extol thee.

An Offering

Come, bring thy gift. If blessings were as slow
As men's returns, what would become of fools?
What hast thou there? a heart? but is it pure?
Search well and see; for hearts have many holes.
Yet one pure heart is nothing to bestow:
In Christ two natures met to be thy cure.

O that within us hearts had propagation,
Since many gifts do challenge many hearts!
Yet one, if good, may title to a number;
And single things grow fruitful by deserts.   10
In public judgements one may be a nation,°
And fence a plague, while others sleep and slumber.

But all I fear is lest thy heart displease,
As neither good, nor one: so oft divisions
Thy lusts have made, and not thy lusts alone;
Thy passions also have their set partitions.
These parcel out thy heart: recover these,
And thou mayst offer many gifts in one.

There is a balsam, or indeed a blood,
Dropping from heav'n, which doth both cleanse and close   20
All sorts of wounds; of such strange force it is.
Seek out this All-heal, and seek no repose,°
Until thou find and use it to thy good:
Then bring thy gift, and let thy hymn be this:

                    Since my sadness
                    Into gladness
            Lord thou dost convert,
                    O accept
                    What thou hast kept,
            As thy due desert.   30

                    Had I many,
                    Had I any,
            (For this heart is none)

All were thine
And none of mine:
Surely thine alone.

Yet thy favour
May give savour
To this poor oblation;
And it raise   40
To be thy praise,
And be my salvation.

Longing

With sick and famished eyes,
With doubling knees and weary bones,
To thee my cries,
To thee my groans,
To thee my sighs, my tears ascend:
No end?

My throat, my soul is hoarse;
My heart is withered like a ground
Which thou dost curse.°
My thoughts turn round,   10
And make me giddy; Lord, I fall,
Yet call.

From thee all pity flows.
Mothers are kind, because thou art,
And dost dispose
To them a part:
Their infants, them; and they suck thee
More free.

Bowels of pity, hear!°
Lord of my soul, love of my mind,   20
Bow down thine ear!°
Let not the wind
Scatter my words, and in the same
Thy name!

Look on my sorrow's round!
Mark well my furnace! O what flames,°
　　　　What heats abound!
　　　　What griefs, what shames!
Consider, Lord; Lord, bow thine ear,
　　　　　　And hear!   30

Lord Jesu, thou didst bow
Thy dying head upon the tree:
　　　　O be not now
　　　　More dead to me!
Lord hear! *Shall he that made the ear,*°
　　　　　　Not hear?

Behold, thy dust doth stir,
It moves, it creeps, it aims at thee:
　　　　Wilt thou defer
　　　　To succour me,
Thy pile of dust, wherein each crumb   40
　　　　　　Says, Come?

To thee help appertains.
Hast thou left all things to their course,
　　　　And laid the reins
　　　　Upon the horse?
Is all locked? hath a sinner's plea
　　　　　　No key?

Indeed the world's thy book,
Where all things have their leaf assigned: 50
　　　　Yet a meek look
　　　　Hath interlined.
Thy board is full, yet humble guests°
　　　　　　Find nests.

Thou tarriest, while I die,
And fall to nothing: thou dost reign,
　　　　And rule on high,
　　　　While I remain
In bitter grief: yet am I styled°
　　　　　　Thy child.   60

Lord, didst thou leave thy throne,
Not to relieve? how can it be,
That thou art grown
Thus hard to me?
Were sin alive, good cause there were
To bear.

But now both sin is dead,
And all thy promises live and bide.
That wants his head;
These speak and chide,   70
And in thy bosom pour my tears,
As theirs.

Lord JESU, hear my heart,
Which hath been broken now so long,
That ev'ry part
Hath got a tongue!
Thy beggars grow; rid them away
Today.

My love, my sweetness, hear!
By these thy feet, at which my heart   80
Lies all the year,
Pluck out thy dart,
And heal my troubled breast which cries,
Which dies.

The Bag°

Away despair! my gracious Lord doth hear.
   Though winds and waves assault my keel,°
   He doth preserve it: he doth steer,
   Ev'n when the boat seems most to reel.
   Storms are the triumph of his art:
Well may he close his eyes, but not his heart.

Hast thou not heard, that my Lord Jesus died?
    Then let me tell thee a strange story.
    The God of power, as he did ride
    In his majestic robes of glory,   10
    Resolved to light; and so one day°
He did descend, undressing all the way.

The stars his tire of light and rings obtained,°
    The cloud his bow, the fire his spear,°
    The sky his azure mantle gained.
    And when they asked, what he would wear,
    He smiled and said as he did go,
He had new clothes a-making here below.

When he was come, as travellers are wont,
    He did repair unto an inn.   20
    Both then, and after, many a brunt
    He did endure to cancel sin:
    And having giv'n the rest before,
Here he gave up his life to pay our score.

But as he was returning, there came one
    That ran upon him with a spear.
    He, who came hither all alone,
    Bringing nor man, nor arms, nor fear,
    Received the blow upon his side,
And straight he turned, and to his brethren cried,   30

If ye have anything to send or write,
    I have no bag, but here is room:
    Unto my Father's hands and sight,
    Believe me, it shall safely come.
    That I shall mind, what you impart,
Look, you may put it very near my heart.

Or if hereafter any of my friends
    Will use me in this kind, the door°
    Shall still be open; what he sends
    I will present, and somewhat more,   40
    Not to his hurt. Sighs will convey
Anything to me. Hark, Despair away.

The Jews

Poor nation, whose sweet sap and juice
Our scions have purloined, and left you dry:°
Whose streams we got by the Apostles' sluice,
And use in baptism, while ye pine and die:
Who by not keeping once, became a debtor;°
    And now by keeping lose the letter:°

Oh that my prayers! mine, alas!
Oh that some angel might a trumpet sound;°
At which the Church falling upon her face
Should cry so loud, until the trump were drowned,   10
And by that cry of her dear Lord obtain,
    That your sweet sap might come again!

The Collar°

I struck the board, and cried, No more.°
        I will abroad.
    What? shall I ever sigh and pine?
My lines and life are free; free as the road,
    Loose as the wind, as large as store.
        Shall I be still in suit?°
Have I no harvest but a thorn
To let me blood, and not restore
What I have lost with cordial fruit?°
        Sure there was wine   10
Before my sighs did dry it: there was corn°
        Before my tears did drown it.
    Is the year only lost to me?
        Have I no bays to crown it?°
No flowers, no garlands gay? all blasted?
        All wasted?
    Not so, my heart: but there is fruit,
        And thou hast hands.
    Recover all thy sigh-blown age
On double pleasures: leave thy cold dispute   20

Of what is fit, and not. Forsake thy cage,
                    Thy rope of sands,
Which petty thoughts have made, and made to thee
            Good cable, to enforce and draw,
                    And be thy law,
        While thou didst wink and wouldst not see.°
                Away, Take Heed,°
                I will abroad,
Call in thy death's head there: tie up thy fears.
                He that forbears   30
            To suit and serve his need,
                Deserves his load.
But as I raved and grew more fierce and wild
                At every word,
Me thoughts I heard one calling, *Child!*°
            And I replied, *My Lord.*

The Glimpse

        Whither away delight?
Thou cam'st but now; wilt thou so soon depart,
        And give me up to night?
For many weeks of ling'ring pain and smart
But one half hour of comfort to my heart?

        Me thinks delight should have°
More skill in music, and keep better time.
        Wert thou a wind or wave,
They quickly go and come with lesser crime:
Flowers look about, and die not in their prime.   10

        Thy short abode and stay
Feeds not, but adds to the desire of meat.
        Lime begged of old, they say,°
A neighbour spring to cool his inward heat;
Which by the spring's access grew much more great.

In hope of thee my heart
Picked here and there a crumb, and would not die;
But constant to his part,
Whenas my fears foretold this, did reply,
A slender thread a gentle guest will tie.   20

Yet if the heart that wept
Must let thee go, return when it doth knock.
Although thy heap be kept
For future times, the droppings of the stock
May oft break forth, and never break the lock.

If I have more to spin,
The wheel shall go, so that thy stay be short.°
Thou know'st how grief and sin
Disturb the work. O make me not their sport,°
Who by thy coming may be made a court!   30

Assurance

O spiteful bitter thought!
Bitterly spiteful thought! Couldst thou invent
So high a torture? Is such poison bought?
Doubtless, but in the way of punishment.
When wit contrives to meet with thee,
No such rank poison can there be.

Thou said'st but even now,
That all was not so fair, as I conceived,
Betwixt my God and me; that I allow
And coin large hopes, but that I was deceived: 10
Either the league was broke, or near it;
And, that I had great cause to fear it.

And what to this? what more
Could poison, if it had a tongue, express?
What is thy aim? wouldst thou unlock the door
To cold despairs, and gnawing pensiveness?
Wouldst thou raise devils? I see, I know,°
I writ thy purpose long ago.

But I will to my Father,
Who heard thee say it. O most gracious Lord,   20
If all the hope and comfort that I gather,
Were from myself, I had not half a word,
    Not half a letter to oppose
    What is objected by my foes.

    But thou art my desert:°
And in this league, which now my foes invade,°
Thou art not only to perform thy part,
But also mine; as when the league was made
    Thou didst at once thyself indite,°
    And hold my hand, while I did write.   30

    Wherefore if thou canst fail,
Then can thy truth and I: but while rocks stand,
And rivers stir, thou canst not shrink or quail:
Yea, when both rocks and all things shall disband,
    Then shalt thou be my rock and tower,°
    And make their ruin praise thy power.

    Now foolish thought go on,
Spin out thy thread, and make thereof a coat
To hide thy shame: for thou hast cast a bone
Which bounds on thee, and will not down thy throat: 40
    What for itself love once began,
    Now love and truth will end in man.

The Call

    Come, my Way, my Truth, my Life:°
    Such a Way, as gives us breath:
    Such a Truth, as ends all strife:
    Such a Life, as killeth death.

    Come, my Light, my Feast, my Strength:
    Such a Light, as shows a feast:
    Such a Feast, as mends in length:°
    Such a Strength, as makes his guest.

Come, my Joy, my Love, my Heart:
Such a Joy, as none can move:°   10
Such a Love, as none can part:
Such a Heart, as joys in love.

Clasping of Hands

Lord, thou art mine, and I am thine,
If mine I am: and thine much more,
Than I or ought, or can be mine.
Yet to be thine, doth me restore;
So that again I now am mine,
And with advantage mine the more,
Since this being mine, brings with it thine,
And thou with me dost thee restore.
    If I without thee would be mine,
    I neither should be mine nor thine.   10

Lord, I am thine, and thou art mine:
So mine thou art, that something more
I may presume thee mine, than thine.
For thou didst suffer to restore
Not thee, but me, and to be mine,
And with advantage mine the more,
Since thou in death wast none of thine,
Yet then as mine didst me restore.
    O be mine still! still make me thine!
    Or rather make no Thine and Mine!   20

Praise (III)

Lord, I will mean and speak thy praise,
    Thy praise alone.
My busy heart shall spin it all my days:
    And when it stops for want of store,
Then will I wring it with a sigh or groan,
    That thou mayst yet have more.

When thou dost favour any action,
         It runs, it flies:
All things concur to give it a perfection.
    That which had but two legs before,   10
When thou dost bless, hath twelve: one wheel doth rise
        To twenty then, or more.

But when thou dost on business blow,
         It hangs, it clogs:
Not all the teams of Albion in a row
    Can hale or draw it out of door.
Legs are but stumps, and Pharaoh's wheels but logs,°
        And struggling hinders more.

Thousands of things do thee employ
         In ruling all   20
This spacious globe: angels must have their joy,
    Devils their rod, the sea his shore,
The winds their stint: and yet when I did call,°
        Thou heardst my call, and more.

I have not lost one single tear:
         But when mine eyes
Did weep to heav'n, they found a bottle there°
    (As we have boxes for the poor)
Ready to take them in; yet of a size
        That would contain much more.   30

But after thou hadst slipped a drop
         From thy right eye,
(Which there did hang like streamers near the top°
    Of some fair church, to show the sore
And bloody battle which thou once didst try)
        The glass was full and more.

Wherefore I sing. Yet since my heart,
         Though pressed, runs thin;
O that I might some other hearts convert,
    And so take up at use good store:°   40
That to thy chest there might be coming in
        Both all my praise, and more!

Joseph's Coat°

Wounded I sing, tormented I indite,°
Thrown down I fall into a bed, and rest:
Sorrow hath changed its note: such is his will,
Who changeth all things, as him pleaseth best.
    For well he knows, if but one grief and smart
Among my many had his full career,
Sure it would carry with it ev'n my heart,
And both would run until they found a bier°
    To fetch the body; both being due to grief.°
But he hath spoiled the race; and giv'n to anguish   10
One of Joy's coats, ticing it with relief°
To linger in me, and together languish.
    I live to show his power, who once did bring
My *joys* to *weep*, and now my *griefs* to *sing*.

The Pulley

    When God at first made man,
Having a glass of blessings standing by;
Let us (said he) pour on him all we can:
Let the world's riches, which dispersèd lie,
    Contract into a span.°

    So strength first made a way;
Then beauty flowed, then wisdom, honour, pleasure:
When almost all was out, God made a stay,
Perceiving that alone of all his treasure
    Rest in the bottom lay.   10

    For if I should (said he)
Bestow this jewel also on my creature,
He would adore my gifts instead of me,
And rest in Nature, not the God of Nature:
    So both should losers be.

Yet let him keep the rest, *remainder*
But keep them with repining restlessness:
Let him be rich and weary, that at least,
If goodness lead him not, yet weariness
        May toss him to my breast.   20

greatest Gift to MAN

emblematic
God's way of pulling

The Priesthood

Blest Order, which in power dost so excel,°
That with th' one hand thou liftest to the sky,
And with the other throwest down to hell
In thy just censures; fain would I draw nigh,
Fain put thee on, exchanging my lay-sword
        For that of th' holy Word.

But thou art fire, sacred and hallowed fire;
And I but earth and clay: should I presume
To wear thy habit, the severe attire°
My slender compositions might consume.°   10
I am both foul and brittle; much unfit
        To deal in holy Writ.

Yet have I often seen, by cunning hand°
And force of fire, what curious things are made
Of wretched earth. Where once I scorned to stand,
That earth is fitted by the fire and trade
Of skilful artists, for the boards of those
        Who make the bravest shows.

But since those great ones, be they ne'er so great,
Come from the earth, from whence those vessels come;°   20
So that at once both feeder, dish, and meat
Have one beginning and one final sum:
I do not greatly wonder at the sight,
        If earth in earth delight.

But th' holy men of God such vessels are,°
As serve him up, who all the world commands:
When God vouchsafeth to become our fare,
Their hands convey him, who conveys their hands.
O what pure things, most pure must those things be,
      Who bring my God to me!   30

Wherefore I dare not, I, put forth my hand°
To hold the Ark, although it seem to shake
Through th' old sins and new doctrines of our land.
Only, since God doth often vessels make
Of lowly matter for high uses meet,°
      I throw me at his feet.

There will I lie, until my Maker seek°
For some mean stuff whereon to show his skill:
Then is my time. The distance of the meek
Doth flatter power. Lest good come short of ill   40
In praising might, the poor do by submission
      What pride by opposition.

The Search

Whither, O, whither art thou fled,
      My Lord, my Love?
My searches are my daily bread;
      Yet never prove.°

My knees pierce th' earth, mine eyes the sky;
      And yet the sphere
And centre both to me deny°
      That thou art there.

Yet can I mark how herbs below
      Grow green and gay,   10
As if to meet thee they did know,
      While I decay.

Yet can I mark how stars above
            Simper and shine,°
As having keys unto thy love,
            While poor I pine.

I sent a sigh to seek thee out,
            Deep drawn in pain,
Winged like an arrow: but my scout
            Returns in vain.   20

I tuned another (having store)
            Into a groan;
Because the search was dumb before:
            But all was one.

Lord, dost thou some new fabric mould,
            Which favour wins,
And keeps thee present, leaving th' old
            Unto their sins?

Where is my God? what hidden place
            Conceals thee still?   30
What covert dare eclipse thy face?°
            Is it thy will?

O let not that of anything;°
            Let rather brass,
Or steel, or mountains be thy ring,
            And I will pass.

Thy will such an entrenching is,
            As passeth thought:
To it all strength, all subtilties
            Are things of nought.   40

Thy will such a strange distance is,
            As that to it
East and West touch, the poles do kiss,
            And parallels meet.

Since then my grief must be as large,
           As is thy space,
Thy distance from me; see my charge,°
           Lord, see my case.

O take these bars, these lengths away;
           Turn, and restore me: 50
Be not Almighty, let me say,
           Against, but for me.

When thou dost turn, and wilt be near;
           What edge so keen,
What point so piercing can appear
           To come between?

For as thy absence doth excel
           All distance known:
So doth thy nearness bear the bell,°
           Making two one.   60

Grief

O who will give me tears? Come all ye springs,
Dwell in my head and eyes: come clouds, and rain:
My grief hath need of all the wat'ry things,
That nature hath produced. Let ev'ry vein
Suck up a river to supply mine eyes,
My weary weeping eyes, too dry for me,
Unless they get new conduits, new supplies
To bear them out, and with my state agree.
What are two shallow fords, two little spouts
Of a less world? The greater is but small,°   10
A narrow cupboard for my griefs and doubts,
Which want provision in the midst of all.
Verses, ye are too fine a thing, too wise
For my rough sorrows: cease, be dumb and mute,
Give up your feet and running to mine eyes,
And keep your measures for some lover's lute,
Whose grief allows him music and a rhyme:
For mine excludes both measure, tune, and time.
           Alas, my God!

The Cross° Burden

What is this strange and uncouth thing?° difficult to understand
To make me sigh, and seek, and faint, and die,
Until I had some place, where I might sing,
    And serve thee; and not only I,
But all my wealth and family might combine
To set thy honour up, as our design.

And then when after much delay,
Much wrastling, many a combat, this dear end,
So much desired, is giv'n, to take away
    My power to serve thee; to unbend   10
All my abilities, my designs confound,
And lay my threat'nings bleeding on the ground.° vows

One ague dwelleth in my bones,
Another in my soul (the memory
What I would do for thee, if once my groans
    Could be allowed for harmony):° Judged as
I am in all a weak disabled thing,° when views Cross
Save in the sight thereof, where strength doth sting.

Besides, things sort not to my will,
Ev'n when my will doth study thy renown: 20
Thou turnest th' edge of all things on me still,
    Taking me up to throw me down:
So that, ev'n when my hopes seem to be sped,° successfully Accomplished
I am to grief alive, to them as dead.

To have my aim, and yet to be
Further from it than when I bent my bow;
To make my hopes my torture, and the fee
    Of all my woes another woe,
Is in the midst of delicates to need,° luxuries, delicacies
And ev'n in Paradise to be a weed.   30

Ah my dear Father, ease my smart!
These contrarieties crush me: these cross actions
Do wind a rope about, and cut my heart:
    And yet since these thy contradictions
Are properly a cross felt by thy Son,
With but four words, my words, *Thy will be done.*

The Flower

How fresh, O Lord, how sweet and clean
Are thy returns! ev'n as the flowers in spring;
    To which, besides their own demean,°
The late-past frosts tributes of pleasure bring.
        Grief melts away
        Like snow in May,
As if there were no such cold thing.

Who would have thought my shrivelled heart
Could have recovered greenness? It was gone
    Quite under ground; as flowers depart   10
To see their mother-root, when they have blown;°
        Where they together
        All the hard weather,
Dead to the world, keep house unknown.

These are thy wonders, Lord of power,
Killing and quick'ning, bringing down to hell°
    And up to heaven in an hour;
Making a chiming of a passing-bell.°
        We say amiss,
        This or that is: 20
Thy word is all, if we could spell.

O that I once past changing were,
Fast in thy Paradise, where no flower can wither!
    Many a spring I shoot up fair,
Off'ring at heav'n, growing and groaning thither:
        Nor doth my flower
        Want a spring-shower,
My sins and I joining together.

But while I grow in a straight line,
Still upwards bent, as if heav'n were mine own, 30
   Thy anger comes, and I decline:
What frost to that? what pole is not the zone,
      Where all things burn,
      When thou dost turn,
   And the least frown of thine is shown?

   And now in age I bud again,
After so many deaths I live and write;
   I once more smell the dew and rain,
And relish versing: O my only light,
      It cannot be 40
      That I am he
On whom thy tempests fell all night.

   These are thy wonders, Lord of love,
To make us see we are but flowers that glide:
   Which when we once can find and prove,
Thou hast a garden for us, where to bide.
      Who would be more,
      Swelling through store,
Forfeit their Paradise by their pride.

Dotage

False glozing pleasures, casks of happiness,
Foolish night-fires, women's and children's wishes,°
Chases in arras, gilded emptiness,°
Shadows well mounted, dreams in a career,°
Embroidered lies, nothing between two dishes;
      These are the pleasures here.

True earnest sorrows, rooted miseries,
Anguish in grain, vexations ripe and blown,°
Sure-footed griefs, solid calamities,
Plain demonstrations, evident and clear, 10
Fetching their proofs ev'n from the very bone;
      These are the sorrows here.

But oh the folly of distracted men,
Who griefs in earnest, joys in jest pursue;
Preferring, like brute beasts, a loathsome den
Before a court, ev'n that above so clear,
Where are no sorrows, but delights more true
               Than miseries are here!

The Son

Let foreign nations of their language boast,
What fine variety each tongue affords:
I like our language, as our men and coast:°
Who cannot dress it well, want wit, not words.
How neatly do we give one only name
To parents' issue and the sun's bright star!
A son is light and fruit; a fruitful flame
Chasing the father's dimness, carried far
From the first man in th' East, to fresh and new
Western discov'ries of posterity.   10
So in one word our Lord's humility
We turn upon him in a sense most true:
     For what Christ once in humbleness began,
     We him in glory call, *The Son of Man*.

A True Hymn

        My joy, my life, my crown!
      My heart was meaning all the day,
         Somewhat it fain would say:
And still it runneth mutt'ring up and down
With only this, *My joy, my life, my crown.*

        Yet slight not these few words:
      If truly said, they may take part
         Among the best in art.
The fineness which a hymn or psalm affords,
Is, when the soul unto the lines accords.   10

He who craves all the mind,
And all the soul, and strength, and time,
If the words only rhyme,
Justly complains, that somewhat is behind°
To make his verse, or write a hymn in kind.°

Whereas if th' heart be moved,
Although the verse be somewhat scant,
God doth supply the want.
As when th' heart says (sighing to be approved)
O, could I love! and stops: God writeth, *Loved.*   20

The Answer

My comforts drop and melt away like snow:
I shake my head, and all the thoughts and ends,
Which my fierce youth did bandy, fall and flow
Like leaves about me: or like summer friends,
Flies of estates and sunshine. But to all,
Who think me eager, hot, and undertaking,
But in my prosecutions slack and small;
As a young exhalation, newly waking,°
Scorns his first bed of dirt, and means the sky;°
But cooling by the way, grows pursy and slow,   10
And settling to a cloud, doth live and die
In that dark state of tears: to all, that so
        Show me, and set me, I have one reply,°
        Which they that know the rest, know more than I.

A Dialogue-Anthem°

Christian. Death.

Chr. Alas, poor Death, where is thy glory?°
        Where is thy famous force, thy ancient sting?
Dea. *Alas poor mortal, void of story,*°
        Go spell and read how I have killed thy King.

Chr.　Poor Death! and who was hurt thereby?
　　　　Thy curse being laid on him, makes thee accurst.°
Dea.　*Let losers talk: yet thou shalt die;*
　　　　These arms shall crush thee.
Chr.　　　　　　　　　　Spare not, do thy worst.
　　　　I shall be one day better than before:
　　　　Thou so much worse, that thou shalt be no more.　　10

The Water-course

Thou who dost dwell and linger here below,
Since the condition of this world is frail,
Where of all plants afflictions soonest grow;
If troubles overtake thee, do not wail:

　　For who can look for less, that loveth $\begin{cases} \text{Life?} \\ \text{Strife?} \end{cases}$

But rather turn the pipe and water's course
To serve thy sins, and furnish thee with store
Of sov'reign tears, springing from true remorse:°
That so in pureness thou mayst him adore,

　　Who gives to man, as he sees fit, $\begin{cases} \text{Salvation.°} \\ \text{Damnation.} \end{cases}$　　10

Self-condemnation

Thou who condemnest Jewish hate,
For choosing Barrabas a murderer°
　　Before the Lord of glory;
Look back upon thine own estate,
Call home thine eye (that busy wanderer):
　　That choice may be thy story.°

He that doth love, and love amiss,
This world's delights before true Christian joy,
　　Hath made a Jewish choice:
The world an ancient murderer is;　　10
Thousands of souls it hath and doth destroy
　　With her enchanting voice.

He that hath made a sorry wedding
Between his soul and gold, and hath preferred
    False gain before the true,
  Hath done what he condemns in reading:
For he hath sold for money his dear Lord,
    And is a Judas-Jew.

Thus we prevent the last great day,°
And judge ourselves. That light, which sin and passion   20
    Did before dim and choke,
  When once those snuffs are ta'en away,°
Shines bright and clear, ev'n unto condemnation,
    Without excuse or cloak.

Bitter-sweet

  Ah my dear angry Lord,
  Since thou dost love, yet strike;
  Cast down, yet help afford;
  Sure I will do the like.

  I will complain, yet praise;
  I will bewail, approve:
  And all my sour-sweet days
  I will lament, and love.

The Glance

  When first thy sweet and gracious eye
Vouchsafed ev'n in the midst of youth and night
To look upon me, who before did lie
    Welt'ring in sin;
  I felt a sugared strange delight,
Passing all cordials made by any art,°
Bedew, embalm, and overrun my heart,°
    And take it in.

Since that time many a bitter storm
My soul hath felt, ev'n able to destroy,   10
Had the malicious and ill-meaning harm
           His swing and sway:
But still thy sweet original joy,
Sprung from thine eye, did work within my soul,
And surging griefs, when they grew bold, control,
           And got the day.

If thy first glance so powerful be,
A mirth but opened and sealed up again;
What wonders shall we feel, when we shall see
           Thy full-eyed love!   20
When thou shalt look us out of pain,
And one aspect of thine spend in delight
More than a thousand suns disburse in light,
           In heav'n above.

The 23d Psalm°

The God of love my shepherd is,
           And he that doth me feed:
While he is mine, and I am his,
           What can I want or need?

He leads me to the tender grass,
           Where I both feed and rest;
Then to the streams that gently pass:
           In both I have the best.

Or if I stray, he doth convert
           And bring my mind in frame:°   10
And all this not for my desert,
           But for his holy name.

Yea, in death's shady black abode
           Well may I walk, not fear:
For thou art with me; and thy rod
           To guide, thy staff to bear.

Nay, thou dost make me sit and dine,
    Ev'n in my enemies' sight:
My head with oil, my cup with wine
    Runs over day and night.   20

Surely thy sweet and wondrous love
    Shall measure all my days;
And as it never shall remove,
    So neither shall thy praise.°

Mary Magdalene°

When blessed Mary wiped her Saviour's feet,
(Whose precepts she had trampled on before)
And wore them for a jewel on her head,
    Showing his steps should be the street,
    Wherein she thenceforth evermore
With pensive humbleness would live and tread:

She being stained herself, why did she strive
To make him clean, who could not be defiled?
Why kept she not her tears for her own faults,
    And not his feet? Though we could dive   10
    In tears like seas, our sins are piled
Deeper than they, in words, and works, and thoughts.

Dear soul, she knew who did vouchsafe and deign
To bear her filth; and that her sins did dash°
Ev'n God himself: wherefore she was not loth,
    As she had brought wherewith to stain,
    So to bring in wherewith to wash:
And yet in washing one, she washèd both.

Aaron

    Holiness on the head,°
    Light and perfections on the breast,°
Harmonious bells below, raising the dead
    To lead them unto life and rest:
        Thus are true Aarons drest.°

identity of poet with Christ

Profaneness in my head,
Defects and darkness in my breast,
A noise of passions ringing me for dead
Unto a place where is no rest:
    Poor priest thus am I drest.   10

Only another head *Christ*
I have, another heart and breast,
Another music, making live not dead,
Without whom I could have no rest:
    In him I am well drest.

Lord

Christ is my only head,   *D.*
My alone only heart and breast,
My only music, striking me ev'n dead;
That to the old man I may rest,°
    And be in him new drest.   20

So holy in my head,
Perfect and light in my dear breast,
My doctrine tuned by Christ, (who is not dead,
But lives in me while I do rest)
    Come people; Aaron's drest.   *put on Christ*
                                        in Christ

The Odour. 2. Cor. 2. 15°

How sweetly doth *My Master* sound! *My Master*!
    As ambergris leaves a rich scent°
            Unto the taster:
    So do these words a sweet content,
An oriental fragrancy, *My Master*.

With these all day I do perfume my mind,
    My mind ev'n thrust into them both:
            That I might find
    What cordials make this curious broth,
This broth of smells, that feeds and fats my mind.   10

My Master, shall I speak? O that to thee
      My servant were a little so,
             As flesh may be;
    That these two words might creep and grow
To some degree of spiciness to thee!

Then should the pomander, which was before,°
      A speaking sweet, mend by reflection,
             And tell me more:
    For pardon of my imperfection
Would warm and work it sweeter than before.   20

For when *My Master*, which alone is sweet,
      And ev'n in my unworthiness pleasing,
             Shall call and meet,
    My servant, as thee not displeasing,
That call is but the breathing of the sweet.

This breathing would with gains by sweet'ning me
      (As sweet things traffic when they meet)°
             Return to thee.
    And so this new commerce and sweet
Should all my life employ and busy me.   30

The Foil°

        If we could see below
    The sphere of virtue, and each shining grace
      As plainly as that above doth show;
    This were the better sky, the brighter place.

        God hath made stars the foil
    To set off virtues; griefs to set off sinning:
      Yet in this wretched world we toil,
    As if grief were not foul, nor virtue winning.

The Forerunners

The harbingers are come. See, see their mark;°
White is their colour, and behold my head.
But must they have my brain? must they dispark°
Those sparkling notions, which therein were bred?
        Must dullness turn me to a clod?
Yet have they left me, *Thou art still my God.*°

Good men ye be, to leave me my best room,
Ev'n all my heart, and what is lodgèd there:
I pass not, I, what of the rest become,°
So *Thou art still my God*, be out of fear.   10
        He will be pleasèd with that ditty;°
And if I please him, I write fine and witty.

Farewell sweet phrases, lovely metaphors.
But will ye leave me thus? when ye before
Of stews and brothels only knew the doors,
Then did I wash you with my tears, and more,
        Brought you to Church well dressed and clad:
My God must have my best, ev'n all I had.

Lovely enchanting language, sugar-cane,
Honey of roses, whither wilt thou fly?   20
Hath some fond lover ticed thee to thy bane?°
And wilt thou leave the Church, and love a sty?
        Fie, thou wilt soil thy broidered coat,
And hurt thyself, and him that sings the note.

Let foolish lovers, if they will love dung,
With canvas, not with arras, clothe their shame:°
Let folly speak in her own native tongue.
True beauty dwells on high: ours is a flame
        But borrowed thence to light us thither.
Beauty and beauteous words should go together.   30

Yet if you go, I pass not; take your way:
For, *Thou art still my God*, is all that ye
Perhaps with more embellishment can say.
Go birds of spring: let winter have his fee;
      Let a bleak paleness chalk the door,
So all within be livelier than before.

The Rose

Press me not to take more pleasure
      In this world of sugared lies,
And to use a larger measure
      Than my strict, yet welcome size.

First, there is no pleasure here:
      Coloured griefs indeed there are,
Blushing woes, that look as clear
      As if they could beauty spare.

Or if such deceits there be,
      Such delights I meant to say;   10
There are no such things to me,
      Who have passed my right away.

But I will not much oppose
      Unto what you now advise:
Only take this gentle rose,
      And therein my answer lies.

What is fairer than a rose?
      What is sweeter? yet it purgeth.°
Purgings enmity disclose,
      Enmity forbearance urgeth.   20

If then all that worldlings prize
      Be contracted to a rose;
Sweetly there indeed it lies,
      But it biteth in the close.

So this flower doth judge and sentence
        Worldly joys to be a scourge:
For they all produce repentance,
        And repentance is a purge.

But I health, not physic choose:°
        Only though I you oppose,   30
Say that fairly I refuse,
        For my answer is a rose.

Discipline

Throw away thy rod,
Throw away thy wrath:
        O my God,
Take the gentle path.

For my heart's desire
Unto thine is bent:
        I aspire
To a full consent.

Not a word or look
I affect to own,
        But by book,   10
And thy book alone.

Though I fail, I weep:
Though I halt in pace,
        Yet I creep
To the throne of grace.

Then let wrath remove;
Love will do the deed:
        For with love
Stony hearts will bleed.   20

Love is swift of foot;
Love's a man of war,°
                    And can shoot,
And can hit from far.

Who can scape his bow?
That which wrought on thee,
                    Brought thee low,
Needs must work on me.

Throw away thy rod;
Though man frailties hath,   30
                    Thou art God:
Throw away thy wrath.

The Invitation°

Come ye hither All, whose taste°
                    Is your waste;
Save your cost, and mend your fare.
God is here prepared and dressed°
                    And the feast,
God, in whom all dainties are.

Come ye hither All, whom wine
                    Doth define,°
Naming you not to your good:
Weep what ye have drunk amiss,   10
                    And drink this,
Which before ye drink is blood.

Come ye hither All, whom pain
                    Doth arraign,
Bringing all your sins to sight:
Taste and fear not: God is here
                    In this cheer,°
And on sin doth cast the fright.

Come ye hither All, whom joy
                    Doth destroy,   20
While ye graze without your bounds:
Here is joy that drowneth quite
                    Your delight,
As a flood the lower grounds.°

Come ye hither All, whose love
                    Is your dove,
And exalts you to the sky:
Here is love, which having breath
                    Ev'n in death,
After death can never die.   30

Lord I have invited all,
                    And I shall
Still invite, still call to thee:
For it seems but just and right
                    In my sight,
Where is All, there All should be.

The Banquet°

Welcome sweet and sacred cheer,°
                    Welcome dear;
With me, in me, live and dwell:
For thy neatness passeth sight,°
                    Thy delight
Passeth tongue to taste or tell.

O what sweetness from the bowl°
                    Fills my soul,
Such as is, and makes divine!
Is some star (fled from the sphere)   10
                    Melted there,
As we sugar melt in wine?

Or hath sweetness in the bread
        Made a head°
To subdue the smell of sin;
Flowers, and gums, and powders giving
        All their living,
Lest the Enemy should win?

Doubtless, neither star nor flower
        Hath the power   20
Such a sweetness to impart:
Only God, who gives perfumes,
        Flesh assumes,
And with it perfumes my heart.

But as pomanders and wood°
        Still are good,
Yet being bruised are better scented:
God, to show how far his love
        Could improve,
Here, as broken, is presented.   30

When I had forgot my birth,
        And on earth
In delights of earth was drowned;
God took blood, and needs would be
        Spilt with me,
And so found me on the ground.

Having raised me to look up,
        In a cup
Sweetly he doth meet my taste.
But I still being low and short,
        Far from court,   40
Wine becomes a wing at last.

For with it alone I fly
        To the sky:
Where I wipe mine eyes, and see
What I seek, for what I sue;
        Him I view,
Who hath done so much for me.

Let the wonder of his pity°
    Be my ditty,   50
And take up my lines and life:
Hearken under pain of death,
    Hands and breath;
Strive in this, and love the strife.

The Posy°

    Let wits contest,
And with their words and posies windows fill:
    Less than the least
Of all thy mercies, is my posy still.°

    This on my ring,
This by my picture, in my book I write:
    Whether I sing,
Or say, or dictate, this is my delight.

    Invention rest,
Comparisons go play, wit use thy will: 10
    Less than the least
Of all God's mercies, is my posy still.

A Parody°

    Soul's joy, when thou art gone,
    And I alone,
    Which cannot be,
Because thou dost abide with me,
And I depend on thee;

    Yet when thou dost suppress
    The cheerfulness
    Of thy abode,
And in my powers not stir abroad,
But leave me to my load: 10

O what a damp and shade
        Doth me invade!
        No stormy night
Can so afflict or so affright,
        As thy eclipsèd light.

Ah Lord! do not withdraw,
        Lest want of awe
        Make Sin appear;
And when thou dost but shine less clear,
        Say, that thou art not here.   20

And then what life I have,
        While Sin doth rave,
        And falsely boast,
That I may seek, but thou art lost;
        Thou and alone thou know'st.

O what a deadly cold
        Doth me infold!
        I half believe,
That Sin says true: but while I grieve,
        Thou com'st and dost relieve.   30

The Elixir°

Teach me, my God and King,
        In all things thee to see,
And what I do in anything,
        To do it as for thee:

Not rudely, as a beast,
        To run into an action;
But still to make thee prepossessed,°
        And give it his perfection.°

A man that looks on glass,
        On it may stay his eye;   10
Or if he pleaseth, through it pass,
        And then the heav'n espy.

All may of thee partake:
Nothing can be so mean,
Which with his tincture (for thy sake)°
Will not grow bright and clean.

A servant with this clause
Makes drudgery divine:
Who sweeps a room, as for thy laws,
Makes that and th' action fine.   20

This is the famous stone
That turneth all to gold:
For that which God doth touch and own°
Cannot for less be told.°

A Wreath

A wreathèd garland of deservèd praise,
Of praise deservèd, unto thee I give,
I give to thee, who knowest all my ways,
My crooked winding ways, wherein I live,
Wherein I die, not live: for life is straight,
Straight as a line, and ever tends to thee,
To thee, who art more far above deceit,
Than deceit seems above simplicity.
Give me simplicity, that I may live,
So live and like, that I may know thy ways,   10
Know them and practise them: then shall I give
For this poor wreath, give thee a crown of praise.

Death

Death, thou wast once an uncouth hideous thing,°
Nothing but bones,
The sad effect of sadder groans:
Thy mouth was open, but thou couldst not sing.

For we considered thee as at some six
        Or ten years hence,
    After the loss of life and sense,
Flesh being turned to dust, and bones to sticks.

We looked on this side of thee, shooting short;
        Where we did find   10
    The shells of fledge souls left behind,°
Dry dust, which sheds no tears, but may extort.

But since our Saviour's death did put some blood
        Into thy face;
    Thou art grown fair and full of grace,
Much in request, much sought for as a good.

For we do now behold thee gay and glad,
        As at doomsday;
    When souls shall wear their new array,
And all thy bones with beauty shall be clad.   20

Therefore we can go die as sleep, and trust
        Half that we have
    Unto an honest faithful grave;
Making our pillows either down, or dust.

Doomsday

        Come away,
      Make no delay.
Summon all the dust to rise,
Till it stir, and rub the eyes;
While this member jogs the other,
Each one whisp'ring, *Live you brother?*

        Come away,
      Make this the day.
Dust, alas, no music feels,
But thy trumpet: then it kneels,   10
As peculiar notes and strains
Cure tarantula's raging pains.°

Come away,
O make no stay!
Let the graves make their confession,
Lest at length they plead possession:
Flesh's stubbornness may have
Read that lesson to the grave.

Come away,
Thy flock doth stray.   20
Some to winds their body lend,
And in them may drown a friend:
Some in noisome vapours grow
To a plague and public woe.

Come away,
Help our decay.
Man is out of order hurled,
Parcelled out to all the world.
Lord, thy broken consort raise,°
And the music shall be praise.   30

Judgement

Almighty Judge, how shall poor wretches brook
                    Thy dreadful look,
Able a heart of iron to appal,
                    When thou shalt call
For ev'ry man's peculiar book?°

What others mean to do, I know not well;
                    Yet I hear tell,
That some will turn thee to some leaves therein
                    So void of sin,
That they in merit shall excel.   10

But I resolve, when thou shalt call for mine,
                    That to decline,
And thrust a Testament into thy hand:
                    Let that be scanned.
There thou shalt find my faults are thine.

Heaven°

O who will show me those delights on high?
        Echo.   I.
Thou Echo, thou art mortal, all men know.
        Echo.   No.
Wert thou not born among the trees and leaves?
        Echo.   Leaves.
And are there any leaves, that still abide?
        Echo.   Bide.
What leaves are they? impart the matter wholly.
        Echo.   Holy.   10
Are holy leaves the Echo then of bliss?
        Echo.   Yes.
Then tell me, what is that supreme delight?
        Echo.   Light.
Light to the mind: what shall the will enjoy?
        Echo.   Joy.
But are there cares and business with the pleasure?
        Echo.   Leisure.
Light, joy, and leisure; but shall they persever?°
        Echo.   Ever.   20

Love (III)

Love bade me welcome: yet my soul drew back,
        Guilty of dust and sin.
But quick-eyed Love, observing me grow slack
        From my first entrance in,
Drew nearer to me, sweetly questioning,
        If I lacked anything.

A guest, I answered, worthy to be here:
        Love said, You shall be he.
I the unkind, ungrateful? Ah my dear,
        I cannot look on thee.
Love took my hand, and smiling did reply,   10
        Who made the eyes but I?°

Truth Lord, but I have marred them: let my shame
Go where it doth deserve.
And know you not, says Love, who bore the blame?
My dear, then I will serve.
You must sit down, says Love, and taste my meat:°
So I did sit and eat.

FINIS

Glory be to God *on high*
And on earth peace
Goodwill towards men.

THE CHURCH MILITANT°

Almighty Lord, who from thy glorious throne
Seest and rulest all things ev'n as one:
The smallest ant or atom knows thy power,
Known also to each minute of an hour:
Much more do Commonweals acknowledge thee,°
And wrap their policies in thy decree,
Complying with thy counsels, doing nought
Which doth not meet with an eternal thought.
But above all, thy Church and Spouse doth prove
Not the decrees of power, but bands of love.   10
Early didst thou arise to plant this vine,
Which might the more endear it to be thine.
Spices come from the East; so did thy Spouse,
Trim as the light, sweet as the laden boughs
Of Noah's shady vine, chaste as the dove;°
Prepared and fitted to receive thy love.
The course was westward, that the sun might light
As well our understanding as our sight.
Where th' Ark did rest, there Abraham began
To bring the other Ark from Canaan.°   20
Moses pursued this: but King Solomon
Finished and fixed the old religion.
When it grew loose, the Jews did hope in vain
By nailing Christ to fasten it again.
But to the Gentiles he bore cross and all,
Rending with earthquakes the partition-wall:°
Only whereas the Ark in glory shone,
Now with the cross, as with a staff, alone,
Religion, like a pilgrim, westward bent,
Knocking at all doors, ever as she went.   30
Yet as the sun, though forward be his flight,
Listens behind him, and allows some light,
Till all depart: so went the Church her way,
Letting, while one foot stepped, the other stay
Among the eastern nations for a time,
Till both removèd to the western clime.
To Egypt first she came, where they did prove
Wonders of anger once, but now of love.

The ten Commandments there did flourish more
Than the ten bitter plagues had done before.   40
Holy Macarius and great Anthony°
Made Pharaoh Moses, changing th' history.
Goshen was darkness, Egypt full of lights,
Nilus for monsters brought forth Israelites.
Such power hath mighty Baptism to produce
For things misshapen, things of highest use.
How dear to me, O God, thy counsels are!°
                   Who may with thee compare?
Religion thence fled into Greece, where arts
Gave her the highest place in all men's hearts.   50
Learning was posed, philosophy was set,°
Sophisters taken in a fisher's net.
Plato and Aristotle were at a loss,
And wheeled about again to spell *Christ-Cross.*°
Prayers chased syllogisms into their den,
And *Ergo* was transformed into *Amen.*°
Though Greece took horse as soon as Egypt did,
And Rome as both; yet Egypt faster rid,
And spent her period and prefixèd time
Before the other. Greece being past her prime,   60
Religion went to Rome, subduing those,
Who, that they might subdue, made all their foes.
The warrior his dear scars no more resounds,°
But seems to yield Christ hath the greater wounds,
Wounds willingly endured to work his bliss,
Who by an ambush lost his Paradise.
The great heart stoops, and taketh from the dust
A sad repentance, not the spoils of lust:
Quitting his spear, lest it should pierce again
Him in his members, who for him was slain.   70
The Shepherd's hook grew to a sceptre here,
Giving new names and numbers to the year.°
But th' empire dwelt in Greece, to comfort them°
Who were cut short in Alexander's stem.
In both of these prowess and arts did tame
And tune men's hearts against the Gospel came:°
Which using, and not fearing skill in th' one,
Or strength in th' other, did erect her throne.
Many a rent and struggling th' empire knew,

(As dying things are wont) until it flew   80
At length to Germany, still westward bending,
And there the Church's festival attending:
That as before empire and arts made way,
(For no less harbingers would serve than they)
So they might still, and point us out the place
Where first the Church should raise her downcast face.
Strength levels grounds, art makes a garden there;
Then showers Religion, and makes all to bear.
Spain in the empire shared with Germany,°
But England in the higher victory: 90
Giving the Church a crown to keep her state,
And not go less than she had done of late.
Constantine's British line meant this of old,°
And did this mystery wrap up and fold
Within a sheet of paper, which was rent
From time's great Chronicle, and hither sent.
Thus both the Church and sun together ran
Unto the farthest old meridian.
How dear to me, O God, thy counsels are!
                    Who may with thee compare?   100
Much about one and the same time and place,
Both where and when the Church began her race,
Sin did set out of eastern Babylon,
And travelled westward also: journeying on
He chid the Church away, where'er he came,
Breaking her peace, and tainting her good name.
At first he got to Egypt, and did sow
Gardens of gods, which ev'ry year did grow
Fresh and fine deities. They were at great cost,
Who for a god clearly a sallet lost.°   110
Ah, what a thing is man devoid of grace,
Adoring garlic with an humble face,°
Begging his food of that which he may eat,
Starving the while he worshippeth his meat!
Who makes a root his god, how low is he,
If God and man be severed infinitely!
What wretchedness can give him any room,
Whose house is foul, while he adores his broom?
None will believe this now, though money be
In us the same transplanted foolery.   120

Thus Sin in Egypt sneakèd for a while;
His highest was an ox or crocodile,
And such poor game. Thence he to Greece doth pass,
And being craftier much than Goodness was,
He left behind him garrisons of sins
To make good that which ev'ry day he wins.
Here Sin took heart, and for a garden-bed
Rich shrines and oracles he purchasèd:
He grew a gallant, and would needs foretell
As well what should befall, as what befell.   130
Nay, he became a poet, and would serve°
His pills of sublimate in that conserve.°
The world came in with hands and purses full
To this great lottery, and all would pull.°
But all was glorious cheating, brave deceit,
Where some poor truths were shuffled for a bait
To credit him, and to discredit those
Who after him should braver truths disclose.
From Greece he went to Rome: and as before
He was a god, now he's an emperor.   140
Nero and others lodged him bravely there,
Put him in trust to rule the Roman sphere.
Glory was his chief instrument of old:
Pleasure succeeded straight, when that grew cold.
Which soon was blown to such a mighty flame,
That though our Saviour did destroy the game,
Disparking oracles, and all their treasure,°
Setting affliction to encounter pleasure;
Yet did a rogue with hope of carnal joy°
Cheat the most subtle nations. Who so coy,°   150
So trim, as Greece and Egypt? yet their hearts
Are given over, for their curious arts,°
To such Mahometan stupidities,
As the old heathen would deem prodigies.
How dear to me, O God, thy counsels are!
            Who may with thee compare?
Only the West and Rome do keep them free
From this contagious infidelity.
And this is all the Rock, whereof they boast,
As Rome will one day find unto her cost.   160
Sin being not able to extirpate quite

The Churches here, bravely resolved one night
To be a Churchman too, and wear a Mitre:
The old debauchèd ruffian would turn writer.
I saw him in his study, where he sate
Busy in controversies sprung of late.
A gown and pen became him wondrous well:
His grave aspect had more of heav'n than hell:
Only there was a handsome picture by,
To which he lent a corner of his eye. 170
As Sin in Greece a prophet was before,
And in old Rome a mighty emperor;
So now being priest he plainly did profess
To make a jest of Christ's three offices:°
The rather since his scattered jugglings were
United now in one both time and sphere.
From Egypt he took petty deities,
From Greece oracular infallibilities,
And from old Rome the liberty of pleasure
By free dispensings of the Church's treasure. 180
Then in memorial of his ancient throne
He did surname his palace, Babylon.°
Yet that he might the better gain all nations,
And make that name good by their transmigrations,°
From all these places, but at divers times,
He took fine vizards to conceal his crimes:°
From Egypt anchorism and retiredness,°
Learning from Greece, from old Rome stateliness:
And blending these he carried all men's eyes,
While Truth sat by, counting his victories: 190
Whereby he grew apace and scorned to use
Such force as once did captivate the Jews;°
But did bewitch, and finely work each nation
Into a voluntary transmigration.
All post to Rome: Princes submit their necks°
Either t' his public foot or private tricks.
It did not fit his gravity to stir,
Nor his long journey, nor his gout and fur.
Therefore he sent out able ministers,
Statesmen within, without doors cloisterers:° 200
Who without spear, or sword, or other drum
Than what was in their tongue, did overcome;

And having conquered, did so strangely rule,
That the whole world did seem but the Pope's mule.°
As new and old Rome did one empire twist;
So both together are one Antichrist,
Yet with two faces, as their Janus was,
Being in this their old cracked looking-glass.
How dear to me, O God, thy counsels are!
              Who may with thee compare?   210
Thus Sin triumphs in western Babylon;
Yet not as Sin, but as Religion.
Of his two thrones he made the latter best,
And to defray his journey from the east.
Old and new Babylon are to hell and night,
As is the moon and sun to heav'n and light.
When th' one did set, the other did take place,
Confronting equally the Law and Grace.
They are hell's landmarks, Satan's double crest:°
They are Sin's nipples, feeding th' east and west.   220
But as in vice the copy still exceeds
The pattern, but not so in virtuous deeds;
So though Sin made his latter seat the better,
The latter Church is to the first a debtor.
The second Temple could not reach the first:
And the late reformation never durst
Compare with ancient times and purer years;
But in the Jews and us deserveth tears.
Nay, it shall ev'ry year decrease and fade;
Till such a darkness do the world invade   230
At Christ's last coming, as his first did find:
Yet must there such proportion be assigned°
To these diminishings, as is between
The spacious world and Jewry to be seen.
Religion stands on tip-toe in our land,°
Ready to pass to the American strand.
When height of malice, and prodigious lusts,
Impudent sinning, witchcrafts, and distrusts
(The marks of future bane) shall fill our cup
Unto the brim, and make our measure up;   240
When Seine shall swallow Tiber, and the Thames
By letting in them both pollutes her streams:
When Italy of us shall have her will,

And all her calendar of sins fulfil;
Whereby one may foretell, what sins next year
Shall both in France and England domineer:
Then shall Religion to America flee:
They have their times of Gospel, ev'n as we.
My God, thou dost prepare for them a way
By carrying first their gold from them away: 250
For gold and grace did never yet agree:
Religion always sides with poverty.
We think we rob them, but we think amiss:
We are more poor, and they more rich by this.
Thou wilt revenge their quarrel, making grace
To pay our debts, and leave her ancient place
To go to them, while that which now their nation
But lends to us, shall be our desolation.
Yet as the Church shall thither westward fly,
So Sin shall trace and dog her instantly:°   260
They have their period also and set times
Both for their virtuous actions and their crimes.
And where of old the empire and the arts
Ushered the Gospel ever in men's hearts,
Spain hath done one; when arts perform the other,
The Church shall come, and Sin the Church shall smother:
That when they have accomplishèd their round,
And met in th' east their first and ancient sound,°
Judgement may meet them both and search them round.
Thus do both lights, as well in Church as sun,   270
Light one another, and together run.
Thus also Sin and darkness follow still
The Church and sun with all their power and skill.
But as the sun still goes both west and east;
So also did the Church by going west
Still eastward go; because it drew more near
To time and place, where judgement shall appear.
How dear to me, O God, thy counsels are!
                    Who may with thee compare?

L'Envoy

King of Glory, King of Peace,
With the one make war to cease;°
With the other bless thy sheep,
Thee to love, in thee to sleep.
Let not Sin devour thy fold,
Bragging that thy blood is cold,
That thy death is also dead,
While his conquests daily spread;
That thy flesh hath lost his food,
And thy Cross is common wood.   10
Choke him, let him say no more,
But reserve his breath in store,
Till thy conquests and his fall
Make his sighs to use it all,
And then bargain with the wind
To discharge what is behind.

Blessed be God *alone,*
Thrice blessed Three in One.

FINIS

POEMS NOT INCLUDED
IN *THE TEMPLE*

I. From the Williams Manuscript

The H. Communion

O gracious Lord, how shall I know
Whether in these gifts thou be so
   As thou art ev'rywhere;
Or rather so, as thou alone°
Tak'st all the lodging, leaving none
   For thy poor creature there?°

First I am sure, whether bread stay
Or whether bread do fly away
   Concerneth bread, not me.
But that both thou and all thy train   10
Be there, to thy truth, and my gain,
   Concerneth me and Thee.

And if in coming to thy foes°
Thou dost come first to them, that shows
   The haste of thy good will.
Or if that thou two stations makest
In bread and me, the way thou takest
   Is more, but for me still.

Then of this also I am sure
That thou didst all those pains endure   20
   To abolish Sin, not wheat.
Creatures are good, and have their place;
Sin only, which did all deface,
   Thou drivest from his seat.

I could believe an Impanation°
At the rate of an Incarnation,°
   If thou hadst died for bread.

But that which made my soul to die,
My flesh, and fleshly villainy,
    That also made thee dead.   30

That flesh is there, mine eyes deny:
And what should flesh but flesh descry,
    The noblest sense of five?
If glorious bodies pass the sight,
Shall they be food and strength and might
    Even there, where they deceive?

Into my soul this cannot pass;
Flesh (though exalted) keeps his grass
    And cannot turn to soul.
Bodies and minds are different spheres,   40
Nor can they change their bounds and meres,°
    But keep a constant pole.

This gift of all gifts is the best,
Thy flesh the least that I request.
    Thou took'st that pledge from me:
Give me not that I had before,
Or give me that, so I have more;
    My God, give me all Thee.

Love

Thou art too hard for me in Love:
There is no dealing with thee in that art:
    That is thy masterpiece I see.
    When I contrive and plot to prove
Something that may be conquest on my part,
    Thou still, O Lord, outstrippest me.

Sometimes, whenas I wash, I say,
And shrewdly, as I think, Lord wash my soul
    More spotted than my flesh can be.

But then there comes into my way
Thy ancient baptism, which when I was foul
   And knew it not, yet cleansèd me.

I took a time when thou didst sleep,°
Great waves of trouble combating my breast:
   I thought it brave to praise thee then,
   Yet then I found, that thou didst creep
Into my heart with joy, giving more rest
   Than flesh did lend thee back again.

Let me but once the conquest have
Upon the matter, 'twill thy conquest prove:
   If thou subdue mortality,
   Thou dost no more than doth the grave:
Whereas if I o'ercome thee and thy Love,
   Hell, Death and Devil come short of me.

Trinity Sunday

   He that is one,
      Is none.
   Two reacheth thee
   In some degree.
   Nature and Grace
With Glory may attain thy Face.
   Steel and a flint strike fire,
      Wit and desire
   Never to thee aspire,
Except life catch and hold those fast.
   That which belief
Did not confess in the first thief
   His fall can tell,
   From Heaven, through Earth, to Hell.
   Let two of those alone
      To them that fall,
Who God and Saints and Angels lose at last.
   He that has one,
      Has all.

Evensong°

The day is spent, and hath his will on me:
    I and the sun have run our races,
    I went the slower, yet more paces,
        For I decay, not he.

Lord make my losses up, and set me free:
    That I who cannot now by day
    Look on his daring brightness may
        Shine then more bright than he.

If thou defer this light, then, shadow me:
    Lest that the night, earth's gloomy shade,   10
    Fouling her nest, my earth invade,
        As if shades knew not thee.

But thou art light and darkness both together:
    If that be dark we cannot see,
    The sun is darker than a tree,
        And thou more dark than either.

Yet thou art not so dark, since I know this,
    But that my darkness may touch thine,
    And hope, that may teach it to shine,
        Since light thy darkness is.   20

O let my soul, whose keys I must deliver
    Into the hands of senseless dreams
    Which know not thee, suck in thy beams
        And wake with thee forever.

The Knell

    The bell doth toll:
Lord help thy servant whose perplexèd soul
    Doth wishly look°
    On either hand
And sometimes offers, sometimes makes a stand,°
    Struggling on th' hook.

Now is the season,
Now the great combat of our flesh and reason:
  O help, my God!
  See, they break in,   10
Disbanded humours, sorrows, troops of Sin,
  Each with his rod.

  Lord make thy Blood
Convert and colour all the other flood
  And streams of grief,
  That they may be
Juleps and cordials when we call on thee°
  For some relief.

Perseverance°

My God, the poor expressions of my love
Which warm these lines and serve them up to thee
Are so, as for the present I did move,
 Or rather as thou movedst me.

But what shall issue, whether these my words
Shall help another, but my judgement be,
As a burst fowling-piece doth save the birds
 But kill the man, is sealed with thee.

For who can tell, though thou hast died to win
And wed my soul in glorious paradise,   10
Whether my many crimes and use of sin
 May yet forbid the banns and bliss?°

Only my soul hangs on thy promises°
With face and hands clinging unto thy breast,
Clinging and crying, crying without cease,
 Thou art my rock, thou art my rest.°

II. From Walton's *Life of Herbert*°

Sonnets

My God, where is that ancient heat towards thee,
  Wherewith whole shoals of Martyrs once did burn,
  Besides their other flames? Doth Poetry
Wear Venus' livery? only serve her turn?
Why are not sonnets made of thee? and lays
  Upon thine Altar burnt? Cannot thy love
  Heighten a spirit to sound out thy praise
As well as any she? Cannot thy Dove
Outstrip their Cupid easily in flight?
  Or, since thy ways are deep, and still the same,   10
  Will not a verse run smooth that bears thy name?
Why doth that fire, which by thy power and might
  Each breast does feel, no braver fuel choose
  Than that, which one day worms may chance refuse?

Sure, Lord, there is enough in thee to dry
  Oceans of ink; for, as the Deluge did
  Cover the earth, so doth thy Majesty:
Each cloud distills thy praise, and doth forbid
Poets to turn it to another use.
  Roses and lilies speak thee; and to make
  A pair of cheeks of them, is thy abuse.
Why should I women's eyes for crystal take?
Such poor invention burns in their low mind
  Whose fire is wild, and doth not upward go   10
  To praise, and on thee, Lord, some ink bestow.
Open the bones, and you shall nothing find
  In the best face but filth, when, Lord, in thee
  The beauty lies in the discovery.°

To my Successor

If thou chance for to find
A new house to thy mind,
And built without thy cost:
Be good to the poor,
As God gives thee store,
And then, my labour's not lost.

A PRIEST
To the
TEMPLE,

OR,
The Countrey PARSON
HIS
CHARACTER,
AND
Rule of Holy Life.

The AUTHOUR,
Mr *G.H.*

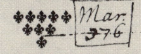

LONDON,
Printed by *T. Maxey* for *T. Garthwait*, at the
little North door of St *Paul's*: 1652.

The Author to the Reader

Being desirous (through the mercy of God) to please him, for whom I am, and live, and who giveth me my desires and performances; and considering with myself that the way to please him is to feed my flock diligently and faithfully, since our Saviour hath made that the argument of a pastor's love,° I have resolved to set down the form and character of a true pastor, that I may have a mark to aim at: which also I will set as high as I can, since he shoots higher that threatens the moon, than he that aims at a tree. Not that I think, if a man do not all which is here expressed, he presently sins and displeases God, but that it is a good strife to go as far as we can in pleasing of him who hath done so much for us. The Lord prosper the intention to myself and others, who may not despise my poor labours, but add to those points which I have observed, until the book grow to a complete pastoral.°

1632

GEO. HERBERT

A PRIEST TO THE TEMPLE

OR,

THE COUNTRY PARSON
HIS CHARACTER, etc.

CHAP. I

Of a Pastor

A pastor is the deputy of Christ for the reducing° of man to the obedience of God. This definition is evident, and contains the direct steps of pastoral duty and authority. For first, man fell from God by disobedience. Secondly, Christ is the glorious instrument of God for the revoking° of man. Thirdly, Christ being not to continue on earth, but after he had fulfilled the work of reconciliation, to be received up into heaven, he constituted deputies in his place, and these are priests. And therefore St. Paul in the beginning of his Epistles° professeth this: and in the first to the Colossians plainly avoucheth, that he *fills up that which is behind of the afflictions of Christ in his flesh, for his body's sake, which is the Church.°* Wherein is contained the complete definition of a minister. Out of this charter of the priesthood may be plainly gathered both the dignity thereof and the duty: the dignity, in that a priest may do that which Christ did, and by his authority, and as his vicegerent; the duty, in that a priest is to do that which Christ did, and after his manner, both for doctrine and life.

CHAP. II

Their Diversities

Of pastors (intending mine own nation only, and also therein setting aside the reverend prelates of the Church, to whom this discourse ariseth not) some live in the universities, some in noble houses, some in parishes residing on their cures.° Of those that live in the universities, some live there in office, whose rule is that of the Apostle, Rom. 12. 6. *Having gifts differing, according to the grace that is given to us, whether prophecy, let us prophesy according to the proportion of faith; or ministry, let us wait on our ministering; or he that teacheth, on teaching,* etc. *he that ruleth, let him do it with diligence,* etc. Some in a preparatory way, whose aim and labour must be not only to get knowledge, but to subdue and mortify all lusts and affections: and not to think, that when they have read the Fathers, or schoolmen,° a minister is made, and the thing done. The greatest and hardest preparation is within: for, *Unto the ungodly, saith God, Why dost thou preach my laws, and takest my covenant in thy mouth?* Psal. 50. 16.° Those that live in noble houses are called chaplains, whose duty and obligation being the same to the houses they live in, as a parson's to his parish, in describing the one (which is indeed the bent of my discourse) the other will be manifest. Let not chaplains think themselves so free, as many of them do, and because they have different names, think their office different. Doubtless they are parsons of the families they live in, and are entertained to that end, either by an open, or implicit covenant. Before they are in orders, they may be received for companions, or discoursers; but after a man is once minister, he cannot agree to come into any house, where he shall not exercise what he is, unless he forsake his plough, and look back. Wherefore they are not to be over-submissive and base, but to keep up with the lord and lady of the house, and to preserve a boldness with them and all, even so far as reproof to their very face, when occasion calls, but seasonably° and discreetly. They who do not thus, while they remember their earthly lord, do much forget their heavenly; they wrong the priesthood, neglect their duty, and shall be so far from that which they seek with their over-submissiveness and cringings, that they shall ever be despised. They who for the hope of promotion neglect any necessary admonition or reproof, sell (with Judas) their Lord and Master.

Chap. III

The Parson's Life

The country parson is exceeding exact in his life, being holy, just, prudent, temperate, bold, grave in all his ways. And because the two highest points of life, wherein a Christian is most seen, are patience and mortification (patience in regard of afflictions, mortification in regard of lusts and affections, and the stupifying and deading of all the clamorous powers of the soul) therefore he hath thoroughly studied these, that he may be an absolute master and commander of himself, for all the purposes which God hath ordained him. Yet in these points he labours most in those things which are most apt to scandalize his parish. And first, because country people live hardly, and therefore as feeling their own sweat, and consequently knowing the price of money, are offended much with any who by hard usage increase their travail, the country parson is very circumspect in avoiding all covetousness, neither being greedy to get, nor niggardly to keep, nor troubled to lose any worldly wealth; but in all his words and actions slighting and disesteeming it, even to a wondering that the world should so much value wealth, which in the day of wrath hath not one dram of comfort for us. Secondly, because luxury° is a very visible sin, the parson is very careful to avoid all the kinds thereof, but especially that of drinking, because it is the most popular vice; into which if he come, he prostitutes himself both to shame and sin, and by having *fellowship with the unfruitful works of darkness*, he disableth himself of authority *to reprove them*:° for sins make all equal whom they find together; and then they are worst, who ought to be best. Neither is it for the servant of Christ to haunt inns, or taverns, or alehouses, to the dishonour of his person and office. The parson doth not so, but orders his life in such a fashion, that when death takes him, as the Jews and Judas did Christ, he may say as he did, *I sat daily with you teaching in the Temple.*° Thirdly, because country people (as indeed all honest men) do much esteem their word, it being the life of buying and selling, and dealing in the world; therefore the parson is very strict in keeping his word, though it be to his own hindrance,° as knowing, that if he be not so, he will quickly be discovered and disregarded: neither will they believe him in the pulpit, whom they cannot trust in his conversation.° As for oaths and apparel, the disorders thereof are also very manifest. The parson's yea is yea, and nay, nay; and his apparel plain, but reverend and clean, without spots, or dust, or smell; the purity of his mind breaking out and dilating itself even to his body, clothes, and habitation.

CHAP. IIII

The Parson's Knowledge

The country parson is full of all knowledge. They say, it is an ill mason that refuseth any stone: and there is no knowledge, but, in a skilful hand, serves either positively as it is, or else to illustrate some other knowledge. He condescends even to the knowledge of tillage and pastorage, and makes great use of them in teaching, because people by what they understand, are best led to what they understand not. But the chief and top of his knowledge consists in the book of books, the storehouse and magazine of life and comfort, the holy Scriptures. There he sucks, and lives. In the Scriptures he finds four things: precepts for life, doctrines for knowledge, examples for illustration, and promises for comfort; these he hath digested severally.° But for the understanding of these, the means he useth are first, a holy life, remembering what his Master saith, that *if any do God's will, he shall know of the doctrine, John* 7. [17], and assuring himself, that wicked men, however learned, do not know the Scriptures, because they feel them not, and because they are not understood but with the same Spirit that writ them. The second means is prayer, which if it be necessary even in temporal things, how much more in things of another world, where the well is deep, and we have nothing of ourselves to draw with?° Wherefore he ever begins the reading of the Scripture with some short inward ejaculation, as, *Lord, open mine eyes, that I may see the wondrous things of thy Law*, etc.° The third means is a diligent collation of Scripture with Scripture. For all truth being consonant to itself, and all being penned by one and the self-same Spirit, it cannot be, but that an industrious and judicious comparing of place with place must be a singular help for the right understanding of the Scriptures. To this may be added the consideration of any text with the coherence thereof, touching what goes before, and what follows after, as also the scope° of the Holy Ghost. When the Apostles would have called down fire from Heaven, they were reproved, as ignorant of what spirit they were. For the Law required one thing, and the Gospel another: yet as diverse, not as repugnant: therefore the spirit of both is to be considered and weighed. The fourth means are commenters and Fathers, who have handled the places controverted, which the parson by no means refuseth. As he doth not so study others, as to neglect the grace of God in himself, and what the Holy Spirit teacheth him, so doth he assure himself that God in all ages hath had his servants, to whom he hath revealed his Truth, as well as to him; and that as one country doth not bear all things, that there may be a commerce, so neither hath God opened, or will open all to one, that there may be a traffic in knowledge between the servants of God, for the planting both of love and humility. Wherefore he hath one Comment° at least upon every book of Scripture, and ploughing with this, and his own meditations, he enters into the secrets of God treasured in the holy Scripture.

CHAP. V
The Parson's Accessory Knowledges

The country parson hath read the Fathers also, and the school-men, and the later writers, or a good proportion of all, out of all which he hath compiled a book and body of divinity, which is the storehouse of his sermons, and which he preacheth all his life; but diversely clothed, illustrated, and enlarged. For though the world is full of such composures, yet every man's own is fittest, readiest, and most savoury to him. Besides, this being to be done in his younger and preparatory times, it is an honest joy ever after to look upon his well spent hours. This body he made by way of expounding the Church Catechism, to which all divinity may easily be reduced. For it being indifferent in itself to choose any method, that is best to be chosen, of which there is likeliest to be most use. Now catechizing being a work of singular and admirable benefit to the Church of God, and a thing required under canonical obedience, the expounding of our Catechism must needs be the most useful form. Yet hath the parson, besides this laborious work, a slighter form of catechizing, fitter for country people; according as his audience is, so he useth one, or other; or sometimes both, if his audience be inter-mixed. He greatly esteems also of cases of conscience, wherein he is much versed. And indeed, herein is the greatest ability of a parson to lead his people exactly in the ways of Truth, so that they neither decline to the right hand, nor to the left. Neither let any think this a slight thing. For every one hath not digested, when it is a sin to take something for money lent, or when not; when it is a fault to discover another's fault, or when not; when the affections of the soul in desiring and procuring increase of means or honour, be a sin of covet-ousness or ambition, and when not; when the appetites of the body in eating, drinking, sleep, and the pleasure that comes with sleep, be sins of gluttony, drunkenness, sloth, lust, and when not, and so in many circumstances of actions. Now if a shepherd know not which grass will bane,° or which not, how is he fit to be a shepherd? Wherefore the parson hath thoroughly canvassed all the particulars of human actions, at least all those which he observeth are most incident to his parish.

CHAP. VI

The Parson Praying

The country parson, when he is to read divine services, composeth himself to all possible reverence, lifting up his heart and hands and eyes, and using all other gestures which may express a hearty and unfeigned devotion. This he doth, first, as being truly touched and amazed with the Majesty of God, before whom he then presents himself; yet not as himself alone, but as presenting with himself the whole congregation, whose sins he then bears, and brings with his own to the heavenly altar to be bathed and washed in the sacred laver of Christ's blood. Secondly, as this is the true reason of his inward fear, so he is content to express this outwardly to the utmost of his power; that being first affected himself, he may affect also his people, knowing that no sermon moves them so much to a reverence, which they forget again, when they come to pray, as a devout behaviour in the very act of praying. Accordingly his voice is humble, his words treatable° and slow; yet not so slow neither, as to let the fervency of the supplicant hang and die between speaking, but with a grave liveliness, between fear and zeal, pausing yet pressing, he performs his duty. Besides his example, he having often instructed his people how to carry themselves in divine service, exacts of them all possible reverence, by no means enduring either talking, or sleeping, or gazing, or leaning, or half-kneeling, or any undutiful behaviour in them, but causing them, when they sit, or stand, or kneel, to do all in a straight and steady posture, as attending to what is done in the church, and everyone, man and child, answering aloud both Amen, and all other answers which are on the clerk's° and people's part to answer; which answers also are to be done not in a huddling or slubbering fashion, gaping, or scratching the head, or spitting even in the midst of their answer, but gently and pausably,° thinking what they say; so that while they answer, *As it was in the beginning,* etc. they meditate as they speak, that God hath ever had his people that have glorified him as well as now, and that he shall have so forever. And the like in other answers. This is that which the Apostle calls a reasonable service,° Rom. 12., when we speak not as parrots, without reason, or offer up such sacrifices as they did of old, which was of beasts devoid of reason; but when we use our reason, and apply our powers to the service of him that gives them. If there be any of the gentry or nobility of the parish, who sometimes make it a piece of state° not to come at the beginning of service with their poor neighbours, but at mid-prayers, both to their own loss, and of theirs also who gaze upon them when they come in, and neglect the present service of God, he by no means suffers it, but after divers gentle admonitions, if they persevere, he causes them to be presented;° or if the poor churchwardens° be affrighted with their greatness, notwithstanding his instruction that they ought not to be so, but even to let the world sink, so they do their duty, he presents them himself, only protesting to them, that not any ill will draws him to it, but the debt and obligation of his calling, being to obey God rather than men.

CHAP. VII

The Parson Preaching

The country parson preacheth constantly, the pulpit is his joy and his throne: if he at any time intermit, it is either for want of health, or against some great festival,° that he may the better celebrate it, or for the variety of the hearers, that he may be heard at his return more attentively. When he intermits, he is ever very well supplied by some able man who treads in his steps, and will not throw down what he hath built; whom also he entreats to press some point that he himself hath often urged with no great success, that so in the mouth of two or three witnesses the truth may be more established.° When he preacheth, he procures attention by all possible art, both by earnestness of speech, it being natural to men to think that where is much earnestness, there is somewhat worth hearing; and by a diligent and busy cast of his eye on his auditors, with letting them know that he observes who marks, and who not; and with particularizing of his speech now to the younger sort, then to the elder, now to the poor, and now to the rich. This is for you, and, This is for you; for particulars ever touch and awake more than generals. Herein also he serves himself of the judgements of God, as of those of ancient times, so especially of the late ones; and those most, which are nearest to his parish; for people are very attentive at such discourses, and think it behoves them to be so, when God is so near them, and even over their heads. Sometimes he tells them stories and sayings of others, according as his text invites him; for them also men heed and remember better than exhortations; which though earnest, yet often die with the sermon, especially with country people, which are thick and heavy, and hard to raise to a point of zeal and fervency, and need a mountain of fire to kindle them; but stories and sayings they will well remember. He often tells them that sermons are

[handwritten margin notes: "1. right kind of text 2. 3. making apostrophes to God", "how to", and circled numbers 1, 2, 3]

dangerous things, that none goes out of church as he came in, but
either better, or worse; that none is careless before his judge, and
that the word of God shall judge us. By these and other means the
parson procures attention; but the character of his sermon is holiness; he is not witty, or learned, or eloquent, but holy. A character
that Hermogenes° never dreamed of, and therefore he could give no
precepts thereof. But it is gained, first, by choosing texts of devotion,
not controversy, moving and ravishing texts, whereof the Scriptures
are full. Secondly, by dipping and seasoning all our words and sen-
tences in our hearts, before they come into our mouths, truly
affecting° and cordially° expressing all that we say; so that the auditors may plainly perceive that every word is heart-deep. Thirdly, by
turning often, and making many apostrophes to God, as, Oh Lord,
bless my people, and teach them this point; or, Oh my Master, on
whose errand I come, let me hold my peace, and do thou speak
thyself; for thou art Love, and when thou teachest, all are scholars.
Some such irradiations scatteringly in the sermon carry great holiness in them. The Prophets are admirable in this. So Isa. 64. [1], *Oh
that thou wouldst rent the heavens, that thou wouldst come down*, etc.
And Jeremy, chapt. 10, after he had complained of the desolation of
Israel, turns to God suddenly, *Oh Lord, I know that the way of man is
not in himself*, etc.° Fourthly, by frequent wishes of the people's good,
and joying therein, though he himself were with Saint Paul even
sacrificed upon the service of their faith. For there is no greater sign
of holiness, than the procuring and rejoicing in another's good. And
herein St Paul excelled in all his Epistles. How did he put the
Romans in all his prayers! Rom. 1. 9. And ceased not to give thanks
for the Ephesians, Eph. 1. 16. And for the Corinthians, chap. 1. 4.
And for the Philippians made request with joy, ch. 1. 4. And is in
contention for them whether to live or die, be with them, or Christ,
verse 23, which, setting aside his care of his flock, were a madness
to doubt of. What an admirable Epistle is the second to the Corinthians! how full of affections! He joys, and he is sorry, he grieves, and
he glories, never was there such care of a flock expressed, save in
the great shepherd of the fold, who first shed tears over Jerusalem,
and afterwards blood. Therefore this care may be learned there, and
then woven into sermons, which will make them appear exceeding
reverend and holy. Lastly, by an often urging of the presence and
majesty of God, by these, or such-like speeches. Oh let us all take
heed what we do, God sees us, he sees whether I speak as I ought,
or you hear as you ought, he sees hearts, as we see faces: he is

among us; for if we be here, he must be here, since we are here by
him, and without him could not be here. Then turning the discourse
to his Majesty, And he is a great God and terrible, as great in mercy,
so great in judgement: there are but two devouring elements, fire
and water, he hath both in him; *his voice is as the sound of many
waters*, Revelations 1. [15], and he himself *is a consuming fire*, Hebrews 12. [29]. Such discourses show very holy. The parson's method
in handling of a text consists of two parts; first, a plain and evident
declaration of the meaning of the text; and secondly, some choice
observations drawn out of the whole text, as it lies entire and un-
broken in the Scripture itself. This he thinks natural, and sweet, and
grave. Whereas the other way of crumbling a text into small parts, as,
the person speaking, or spoken to, the subject, and object, and the
like, hath neither in it sweetness, nor gravity, nor variety, since the
words apart are not Scripture, but a dictionary, and may be considered alike in all the Scripture. The parson exceeds not an hour in
preaching, because all ages have thought that a competency, and he
that profits not in that time, will less afterwards, the same affection°
which made him not profit before, making him then weary, and so
he grows from not relishing, to loathing.

Chap. VIII

The Parson on Sundays

The country parson, as soon as he awakes on Sunday morning,
presently° falls to work, and seems to himself so as a market-man is,
when the market day comes, or a shopkeeper, when customers use
to° come in. His thoughts are full of making the best of the day, and
contriving it to his best gains. To this end, besides his ordinary
prayers, he makes a peculiar one for a blessing on the exercises of
the day, that nothing befall him unworthy of that Majesty before
which he is to present himself, but that all may be done with reverence to his glory, and with edification to his flock, humbly beseeching his Master, that how or whenever he punish him, it be not
in his ministry: then he turns to request for his people, that the Lord
would be pleased to sanctify them all, that they may come with holy
hearts and awful minds into the congregation, and that the good
God would pardon all those, who come with less prepared hearts
than they ought. This done, he sets himself to the consideration of
the duties of the day, and if there be any extraordinary addition to
the customary exercises, either from the time of the year, or from

the State, or from God by a child born or dead, or any other accident, he contrives how and in what manner to induce° it to the best
advantage. Afterwards when the hour calls, with his family attending
him, he goes to church, at his first entrance humbly adoring and
worshipping the invisible majesty and presence of Almighty God,
and blessing the people either openly, or to himself. Then having
read divine service twice fully, and preached in the morning, and
catechized in the afternoon, he thinks he hath in some measure,
according to poor and frail man, discharged the public duties of the
congregation. The rest of the day he spends either in reconciling
neighbours that are at variance, or in visiting the sick, or in exhortations to some of his flock by themselves, whom his sermons cannot,
or do not reach. And everyone is more awaked, when we come and
say, *Thou art the man.*° This way he finds exceeding useful and winning; and these exhortations he calls his privy purse,° even as princes
have theirs, besides their public disbursements. At night he thinks it
a very fit time, both suitable to the joy of the day, and without hindrance to public duties, either to entertain some of his neighbours,
or to be entertained of them, where he takes occasion to discourse of
such things as are both profitable and pleasant, and to raise up their
minds to apprehend God's good blessing to our Church and State;
that order is kept in the one, and peace in the other, without disturbance or interruption of public divine offices. As he opened the
day with prayer, so he closeth it, humbly beseeching the Almighty to
pardon and accept our poor services, and to improve them, that we
may grow therein, and that our feet may be like hinds' feet° ever
climbing up higher and higher unto him.

CHAP. IX

The Parson's State of Life

The country parson, considering that virginity is a higher state
than matrimony, and that the ministry requires the best and highest
things, is rather unmarried, than married. But yet as the temper° of
his body may be, or as the temper of his parish may be, where he
may have occasion to converse with women, and that among sus-
picious men, and other like circumstances considered, he is rather
married than unmarried. Let him communicate the thing often by
prayer unto God, and as his grace shall direct him, so let him proceed. If he be unmarried, and keep house, he hath not a woman in
his house, but finds opportunities of having his meat dressed° and

other services done by men-servants at home, and his linen washed abroad. If he be unmarried, and sojourn,° he never talks with any woman alone, but in the audience of others, and that seldom, and then also in a serious manner, never jestingly or sportfully. He is very circumspect in all companies, both of his behaviour, speech, and very looks, knowing himself to be both suspected and envied. If he stand steadfast in his heart, having no necessity, but hath power over his own will, and hath so decreed in his heart, that he will keep himself a virgin, he spends his days in fasting and prayer, and blesseth God for the gift of continency, knowing that it can no way be preserved, but only by those means, by which at first it was obtained. He therefore thinks it not enough for him to observe the fasting days of the Church, and the daily prayers enjoined him by authority, which he observeth out of humble conformity and obedience; but adds to them, out of choice and devotion, some other days for fasting, and hours for prayers; and by these he keeps his body tame, serviceable, and healthful, and his soul fervent, active, young, and lusty as an eagle. He often readeth the Lives of the primitive monks, hermits, and virgins, and wondereth not so much at their patient suffering, and cheerful dying under persecuting emperors (though that indeed be very admirable), as at their daily temperance, abstinence, watchings, and constant prayers and mortifications in the times of peace and prosperity. To put on the profound humility and the exact temperance of our Lord Jesus, with other exemplary virtues of that sort, and to keep them on in the sunshine and noon of prosperity, he findeth to be as necessary, and as difficult at least, as to be clothed with perfect patience and Christian fortitude in the cold midnight storms of persecution and adversity. He keepeth his watch and ward, night and day, against the proper and peculiar temptations of his state of life, which are principally these two, spiritual pride and impurity of heart: against these ghostly° enemies he girdeth up his loins, keeps the imagination from roving, puts on the whole armour of God, and by the virtue of the shield of faith,° he is not afraid of the pestilence that walketh in darkness (carnal impurity), nor of the sickness that destroyeth at noonday° (ghostly pride and self-conceit). Other temptations he hath, which, like mortal enemies, may sometimes disquiet him likewise; for the human soul being bounded and kept in, in her sensitive faculty, will run out more or less in her intellectual. Original concupiscence is such an active thing, by reason of continual inward or outward temptations, that it is ever attempting, or doing one mischief or other. Ambition, or untimely desire of promotion to an higher state or place, under colour of accommodation° or necessary provision, is a common temptation to men of any eminency, especially being single men. Curiosity in prying into high speculative and unprofitable questions is another great stumbling block to the holiness of scholars. These and many other spiritual wickednesses in high places° doth the parson fear, or experiment,° or both; and that much more being single, than if he were married; for then commonly the stream of temptations is turned another way, into covetousness, love of pleasure or ease, or the like. If the parson be unmarried, and means to continue so, he doth at least as much as hath been said. If he be married, the choice of his wife was made rather by his ear, than by his eye; his judgement, not his affection found out a fit wife for him, whose humble and liberal disposition he preferred before beauty, riches, or honour. He knew that (the good instrument of God to bring women to heaven) a wise and loving husband could, out of humility, produce any special grace of faith, patience, meekness, love, obedience, etc., and out of liberality, make her fruitful in all good works. As he is just in all things, so is he to his wife also, counting nothing so much his own, as that he may be unjust unto it. Therefore he gives her respect both afore her servants and others, and half at least of the government of the house, reserving so much of the affairs as serve for a diversion for him; yet never so giving over the reins, but that he sometimes looks how things go, demanding an account, but not by the way of an account. And this must be done the oftener, or the seldomer, according as he is satisfied of his wife's discretion.

Chap. X

The Parson in his House

The parson is very exact in the governing of his house, making it a copy and model for his parish. He knows the temper and pulse of every person in his house, and accordingly either meets with their vices, or advanceth their virtues. His wife is either religious, or night and day he is winning her to it. Instead of the qualities of the world, he requires only three of her; first, a training up of her children and maids in the fear of God, with prayers, and catechizing, and all religious duties. Secondly, a curing and healing of all wounds and sores with her own hands; which skill either she brought with her, or he takes care she shall learn it of some religious neighbour. Thirdly, a providing for her family in such sort, as that neither they want a competent sustentation,° nor her husband be brought in debt. His children he first makes Christians, and then commonwealth's-men; the one he owes to his heavenly country, the other to his earthly, having no title to either, except he do good to both. Therefore having seasoned them with all piety, not only of words in praying and reading, but in actions, in visiting other sick children, and tending their wounds, and sending his charity by them to the poor, and sometimes giving them a little money to do it of themselves, that they get a delight in it, and enter favour with God, who weighs even children's actions, 1 King. 14. 12, 13. He afterwards turns his care to fit all their dispositions with some calling, not sparing the eldest, but giving him the prerogative of his father's profession, which haply for his other children he is not able to do.° Yet in binding them prentices° (in case he think fit to do so) he takes care not to put them into vain trades, and unbefitting the reverence of their father's calling, such as are taverns for men, and lace-making for women; because those trades, for the most part, serve but the vices and vanities of the world, which he is to deny, and not augment. However, he resolves with himself never to omit any present good deed of charity, in consideration of providing a stock for his children; but assures himself, that money thus lent to God is placed surer for his children's advantage, than if it were given to the Chamber of London.° Good deeds and good breeding are his two great stocks for his children; if God give anything above those, and not spent in them, he blesseth God, and lays it out as he sees cause. His servants are all religious, and were it not his duty to have them so, it were his profit, for none are so well served, as by religious servants, both because they do best, and because what they do is blessed and prospers. After religion, he teacheth them that three things make a complete servant, truth, and diligence, and neatness, or cleanliness. Those that can read are allowed times for it, and those that cannot are taught; for all in his house are either teachers or learners, or both, so that his family is a school of religion, and they all account that to teach the ignorant is the greatest alms. Even the walls are not idle, but something is written or painted there, which may excite the reader to a thought of piety; especially the 101 Psalm, which is expressed in a fair table,° as being the rule of a family. And when they go abroad, his wife among her neighbours is the beginner of good discourses, his children among children, his servants among other servants; so that as in the house of those that are skilled in music, all are musicians, so in the house of a preacher, all are preachers. He suffers not a lie or equivocation by any means in his house, but counts it the art and secret of governing to preserve a directness and open plainness in all things; so that all his house knows that there is no help for a fault done, but confession. He himself, or his wife, takes account of sermons, and how everyone profits, comparing this year with the last: and besides the common prayers of the family, he straitly° requires of all to pray by themselves before they sleep at night, and stir out in the morning, and knows what prayers they say, and till they have learned them, makes them kneel by him; esteeming that this private praying is a more voluntary act in them, than when they are called to others' prayers, and that which, when they leave the family, they carry with them. He keeps his servants between love and fear, according as he finds them; but generally he distributes it thus: to his children he shows more love than terror, to his servants more terror than love; but an old good servant boards° a child. The furniture of his house is very plain, but clean, whole, and sweet, as sweet as his garden can make; for he hath no money for such things, charity being his only perfume, which deserves cost when he can spare it. His fare is plain and common, but wholesome; what he hath is little, but very good; it consisteth most of mutton, beef, and veal, if he adds anything for a great day, or a stranger, his garden or orchard supplies it, or his barn and back-side:° he goes no further for any entertainment, lest he go into the world, esteeming it absurd, that he should exceed, who teacheth others temperance. But those which his home produceth, he refuseth not, as coming cheap and easy, and arising from the improvement of things which otherwise would be lost. Wherein he admires and imitates the wonderful providence and thrift of the great householder of the world: for there being two things, which as they are, are unuseful to man, the one for smallness, as crumbs and scattered corn,° and the like, the other for the foulness, as wash, and dirt, and things thereinto fallen; God hath provided creatures for both; for the first, poultry; for the second, swine. These save man the labour, and doing that which either he could not do, or was not fit for him to do, by taking both sorts of food into them, do as it were dress and prepare both for man in themselves, by growing themselves fit for his table. The parson in his house observes fasting days; and particularly, as Sunday is his day of joy, so Friday his day of humiliation, which he celebrates not only with abstinence of diet, but also of company, recreation, and all outward contentments; and besides, with confession of sins, and all acts of mortification. Now fasting days contain a treble obligation; first, of eating less that day, than on other days; secondly, of eating no pleasing, or over-nourishing things, as the Israelites did eat sour herbs; thirdly, of eating no flesh, which is but the determination of the second rule by authority to this particular. The two former obligations are much more essential to a true fast, than the third and last; and fasting days were fully performed by keeping of the two former, had not authority interposed: so that to eat little, and that unpleasant, is the natural rule of fasting, although it be flesh. For since fasting in Scripture language is an afflicting of our souls, if a piece of dry flesh at my table be more unpleasant to me, than some fish there, certainly to eat the flesh, and not the fish, is to keep the fasting day naturally. And it is observable, that the prohibiting of flesh came from hot countries, where both flesh alone, and much more with wine, is apt to nourish more than in cold regions, and where flesh may be much better spared, and with more safety than elsewhere, where both the people and the drink being cold and phlegmatic, the eating of flesh is an antidote to both. For it is certain that a weak stomach, being prepossessed with flesh, shall much better brook and bear a draught of beer, than if it had taken before either fish, or roots, or such things; which will discover itself by spitting, and rheum, or phlegm. To conclude, the parson, if he be in full health, keeps the three obligations, eating fish, or roots, and that for quantity little, for quality unpleasant. If his body be weak and obstructed, as most students are, he cannot keep the last obligation, nor suffer others in his house that are so, to keep it; but only the two former, which also in diseases of exinanition° (as consumptions) must be broken: for meat was made for man, not man for meat. To all this may be added, not for emboldening the unruly, but for the comfort of the weak, that not only sickness breaks these obligations of fasting, but sickliness also. For it is as unnatural to do anything that leads me to a sickness, to which I am inclined, as not to get out of that sickness, when I am in it, by any diet. One thing is evident, that an English body, and a student's body, are two great obstructed vessels, and there is nothing that is food, and not physic, which doth less obstruct, than flesh moderately taken; as being immoderately taken, it is exceeding obstructive. And obstructions are the cause of most diseases.

Chap. XI

The Parson's Courtesy

The country parson owing a debt of charity to the poor, and of courtesy to his other parishioners, he so distinguisheth, that he keeps his money for the poor, and his table for those that are above alms. Not but that the poor are welcome also to his table, whom he sometimes purposely takes home with him, setting them close by him, and carving for them, both for his own humility, and their comfort, who are much cheered with such friendliness. But since both is to be done, the better sort invited, and meaner relieved, he chooseth rather to give the poor money, which they can better employ to their own advantage, and suitably to their needs, than so much given in meat at dinner. Having then invited some of his parish, he taketh his times to do the like to the rest; so that in the compass of the year, he hath them all with him, because country people are very observant of such things, and will not be persuaded but, being not invited, they are hated. Which persuasion the parson by all means avoids, knowing that where there are such conceits,° there is no room for his doctrine to enter. Yet doth he oftenest invite those whom he sees take best courses, that so both they may be encouraged to persevere, and others spurred to do well, that they may enjoy the like courtesy. For though he desire that all should live well and virtuously, not for any reward of his, but for virtue's sake, yet that will not be so: and therefore as God, although we should love him only for his own sake, yet out of his infinite pity hath set forth heaven for a reward to draw men to piety, and is content, if at least so, they will become good, so the country parson, who is a diligent observer and tracker of God's ways, sets up as many encouragements to goodness as he can, both in honour, and profit, and fame; that he may, if not the best way, yet any way, make his parish good.

Chap. XII

The Parson's Charity

The country parson is full of charity; it is his predominant element. For many and wonderful things are spoken of thee, thou great virtue. To charity is given the covering of sins, 1 Pet. 4. 8. and the forgiveness of sins, Matthew 6. 14. Luke 7. 47. The fulfilling of the Law, Romans 13. 10. The life of faith, James 2. 26. The blessings of this life, Proverbs 22. 9. Psalm 41. 2. And the reward of the next, Matth. 25. 35. In brief, it is the body of Religion, John 13. 35. And the top of Christian virtues, 1 Corin. 13. Wherefore all his works relish of charity. When he riseth in the morning, he bethinketh himself what good deeds he can do that day, and presently doth them; counting that day lost, wherein he hath not exercised his charity. He first considers his own parish, and takes care that there be not a beggar or idle person in his parish, but that all be in a competent way of getting their living. This he effects either by bounty, or persuasion, or by authority, making use of that excellent statute,° which binds all parishes to maintain their own. If his parish be rich, he exacts this of them; if poor, and he able, he easeth them therein. But he gives no set pension to any; for this in time will lose the name and effect of charity with the poor people, though not with God: for then they will reckon upon it, as on a debt; and if it be taken away, though justly, they will murmur and repine as much as he that is disseized° of his own inheritance. But the parson, having a double aim, and making a hook of his charity, causeth them still to depend on him; and so by continual and fresh bounties, unexpected to them, but resolved to himself, he wins them to praise God more, to live more religiously, and to take more pains in their vocation, as not knowing when they shall be relieved; which otherwise they would reckon upon, and turn to idleness. Besides this general provision, he hath other times of opening his hand; as at great festivals and Communions; not suffering any that day that he receives, to want a good meal suiting to the joy of the occasion. But specially, at hard times and dearths, he even parts his living and life among them, giving some corn outright, and selling other at under rates; and when his own stock serves not, working those that are able to the same charity, still pressing it in the pulpit, and out of the pulpit, and never leaving them, till he obtain his desire. Yet in all his charity, he distinguisheth, giving them most, who live best, and take most pains and are most charged:° so is his charity in effect a sermon. After the consideration of his own parish, he enlargeth himself, if he be able, to the neighbourhood; for that also is some kind of obligation; so doth he also to those at his door, whom God puts in his way, and makes his neighbours. But these he helps not without some testimony, except the evidence of the misery bring testimony with it. For though these testimonies also may be falsified, yet considering that the law allows these in case they be true, but allows by no means to give without testimony, as he obeys authority in the one, so, that being once satisfied, he allows his charity some blindness in the other; especially, since of the two commands, we are more enjoined to be charitable, than wise. But evident miseries have a natural privilege and exemption from all law. Whenever he gives anything, and sees them labour in thanking of him, he exacts of them to let him alone, and say rather, God be praised, God be glorified; that so the thanks may go the right way, and thither only, where they are only due. So doth he also before giving make them say their prayers first, or the Creed, and ten Commandments, and as he finds them perfect, rewards them the more. For other givings are lay and secular, but this is to give like a priest.

CHAP. XIII

The Parson's Church

The country parson hath a special care of his church, that all things there be decent, and befitting his Name by which it is called. Therefore first he takes order that all things be in good repair; as walls plastered, windows glazed, floor paved, seats whole, firm, and uniform, especially that the pulpit, and desk, and Communion table, and font be as they ought, for those great duties that are performed in them. Secondly, that the church be swept, and kept clean without dust or cobwebs, and at great festivals strawed,° and stuck with boughs, and perfumed with incense. Thirdly, that there be fit and proper texts of Scripture everywhere painted, and that all the painting be grave and reverend, not with light colours, or foolish antics.° Fourthly, that all the books appointed by authority be there, and those not torn or fouled, but whole and clean, and well bound; and that there be a fitting and sightly Communion cloth of fine linen, with an handsome and seemly carpet of good and costly stuff or cloth, and all kept sweet and clean, in a strong and decent chest, with a chalice and cover, and a stoup or flagon; and a basin for alms and offerings; besides which, he hath a poor-man's box conveniently seated, to receive the charity of well-minded people, and to lay up treasure for the sick and needy. And all this he doth, not as out of necessity, or as putting a holiness in the things, but as desiring to keep the middle way between superstition and slovenliness, and as following the Apostle's two great and admirable rules in things of this nature: the first whereof is, *Let all things be done decently, and in order*, the second, *Let all things be done to edification*, 1 Cor. 14 [26, 40]. For these two rules comprise and include the double object of our duty, God and our neighbour; the first being for the honour of

God; the second for the benefit of our neighbour. So that they excellently score out the way, and fully and exactly contain, even in external and indifferent things, what course is to be taken; and put them to great shame, who deny the Scripture to be perfect.

CHAP. XIV

The Parson in Circuit

The country parson upon the afternoons in the weekdays takes occasion sometimes to visit in person, now one quarter of his parish, now another. For there he shall find his flock most naturally as they are, wallowing in the midst of their affairs: whereas on Sundays it is easy for them to compose themselves to order, which they put on as their holy-day clothes, and come to church in frame,° but commonly the next day put off both. When he comes to any house, first he blesseth it, and then as he finds the persons of the house employed, so he forms his discourse. Those that he finds religiously employed, he both commends them much, and furthers them when he is gone, in their employment; as, if he finds them reading, he furnisheth them with good books; if curing poor people, he supplies them with receipts,° and instructs them further in that skill, showing them how acceptable such works are to God, and wishing them ever to do the cures with their own hands, and not to put them over to servants. Those that he finds busy in the works of their calling, he commendeth them also: for it is a good and just thing for everyone to do their own business. But then he admonisheth them of two things; first, that they dive not too deep into worldly affairs, plunging themselves over head and ears into carking° and caring; but that they so labour, as neither to labour anxiously, nor distrustfully, nor profanely. Then they labour anxiously, when they overdo it, to the loss of their quiet and health: then distrustfully, when they doubt God's providence, thinking that their own labour is the cause of their thriving, as if it were in their own hands to thrive, or not to thrive. Then they labour profanely, when they set themselves to work like brute beasts, never raising their thoughts to God, nor sanctifying their labour with daily prayer; when on the Lord's day they do unnecessary servile work, or in time of divine service on other holy days, except in the cases of extreme poverty, and in the seasons of seed-time and harvest. Secondly, he adviseth them so to labour for wealth and maintenance, as that they make not that the end of their labour, but that they may have wherewithal to serve God the better, and to do good deeds. After these discourses, if they be poor and needy, whom he thus finds labouring, he gives them somewhat; and opens not only his mouth, but his purse to their relief, that so they go on more cheerfully in their vocation, and himself be ever the more welcome to them. Those that the parson finds idle, or ill employed, he chides not at first, for that were neither civil nor profitable; but always in the close, before he departs from them: yet in this he distinguisheth; for if he be a plain countryman, he reproves him plainly, for they are not sensible of fineness; if they be of higher quality, they commonly are quick, and sensible, and very tender of reproof: and therefore he lays his discourse so, that he comes to the point very leisurely, and oftentimes, as Nathan did,° in the person of another, making them to reprove themselves. However, one way or other, he ever reproves them, that he may keep himself pure, and not be entangled in others' sins. Neither in this doth he forbear, though there be company by: for as when the offence is particular and against me, I am to follow our Saviour's rule,° and to take my brother aside and reprove him; so when the offence is public and against God, I am then to follow the Apostle's rule, 1 Timothy 5. 20, and to *rebuke openly* that which is done openly. Besides these occasional discourses, the parson questions what order is kept in the house, as about prayers morning and evening on their knees, reading of Scripture, catechizing, singing of Psalms at their work, and on holy days; who can read, who not; and sometimes he hears the children read himself, and blesseth them, encouraging also the servants to learn to read, and offering to have them taught on holy-days by his servants. If the parson were ashamed of particularizing in these things, he were not fit to be a parson; but he holds the rule, that nothing is little in God's service: if it once have the honour of that Name, it grows great instantly. Wherefore neither disdaineth he to enter into the poorest cottage, though he even creep into it, and though it smell never so loathsomely. For both God is there also, and those for whom God died: and so much the rather doth he so, as his access to the poor is more comfortable,° than to the rich; and in regard of himself, it is more humiliation. These are the parson's general aims in his circuit; but with these he mingles other discourses for conversation sake, and to make his higher purposes slip the more easily.

CHAP. XV

The Parson Comforting

The country parson, when any of his cure is sick, or afflicted with loss of friend or estate, or any ways distressed, fails not to afford his best comforts, and rather goes to them, than sends for the afflicted, though they can, and otherwise ought to come to him. To this end he hath thoroughly digested all the points of consolation, as having continual use of them, such as are from God's general providence extended even to lilies;° from his particular, to his Church; from his promises, from the examples of all Saints that ever were; from Christ himself, perfecting our Redemption no other way, than by sorrow; from the benefit of affliction, which softens and works the stubborn heart of man; from the certainty both of deliverance and reward, if we faint not; from the miserable comparison of the moment of griefs here with the weight of joys hereafter. Besides this, in his visiting the sick, or otherwise afflicted, he followeth the Church's counsel, namely, in persuading them to particular confession, labouring to make them understand the great good use of this ancient and pious ordinance, and how necessary it is in some cases; he also urgeth them to do some pious charitable works, as a necessary evidence and fruit of their faith, at that time especially; the participation of the holy Sacrament, how comfortable and sovereign a medicine it is to all sin-sick souls; what strength, and joy, and peace it administers against all temptations, even to death itself, he plainly and generally intimateth to the disaffected° or sick person, that so the hunger and thirst after it may come rather from themselves, than from his persuasion.

CHAP. XVI

The Parson a Father

The country parson is not only a father to his flock, but also professeth himself thoroughly of the opinion, carrying it about with him as fully, as if he had begot his whole parish. And of this he makes great use. For by this means, when any sins, he hateth him not as an officer, but pities him as a father; and even in those wrongs which either in tithing or otherwise are done to his own person, he considers the offender as a child, and forgives, so he may have any sign of amendment; so also when after many admonitions, any continue to be refractory, yet he gives him not over, but is long before he proceed to disinheriting, or perhaps never goes so far; knowing that some are called at the eleventh hour, and therefore he still expects and waits, lest he should determine God's hour of coming; which as he cannot, touching the last day, so neither touching the intermediate days of conversion.

CHAP. XVII

The Parson in Journey

The country parson, when a just occasion calleth him out of his parish (which he diligently and strictly weigheth, his parish being all his joy and thought), leaveth not his ministry behind him, but is himself wherever he is. Therefore those he meets on the way he blesseth audibly, and with those he overtakes or that overtake him, he begins good discourses, such as may edify, interposing sometimes some short and honest refreshments, which may make his other discourses more welcome and less tedious. And when he comes to his inn, he refuseth not to join, that he may enlarge the glory of God to the company he is in, by a due blessing of God for their safe arrival, and saying grace at meat, and at going to bed by giving the host notice that he will have prayers in the hall, wishing him to inform his guests thereof, that if any be willing to partake, they may resort thither. The like he doth in the morning, using pleasantly the outlandish° proverb, that *Prayers and provender never hinder journey.* When he comes to any other house, where his kindred or other relations give him any authority over the family, if he be to stay for a time, he considers diligently the state thereof to Godward, and that in two points: first, what disorders there are either in apparel, or diet, or too open a buttery, or reading vain books, or swearing, or breeding up children to no calling, but in idleness, or the like. Secondly, what means of piety, whether daily prayers be used, grace, reading of Scriptures, and other good books, how Sundays, holy days, and fasting days are kept. And accordingly, as he finds any defect in these, he first considers with himself, what kind of remedy fits the temper of the house best, and then he faithfully and boldly applieth it; yet seasonably° and discreetly, by taking aside the lord or lady, or master and mistress of the house, and showing them clearly, that they respect them most, who wish them best, and that not a desire to meddle with others' affairs, but the earnestness to do all the good he can, moves him to say thus and thus.

CHAP. XVIII

The Parson in Sentinel

The country parson, wherever he is, keeps God's watch; that is, there is nothing spoken or done in the company where he is, but comes under his test and censure. If it be well spoken or done, he takes occasion to commend and enlarge it; if ill, he presently lays hold of it, lest the poison steal into some young and unwary spirits, and possess them even before they themselves heed it. But this he doth discreetly, with mollifying and suppling words: This was not so well said, as it might have been forborne; We cannot allow this; or else if the thing will admit interpretation, Your meaning is not thus, but thus; or, So far indeed what you say is true, and well said, but this will not stand. This is called keeping God's watch, when the baits which the enemy lays in company are discovered and avoided. This is to be on God's side, and be true to his party. Besides, if he perceive in company any discourse tending to ill, either by the wickedness or quarrelsomeness thereof, he either prevents it judiciously, or breaks it off seasonably by some diversion. Wherein a pleasantness of disposition is of great use, men being willing to sell the interest and engagement of their discourses for no price sooner, than that of mirth; whither the nature of man, loving refreshment, gladly betakes itself, even to the loss of honour.

CHAP. XIX

The Parson in Reference°

The country parson is sincere and upright in all his relations. And first, he is just to his country; as when he is set at° an armour or horse, he borrows them not to serve the turn, nor provides slight and unuseful, but such as are every way fitting to do his country true and laudable service, when occasion requires. To do otherwise is deceit; and therefore not for him, who is hearty and true in all his ways, as being the servant of him in whom there was no guile. Likewise in any other country-duty,° he considers what is the end of any command, and then he suits things faithfully according to that end. Secondly, he carries himself very respectively,° as to all the Fathers of the Church, so especially to his Diocesan,° honouring him both in word and behaviour, and resorting unto him in any difficulty, either in his studies or in his parish. He observes Visitations,° and being there, makes due use of them, as of clergy councils, for the benefit of the diocese. And therefore before he comes, having observed some defects in the ministry, he then either in sermon, if he preach, or at some other time of the day, propounds among his brethren what were fitting to be done. Thirdly, he keeps good correspondence° with all the neighbouring pastors round about him, performing for them any ministerial office which is not to the prejudice of his own parish. Likewise he welcomes to his house any minister, how poor or mean soever, with as joyful a countenance, as if he were to entertain some great lord. Fourthly, he fulfils the duty and debt of neighbourhood° to all the parishes which are near him. For the Apostle's rule Philip. 4. being admirable and large, that *we should do whatsoever things are honest, or just, or pure, or lovely, or of good report, if there be any virtue, or any praise;*° and neighbourhood being ever reputed, even among the heathen, as an obligation to do good, rather than to those that are further, where things are otherwise equal, therefore he satisfies this duty also. Especially, if God have sent any calamity, either by fire or famine, to any neighbouring parish, then he expects no brief;° but taking his parish together the next Sunday or holy day, and exposing to them the uncertainty of human affairs, none knowing whose turn may be next, and then when he hath affrighted them with this, exposing the obligation of charity and neighbourhood, he first gives himself liberally, and then incites them to give; making together a sum either to be sent, or, which were more comfortable, all together choosing some fit day to carry it themselves, and cheer the afflicted. So, if any neighbouring village be overburdened with poor, and his own less charged, he finds some way of relieving it, and reducing the manna and bread of charity to some equality, representing to his people that the blessing of God to them ought to make them the more charitable, and not the less, lest he cast their neighbours' poverty on them also.

Chap. XX

The Parson in God's Stead

The country parson is in God's stead to his parish, and dischargeth God what he can of his promises. Wherefore there is nothing done, either well or ill, whereof he is not the rewarder or punisher. If he chance to find any reading in another's Bible, he provides him one of his own. If he find another giving a poor man a penny, he gives him a tester° for it, if the giver be fit to receive it; or if he be of a condition above such gifts, he sends him a good book, or easeth him in his tithes, telling him when he hath forgotten it, This I do, because at such and such a time you were charitable. This is in some sort a discharging of God, as concerning this life, who hath promised that godliness shall be gainful: but in the other God is his own immediate paymaster, rewarding all good deeds to their full proportion. The parson's punishing of sin and vice is rather by withdrawing his bounty and courtesy from the parties offending, or by private or public reproof, as the case requires, than by causing them to be presented, or otherwise complained of. And yet as the malice of the person, or heinousness of the crime may be, he is careful to see condign punishment inflicted, and with truly godly zeal, without hatred to the person, hungereth and thirsteth after righteous punishment of unrighteousness. Thus both in rewarding virtue, and in punishing vice, the parson endeavoureth to be in God's stead, knowing that country people are drawn or led by sense, more than by faith; by present rewards or punishments, more than by future.

CHAP. XXI

The Parson Catechizing

The country parson values catechizing highly: for there being three points of his duty, the one, to infuse a competent knowledge of salvation in every one of his flock; the other, to multiply and build up this knowledge to a spiritual Temple; the third, to inflame this knowledge, to press and drive it to practice, turning it to reformation of life, by pithy and lively exhortations; catechizing is the first point, and but by catechizing, the other cannot be attained. Besides, whereas in sermons there is a kind of state, in catechizing there is an humbleness very suitable to Christian regeneration, which exceedingly delights him as by way of exercise upon himself, and by way of preaching to himself, for the advancing of his own mortification; for in preaching to others, he forgets not himself, but is first a sermon to himself, and then to others, growing with the growth of his parish. He useth and preferreth the ordinary Church-catechism, partly for obedience to authority, partly for uniformity sake, that the same common truths may be everywhere professed, especially since many remove from parish to parish, who like Christian soldiers are to give the word, and to satisfy the congregation by their catholic answers. He exacts of all the doctrine of the catechism; of the younger sort, the very words; of the elder, the substance. Those he catechizeth publicly, these privately, giving age honour, according to the Apostle's rule, 1 Tim. 5. 1. He requires all to be present at catechizing: first, for the authority of the work; secondly, that parents and masters, as they hear the answers prove, may when they come home, either commend or reprove, either reward or punish. Thirdly, that those of the elder sort who are not well grounded may then by an honourable way take occasion to be better instructed. Fourthly, that those who are well grown in the knowledge of Religion may examine their grounds, renew their vows, and by occasion of both, enlarge their meditations. When once all have learned the words of the catechism, he thinks it the most useful way that a pastor can take, to go over the same, but in other words: for many say the catechism by rote, as parrots, without ever piercing into the sense of it. In this course the order of the catechism would be kept, but the rest varied: as thus, in the Creed: How came this world to be as it is? Was it made, or came it by chance? Who made it? Did you see God make it? Then are there some things to be believed that are not seen? Is this the nature of belief? Is not Christianity full of such things, as are not to be seen, but believed? You said, God made the world; Who is God? And so forward, requiring answers to all these, and helping and cherishing the answerer by making the question very plain with comparisons, and making much even of a word of truth from him. This order being used to one, would be a little varied to another. And this is an admirable way of teaching, wherein the catechized will at length find delight, and by which the cat-echizer, if he once get the skill of it, will draw out of ignorant and silly° souls even the dark and deep points of Religion. Socrates did thus in philosophy, who held that the seeds of all truths lay in every-body, and accordingly by questions well ordered he found philosophy in silly tradesmen. That position will not hold in Christianity, be-cause it contains things above nature; but after that the catechism is once learned, that which nature is towards philosophy, the catechism is towards divinity. To this purpose, some dialogues in Plato were worth the reading, where the singular dexterity of Socrates in this kind may be observed and imitated. Yet the skill consists but in these three points: first, an aim and mark of the whole discourse, whither to drive the answerer, which the questionist must have in his mind before any question be propounded, upon which and to which the questions are to be chained. Secondly, a most plain and easy framing the question, even containing in virtue° the answer also, especially to the more ignorant. Thirdly, when the answerer sticks, an illustrating the thing by something else which he knows, making what he knows to serve him in that which he knows not: as, when the parson once demanded after other questions about man's misery, since man is so miserable, what is to be done? And the answerer could not tell. He asked him again, what he would do, if he were in a ditch? This familiar illustration made the answer so plain that he was even ashamed of his ignorance; for he could not but say, he would haste out of it as fast as he could. Then he proceeded to ask, whether he could get out of the ditch alone, or whether he needed a helper, and who was that helper. This is the skill, and doubtless the Holy Scripture intends thus much, when it condescends to the naming of a plough, a hatchet, a bushel, leaven, boys piping and dancing; showing that things of ordinary use are not only to serve in the way of drudgery, but to be washed, and cleansed, and serve for lights even of Heavenly Truths. This is the practice which the parson so much commends to all his fellow-labourers; the secret of whose good consists in this, that at sermons and prayers, men may sleep or wander; but when one is asked a question, he must discover what he is. This practice exceeds even sermons in teaching: but there being two things in sermons, the one informing, the other inflaming; as sermons come short of questions in the one, so they far exceed them in the other. For questions cannot inflame or ravish; that must be done by a set, and laboured, and continued speech.

Chap. XXII

The Parson in Sacraments

The country parson, being to administer the Sacraments, is at a stand with himself, how or what behaviour to assume for so holy things. Especially at Communion times he is in a great confusion, as being not only to receive God, but to break and administer him. Neither finds he any issue in this, but to throw himself down at the throne of grace, saying, Lord, thou knowest what thou didst, when thou appointedst it to be done thus; therefore do thou fulfil what thou didst appoint; for thou art not only the feast, but the way to it. At baptism, being himself in white, he requires the presence of all, and baptizeth not willingly but on Sundays or great days. He admits no vain or idle names, but such as are usual and accustomed. He says that prayer with great devotion, where God is thanked for calling us to the knowledge of his grace, baptism being a blessing that the world hath not the like. He willingly and cheerfully crosseth the child, and thinketh the ceremony not only innocent, but reverend. He instructeth the godfathers and godmothers, that it is no com- plemental° or light thing to sustain that place, but a great honour, and no less burden, as being done both in the presence of God and his Saints, and by way of undertaking for a Christian soul. He adviseth all to call to mind their baptism often; for if wise men have thought it the best way of preserving a state to reduce it to its prin- ciples by which it grew great, certainly it is the safest course for Christians also to meditate on their baptism often (being the first step into their great and glorious calling) and upon what terms, and with what vows they were baptized. At the times of the Holy Communion, he first takes order with the churchwardens that the elements be of the best, not cheap or coarse, much less ill-tasted or unwholesome. Secondly, he considers and looks into the ignorance or carelessness of his flock, and accordingly applies himself with catechizings and lively exhortations, not on the Sunday of the Com- munion only (for then it is too late) but the Sunday or Sundays before the Communion, or on the eves of all those days. If there be any, who having not received yet, are to enter into this great work, he takes the more pains with them, that he may lay the foundation of future blessings. The time of everyone's first receiving is not so much by years as by understanding; particularly, the rule may be this: when anyone can distinguish the sacramental from common bread, knowing the institution and the difference, he ought to re- ceive, of what age soever. Children and youths are usually deferred too long, under pretence of devotion to the Sacrament, but it is for want of instruction; their understandings being ripe enough for ill things, and why not then for better? But parents and masters should make haste in this, as to a great purchase for their children and servants, which while they defer, both sides suffer; the one, in want- ing many excitings of grace; the other, in being worse served and obeyed. The saying of the catechism is necessary, but not enough; because to answer in form may still admit ignorance; but the ques- tions must be propounded loosely and wildly, and then the answerer will discover what he is. Thirdly, for the manner of receiving, as the parson useth all reverence himself, so he administers to none but to the reverent. The feast indeed requires sitting, because it is a feast; but man's unpreparedness asks kneeling. He that comes to the Sacrament hath the confidence of a guest, and he that kneels con- fesseth himself an unworthy one, and therefore differs from other feasters; but he that sits or lies, puts up to an Apostle:° contentiousness in a feast of charity is more scandal than any posture. Fourthly, touching the frequency of the Communion, the parson celebrates it, if not duly once a month, yet at least five or six times in the year; as, at Easter, Christmas, Whitsuntide, afore and after harvest, and the beginning of Lent. And this he doth, not only for the benefit of the work, but also for the discharge of the churchwardens, who, being to present all that receive not thrice a year, if there be but three Communions, neither can all the people so order their affairs as to receive just at those times, nor the churchwardens so well take notice who receive thrice, and who not.

Chap. XXIII

The Parson's Completeness

The country parson desires to be all to his parish, and not only a pastor, but a lawyer also, and a physician. Therefore he endures not that any of his flock should go to law; but in any controversy, that they should resort to him as their judge. To this end, he hath gotten to himself some insight in things ordinarily incident and controverted, by experience, and by reading some initiatory treatises in the law, with Dalton's Justice of Peace,° and the Abridgements of the Statutes, as also by discourse with men of that profession, whom he hath ever some cases to ask, when he meets with them; holding that rule, that to put men to discourse of that wherein they are most eminent, is the most gainful way of conversation. Yet whenever any controversy is brought to him, he never decides it alone, but sends for three or four of the ablest of the parish to hear the cause with him, whom he makes to deliver their opinion first; out of which he gathers, in case he be ignorant himself, what to hold; and so the thing passeth with more authority and less envy. In judging, he follows that which is altogether right; so that if the poorest man of the parish detain but a pin unjustly from the richest, he absolutely restores it as a judge; but when he hath so done, then he assumes the parson, and exhorts to charity. Nevertheless, there may happen sometimes some cases, wherein he chooseth to permit his parishioners rather to make use of the law, than himself: as in cases of an obscure and dark nature, not easily determinable by lawyers themselves; or in cases of high consequence, as establishing of inheritances; or lastly, when the persons in difference are of a contentious disposition, and cannot be gained, but that they still fall from all compromises that have been made. But then he shows them how to go to law, even as brethren, and not as enemies, neither avoiding therefore one another's company, much less defaming one another. Now as the parson is in law, so is he in sickness also: if there be any of his flock sick, he is their physician, or at least his wife, of whom instead of the qualities of the world, he asks no other, but to have the skill of healing a wound, or helping the sick. But if neither himself nor his wife have the skill, and his means serve, he keeps some young practitioner in his house for the benefit of his parish, whom yet he ever exhorts not to exceed his bounds, but in tickle cases° to call in help. If all fail, then he keeps good correspondence with some neighbour physician, and entertains him for the cure of his parish. Yet is it easy for any scholar to attain to such a measure of physic as may be of much use to him both for himself and others. This is done by seeing one anatomy,° reading one book of physic, having one herbal by him. And let Fernelius° be the physic author, for he writes briefly, neatly, and judiciously; especially let his method of physic be diligently perused, as being the practical part, and of most use. Now both the reading of him, and the knowing of herbs may be done at such times, as they may be an help and a recreation to more divine studies, Nature serving Grace both in comfort of diversion, and the benefit of application when need requires; as also by way of illustration, even as our Saviour made plants and seeds to teach the people: for he was the true householder, who bringeth out of his treasure things new and old; the old things of philosophy, and the new of Grace; and maketh the one serve the other. And I conceive, our Saviour did this for three reasons: first, that by familiar things he might make his doctrine slip the more easily into the hearts even of the meanest. Secondly, that labouring people (whom he chiefly considered) might have everywhere monuments of his doctrine, remembering in gardens, his mustard-seed and lilies; in the field, his seed-corn and tares; and so not be drowned altogether in the works of their vocation, but sometimes lift up their minds to better things, even in the midst of their pains. Thirdly, that he might set a copy for parsons. In the knowledge of simples,° wherein the manifold wisdom of God is wonderfully to be seen, one thing would be carefully observed; which is, to know what herbs may be used instead of drugs of the same nature, and to make the garden the shop: for home-bred medicines are both more easy for the parson's purse, and more familiar for all men's bodies. So, where the apothecary useth either for loosing, rhubarb, or for binding, bolearmena,° the parson useth damask or white roses for the one, and plantain, shepherd's purse, knot-grass for the other, and that with better success. As for spices, he doth not only prefer home-bred things before them, but condemns them for vanities, and so shuts them out of his family, esteeming that there is no spice comparable for herbs, to rosemary, thyme, savory, mints; and for seeds, to fennel and caraway seeds. Accordingly, for salves, his wife seeks not the city, but prefers her garden and fields before all outlandish gums. And surely hyssop, valerian, mercury, adder's tongue, yarrow, melilot, and Saint-John's-wort, made into a salve, and elder, camomile, mallows, comfrey, and smallage, made into a poultice, have done great and rare cures. In curing of any, the parson and his family use to premise° prayers, for this is to cure like a parson, and this raiseth the action from the shop to the church. But though the parson sets forward all charitable deeds, yet he looks not in this point of curing beyond his own parish, except the person be so poor that he is not able to reward the physician: for as he is charitable, so he is just also. Now it is a justice and debt to the commonwealth he lives in, not to encroach on others' professions, but to live on his own. And justice is the ground of charity.

CHAP. XXIV

The Parson Arguing

The country parson, if there be any of his parish that hold strange doctrines, useth all possible diligence to reduce° them to the common faith. The first means he useth is prayer, beseeching the Father of lights to open their eyes, and to give him power so to fit his discourse to them, that it may effectually pierce their hearts and convert them. The second means is a very loving and sweet usage of them, both in going to and sending for them often, and in finding out courtesies to place on them; as in their tithes, or otherwise. The third means is the observation what is the main foundation and pillar of their cause, whereon they rely; as if he be a Papist, the Church is the hinge he turns on; if a schismatic, scandal.° Wherefore the parson hath diligently examined these two with himself, as what the Church is, how it began, how it proceeded, whether it be a rule to itself, whether it hath a rule, whether having a rule, it ought not to be guided by it; whether any rule in the world be obscure, and how then should the best be so, at least in fundamental things, the obscurity in some points being the exercise of the Church, the light in the foundations being the guide; the Church needing both an evidence and an exercise. So for scandal: what scandal is, when given or taken; whether, there being two precepts, one of obeying authority, the other of not giving scandal, that ought not to be preferred, especially since in disobeying there is scandal also; whether things once indifferent, being made by the precept of authority more than indifferent, it be in our power to omit or refuse them. These and the like points he hath accurately digested, having ever besides two great helps and powerful persuaders on his side; the one, a strict religious life; the other, an humble and ingenuous search of truth, being unmoved in arguing and void of all contentiousness: which are two great lights able to dazzle the eyes of the misled, while they consider that God cannot be wanting to them in doctrine, to whom he is so gracious in life.

Chap. XXV

The Parson Punishing

Whensoever the country parson proceeds so far as to call in authority, and to do such things of legal opposition either in the presenting or punishing of any, as the vulgar ever construes for signs of ill will, he forbears not in any wise to use the delinquent as before, in his behaviour and carriage towards him, not avoiding his company, or doing anything of averseness, save in the very act of punishment: neither doth he esteem him for an enemy, but as a brother still, except some small and temporary estranging may corroborate the punishment to a better subduing and humbling of the delinquent; which if it happily take effect, he then comes on the faster, and makes so much the more of him, as before he alienated himself, doubling his regards, and showing by all means that the delinquent's return is to his advantage.

Chap. XXVI

The Parson's Eye

The country parson at spare times from action, standing on a hill, and considering his flock, discovers two sorts of vices, and two sorts of vicious persons. There are some vices whose natures are always clear and evident, as adultery, murder, hatred, lying, etc. There are other vices whose natures, at least in the beginning, are dark and obscure: as covetousness and gluttony. So likewise there are some persons who abstain not even from known sins; there are others who, when they know a sin evidently, they commit it not. It is true, indeed, they are long a-knowing it, being partial to themselves, and witty to others who shall reprove them from it. A man may be both covetous and intemperate, and yet hear sermons against both, and himself condemn both in good earnest: and the reason hereof is, because the natures of these vices being not evidently discussed, or known commonly, the beginnings of them are not easily observable; and the beginnings of them are not observed, because of the sudden passing from that which was just now lawful, to that which is presently unlawful, even in one continued action. So a man dining, eats at first lawfully; but proceeding on, comes to do unlawfully, even before he is aware; not knowing the bounds of the action, nor when his eating begins to be unlawful. So a man storing up money for his necessary provisions, both in present for his family, and in future for his children, hardly perceives when his storing becomes unlawful: yet is there a period for his storing, and a point, or centre, when his storing, which was even now good, passeth from good to bad. Wherefore the parson, being true to his business, hath exactly sifted the definitions of all virtues and vices, especially canvassing those whose natures are most stealing and beginnings uncertain. Particularly, concerning these two vices, not because they are all that are of this dark and creeping disposition, but for example sake, and because they are most common, he thus thinks: first, for covetousness he lays this ground: whosoever, when a just occasion calls, either spends not at all, or not in some proportion to God's blessing upon him, is covetous. The reason of the ground is manifest, because wealth is given to that end to supply our occasions. Now, if I do not give everything its end, I abuse the creature, I am false to my reason which should guide me, I offend the supreme judge in perverting that order which he hath set both to things and to reason. The application of the ground would be infinite; but in brief, a poor man is an occasion, my country is an occasion, my friend is an occasion, my table is an occasion, my apparel is an occasion: if in all these, and those more which concern me, I either do nothing, or pinch, and scrape, and squeeze blood undecently to the station° wherein God hath placed me, I am covetous. More particularly, and to give one instance for all, if God have given me servants, and I either provide too little for them, or that which is unwholesome, being sometimes baned° meat, sometimes too salt, and so not competent nourishment, I am covetous. I bring this example, because men usually think that servants for their money are as other things that they buy, even as a piece of wood, which they may cut, or hack, or throw into the fire, and so they pay them their wages, all is well. Nay, to descend yet more particularly, if a man hath wherewithal to buy a spade, and yet he chooseth rather to use his neighbour's, and wear out that, he is covetous. Nevertheless, few bring covetousness thus low, or consider it so narrowly, which yet ought to be done, since there is a justice in the least things, and for the least there shall be a judgement. Country people are full of these petty injustices, being cunning to make use of another, and spare themselves. And scholars ought to be diligent in the observation of these, and driving of their general school rules° ever to the smallest actions of life; which while they dwell in their books, they will never find; but being seated in the country, and doing their duty faithfully, they will soon discover: especially if they carry their eyes ever open, and fix them on their charge, and not on their preferment. Secondly, for gluttony, the parson lays this ground: he that either for quantity eats more than his health or employments will bear, or for quality is licorous° after dainties, is a glutton; as he that eats more than his estate will bear is a prodigal; and he that eats offensively to the company, either in his order or length of eating, is scandalous and uncharitable. These three rules generally comprehend the faults of eating, and the truth of them needs no proof: so that men must eat neither to the disturbance of their health, nor of their affairs (which being overburdened, or studying dainties too much, they cannot well dispatch), nor of their estate, nor of their brethren. One act in these things is bad, but it is the custom and habit that names a glutton. Many think they are at more liberty than they are, as if they were masters of their health, and so they will stand to the pain, all is well. But to eat to one's hurt, comprehends, besides the hurt, an act against reason, because it is unnatural to hurt oneself; and this they are not masters of. Yet of hurtful things, I am more bound to abstain from those which by mine own experience I have found hurtful, than from those which by a common tradition and vulgar knowledge are reputed to be so. That which is said of hurtful meats extends to hurtful drinks also. As for the quantity, touching our employments, none must eat so as to disable themselves from a fit discharging either of divine duties, or duties of their calling. So that if after dinner they are not fit (or unwieldy) either to pray or work, they are gluttons. Not that all must presently work after dinner (for they rather must not work, especially students, and those that are weakly); but that they must rise so, as that it is not meat or drink that hinders them from working. To guide them in this, there are three rules: first, the custom and knowledge of their own body, and what it can well disgest;° the second, the feeling of themselves in time of eating, which because it is deceitful (for one thinks in eating, that he can eat more, than afterwards he finds true): the third is the observation with what appetite they sit down. This last rule, joined with the first, never fails. For knowing what one usually can well disgest, and feeling when I go to meat in what disposition I am, either hungry or not, according as I feel myself, either I take my wonted proportion, or diminish of it. Yet physicians bid those that would live in health not keep an uniform diet, but to feed variously, now more, now less: and Gerson,° a spiritual man, wisheth all to incline rather to too much, than to too little; his reason is, because diseases of exinanition are more dangerous than diseases of repletion. But the parson distinguisheth according to his double aim, either of abstinence, a moral virtue, or mortification, a divine. When he deals with any that is heavy and carnal, he gives him those freer rules: but when he meets with a refined and heavenly disposition, he carries them higher, even sometimes to a forgetting of themselves, knowing that there is one, who when they forget, remembers for them; as when the people hungered and thirsted after our Saviour's doctrine, and tarried so long at it, that they would have fainted, had they returned empty, he suffered it not; but rather made food miraculously,° than suffered so good desires to miscarry.

Chap. XXVII

The Parson in Mirth

The country parson is generally sad, because he knows nothing but the Cross of Christ, his mind being defixed on it with those nails wherewith his master was; or if he have any leisure to look off from thence, he meets continually with two most sad spectacles, sin and misery; God dishonoured every day, and man afflicted. Nevertheless, he sometimes refresheth himself, as knowing that nature will not bear everlasting droopings, and that pleasantness of disposition is a great key to do good; not only because all men shun the company of perpetual severity, but also for that when they are in company, instructions seasoned with pleasantness both enter sooner and root deeper. Wherefore he condescends to human frailties both in himself and others; and intermingles some mirth in his discourses occasionally, according to the pulse of the hearer.

Chap. XXVIII

The Parson in Contempt

The country parson knows well, that both for the general ig-
nominy which is cast upon the profession, and much more for those
rules, which out of his choicest judgement he hath resolved to
observe, and which are described in this book, he must be despised;
because this hath been the portion of God his Master, and of God's
Saints his brethren, and this is foretold, that it shall be so still, until
things be no more. Nevertheless, according to the Apostle's rule,° he
endeavours that none shall despise him; especially in his own parish
he suffers it not to his utmost power; for that, where contempt is,
there is no room for instruction. This he procures, first, by his holy
and unblameable life; which carries a reverence with it, even above
contempt. Secondly, by a courteous carriage and winning behaviour:
he that will be respected, must respect; doing kindnesses, but receiving none, at least of those who are apt to despise: for this argues a
height and eminency of mind which is not easily despised, except it
degenerate to pride. Thirdly, by a bold and impartial reproof, even
of the best in the parish, when occasion requires: for this may produce hatred in those that are reproved, but never contempt either in
them or others. Lastly, if the contempt shall proceed so far as to do
anything punishable by law, as contempt is apt to do, if it be not
thwarted, the parson, having a due respect both to the person and to
the cause, referreth the whole matter to the examination and punishment of those which are in authority; that so the sentence lighting
upon one, the example may reach to all. But if the contempt be not
punishable by law, or being so, the parson think it in his discretion
either unfit or bootless° to contend, then when any despises him, he
takes it either in an humble way, saying nothing at all; or else in a
slighting way, showing that reproaches touch him no more than a
stone thrown against heaven, where he is and lives; or in a sad way,
grieved at his own and others' sins, which continually break God's
laws, and dishonour him with those mouths which he continually fills
and feeds; or else in a doctrinal way, saying to the contemner, Alas,
why do you thus? you hurt yourself, not me; he that throws a stone
at another, hits himself; and so between gentle reasoning, and
pitying, he overcomes the evil; or lastly, in a triumphant way, being
glad and joyful that he is made conformable to his Master; and being
in the world as he was, hath this undoubted pledge of his salvation.
These are the five shields, wherewith the godly receive the darts of

the wicked; leaving anger, and retorting, and revenge to the children of the world, whom another's ill mastereth and leadeth captive without any resistance, even in resistance, to the same destruction. For while they resist the person that reviles, they resist not the evil which takes hold of them, and is far the worse enemy.

CHAP. XXIX

The Parson with his Churchwardens

The country parson doth often, both publicly and privately, instruct his churchwardens what a great charge lies upon them, and that indeed the whole order and discipline of the parish is put into their hands. If himself reform anything, it is out of the overflowing of his conscience, whereas they are to do it by command and by oath. Neither hath the place its dignity from the ecclesiastical laws only, since even by the common statute-law they are taken for a kind of corporation, as being persons enabled by that name to take moveable goods, or chattels, and to sue and to be sued at the law concerning such goods for the use and profit of their parish: and by the same law they are to levy penalties for negligence in resorting to church, or for disorderly carriage in time of divine service. Wherefore the parson suffers not the place to be vilified or debased, by being cast on the lower rank of people, but invites and urges the best unto it, showing that they do not lose, or go less, but gain by it; it being the greatest honour of this world, to do God and his chosen service; or as David says, to be even a door-keeper in the house of God.° Now the Canons° being the churchwardens' rule, the parson adviseth them to read or hear them read often, as also the Visitation Articles,° which are grounded upon the Canons, that so they may know their duty, and keep their oath the better; in which regard, considering the great consequence of their place, and more of their oath, he wisheth them by no means to spare any, though never so great; but if after gentle and neighbourly admonitions they still persist in ill, to present them; yea though they be tenants, or otherwise engaged to the delinquent: for their obligation to God, and their own soul, is above any temporal tie. Do well and right, and let the world sink.

Chap. XXX

The Parson's Consideration of Providence

The country parson—considering the great aptness country people have to think that all things come by a kind of natural course; and that if they sow and soil° their grounds, they must have corn; if they keep and fodder well their cattle, they must have milk and calves—labours to reduce them to see God's hand in all things, and to believe that things are not set in such an inevitable order, but that God often changeth it according as he sees fit, either for reward or punishment. To this end he represents to his flock, that God hath and exerciseth a threefold power in everything which concerns man. The first is a sustaining power; the second a governing power; the third a spiritual power. By his sustaining power he preserves and actuates everything in his being; so that corn doth not grow by any other virtue, than by that which he continually supplies, as the corn needs it; without which supply the corn would instantly dry up, as a river would if the fountain were stopped. And it is observable, that if anything could presume of an inevitable course and constancy in its operations, certainly it should be either the sun in heaven, or the fire on earth, by reason of their fierce, strong, and violent natures: yet when God pleased, the sun stood still, the fire burned not.° By God's governing power he preserves and orders the references of things one to the other, so that though the corn do grow, and be preserved in that act by his sustaining power, yet if he suit not other things to the growth, as seasons, and weather, and other accidents by his governing power, the fairest harvests come to nothing. And it is observable, that God delights to have men feel, and acknowledge, and reverence his power, and therefore he often overturns things, when they are thought past danger; that is his time of interposing: as when a merchant hath a ship come home after many a storm, which it hath escaped, he destroys it sometimes in the very haven; or if the goods be housed, a fire hath broken forth, and suddenly consumed them. Now this he doth, that men should perpetuate, and not break off their acts of dependence, how fair soever the opportunities present themselves. So that if a farmer should depend upon God all the year, and being ready to put hand to sickle, shall then secure himself, and think all cock-sure; then God sends such weather, as lays the corn and destroys it: or if he depend on God further, even till he imbarn his corn, and then think all sure; God sends a fire, and consumes all that he hath: for that he ought not to break off, but to continue his dependence on God, not only before the corn is inned, but after also; and indeed, to depend and fear continually. The third power is spiritual, by which God turns all outward blessings to inward advantages. So that if a farmer hath both a fair harvest, and that also well inned and imbarned, and continuing safe there; yet if God give him not the grace to use and utter° this well, all his advantages are to his loss. Better were his corn burnt, than not spiritually improved. And it is observable in this, how God's goodness strives with man's refractoriness; man would sit down at this world, God bids him sell it, and purchase a better: just as a father, who hath in his hand an apple, and a piece of gold under it; the child comes, and with pulling, gets the apple out of his father's hand: his father bids him throw it away, and he will give him the gold for it, which the child utterly refusing, eats it, and is troubled with worms: so is the carnal and wilful man with the worm of the grave in this world, and the worm of conscience in the next.

CHAP. XXXI

The Parson in Liberty

The country parson observing the manifold wiles of Satan (who plays his part sometimes in drawing God's servants from him, sometimes in perplexing them in the service of God) stands fast in the liberty wherewith Christ hath made us free. This liberty he compasseth by one distinction, and that is, of what is necessary, and what is additionary. As for example: it is necessary, that all Christians should pray twice a day, every day of the week, and four times on Sunday, if they be well. This is so necessary and essential to a Christian, that he cannot without this maintain himself in a Christian state. Besides this, the godly have ever added some hours of prayer, as at nine, or at three, or at midnight, or as they think fit and see cause, or rather as God's spirit leads them. But these prayers are not necessary, but additionary. Now it so happens, that the godly petitioner, upon some emergent° interruption in the day, or by oversleeping himself at night, omits his additionary prayer. Upon this his mind begins to be perplexed and troubled, and Satan, who knows the exigent,° blows the fire, endeavouring to disorder the Christian, and put him out of his station, and to enlarge the perplexity, until it spread and taint his other duties of piety, which none can perform so well in trouble as in calmness. Here the parson interposeth with his distinction, and shows the perplexed Christian that this prayer being additionary, not necessary, taken in, not commanded, the omission thereof upon just occasion ought by no means to trouble him. God knows the occasion as well as he, and he is as a gracious father, who more accepts a common course of devotion, than dislikes an occasional interruption. And of this he is so to assure himself, as to admit no scruple, but to go on as cheerfully, as if he had not been interrupted. By this it is evident that the distinction is of singular use and comfort, especially to pious minds, which are ever tender and delicate. But here there are two cautions to be added. First, that this interruption proceed not out of slackness or coldness, which will appear if the pious soul foresee and prevent such interruptions, what he may, before they come, and when for all that they do come, he be a little affected therewith, but not afflicted or troubled; if he resent° it to a mislike, but not a grief. Secondly, that this interruption proceed not out of shame. As for example: a godly man, not out of superstition, but of reverence to God's house, resolves, whenever he enters into a church, to kneel down and pray, either blessing God, that he will be pleased to dwell among men; or beseeching him, that whenever he repairs to his house, he may behave himself so as befits so great a presence; and this briefly. But it happens, that near the place where he is to pray, he spies some scoffing ruffian, who is likely to deride him for his pains: if he now shall, either for fear or shame, break his custom, he shall do passing° ill: so much the rather ought he to proceed, as that by this he may take into his prayer humiliation also. On the other side, if I am to visit the sick in haste, and my nearest way lie through the church, I will not doubt° to go without staying to pray there (but only, as I pass, in my heart) because this kind of prayer is additionary, not necessary, and the other duty overweighs it: so that if any scruple arise, I will throw it away, and be most confident that God is not displeased. This distinction may run through all Christian duties, and it is a great stay and settling to religious souls.

CHAP. XXXII

The Parson's Surveys

The country parson hath not only taken a particular survey of the faults of his own parish, but a general also of the diseases of the time, that so, when his occasions carry him abroad, or bring strangers to him, he may be the better armed to encounter them. The great and national sin of this land he esteems to be idleness;

great in itself, and great in consequence: for when men have nothing to do, then they fall to drink, to steal, to whore, to scoff, to revile, to all sorts of gamings. Come, say they, we have nothing to do, let's go to the tavern, or to the stews, or what not. Wherefore the parson strongly opposeth this sin, wheresoever he goes. And because idleness is twofold, the one in having no calling, the other in walking carelessly in our calling, he first represents to everybody the necessity of a vocation. The reason of this assertion is taken from the nature of man, wherein God hath placed two great instruments, reason in the soul, and a hand in the body, as engagements of working: so that even in Paradise man had a calling, and how much more out of Paradise, when the evils which he is now subject unto may be prevented or diverted by reasonable employment. Besides, every gift or ability is a talent to be accounted for, and to be improved to our Master's advantage. Yet is it also a debt to our country to have a calling, and it concerns the commonwealth that none should be idle, but all busied. Lastly, riches are the blessing of God, and the great instrument of doing admirable good; therefore all are to procure them honestly and seasonably, when they are not better employed. Now this reason crosseth not our Saviour's precept° of selling what we have, because when we have sold all, and given it to the poor, we must not be idle, but labour to get more, that we may give more, according to St. Paul's rule, Ephes. 4. 28. 1 Thes. 4. 11, 12. So that our Saviour's selling is so far from crossing Saint Paul's working, that it rather establisheth it, since they that have nothing are fittest to work. Now because the only opposer to this doctrine is the gallant, who is witty enough to abuse both others and himself, and who is ready to ask, if he shall mend shoes, or what he shall do? Therefore the parson, unmoved, showeth that ingenuous and fit employment is never wanting to those that seek it. But if it should be, the assertion stands thus: all are either to have a calling, or prepare for it: he that hath or can have yet no employment, if he truly and seriously prepare for it, he is safe and within bounds. Wherefore all are either presently to enter into a calling, if they be fit for it, and it for them; or else to examine with care and advice, what they are fittest for, and to prepare for that with all diligence. But it will not be amiss in this exceeding useful point to descend to particulars: for exactness lies in particulars. Men are either single or married: the married and housekeeper hath his hands full, if he do what he ought to do. For there are two branches of his affairs; first, the improvement of his family, by bringing them up in the fear and nurture of the Lord; and

secondly, the improvement of his grounds, by drowning,° or drain-
ing, or stocking, or fencing, and ordering his land to the best advantage both of himself and his neighbours. The Italian says, None
fouls his hands in his own business: and it is an honest and just
care, so it exceed not bounds, for everyone to employ himself to the
advancement of his affairs, that he may have wherewithal to do good.
But his family is his best care, to labour Christian souls, and raise
them to their height, even to heaven; to dress and prune them, and
take as much joy in a straight-growing child or servant, as a gardener
doth in a choice tree. Could men find out this delight, they would
seldom be from home; whereas now, of any place, they are least
there. But if after all this care well dispatched, the housekeeper's
family be so small, and his dexterity so great, that he have leisure to
look out, the village or parish which either he lives in, or is near
unto it, is his employment. He considers everyone there, and either
helps them in particular, or hath general propositions to the whole
town or hamlet, of advancing the public stock, and managing com-
mons or woods, according as the place suggests. But if he may be of
the Commission of Peace, there is nothing to that: no commonwealth in the world hath a braver institution than that of Justices of
the Peace: for it is both a security to the King, who hath so many
dispersed officers at his beck throughout the kingdom, accountable
for the public good; and also an honourable employment of a gentle
or noble-man in the country he lives in, enabling him with power to
do good, and to restrain all those who else might both trouble him
and the whole State. Wherefore it behoves all, who are come to the
gravity and ripeness of judgement for so excellent a place, not to
refuse, but rather to procure it. And whereas there are usually three
objections made against the place; the one, the abuse of it, by taking
petty country bribes; the other, the casting of it on mean persons,
especially in some shires; and lastly, the trouble of it. These are so
far from deterring any good man from the place, that they kindle
them rather to redeem the dignity either from true faults or unjust
aspersions. Now, for single men, they are either heirs or younger
brothers. The heirs are to prepare in all the fore-mentioned points
against the time of their practice. Therefore they are to mark their
father's discretion in ordering his house and affairs; and also elsewhere, when they see any remarkable point of education or good
husbandry, and to transplant it in time to his own home, with the
same care as others, when they meet with good fruit, get a graff° of
the tree, enriching their orchard and neglecting their house. Besides,

they are to read books of law and justice; especially, the Statutes at large. As for better books of divinity, they are not in this consideration, because we are about a calling, and a preparation thereunto. But chiefly, and above all things, they are to frequent Sessions and Sizes;° for it is both an honour which they owe to the reverend judges and magistrates, to attend them, at least in their shire; and it is a great advantage to know the practice of the land; for our law is practice.° Sometimes he may go to court, as the eminent place both of good and ill. At other times he is to travel over the King's dominions, cutting out the kingdom into portions, which every year he surveys piece-meal. When there is a Parliament, he is to endeavour by all means to be a Knight or Burgess there; for there is no school to a Parliament. And when he is there, he must not only be a morning man, but at committees also; for there the particulars are exactly discussed, which are brought from thence to the House but in general. When none of these occasions call him abroad, every morning that he is at home he must either ride the great horse,° or exercise some of his military gestures. For all gentlemen, that are now weakened and disarmed with sedentary lives, are to know the use of their arms: and as the husbandman labours for them, so must they fight for and defend them, when occasion calls. This is the duty of each to other, which they ought to fulfill: and the parson is a lover of and exciter to justice in all things, even as John the Baptist squared out to every one (even to soldiers) what to do. As for younger brothers, those whom the parson finds loose, and not engaged into some profession by their parents, whose neglect in this point is intolerable, and a shameful wrong both to the commonwealth and their own house: to them, after he hath showed the unlawfulness of spending the day in dressing, complimenting, visiting, and sporting, he first commends the study of the civil law, as a brave and wise knowledge, the professors whereof were much employed by Queen Elizabeth, because it is the key of commerce, and discovers the rules of foreign nations. Secondly, he commends the mathematics, as the only wonder-working knowledge, and therefore requiring the best spirits. After the several knowledge of these, he adviseth to insist and dwell chiefly on the two noble branches thereof, of fortification and navigation; the one being useful to all countries, and the other especially to islands. But if the young gallant think these courses dull and phlegmatic, where can he busy himself better, than in those new plantations and discoveries, which are not only a noble, but also, as they may be handled, a religious employment? Or let him travel into

Germany and France, and observing the artifices and manufactures there, transplant them hither, as divers have done lately, to our country's advantage.

CHAP. XXXIII

The Parson's Library

The country parson's library is a holy life: for besides the blessing that that brings upon it, there being a promise, that if the Kingdom of God be first sought, all other things shall be added,° even itself is a sermon. For the temptations with which a good man is beset, and the ways which he used to overcome them, being told to another, whether in private conference, or in the church, are a sermon. He that hath considered how to carry himself at table about his appetite, if he tell this to another, preacheth; and much more feelingly and judiciously, than he writes his rules of temperance out of books. So that the parson, having studied and mastered all his lusts and affections within, and the whole army of temptations without, hath ever so many sermons ready penned, as he hath victories. And it fares in this as it doth in physic: he that hath been sick of a consumption, and knows what recovered him, is a physician so far as he meets with the same disease and temper; and can much better and particularly do it, than he that is generally learned, and was never sick. And if the same person had been sick of all diseases, and were recovered of all by things that he knew, there were no such physician as he, both for skill and tenderness. Just so it is in divinity, and that not without manifest reason: for though the temptations may be diverse in divers Christians, yet the victory is alike in all, being by the self-same Spirit. Neither is this true only in the military state of a Christian life, but even in the peaceable also; when the servant of God, freed for a while from temptation, in a quiet sweetness seeks how to please his God. Thus the parson, considering that repentance is the great virtue of the Gospel, and one of the first steps of pleasing God, having for his own use examined the nature of it, is able to explain it after to others. And particularly, having doubted sometimes whether his repentance were true, or at least in that degree it ought to be, since he found himself sometimes to weep more for the loss of some temporal things, than for offending God, he came at length to this resolution, that repentance is an act of the mind, not of the body, even as the original° signifies; and that the chief thing which God in Scriptures requires is the heart and the spirit, and to worship him in truth and spirit. Wherefore in case a Christian endeavour to weep, and cannot, since we are not masters of our bodies, this sufficeth. And consequently he found that the essence of repentance, that it may be alike in all God's children (which as concerning weeping it cannot be, some being of a more melting temper than others) consisteth in a true detestation of the soul, abhorring and renouncing sin, and turning unto God in truth of heart and newness of life: which acts of repentance are and must be found in all God's servants: not that weeping is not useful, where it can be, that so the body may join in the grief, as it did in the sin; but that, so the other acts be, that is not necessary: so that he as truly repents, who performs the other acts of repentance, when he cannot more, as he that weeps a flood of tears. This instruction and comfort the parson getting for himself, when he tells it to others, becomes a sermon. The like he doth in other Christian virtues, as of faith and love, and the cases of conscience belonging thereto, wherein (as Saint Paul implies that he ought, Romans 2.)° he first preacheth to himself, and then to others.

Chap. XXXIV

The Parson's Dexterity in applying of Remedies

The country parson knows that there is a double state of a Christian even in this life, the one military, the other peaceable. The military is, when we are assaulted with temptations either from within or from without. The peaceable is, when the Devil for a time leaves us, as he did our Saviour, and the angels minister to us their own food,° even joy, and peace, and comfort in the Holy Ghost. These two states were in our Saviour, not only in the beginning of his preaching, but afterwards also, as Mat. 22. 35: he was tempted; and Luke 10. 21: he rejoiced in spirit; and they must be likewise in all that are his. Now the parson having a spiritual judgement, according as he discovers any of his flock to be in one or the other state, so he applies himself to them. Those that he finds in the peaceable state, he adviseth to be very vigilant, and not to let go the reins as soon as the horse goes easy. Particularly, he counselleth them to two things: first, to take heed lest their quiet betray them (as it is apt to do) to a coldness and carelessness in their devotions, but to labour still to be as fervent in Christian duties, as they remember themselves were, when affliction did blow the coals. Secondly, not to take the full compass and liberty of their peace: not to eat of all those dishes at table which even their present health otherwise admits; nor to store their house with all those furnitures which even their present plenty of wealth otherwise admits; nor when they are among them that are merry, to extend themselves to all that mirth which the present occasion of wit and company otherwise admits; but to put bounds and hoops to their joys: so will they last the longer, and when they depart, return the sooner. If we would judge ourselves, we should not be judged; and if we would bound ourselves, we should not be bounded. But if they shall fear that at such or such a time their peace and mirth have carried them further than this moderation, then to take Job's admirable course, who sacrificed lest his children should have transgressed in their mirth: so let them go and find some poor afflicted soul, and there be bountiful and liberal; for with such sacrifices God is well pleased. Those that the parson finds in the military state, he fortifies and strengthens with his utmost skill. Now in those that are tempted, whatsoever is unruly falls upon two heads; either they think that there is none that can or will look after things, but all goes by chance or wit: or else, though there be a great Governor of all things, yet to them he is lost, as if they said, God doth forsake and persecute them, and there is none to deliver them. If the parson suspect the first, and find sparks of such thoughts now and then to break forth, then without opposing directly (for disputation is no cure for atheism) he scatters in his discourse three sorts of arguments; the first taken from Nature, the second from the Law, the third from Grace.

For Nature, he sees not how a house could be either built without a builder, or kept in repair without a house-keeper. He conceives not possibly, how the winds should blow so much as they can, and the sea rage so much as it can, and all things do what they can, and all, not only without dissolution of the whole, but also of any part, by taking away so much as the usual seasons of summer and winter, earing° and harvest. Let the weather be what it will, still we have bread, though sometimes more, sometimes less; wherewith also a careful Joseph might meet.° He conceives not possibly, how he that would believe a divinity, if he had been at the creation of all things, should less believe it, seeing the preservation of all things; for preservation is a creation; and more, it is a continued creation, and a creation every moment.

Secondly, for the Law, there may be so evident, though unused a proof of divinity taken from thence, that the atheist or epicurean can have nothing to contradict. The Jews yet live and are known: they have their Law and language bearing witness to them, and they to it: they are circumcised to this day, and expect the promises of the Scripture; their country also is known, the places and rivers travelled unto and frequented by others, but to them an unpenetrable rock, an inaccessible desert. Wherefore if the Jews live, all the great wonders of old live in them, and then who can deny the stretched-out arm of a mighty God? Especially since it may be a just doubt, whether, considering the stubbornness of the nation, their living then in their country under so many miracles were a stranger thing, than their present exile and disability to live in their country. And it is observable, that this very thing was intended by God, that the Jews should be his proof and witnesses, as he calls them, Isaiah 43. 12. And their very dispersion in all lands was intended not only for a punishment to them, but for an exciting of others, by their sight, to the acknowledging of God and his power, Psalm 59. 11. And therefore this kind of punishment was chosen rather than any other.

Thirdly, for Grace. Besides the continual succession (since the Gospel) of holy men who have borne witness to the truth (there being no reason, why any should distrust Saint Luke, or Tertullian, or Chrysostom, more than Tully, Virgil, or Livy), there are two prophecies in the Gospel, which evidently argue Christ's divinity by their success: the one concerning the woman that spent the ointment on our Saviour, for which he told, that it should never be forgotten, but with the Gospel itself be preached to all ages, Matth. 26. 13. The other concerning the destruction of Jerusalem; of which our Saviour said, that that generation should not pass, till all were fulfilled, Luke 21. 32. Which Josephus's History confirmeth, and the continuance of which verdict is yet evident. To these might be added the preaching of the Gospel in all nations, Matthew 24. 14, which we see even miraculously effected in these new discoveries, God turning men's covetousness and ambitions to the effecting of his word. Now a prophecy is a wonder sent to posterity, lest they complain of want of wonders. It is a letter sealed and sent, which to the bearer is but paper, but to the receiver and opener is full of power. He that saw Christ open a blind man's eyes, saw not more divinity than he that reads the woman's ointment in the Gospel, or sees Jerusalem destroyed. With some of these heads enlarged and woven into his discourse, at several times and occasions, the parson settleth wavering minds. But if he sees them nearer desperation than atheism, not so much doubting a God, as that he is theirs; then he dives unto the boundless ocean of God's love, and the unspeakable riches of his

3 things

loving kindness. He hath one argument unanswerable. If God hate them, either he doth it as they are creatures, dust and ashes, or as they are sinful. As creatures, he must needs love them; for no perfect artist ever yet hated his own work. As sinful, he must much more love them; because notwithstanding his infinite hate of sin, his love overcame that hate; and with an exceeding great victory, which in the Creation needed not, gave them love for love, even the son of his love out of his bosom of love. So that man, which way soever he turns, hath two pledges of God's love, that in the mouth of two or three witnesses every word may be established;° the one in his being, the other in his sinful being: and this as the more faulty in him, so the more glorious in God. And all may certainly conclude that God loves them, till either they despise that love, or despair of his mercy: not any sin else, but is within his love; but the despising of love must needs be without it. The thrusting away of his arm makes us only not embraced.

CHAP. XXXV

The Parson's Condescending°

The country parson is a lover of old customs, if they be good and harmless; and the rather, because country people are much addicted to them, so that to favour them therein is to win their hearts, and to oppose them therein is to deject them. If there be any ill in the custom that may be severed from the good, he pares the apple, and gives them the clean to feed on. Particularly, he loves Procession° and maintains it, because there are contained therein four manifest advantages. First, a blessing of God for the fruits of the field; secondly, justice in the preservation of bounds; thirdly, charity in loving walking and neighbourly accompanying one another, with reconciling of differences at that time, if there be any; fourthly, mercy in relieving the poor by a liberal distribution and largesse, which at that time is, or ought to be used. Wherefore he exacts of all to be present at the perambulation, and those that withdraw and sever themselves from it, he mislikes and reproves as uncharitable and unneighbourly; and if they will not reform, presents them. Nay, he is so far from condemning such assemblies, that he rather procures them to be often, as knowing that absence breeds strangeness, but presence love. Now love is his business and aim; wherefore he likes well that his parish at good times invite one another to their houses, and he urgeth them to it: and sometimes, where he knows there hath been or is a little difference, he takes one of the parties, and goes with him to the other, and all dine or sup together. There is much preaching in this friendliness. Another old custom there is of saying, when light is brought in, God send us the light of heaven; and the parson likes this very well; neither is he afraid of praising, or praying to God at all times, but is rather glad of catching opportunities to do them. Light is a great blessing, and as great as food, for which we give thanks: and those that think this superstitious, neither know superstition, nor themselves. As for those that are ashamed to use this form, as being old, and obsolete, and not the fashion, he reforms and teaches them that at baptism they professed not to be ashamed of Christ's Cross, or for any shame to leave that which is good. He that is ashamed in small things will extend his pusillanimity to greater. Rather should a Christian soldier take such occasions to harden himself, and to further his exercises of mortification.

Chap. XXXVI

The Parson Blessing

The country parson wonders, that blessing the people is in so little use with his brethren: whereas he thinks it not only a grave and reverend thing, but a beneficial also. Those who use it not, do so either out of niceness,° because they like the salutations, and compliments, and forms of worldly language better; which conformity and fashionableness is so exceeding unbefitting a minister, that it deserves reproof, not refutation: or else, because they think it empty and superfluous. But that which the Apostles used so diligently in their writings, nay, which our Saviour himself used, Mark 10. 16, cannot be vain and superfluous. But this was not proper to° Christ or the Apostles only, no more than to be a spiritual father was appropriated to them. And if temporal fathers bless their children, how much more may and ought spiritual fathers? Besides, the priests of the Old Testament were commanded to bless the people, and the form thereof is prescribed, Numb. 6. [22–6]. Now as the Apostle argues in another case, if the ministration of condemnation did bless, how shall not the ministration of the spirit exceed in blessing?° The fruit of this blessing good Hannah found, and received with great joy, 1 Sam. 1. 18, though it came from a man disallowed by God: for it was not the person, but priesthood, that blessed; so that even ill priests may bless. Neither have the ministers power of blessing only, but also of cursing. So in the Old Testament Elisha cursed the children, 2 Kin. 2. 24, which though our Saviour reproved as unfitting for his particular, who was to show all humility before his Passion, yet he allows in his Apostles. And therefore St. Peter used that fearful imprecation to Simon Magus, Act. 8. [20], *Thy money perish with thee*: and the event confirmed it. So did St. Paul, 2 Tim. 4. 14, and 1 Tim. 1. 20: speaking of Alexander the coppersmith, who had withstood his preaching, *The Lord* (saith he) *reward him according to his works*; and again, of Hymeneus and Alexander, he saith, he had *delivered them to Satan, that they might learn not to blaspheme*. The forms both of blessing and cursing are expounded in the Common-Prayer Book: the one in, The Grace of our Lord Jesus Christ, etc. and The Peace of God, etc. The other in general, in the Commination.° Now blessing differs from prayer, in assurance, because it is not performed by way of request, but of confidence and power, effectually applying God's favour to the blessed, by the interesting of that dignity wherewith God hath invested the priest, and engaging of God's own power and institution for a blessing. The neglect of this duty in ministers themselves hath made the people also neglect it; so that they are so far from craving this benefit from their ghostly father, that they oftentimes go out of church before he hath blessed them. In the time of Popery, the priest's *Benedicite* and his holy water were over-highly valued; and now we are fallen to the clean contrary, even from superstition to coldness and atheism. But the parson first values the gift in himself, and then teacheth his parish to value it. And it is observable, that if a minister talk with a great man in the ordinary course of complimenting language, he shall be esteemed as ordinary complimenters; but if he often interpose a blessing, when the other gives him just opportunity, by speaking any good, this unusual form begets a reverence, and makes him esteemed according to his profession. The same is to be observed in writing letters also. To conclude, if all men are to bless upon occasion, as appears, Rom. 12. 14, how much more those, who are spiritual fathers?

CHAP. XXXVII

Concerning Detraction

The country parson, perceiving that most, when they are at leisure, make others' faults their entertainment and discourse, and that even some good men think, so they speak truth, they may disclose another's fault, finds it somewhat difficult how to proceed in this point. For if he absolutely shut up men's mouths, and forbid all disclosing of faults, many an evil may not only be, but also spread in his parish, without any remedy (which cannot be applied without notice), to the dishonour of God, and the infection of his flock, and the discomfort, discredit, and hindrance of the pastor. On the other side, if it be unlawful to open faults, no benefit or advantage can make it lawful: for we must not do evil, that good may come of it. Now the parson taking this point to task, which is so exceeding useful, and hath taken so deep root, that it seems the very life and substance of conversation, hath proceeded thus far in the discussing of it. Faults are either notorious or private. Again, notorious faults are either such as are made known by common fame (and of these, those that know them may talk, so they do it not with sport, but commiseration) or else such as have passed judgement, and been corrected either by whipping, or imprisoning, or the like. Of these also men may talk, and more, they may discover them to those that know them not: because infamy is a part of the sentence against malefactors, which the law intends, as is evident by those which are branded for rogues, that they may be known; or put into the stocks, that they may be looked upon. But some may say, though the law allow this, the Gospel doth not, which hath so much advanced charity, and ranked backbiters among the generation of the wicked, Rom. 1. 30. But this is easily answered: as the executioner is not uncharitable, that takes away the life of the condemned, except besides his office, he add a tincture of private malice in the joy and haste of acting his part; so neither is he that defames him whom the law would have defamed, except he also do it out of rancour. For in infamy, all are executioners, and the law gives a malefactor to all to be defamed. And as malefactors may lose and forfeit their goods or life, so may they their good name and the possession thereof, which before their offence and judgement they had in all men's breasts: for all are honest till the contrary be proved. Besides, it concerns the commonwealth that rogues should be known, and charity to the public hath the precedence of private charity. So that it is so far from being a fault to discover such offenders, that it is a duty rather, which may do much good, and save much harm. Nevertheless, if the punished delinquent shall be much troubled for his sins, and turn quite another man, doubtless then also men's affections and words must turn, and forbear to speak of that which even God himself hath forgotten.

The Author's Prayer before Sermon

O Almighty and ever-living Lord God! Majesty, and Power, and Brightness, and Glory! How shall we dare to appear before thy face, who are contrary to thee, in all we call thee? For we are darkness, and weakness, and filthiness, and shame. Misery and sin fill our days: yet art thou our Creator, and we thy work. Thy hands both made us, and also made us lords of all thy creatures; giving us one world in ourselves, and another to serve us: then didst thou place us in Paradise, and wert proceeding still on in thy favours, until we interrupted thy counsels, disappointed thy purposes, and sold our God, our glorious, our gracious God for an apple. O write it! O brand it in our foreheads for ever: for an apple once we lost our God, and still lose him for no more; for money, for meat, for diet. But thou, Lord, art patience, and pity, and sweetness, and love; therefore we sons of men are not consumed. Thou hast exalted thy mercy above all things; and hast made our salvation, not our punishment, thy glory: so that then where sin abounded, not death, but grace superabounded; accordingly, when we had sinned beyond any help in heaven or earth, then thou saidest, Lo, I come! Then did the Lord of life, unable of himself to die, contrive to do it. He took flesh, he wept, he died; for his enemies he died; even for those that derided him then, and still despise him. Blessed Saviour! many waters could not quench thy love! nor no pit overwhelm it. But though the streams of thy blood were current through darkness, grave, and hell; yet by these thy conflicts and seemingly hazards, didst thou arise triumphant, and therein madst us victorious.

Neither doth thy love yet stay here! for this word of thy rich peace and reconciliation thou hast committed, not to thunder or angels, but to silly and sinful men: even to me, pardoning my sins, and bidding me go feed the people of thy love.

Blessed be the God of Heaven and Earth! who only doth wondrous things. Awake therefore, my lute and my viol! Awake, all my powers to glorify thee! We praise thee! We bless thee! We magnify thee for ever! And now, O Lord! in the power of thy victories, and in the ways of thy ordinances, and in the truth of thy love, lo, we stand here, beseeching thee to bless thy word, wherever spoken this day throughout the universal Church. O make it a word of power and peace, to convert those who are not yet thine, and to confirm those that are: particularly, bless it in this thy own kingdom, which thou hast made a land of light, a storehouse of thy treasures and mercies. O let not our foolish and unworthy hearts rob us of the continuance of this thy sweet love: but pardon our sins, and perfect what thou hast begun. Ride on Lord, because of the word of truth, and meekness, and righteousness; and thy right hand shall teach thee terrible things. Especially, bless this portion here assembled together, with thy unworthy servant speaking unto them: Lord Jesu! teach thou me, that I may teach them: sanctify and enable all my powers, that in their full strength they may deliver thy message reverently, readily, faithfully, and fruitfully. O make thy word a swift word, passing from the ear to the heart, from the heart to the life and conversation: that as the rain returns not empty, so neither may thy word, but accomplish that for which it is given. O Lord hear, O Lord forgive! O Lord, hearken, and do so for thy blessed Son's sake, in whose sweet and pleasing words, we say, *Our Father*, etc.

of Collar

A Prayer after Sermon

Blessed be God! and the Father of all mercy! who continueth to pour his benefits upon us. Thou hast elected us, thou hast called us, thou hast justified us, sanctified, and glorified us. Thou wast born for us, and thou livedst and diedst for us. Thou hast given us the blessings of this life, and of a better. O Lord! thy blessings hang in clusters, they come trooping upon us! they break forth like mighty waters on every side. And now, Lord, thou hast fed us with the bread of life: so man did eat angels' food: O Lord, bless it: O Lord, make it health and strength unto us, still striving and prospering so long within us, until our obedience reach the measure of thy love, who hast done for us as much as may be. Grant this, dear Father, for thy Son's sake, our only Saviour: to whom with thee, and the Holy Ghost, three Persons, but one most glorious, incomprehensible God, be ascribed all honour, and glory, and praise, ever. Amen.

HENRY VAUGHAN

Silex Scintillans:

or

SACRED POEMS

and

Private Ejaculations

By

Henry Vaughan Silurist

LONDON Printed by T.W. for H. Blunden
at ye Castle in Cornehill . 1650

Authoris (*de se*) Emblema

Tentasti, fateor, sine vulnere saepius, et me
    Consultum voluit Vox, *sine voce, frequens;*
Ambivit placido divinior aura meatu,
    Et frustra sancto murmure praemonuit.
Surdus eram, mutusque Silex: *Tu* (*quanta tuorum*
    Cura tibi est!) *alia das renovare via,*
Permutas curam: iamque irritatus Amorem
    Posse negas, et vim, Vi, *superare paras,*
Accedis propior, molemque, et saxea rumpis
    Pectora, fitque Caro, *quod fuit ante Lapis.*°   10
En lacerum! Coelosque tuos ardentia tandem
    Fragmenta, *et liquidas ex* Adamante *genas.*
Sic olim undantes Petras, Scopulosque *vomentes*°
    Curasti, O populi providus usque tui!
Quam miranda tibi manus est! Moriendo, *revixi;*
    Et fractas *jam sum* ditior *inter* opes.

[The Author's Emblem (concerning himself)

You have often touched me, I confess, without a wound, and your *Voice*, without a voice, has often sought to counsel me; your diviner breath has encompassed me with its calm motion, and in vain has cautioned me with its sacred murmur. I was deaf and dumb: a *Flint*: You (how great care you take of your own!) try to revive another way, you change the remedy; and now angered you say that *Love* has no power, and you prepare to conquer force with *Force*, you come closer, you break through the *Rocky* barrier of my heart, and it is made *Flesh* that was before a *Stone.*° Behold me torn asunder! and at last the *Fragments* burning toward your skies, and the cheeks streaming with tears out of the *Adamant.* Thus once upon a time you made the *Rocks* flow and the *Crags* gush,° oh ever provident of your people! How marvellous toward me is your hand! In *Dying*, I have been born again; and in the midst of my *shattered means* I am now *richer.*]

The Dedication

My God, thou that didst die for me,
These thy death's fruits I offer thee.
Death that to me was life and light
But dark and deep pangs to thy sight.
Some drops of thy all-quick'ning blood
Fell on my heart, these made it bud
And put forth thus, though, Lord, before
The ground was cursed, and void of store.°
   Indeed, I had some here to hire°
Which long resisted thy desire,   10
That stoned thy servants, and did move
To have thee murthered for thy Love,
But, Lord, I have expelled them, and so bent
Beg thou wouldst take thy tenant's rent.

SILEX SCINTILLANS

Regeneration

A ward, and still in bonds, one day°
       I stole abroad,
It was high-spring, and all the way
     Primrosed, and hung with shade;
     Yet, was it frost within,
         And surly winds
Blasted my infant buds, and sin
     Like clouds eclipsed my mind.

2

Stormed thus, I straight perceived my spring
       Mere stage and show,   10
My walk a monstrous, mountained thing
     Rough-cast with rocks and snow;
     And as a pilgrim's eye
         Far from relief,
Measures the melancholy sky
     Then drops, and rains for grief,

3

So sighed I upwards still, at last
             'Twixt steps, and falls
I reached the pinnacle, where placed
        I found a pair of scales,   20
        I took them up and laid
             In th' one late pains,
The other smoke, and pleasures weighed
        But proved the heavier grains;

4

With that, some cried, *Away*; straight I°
        Obeyed, and led
Full East, a fair, fresh field could spy°
        Some called it, *Jacob's Bed*;
        A virgin-soil, which no
             Rude feet e'er trod,   30
Where (since he stepped there) only go
        Prophets, and friends of God.°

5

Here, I reposed; but scarce well set,°
        A grove descried
Of stately height, whose branches met
        And mixed on every side;
        I entered, and once in
             (Amazed to see't)
Found all was changed, and a new spring
        Did all my senses greet;   40

6

The unthrift sun shot vital gold°
        A thousand pieces,
And heaven its azure did unfold
        Chequered with snowy fleeces,
        The air was all in spice
             And every bush
A garland wore; thus fed my eyes
        But all the ear lay hush.

7

Only a little fountain lent
                    Some use for ears,   50
And on the dumb shades language spent,
                    The music of her tears;
          I drew her near, and found
                    The cistern full
Of divers stones, some bright, and round,°
          Others ill-shaped, and dull.

8

The first (pray mark) as quick as light
                    Danced through the flood,
But, th' last more heavy than the night
                    Nailed to the Centre stood;°   60
          I wondered much, but tired
                    At last with thought,
My restless eye that still desired
                    As strange an object brought;

9

It was a bank of flowers, where I descried
                    (Though 'twas mid-day)
Some fast asleep, others broad-eyed
                    And taking in the Ray,
          Here musing long, I heard
                    A rushing wind°   70
Which still increased, but whence it stirred
          Nowhere I could not find;

10

I turned me round, and to each shade
                    Dispatched an eye,
To see, if any leaf had made
                    Least motion or reply,
          But while I list'ning sought
                    My mind to ease
By knowing, where 'twas, or where not,
                    It whispered: *Where I please.*°   80

Lord, then said I, *On me one breath,*
And let me die before my death!

Cant. Cap. 5. ver. 17
Arise O North, and come thou South-wind, and blow upon my garden,
that the spices thereof may flow out.°

end of alleg. journey in a reference to the Bible

Death

A Dialogue

Soul.   'Tis a sad land, that in one day
    Hath dulled thee thus, when death shall freeze
    Thy blood to ice, and thou must stay
    Tenant for years, and centuries,
    How wilt thou brook't?——

Body.   I cannot tell,——
    But if all sense wings not with thee,
    And something still be left the dead,
    I'll wish my curtains off to free
    Me from so dark and sad a bed;   10

    A nest of nights, a gloomy sphere,
    Where shadows thicken, and the cloud
    Sits on the sun's brow all the year,
    And nothing moves without a shroud;

Soul.   'Tis so: but as thou sawest that night
    We travelled in, our first attempts
    Were dull and blind, but custom straight
    Our fears and falls brought to contempt,

    Then, when the ghastly *twelve* was past
    We breathed still for a blushing *East*,   20
    And bade the lazy sun make haste,
    And on sure hopes, though long, did feast;

But when we saw the clouds to crack
And in those crannies light appeared,
We thought the day then was not slack,
And pleased ourselves with what we feared;

Just so it is in death. But thou
Shalt in thy mother's bosom sleep
Whilst I each minute groan to know
How near Redemption creeps.   30

Then shall we meet to mix again, and met,
'Tis last good-night, our Sun shall never set.

Job. Cap: 10. ver. 21. 22

*Before I go whence I shall not return, even to the land of darkness, and
the shadow of death;*
*A land of darkness, as darkness itself, and of the shadow of death,
without any order, and where the light is as darkness.*

Resurrection and Immortality°

Heb. Cap. 10. ver. 20

*By that new and living way, which he hath prepared for us, through the
veil, which is his flesh.°*

Body

I

Oft have I seen, when that renewing breath
      That binds and loosens death
Inspired a quick'ning power through the dead°
        Creatures abed,
      Some drowsy silk-worm creep
      From that long sleep
And in weak, infant hummings chime and knell
      About her silent cell
Until at last full with the vital Ray
        She winged away,   10
      And proud with life and sense,
      Heav'n's rich expense,
Esteemed (vain things!) of two whole elements°

As mean, and span-extents.°
Shall I then think such providence will be
        Less friend to me?
Or that he can endure to be unjust
Who keeps his Covenant even with our dust?

Soul

2

Poor, querulous handful! was't for this
        I taught thee all that is?   20
Unbowelled nature, showed thee her recruits,°
        And change of suits,
        And how of death we make
        A mere mistake,
For no thing can to *Nothing* fall, but still
        Incorporates by skill,°
And then returns, and from the womb of things
        Such treasure brings
        As phoenix-like renew'th
        Both life and youth;   30
For a preserving spirit doth still pass
        Untainted through this mass,
Which doth resolve, produce, and ripen all°
        That to it fall;
        Nor are those births which we
        Thus suffering see
Destroyed at all; but when time's restless wave
        Their substance doth deprave°
And the more noble *Essence* finds his house
        Sickly and loose,   40
        He, ever young, doth wing
        Unto that spring,
And *source* of spirits, where he takes his lot
        Till time no more shall rot
His passive cottage; which (though laid aside)
        Like some spruce bride,
Shall one day rise, and clothed with shining light
        All pure and bright
        Re-marry to the soul, for 'tis most plain
        Thou only fall'st to be refined again.   50

3

Then I that here saw darkly in a glass°
          But mists and shadows pass,
And, by their own weak *shine*, did search the springs
          And course of things,
    Shall with enlightened Rays
          Pierce all their ways;
And as thou saw'st, I in a thought could go
          To heav'n, or earth below
To read some *star*, or *min'ral*, and in state°
          There often sate,   60
    So shalt thou then with me
          (Both winged and free)
Rove in that mighty and eternal light
          Where no rude shade or night
Shall dare approach us; we shall there no more
          Watch stars, or pore
    Through melancholy clouds, and say,
          Would it were day!°
One everlasting *Sabbath* there shall run
Without *succession*, and without a *sun*.   70

Dan. Cap: 12. ver: 13
*But go thou thy way until the end be, for thou shalt rest, and stand up
in thy lot, at the end of the days.*

Day of Judgement

When through the North a fire shall rush
          And roll into the East,
And like a fiery torrent brush
          And sweep up South and West,

When all shall stream, and lighten round
          And with surprising flames
Both stars and elements confound
          And quite blot out their names,

When thou shalt spend thy sacred store
          Of thunders in that heat   10
And low as e'er they lay before
          Thy six-days-buildings beat,

When like a scroll the heavens shall pass°
          And vanish clean away,
And nought must stand of that vast space
          Which held up night and day,

When one loud blast shall rend the deep,
          And from the womb of earth
Summon up all that are asleep
          Unto a second birth,   20

When thou shalt make the clouds thy seat,°
          And in the open air
The quick and dead, both small and great°
          Must to thy bar repair;

O then it will be all too late
          To say, *What shall I do?*
Repentance there is out of date
          And so is *mercy* too;

Prepare, prepare me then, O God!
          And let me now begin   30
To feel my loving father's *rod*
          Killing the man of sin!°

Give me, O give me crosses here,
          Still more afflictions lend,
That pill, though bitter, is most dear
          That brings health in the end;

Lord, God! I beg nor friends, nor wealth
          But pray against them both;
Three things I'd have, my soul's chief health!
          And one of these seem loath,   40

A living *FAITH*, a *HEART* of flesh,°
    The *WORLD* an enemy,
This last will keep the first two fresh,
    And bring me, where I'd be.

1 Pet. 4. 7
  Now the end of all things is at hand, be you therefore sober, and watching in prayer.°

Religion

My God, when I walk in those groves
And leaves thy spirit doth still fan,
I see in each shade that there grows
An angel talking with a man.

Under a *juniper*, some house,°
Or the cool *myrtle's* canopy,°
Others beneath an *oak's* green boughs,°
Or at some *fountain's* bubbling eye;°

Here Jacob dreams, and wrestles; there°
Elias by a raven is fed,°   10
Another time by th' angel, where°
He brings him water with his bread;

In Abr'ham's tent the wingèd guests°
(O how familiar then was heaven!)
Eat, drink, discourse, sit down, and rest
Until the cool and shady *even*;

Nay thou thyself, my God, in *fire*,°
Whirlwinds, and *clouds*, and the *soft voice*°
Speak'st there so much, that I admire°
We have no conf'rence in these days;°   20

Is the truce broke? or 'cause we have
A mediator now with thee,
Dost thou therefore old treaties waive
And by appeals from him decree?

Or is't so, as some green heads say
That now all miracles must cease?
Though thou hast promised they should stay
The tokens of the Church, and peace;

No, no; Religion is a spring
That from some secret, golden mine   30
Derives her birth, and thence doth bring
Cordials in every drop, and wine;°

But in her long and hidden course
Passing through the earth's dark veins,
Grows still from better unto worse,
And both her taste and colour stains,

Then drilling on, learns to increase°
False echoes and confusèd sounds,
And unawares doth often seize
On veins of sulphur under ground;   40

So poisoned, breaks forth in some clime,
And at first sight doth many please,
But drunk, is puddle, or mere slime°
And 'stead of physic, a disease;°

Just such a tainted sink we have°
Like that Samaritan's dead *well*,°
Nor must we for the kernel crave
Because most voices like the *shell*.

Heal then these waters, Lord; or bring thy flock,
Since these are troubled, to the springing rock,°   50
Look down great Master of the feast; O shine,
And turn once more our *water* into *wine*!°

Cant. Cap. 4. ver. 12

*My sister, my spouse is as a garden inclosed, as a spring shut up, and a
fountain sealed up.*

The Search°

'Tis now clear day: I see a Rose
Bud in the bright East, and disclose
The Pilgrim-Sun; all night have I
Spent in a roving ecstasy°
To find my Saviour; I have been
As far as Bethlem, and have seen
His inn and cradle; being there
I met the *Wise-men*, asked them where
He might be found, or what star can
Now point him out, grown up a man?   10
To Egypt hence I fled, ran o'er
All her parched bosom to Nile's shore
Her yearly nurse; came back, enquired
Amongst the *Doctors*, and desired
To see the *Temple*, but was shown°
A little dust, and for the town
A heap of ashes, where some said
A small bright sparkle was a bed,
Which would one day (beneath the pole)°
Awake, and then refine the whole.   20
    Tired here, I come to Sychar; thence°
To Jacob's well, bequeathèd since
Unto his sons (where often they
In those calm, golden evenings lay
Wat'ring their flocks, and having spent
Those white days, drove home to the tent
Their *well-fleeced* train; and here (O fate!)
I sit, where once my Saviour sate;
The angry spring in bubbles swelled
Which broke in sighs still, as they filled,   30
And whispered, *Jesus had been there*
But Jacob's children would not hear.
Loath hence to part, at last I rise
But with the fountain in my eyes,
And here a fresh search is decreed:
He must be found, where he did bleed;
I walk the garden, and there see
Ideas of his Agony,°

And moving anguishments that set
His blest face in a bloody sweat;   40
I climbed the Hill, perused the Cross
Hung with my gain, and his great loss,
Never did tree bear fruit like this,
Balsam of souls, the body's bliss;°
But, O his grave! where I saw lent°
(For he had none) a monument,
An undefiled and new-hewed one,
But there was not the *corner-stone*;°
Sure (then said I) my quest is vain,
He'll not be found, where he was slain,   50
So mild a Lamb can never be
'Midst so much blood and cruelty;
I'll to the wilderness, and can°
Find beasts more merciful than man,
He lived there safe, 'twas his retreat
From the fierce Jew, and Herod's heat,
And forty days withstood the fell
And high temptations of hell;
With Seraphins there talkèd he,
His father's flaming ministry,   60
He heav'ned their walks, and with his eyes
Made those wild shades a Paradise,
Thus was the desert sanctified
To be the refuge of his bride;°
I'll thither then; see, it is day,
The Sun's broke through to guide my way.
    But as I urged thus, and writ down
What pleasures should my journey crown,
What silent paths, what shades, and cells,
Fair, virgin-flowers, and hallow'd *wells*   70
I should rove in, and rest my head
Where my dear Lord did often tread,
Sug'ring all dangers with success,
Me thought I heard one singing thus;°

I

Leave, leave, thy gadding thoughts;
Who pores
and spies

Still out of doors°
descries
Within them nought.   80

2

The skin and shell of things
Though fair,
are not
Thy wish, nor pray'r
but got
By mere despair
of wings.

3

To rack old elements,
or dust
and say   90
Sure here he must
needs stay
Is not the way,
nor just.

Search well another world; who studies this,°
Travels in clouds, seeks *Manna*, where none is.

Acts Cap. 17. ver. 27, 28
That they should seek the Lord, if happily° they might feel after him,
and find him, though he be not far off from every one of us, for in him we
live, and move, and have our being.

Isaac's Marriage°

Gen. Cap. 24. ver. 63°
And Isaac went out to pray in the field at the even-tide, and he lift up
his eyes, and saw, and behold, the camels were coming.

Praying! and to be married? It was rare,
But now 'tis monstrous; and that pious care°
Though of ourselves, is so much out of date,
That to renew't were to degenerate.°
But thou a chosen sacrifice wert given,

And offered up so early unto heaven
Thy flames could not be out; Religion was
Rayed into thee, like beams into a glass,
Where, as thou grewst, it multiplied and shined,
The sacred constellation of thy mind.°　　　　　10
But being for a bride, prayer was such°
A decried course, sure it prevailed not much.
Had'st ne'er an oath, nor compliment? thou wert
An odd dull suitor; hadst thou but the art°
Of these our days, thou couldst have coined thee twenty
New sev'ral oaths, and compliments (too) plenty;°
O sad and wild excess! and happy those
White days, that durst no impious mirth expose!
When conscience by lewd use had not lost sense,°
Nor bold-faced custom banished innocence;　　　　　20
Thou hadst no pompous train, nor *antic* crowd°
Of young, gay swearers, with their needless, loud
Retinue; all was here smooth as thy bride°
And calm like her, or that mild evening-tide;
Yet, hadst thou nobler guests: angels did wind
And rove about thee, guardians of thy mind,
These fetched thee home thy bride, and all the way
Advised thy servant what to do and say;°
These taught him at the *well*, and thither brought
The chaste and lovely object of thy thought;　　　　　30
But here was ne'er a compliment, not one
Spruce, supple cringe, or studied look put on,
All was plain, modest truth: nor did she come
In *rolls* and *curls*, mincing and stately dumb,
But in a virgin's native blush and fears°
Fresh as those roses, which the day-spring wears.
O sweet, divine simplicity! O grace
Beyond a curlèd lock, or painted face!
A pitcher too she had, nor thought it much
To carry that, which some would scorn to touch;　　　　　40
With which in mild, chaste language she did woo
To draw him drink, and for his camels too.

　　And now thou knewst her coming, it was time
To get thee wings on, and devoutly climb
Unto thy God, for marriage of all states
Makes most unhappy, or most fortunates;°

This brought thee forth, where now thou didst undress
Thy soul, and with new pinions refresh
Her wearied wings, which so restored did fly
Above the stars, a track unknown and high,   50
And in her piercing flight perfumed the air,
Scatt'ring the myrrh and incense of thy pray'r.
So from Lahai-roi's well some spicy cloud°
Wooed by the sun swells up to be his shroud,
And from his moist womb weeps a fragrant shower,
Which, scattered in a thousand pearls, each flower
And herb partakes, where having stood awhile
And something cooled the parched and thirsty isle,
The thankful earth unlocks herself, and blends
A thousand odours, which (all mixed) she sends   60
Up in one cloud, and so returns the skies
That dew they lent, a breathing sacrifice.
   Thus soared thy soul, who (though young) didst inherit
Together with his blood, thy father's spirit,
Whose active zeal, and tried faith were to thee
Familiar ever since thy infancy.
Others were timed and trained up to't but thou°
Didst thy swift years in piety out-grow,
Age made them rev'rend, and a snowy head,
But thou wert so, ere time his snow could shed;   70
Then, who would truly limn thee out, must paint
First, a *young Patriarch*, then a *married Saint*.

The British Church°

           Ah! he is fled!
And while these here their *mists* and *shadows* hatch,
           My glorious head
Doth on those hills of myrrh and incense watch.°
           Haste, haste my dear,
           The soldiers here°
         Cast in their lots again,
           That seamless coat
           The Jews touched not,
         These dare divide and stain.   10

2

O get thee wings!
Or if as yet (until these clouds depart,
        And the day springs)
Thou think'st it good to tarry where thou art,
        Write in thy books
        My ravished looks,
    Slain flock, and pillaged fleeces,
        And haste thee so°
        As a young roe
    Upon the mounts of spices.   20

O rosa campi! O lilium convallium! quomodo nunc facta es pabulum aprorum!°

The Lamp

'Tis dead night round about: horror doth creep
And move on with the shades; stars nod and sleep,°
And through the dark air spin a fiery thread
Such as doth gild the lazy glow-worm's bed.
    Yet, burn'st thou here, a full day; while I spend
My rest in cares, and to the dark world lend
These flames, as thou dost thine to me; I watch
That hour, which must thy life and mine dispatch;
But still thou dost out-go me, I can see
Met in thy flames, all acts of piety;   10
Thy light, is *Charity*; thy heat, is *Zeal*;
And thy aspiring, active fires reveal
Devotion still on wing; then, thou dost weep
Still as thou burn'st, and the warm droppings creep
To measure out thy length, as if thou'dst know
What stock, and how much time were left thee now;
Nor dost thou spend one tear in vain, for still
As thou dissolv'st to them, and they distil,
They're stored up in the socket, where they lie,
When all is spent, thy last, and sure supply,   20
And such is true repentance, ev'ry breath
We spend in sighs, is treasure after death;

Only, one point escapes thee; that thy oil
Is still out with thy flame, and so both fail;
But whensoe'er I'm out, both shall be in,
And where thou mad'st an end, there I'll begin.

Mark Cap. 13. ver. 35
Watch you therefore, for you know not when the master of the house
cometh, at even, or at midnight, or at the cock-crowing, or in the morning.

Man's Fall and Recovery

Farewell you everlasting hills! I'm cast°
Here under clouds, where storms and tempests blast
     This sullied flower
Robbed of your calm, nor can I ever make
Transplanted thus, one leaf of his t'awake,
     But ev'ry hour
He sleeps and droops, and in this drowsy state
Leaves me a slave to passions, and my fate;
     Besides I've lost
A train of lights, which in those sunshine days   10
Were my sure guides, and only with me stays
     (Unto my cost)
One sullen beam, whose charge is to dispense°
More punishment, than knowledge to my sense;
     Two thousand years
I sojourned thus; at last Jeshurun's king°
Those famous tables did from Sinai bring;
     These swelled my fears,°
Guilts, trespasses, and all this inward awe,
For sin took strength, and vigour from the Law.   20
     Yet have I found
A plenteous way (thanks to that holy one!)
To cancel all that e'er was writ in stone,
     His saving wound
Wept blood, that broke this adamant, and gave
To sinners confidence, life to the grave;
     This makes me span
My father's journeys, and in one fair step

O'er all their pilgrimage and labours leap,
　　　　For God (made man)　　　　　　　　30
Reduced th' extent of works of faith; so made
Of their *Red Sea*, a *Spring*; I wash, they wade.°

　　　　　　Rom. Cap. 5. ver. 18°
*As by the offence of one, the fault came on all men to condemnation; so
by the righteousness of one, the benefit abounded towards all men to the
justification of life.*

The Shower

'Twas so, I saw thy birth: that drowsy lake
From her faint bosom breathed thee, the disease
Of her sick waters, and infectious ease.
　　　　　　But, now at even
　　　　　　Too gross for heaven,
Thou fall'st in tears, and weep'st for thy mistake.

2

Ah! it is so with me; oft have I pressed
Heaven with a lazy breath, but fruitless this
Pierced not; Love only can with quick access°
　　　　　　Unlock the way,　　　　　　　　10
　　　　　　When all else stray,
The smoke and exhalations of the breast.

3

Yet, if as thou dost melt, and with thy train
Of drops make soft the earth, my eyes could weep
O'er my hard heart, that's bound up and asleep,
　　　　　　Perhaps at last
　　　　　　(Some such shower past)
My God would give a sunshine after rain.

Distraction

O knit me, that am crumbled dust! the heap°
    Is all dispersed and cheap;
      Give for a handful, but a thought
        And it is bought;
          Hadst thou
Made me a star, a pearl, or a rainbow,°
      The beams I then had shot
      My light had lessened not,
        But now
I find myself the less, the more I grow;
      The world
Is full of voices; Man is called and hurled°
      By each, he answers all,
      Knows ev'ry note and call,
        Hence, still
Fresh dotage tempts, or old usurps his will.
Yet, hadst thou clipped my wings, when coffined in
      This quickened mass of sin,
    And saved that light, which freely thou
        Didst then bestow,
         I fear
I should have spurned, and said thou didst forbear;
      Or that thy store was less,
      But now since thou didst bless
        So much,
I grieve, my God! that thou hast made me such.
        I grieve?
O, yes! thou know'st I do; come, and relieve
      And tame, and keep down with thy light
      Dust that would rise, and dim my sight,°
      Lest left alone too long
      Amidst the noise and throng,
        Oppressèd I
Striving to save the whole, by parcels die.°

10

20

30

The Pursuit°

Lord! what a busy, restless thing
    Hast thou made man!
Each day and hour he is on wing,
    Rests not a span;
Then having lost the Sun and light
    By clouds surprised
He keeps a commerce in the night°
    With air disguised;
Hadst thou given to this active dust
    A state untired,   10
The lost son had not left the husk°
    Nor home desired;
That was thy secret, and it is
    Thy mercy too,
For when all fails to bring to bliss,
    Then, this must do.
Ah! Lord! and what a purchase will that be
To take us sick, that sound would not take thee!

Mount of Olives (I)°

Sweet, sacred hill! on whose fair brow
My Saviour sate, shall I allow°
    Language to love
And idolize some shade, or grove,
Neglecting thee? such ill-placed wit,°
Conceit, or call it what you please
    Is the brain's fit,
    And mere disease;

2

Cotswold and Cooper's both have met°
With learned swains, and echo yet   10
    Their pipes and wit;
But thou sleep'st in a deep neglect
Untouched by any; and what need

The sheep bleat thee a silly lay
   That heard'st both reed
   And sheepward play?°

3

Yet, if poets mind thee well
They shall find thou art their hill,
   And fountain too,
Their Lord with thee, had most to do;   20
He wept once, walked whole nights on thee,°
And from thence (his suff'rings ended)°
   Unto glory
   Was attended;

4

Being there, this spacious ball
Is but his narrow footstool all,°
   And what we think
Unsearchable, now with one wink°
He doth comprise; but in this air°
When he did stay to bear our ill   30
   And sin, this hill
   Was then his chair.°

The Incarnation and Passion

Lord! when thou didst thyself undress°
Laying by thy robes of glory,
To make us more, thou wouldst be less,
And becam'st a woeful story.

To put on clouds instead of light,
And clothe the morning-star with dust,°
Was a translation of such height
As, but in thee, was ne'er expressed;

Brave worms and earth! that thus could have
A God enclosed within your cell,   10
Your maker pent up in a grave,
Life locked in death, heav'n in a shell;

Ah, my dear Lord! what couldst thou spy
In this impure, rebellious clay,
That made thee thus resolve to die
For those that kill thee every day?

O what strange wonders could thee move
To slight thy precious blood and breath!
Sure it was *Love*, my Lord; for *Love*°
Is only stronger far than death.   20

The Call

Come my heart! come my head
    In sighs and tears!
'Tis now, since you have lain thus dead
    Some twenty years;
    Awake, awake,
    Some pity take
    Upon yourselves—
Who never wake to groan, nor weep,
Shall be sentenced for their sleep.

2

Do but see your sad estate,   10
    How many sands°
Have left us, while we careless sate
    With folded hands;
    What stock of nights,
    Of days and years
    In silent flights
    Stole by our ears,
How ill have we ourselves bestowed
Whose suns are all set in a cloud?

3

Yet, come, and let's peruse them all;   20
    And as we pass,
What sins on every minute fall
    Score on the glass;

Then weigh and rate
Their heavy state
Until
The glass with tears you fill;
That done, we shall be safe and good,
Those beasts were clean, that chewed the cud.°

¶

Thou that know'st for whom I mourn,°
    And why these tears appear,
That keep'st account, till he return
    Of all his dust left here;
As easily thou mightst prevent
    As now produce these tears,
And add unto that day he went
    A fair supply of years.
But 'twas my sin that forced thy hand
    To cull this *primrose* out,   10
That by thy early choice forewarned
    My soul might look about.
O what a vanity is man!
    How like the eye's quick wink
His cottage fails; whose narrow span
    Begins even at the brink!
Nine months thy hands are fashioning us,
    And many years (alas!)
Ere we can lisp, or ought discuss
    Concerning thee, must pass;   20
Yet have I known thy slightest things,
    A *feather*, or a *shell*,°
A *stick*, or *rod* which some chance brings,
    The best of us excel,
Yea, I have known these shreds outlast
    A fair-compacted frame
And for one *twenty* we have past
    Almost outlive our name.
Thus hast thou placed in man's outside
    Death to the common eye,   30
That heaven within him might abide,

And close eternity;°
Hence, youth and folly (man's first shame)
   Are put unto the slaughter,
And serious thoughts begin to tame
   The wise-man's madness, *laughter*;°
Dull, wretched worms! that would not keep
   Within our first fair bed,
But out of Paradise must creep
   For ev'ry foot to tread;   40
Yet, had our pilgrimage been free,
   And smooth without a thorn,
Pleasures had foiled Eternity,
   And *tares* had choked the *corn*.°
Thus by the Cross Salvation runs,
   Affliction is a mother,
Whose painful throes yield many sons,
   Each fairer than the other;
A silent tear can pierce thy throne,°
   When loud joys want a wing,
And sweeter airs stream from a groan,°   50
   Than any arted string;
Thus, Lord, I see my gain is great,
   My loss but little to it,
Yet something more I must entreat
   And only thou canst do it.
O let me (like him) know my end!°
   And be as glad to find it,
And whatsoe'er thou shalt commend,
   Still let thy servant mind it!   60
Then make my soul white as his own,
   My faith as pure and steady,
And deck me, Lord, with the same crown
   Thou hast crowned him already!

Vanity of Spirit°

Quite spent with thoughts I left my cell, and lay
Where a shrill spring tuned to the early day.
   I begged here long, and groaned to know

Who gave the clouds so brave a bow,°
Who bent the spheres, and circled in
Corruption with this glorious ring,
What is his name, and how I might
Descry some part of his great light.
I summoned nature: pierced through all her store,°
Broke up some seals, which none had touched before,   10
   Her womb, her bosom, and her head
   Where all her secrets lay abed
   I rifled quite, and having passed
   Through all the Creatures, came at last
   To search myself, where I did find°
   Traces, and sounds of a strange kind.
Here of this mighty spring, I found some drills,°
With echoes beaten from th' eternal hills;
   Weak beams, and fires flashed to my sight,
   Like a young East, or moonshine night,   20
   Which showed me in a nook cast by
   A piece of much antiquity,
   With hieroglyphics quite dismembered,
   And broken letters scarce remembered.
I took them up, and (much joyed) went about
T' unite those pieces, hoping to find out
   The mystery; but this near done,
   That little light I had was gone:
   It grieved me much. At last, said I,
   Since in these veils my eclipsed eye   30
   May not approach thee (for at night
   Who can have commerce with the light?),
   I'll disapparel, and to buy
   But one half glance, most gladly die.

The Retreat°

   Happy those early days! when I
   Shined in my angel-infancy.
   Before I understood this place
   Appointed for my second race,°
   Or taught my soul to fancy ought

But a white, celestial thought,
When yet I had not walked above
A mile or two, from my first love,°
And looking back (at that short space)
Could see a glimpse of his bright face;   10
When on some *gilded cloud*, or *flower*
My gazing soul would dwell an hour,
And in those weaker glories spy
Some shadows of eternity;
Before I taught my tongue to wound
My conscience with a sinful sound,
Or had the black art to dispense
A sev'ral sin to ev'ry sense,
But felt through all this fleshly dress
Bright *shoots* of everlastingness.   20
   O how I long to travel back
And tread again that ancient track!
That I might once more reach that plain,
Where first I left my glorious train,
From whence th' inlightened spirit sees
That shady city of palm trees;°
But (ah!) my soul with too much stay°
Is drunk, and staggers in the way.
Some men a forward motion love,
But I by backward steps would move,   30
And when this dust falls to the urn
In that state I came return.

¶

Come, come, what do I here?
   Since he is gone°
Each day is grown a dozen year,
   And each hour, one;
   Come, come!
  Cut off the sum,
  By these soiled tears!
  (Which only thou
  Know'st to be true)
  Days are my fears.   10

2

There's not a wind can stir,
    Or beam pass by,
But straight I think (though far)
    Thy hand is nigh;
    Come, come!
    Strike these lips dumb:
    This restless breath
    That soils thy name,
    Will ne'er be tame
    Until in death.   20

3

Perhaps some think a tomb
    No house of store,
But a dark and sealed up womb,
    Which ne'er breeds more.
    Come, come!
    Such thoughts benumb;
    But I would be
    With him I weep
    Abed, and sleep
    To wake in thee.   30

Midnight

    When to my eyes
(Whilst deep sleep others catches)
    Thine host of spies
The stars shine in their watches,°
    I do survey
    Each busy ray,
And how they work and wind,
    And wish each beam
    My soul doth stream,
With the like ardour shined;   10
    What emanations,
    Quick vibrations
And bright stirs are there!

What thin ejections,
　　Cold affections,
And slow motions here!

2

　　Thy heav'ns (some say)
Are a fiery-liquid light,
　　Which mingling aye°
Streams, and flames thus to the sight.　　20
　　Come then, my God!
　　Shine on this blood°
And water in one beam
　　And thou shalt see
　　Kindled by thee
Both liquors burn and stream.
　　O what bright quickness,
　　Active brightness,
And celestial flows
　　Will follow after　　30
　　On that water,
Which thy spirit blows!

Math. Cap. 3. ver. xi

I indeed baptize you with water unto repentance, but he that cometh after me, is mightier than I, whose shoes I am not worthy to bear, he shall baptize you with the holy Ghost, and with fire.

Content

Peace, peace! I know 'twas brave,°
　　But this coarse fleece
I shelter in, is slave
　　To no such piece.°
　　When I am gone,
I shall no wardrobes leave°
　　To friend, or son
But what their own homes weave,

2

Such, though not proud, nor full,
    May make them weep,   10
And mourn to see the wool
    Outlast the sheep;
    Poor, pious wear!
Hadst thou been rich, or fine
    Perhaps that tear
Had mourned thy loss, not mine.

3

Why then these curled, puffed points,°
    Or a laced story?°
Death sets all out of joint
    And scorns their glory;   20
    Some love a *Rose*
In hand, some in the skin;
    But cross to those,°
I would have mine *within*.

¶

Joy of my life! while left me here,°
    And still my love!
How in thy absence thou dost steer
    Me from above!
    A life well led
    This truth commends,
    With quick or dead
    It never ends.

2

Stars are of mighty use: the night
    Is dark and long;   10
The road foul, and where one goes right,
    Six may go wrong.
    One twinkling ray
    Shot o'er some cloud,
    May clear much way
    And guide a crowd.

3

God's Saints are shining lights; who stays°
    Here long must pass
O'er dark hills, swift streams, and steep ways
    As smooth as glass;   20
    But these all night
    Like candles, shed
    Their beams, and light
    Us into bed.

4

They are (indeed) our pillar-fires°
    Seen as we go,
They are that City's shining spires°
    We travel to;
    A swordlike gleam°
    Kept man for sin   30
    First *Out*; this beam
    Will guide him *In*.

The Storm°

I see the use: and know my blood°
    Is not a sea,
But a shallow, bounded flood
    Though red as he;
Yet have I flows, as strong as his,
    And boiling streams that rave
With the same curling force and hiss,
    As doth the mountained wave.

2

But when his waters billow thus,
    Dark storms and wind   10
Incite them to that fierce discuss,°
    Else not inclined,
Thus the enlarged, enragèd air
    Uncalms these to a flood,
But still the weather that's most fair
    Breeds tempests in my blood;

3

Lord, then round me with weeping clouds,°
          And let my mind
In quick blasts sigh beneath those shrouds
          A spirit-wind,   20
So shall that storm purge this *Recluse*°
          Which sinful ease made foul,
And *wind* and *water* to thy use°
          Both *wash* and *wing* my soul.

Poems of Spiritual Regeneration

The Morning-watch°

un metaphysical

O joys! Infinite sweetness! with what flowers,°
And shoots of glory, my soul breaks and buds!
          All the long hours
          Of night and rest
          Through the still shrouds
          Of sleep and clouds,
     This dew fell on my breast;
          O how it *bloods*,
And *spirits* all my earth! hark! In what rings,   *Ptolemaic universe*
And *hymning circulations* the quick world°   10
          Awakes and sings;
          The rising winds,
          And falling springs,
          Birds, beasts, all things
          Adore him in their kinds.
          Thus all is hurled°   *world on edge of violence*
In sacred *hymns* and *order*, the great *chime*
And *symphony* of nature. Prayer is
          The world in tune,°
          A spirit-voice,   20
          And vocal joys
     Whose echo is heav'n's bliss.°
          O let me climb
When I lie down! The pious soul by night
Is like a clouded star, whose beams though said
          To shed their light
          Under some cloud
          Yet are above,

30

And shine and move
Beyond that misty shroud.
  So in my bed,
That curtained grave, though sleep, like ashes, hide
My lamp and life, both shall in thee abide.

metaphysical conceit [handwritten margin note]

The Evening-watch

A Dialogue

Farewell! I go to sleep; but when   *Body.*
The day-star springs, I'll wake again.°
 Go, sleep in peace; and when thou liest *Soul.*
Unnumbered in thy dust, when all this frame
Is but one dram, and what thou now descriest
 In sev'ral parts shall want a name,
Then may his peace be with thee, and each dust
Writ in his book, who ne'er betrayed man's trust!°
 Amen! but hark, ere we two stray,   *Body.*
 How many hours dost think till day?   10
 Ah! go; th'art weak and sleepy. Heav'n *Soul.*
Is a plain watch, and without figures winds
All ages up; who drew this circle even
 He fills it; days and hours are *blinds.*°
Yet, this take with thee; the last gasp of time
Is thy first breath, and man's *eternal prime.*°

¶°

Silence and stealth of days! 'tis now
  Since thou art gone,
Twelve hundred hours, and not a brow°
  But clouds hang on.
As he that in some cave's thick damp
  Locked from the light,
Fixeth a solitary lamp,
  To brave the night
And walking from his sun, when past°

That glimm'ring ray   10
Cuts through the heavy mists in haste
Back to his day,
So o'er fled minutes I retreat
Unto that hour
Which showed thee last, but did defeat
Thy light and pow'r.
I search and rack my soul to see
Those beams again,
But nothing but the snuff to me°
Appeareth plain;   20
That dark and dead sleeps in its known
And common urn,
But those fled to their Maker's throne,
There shine and burn;
O could I track them! but souls must
Track one the other,
And now the spirit, not the dust
Must be thy brother.
Yet I have one *Pearl* by whose light°
All things I see,   30
And in the heart of earth and night
Find Heaven and thee.

Church Service

Blest be the God of Harmony and Love!
The God above!
And holy dove!
Whose interceding, spiritual groans°
Make restless moans
For dust and stones,
For dust in every part,
But a hard, stony heart.

2

O how in this thy choir of souls I stand
(Propped by thy hand)   10
A heap of sand!

Which busy thoughts (like winds) would scatter quite
          And put to flight,
          But for thy might;
        Thy hand alone doth tame
        Those blasts, and knit my frame,

                3

So that both stones and dust, and all of me
          Jointly agree
          To cry to thee,
And in this music by thy Martyr's blood   20
          Sealed and made good
          Present, O God!
        The echo of these stones
        —My sighs and groans.°

Burial

      O thou! the first fruits of the dead°
              And their dark bed,
      When I am cast into that deep
              And senseless sleep
            The wages of my sin,°
              O then,
      Thou great Preserver of all men!
              Watch o'er that loose
              And empty house,
            Which I sometimes lived in.   10

                2

      It is (in truth!) a ruined piece
              Not worth thy eyes,
      And scarce a room but wind and rain
              Beat through and stain
            The seats and cells within;
              Yet thou
      Led by thy Love wouldst stoop thus low,
              And in this cot
              All filth and spot,
            Didst with thy servant inn.   20

3

And nothing can, I hourly see,
                    Drive thee from me,
Thou art the same, faithful and just
                    In life, or dust;
          Though then (thus crumbed) I stray
                    In blasts,
Or exhalations, and wastes
                    Beyond all eyes
                    Yet thy love spies
          That change, and knows thy clay.   30

4

The world's thy box: how then (there tossed)
                    Can I be lost?
But the delay is all; Time now
                    Is old and slow,
          His wings are dull and sickly;
                    Yet he
Thy servant is, and waits on thee;
                    Cut then the sum,
                    Lord haste, Lord come,
          O come Lord Jesus quickly!°   40

Rom. Cap. 8. ver. 23
*And not only they, but ourselves also, which have the first fruits of the
spirit, even we ourselves groan within ourselves, waiting for the adoption,
to wit, the redemption of our body.*

Cheerfulness

Lord, with what courage and delight
                    I do each thing
When thy least breath sustains my wing!
                    I shine and move
                    Like those above,
                    And (with much gladness
                    Quitting sadness)
Make me fair days of every night.

2

Affliction thus, mere pleasure is,
    And hap what will,   10
If thou be in't, 'tis welcome still;
    But since thy rays
    In sunny days
    Thou dost thus lend
    And freely spend,
Ah! what shall I return for this?

3

O that I were all Soul! that thou
    Wouldst make each part
Of this poor, sinful frame pure heart!
    Then would I drown   20
    My single one,
    And to thy praise°
    A consort raise°
Of *Hallelujahs* here below.

¶

Sure, there's a tie of bodies! and as they
    Dissolve (with it) to clay,
Love languisheth, and memory doth rust
    O'er-cast with that cold dust;
For things thus *centred*, without *beams*, or *action*°
    Nor give, nor take *contaction*,
And man is such a marigold, these fled,°
    That shuts, and hangs the head.

2

Absents within the line conspire, and *sense*°
    Things distant doth unite,   10
Herbs sleep unto the East, and some fowls thence
    Watch the returns of light;
But hearts are not so kind: false, short delights°
    Tell us the world is brave,
And wrap us in imaginary flights
    Wide of a faithful grave;

Thus Lazarus was carried out of town;°
    For 'tis our foe's chief art°
By distance all good objects first to drown,
    And then besiege the heart.   20
But I will be my own *Death's-head*; and though°
    The flatt'rer say, *I live*,
Because incertainties we cannot know
    Be sure, not to believe.

Peace

My soul, there is a country
    Far beyond the stars,
Where stands a wingèd sentry
    All skilful in the wars,
There above noise and danger
    Sweet peace sits crowned with smiles,
And one born in a manger
    Commands the beauteous files,
He is thy gracious friend,
    And (O my soul awake!)   10
Did in pure love descend
    To die here for thy sake,
If thou canst get but thither,
    There grows the flower of peace,
The Rose that cannot wither,
    Thy fortress and thy ease;
Leave then thy foolish ranges;
    For none can thee secure,
But one, who never changes,
    Thy God, thy life, thy cure.   20

The Passion

O my chief good!
My dear, dear God!
When thy blest blood
Did issue forth forced by the rod,°

What pain didst thou
Feel in each blow!
How didst thou weep,
And thyself steep
In thy own precious, saving tears!
What cruel smart   10
Did tear thy heart!
How didst thou groan it
In the spirit,
O thou, whom my soul loves and fears!

2

Most blessèd Vine!°
Whose juice so good
I feel as wine,
But thy fair branches felt as blood,
How wert thou pressed°
To be my feast!   20
In what deep anguish
Didst thou languish,
What springs of sweat and blood did drown thee!
How in one path
Did the full wrath
Of thy great Father
Crowd and gather,
Doubling thy griefs, when none would own thee!°

3

How did the weight
Of all our sins,   30
And death unite
To wrench and rack thy blessed limbs!
How pale and bloody
Looked thy body!
How bruised and broke
With every stroke!
How meek and patient was thy spirit!
How didst thou cry,
And groan on high
Father forgive,°   40
And let them live,
I die to make my foes inherit!

4

O blessèd Lamb!
That took'st my sin,
That took'st my shame
How shall thy dust thy praises sing!
I would I were
One hearty tear!
One constant spring!
Then would I bring   50
Thee two small mites, and be at strife°
Which should most vie,
My heart, or eye,
Teaching my years
In smiles and tears
To weep, to sing, thy *Death*, my *Life*.

Rom. Cap. 8. ver. 19

Etenim res creatae exerto capite observantes expectant revelationem
Filiorum Dei.°

And do they so? have they a sense
Of ought but influence?°
Can they their heads lift, and expect,°
And groan too? why th' Elect°
Can do no more: my volumes said
They were all dull and dead,
They judged them senseless, and their state
Wholly inanimate.
Go, go; seal up thy looks,
And burn thy books.   10

2

I would I were a stone, or tree,
Or flower by pedigree,
Or some poor highway herb, or spring
To flow, or bird to sing!
Then should I (tied to one sure state)
All day expect my date;
But I am sadly loose, and stray
A giddy blast each way;
O let me not thus range!
Thou canst not change.   20

3

Sometimes I sit with thee, and tarry
　　An hour, or so, then vary.
Thy other creatures in this scene
　　Thee only aim, and mean;
Some rise to seek thee, and with heads
　　Erect peep from their beds;
Others, whose birth is in the tomb,
　　And cannot quit the womb,
　　Sigh there, and groan for thee,
　　　Their liberty.　　　　　　　　　　　　30

4

O let not me do less! shall they
　　Watch, while I sleep, or play?
Shall I thy mercies still abuse
　　With fancies, friends, or news?
O brook it not! thy blood is mine,
　　And my soul should be thine;
O brook it not! why wilt thou stop
　　After whole showers one drop?
　　Sure, thou wilt joy to see°
　　　Thy sheep with thee.　　　　　　　　40

The Relapse

My God, how gracious art thou! I had slipped
　　　　Almost to hell,
And on the verge of that dark, dreadful pit
　　　　Did hear them yell,
But O thy love! thy rich, almighty love
　　　　That saved my soul,
And checked their fury, when I saw them move,
　　　　And heard them howl;
O my sole Comfort, take no more these ways,°
　　　　This hideous path,　　　　　　　10
And I will mend my own without delays,
　　　　Cease thou thy wrath!
I have deserved a thick, Egyptian damp,°

Dark as my deeds,
Should *mist* within me, and put out that lamp°
Thy spirit feeds;
A darting conscience full of stabs and fears;
No shade but *yew*,°
Sullen and sad eclipses, cloudy spheres,
These are my due.
But he that with his blood (a price too dear)   20
My scores did pay,°
Bid me, by virtue from him, challenge here°
The brightest day;
Sweet, downy thoughts; soft *lily*-shades; calm streams;°
Joys full and true;
Fresh, spicy mornings; and eternal teams:
These are his due.

The Resolve

I have considered it; and find°
A longer stay
Is but excused neglect. To mind°
One path, and stray
Into another, or to none,
Cannot be love;
When shall that traveller come home,
That will not move?
If thou wouldst thither, linger not,
Catch at the place,°   10
Tell youth and beauty they must rot,
They're but a *case*;°
Loose, parcelled hearts will freeze: the sun°
With scattered locks
Scarce warms, but by contraction
Can heat rocks;
Call in thy *powers*; run and reach°
Home with the light,
Be there, before the shadows stretch,
And *span* up night;°   20
Follow the *cry* no more: there is°

            An ancient way
All strewed with flowers and happiness°
            And fresh as May;
There turn, and turn no more; let wits
            Smile at fair eyes,
Or lips; but who there weeping sits,
            Hath got the *Prize.*

The Match

Dear friend! whose holy, ever-living lines°
            Have done much good
      To many, and have checked my blood,
My fierce, wild blood that still heaves and inclines,
            But is still tamed
      By those bright fires which thee inflamed;
Here I join hands, and thrust my stubborn heart
            Into thy *Deed,*°
      There from no *duties* to be freed,°
And if hereafter *youth,* or *folly* thwart°   10
            And claim their share,
      Here I renounce the pois'nous ware.

ii

Accept, dread Lord, the poor oblation,
            It is but poor,
      Yet through thy mercies may be more.
O thou! that canst not wish my soul's damnation,
            Afford me life,
      And save me from all inward strife!
Two *lifes* I hold from thee, my gracious Lord,°
            Both cost thee dear,   20
      For one, I am thy tenant here;
The other, the true life, in the next world
            And endless is,
      O let me still mind *that* in *this*!
To thee therefore my *Thoughts, Words, Actions*
            I do resign,
      Thy will in all be done, not mine.

Settle my *house*, and shut out all distractions°
      That may unknit
  My heart, and thee planted in it;   30
Lord Jesu! thou didst bow thy blessèd head°
      Upon a tree,
  O do as much, now unto me!
O hear and heal thy servant! Lord, strike dead
      All lusts in me,
  Who only wish life to serve thee!
Suffer no more this dust to overflow
      And drown my eyes,
  But seal, or pin them to thy skies.
And let this *grain* which here in tears I sow°   40
      Though *dead* and *sick*,
  Through thy *increase* grow *new* and *quick*.

Rules and Lessons°

When first thy eyes unveil, give thy soul leave
To do the like; our bodies but forerun
The spirit's duty; true hearts spread and heave
Unto their God, as flow'rs do to the sun.
  Give him thy first thoughts then; so shalt thou keep
  Him company all day, and in him sleep.

Yet, never sleep the sun up; prayer should
Dawn with the day; there are set, awful hours
'Twixt heaven and us; the *manna* was not good°
After sun-rising, far-day sullies flowers.   10
  Rise to prevent the sun; sleep doth sins glut,°
  And heav'ns gate opens, when this world's is shut.

Walk with thy fellow-creatures: note the *hush*
And *whispers* amongst them. There's not a *spring*,
Or *leaf* but hath his *morning-hymn*; Each *bush*
And *oak* doth know *I AM*; canst thou not sing?°
  O leave thy cares and follies! go this way
  And thou art sure to prosper all the day.

Serve God before the world; let him not go°
Until thou hast a blessing, then resign   20
The whole unto him; and remember who
Prevailed by *wrestling* ere the *sun* did *shine*.
     Pour *oil* upon the *stones*, weep for thy sin,°
     Then journey on, and have an eye to heav'n.

Mornings are *mysteries*; the first world's *youth*,
Man's *Resurrection*, and the future's *bud*
Shroud in their births: the Crown of life, light, truth°
Is styled their *star*, the *stone*, and *hidden food*.°
     Three *blessings* wait upon them, two of which
     Should move; they make us *holy*, *happy*, rich.   30

When the world's up, and ev'ry swarm abroad,
Keep thou thy temper, mix not with each clay;°
Dispatch necessities, life hath a load
Which must be carried on, and safely may.
     Yet keep those cares without thee, let the heart
     Be God's alone, and choose the better part.°

Through all thy *actions*, *counsels*, and *discourse*,
Let *mildness* and *Religion* guide thee out,
If truth be thine, what needs a brutish force?
But what's not *good* and *just* ne'er go about.   40
     Wrong not thy conscience for a rotten stick,
     That gain is dreadful, which makes spirits sick.

To God, thy Country, and thy friend be true,
If *priest*, and *people* change, keep thou thy ground.
Who sells Religion, is a Judas Jew,°
And, oaths once broke, the soul cannot be sound.
     The perjurer's a devil let loose: what can
     Tie up his hands, that dares mock God and man?

Seek not the same steps with the *crowd*; stick thou
To thy sure trot; a constant, humble mind°   50
Is both his own joy, and his Maker's too;
Let folly dust it on, or lag behind.
     A sweet *self-privacy* in a right soul
     Out-runs the Earth, and lines the utmost pole.

To all that seek thee, bear an open heart;
Make not thy breast a *Labyrinth*, or *trap*;
If trials come, this will make good thy part,
For honesty is safe, come what can hap;
     It is the good man's *feast*; the prince of flowers
     Which thrives in *storms*, and smells best after *showers*.   60

Seal not thy eyes up from the poor, but give
Proportion to their *merits*, and thy *purse*;
Thou may'st in rags a mighty Prince relieve°
Who, when thy sins call for't, can fence a Curse.°
     Thou shalt not lose one *mite*. Though waters stray,°
     The bread we cast returns in fraughts one day.°

Spend not an hour so, as to weep another,
For tears are not thine own; if thou giv'st words
Dash not thy *friend*, nor *Heav'n*; O smother
A vip'rous thought; some *syllables* are *swords*.   70
     Unbitted tongues are in their penance double,°
     They shame their *owners*, and the *hearers* trouble.

Injure not modest blood, whose *spirits* rise
In judgement against *lewdness*; that's base wit
That voids but *filth and stench*. Hast thou no prize°
But *sickness* or *infection*? stifle it.
     Who makes his jests of sins, must be at least
     If not a very *devil*, worse than a *beast*.

Yet, fly no friend, if he be such indeed,
But meet to quench his *longings*, and thy *thirst*;   80
Allow your joys *Religion*; that done, speed
And bring the same man back, thou wert at first.
     Who so returns not, cannot pray aright,
     But shuts his door, and leaves God out all night.

To heighten thy *devotions*, and keep low
All mutinous thoughts, what busines e'er thou hast
Observe God in his works; here *fountains* flow,
Birds sing, *beasts* feed, *fish* leap, and th' *Earth* stands fast;
     Above are restless *motions*, running *lights*,
     Vast circling *azure*, giddy *clouds*, days, nights.   90

When *seasons* change, then lay before thine eyes
His wondrous *Method*; mark the various *scenes*
In heav'n; *hail, thunder, rainbows, snow*, and *ice,*
Calms, tempests, light, and *darkness* by his means;
    Thou canst not miss his praise; each *tree, herb, flower*
    Are shadows of his *wisdom* and his pow'r.

To *meals* when thou dost come, give him the praise
Whose *Arm* supplied thee; take what may suffice,
And then be thankful; O admire his ways
Who fills the world's unemptied granaries!   100
    A thankless feeder is a *thief*, his feast
    A very *robbery*, and himself no *guest*.

High-noon thus past, thy time decays; provide
Thee other thoughts; away with friends and mirth;
The sun now stoops, and hastes his beams to hide
Under the dark and melancholy Earth.
    All but preludes thy End. Thou art the man
    Whose *rise, height*, and *descent* is but a span.°

Yet, set as he doth, and 'tis well. Have all
Thy beams home with thee: trim thy *lamp*, buy *oil*,°   110
And then set forth; who is thus dressed, the *Fall*
Furthers his glory, and gives death the foil.
    Man is a *summer's day*; whose *youth* and *fire*
    Cool to a glorious *evening*, and expire.

When night comes, list thy deeds; make plain the way
'Twixt Heaven and thee; block it not with delays,
But perfect all before thou sleep'st; then say
There's one sun more strung on my bead of days.
    What's good score up for joy; the bad well scanned
    Wash off with tears, and get thy *Master's* hand.   120

Thy accounts thus made, spend in the grave one hour
Before thy time; be not a stranger there
Where thou may'st sleep whole ages; life's poor flow'r
Lasts not a night sometimes. Bad spirits fear
    This conversation; but the good man lies°
    Intombèd many days before he dies.°

Being laid and dressed for sleep, close not thy eyes
Up with thy curtains; give thy soul the wing
In some good thoughts; so when the day shall rise
And thou *unrak'st* thy *fire*, those *sparks* will bring   130
    New *flames*; besides where these lodge vain *heats* mourn
    And die; that *bush* where God is, shall not burn.°

When thy *nap's* over, stir thy fire, unrake
In that *dead age*; one beam i' th' dark outvies°
Two in the day; then from the *damps* and *ache*
Of night shut up thy *leaves*, be chaste; God pries
    Through thickest nights; though then the sun be far
    Do thou the works of *day*, and rise a *star*.

Briefly, *Do as thou would'st be done unto*,°
Love God, and love thy neighbour; watch, and pray.   140
These are the *Words* and *Works* of life; this do,
And live; who doth not thus, hath lost *Heav'ns way.*
    O lose it not! look up, wilt change those *lights*
    For *chains* of *darkness* and *eternal nights*?

Corruption

    Sure, it was so. Man in those early days
        Was not all stone and earth,
He shined a little, and by those weak rays
        Had some glimpse of his birth.
He saw Heaven o'er his head, and knew from whence
        He came (condemned) hither,
And, as first love draws strongest, so from hence
        His mind sure progressed thither.
Things here were strange unto him: sweat and till,°
        All was a thorn, or weed,°   10
Nor did those last, but (like himself) died still
        As soon as they did *seed*;
They seemed to quarrel with him; for that Act
        That felled him, foiled them all,°
He drew the Curse upon the world, and cracked
        The whole frame with his fall.

This made him long for *home*, as loath to stay
    With murmurers and foes;
He sighed for Eden, and would often say
    Ah! what bright days were those!   20
Nor was Heav'n cold unto him; for each day
    The valley, or the mountain
Afforded visits, and still Paradise lay
    In some green shade, or fountain.
Angels lay *leiger* here; each bush and cell,°
    Each oak and highway knew them,
Walk but the fields, or sit down at some *well*,
    And he was sure to view them.
Almighty *Love*! where art thou now? mad man
    Sits down, and freezeth on,°   30
He raves, and swears to stir nor fire, nor fan,
    But bids the thread be spun.
I see, thy curtains are close-drawn; thy bow
    Looks dim too in the cloud,
Sin triumphs still, and man is sunk below
    The Centre and his shroud;°
All's in deep sleep and night; thick darkness lies°
    And hatcheth o'er thy people;°
But hark! what trumpet's that? what Angel cries°
    Arise! Thrust in thy sickle.   40

H. Scriptures

Welcome dear book, soul's joy and food! The feast
    Of spirits, Heav'n extracted lies in thee;
      Thou art life's charter, the Dove's spotless nest
Where souls are hatched unto Eternity.

In thee the hidden stone, the *manna* lies,°
    Thou art the great *elixir*, rare and choice;°
      The key that opens to all mysteries,
The *Word* in characters, God in the *Voice*.

O that I had deep cut in my hard heart°
    Each line in thee! Then would I plead in groans   10
    Of my Lord's penning, and by sweetest Art
Return upon himself the *Law*, and *stones*.°
    Read here, my faults are thine. This Book and I°
    Will tell thee so; *Sweet Saviour thou didst die!*

Unprofitableness°

How rich, O Lord! how fresh thy visits are!°
'Twas but just now my bleak leaves hopeless hung
    Sullied with dust and mud;
Each snarling blast shot through me, and did share°
Their youth and beauty, cold showers nipped and wrung
    Their spiciness and blood;
But since thou didst in one sweet glance survey
Their sad decays, I flourish, and once more
    Breathe all perfumes and spice;
I smell a dew like *myrrh*, and all the day   10
Wear in my bosom a full Sun; such store
    Hath one beam from thy eyes.
But, ah, my God! what fruit hast thou of this?
What one poor leaf did ever I yet fall
    To wait upon thy wreath?
Thus thou all day a thankless weed dost dress,
And when th' hast done, a stench, or fog is all
    The odour I bequeath.

Christ's Nativity

    Awake, glad heart! get up, and sing,
    It is the birthday of thy King,
        Awake! awake!
        The Sun doth shake
    Light from his locks, and all the way
    Breathing perfumes, doth spice the day.

2

Awake, awake! hark, how th' *wood* rings,°
Winds whisper, and the busy *springs*
    A consort make;°
    Awake, awake!   10
Man is their high-priest, and should rise°
To offer up the sacrifice.

3

I would I were some *bird*, or star,
Flutt'ring in woods, or lifted far
    Above this *inn*
    And road of sin!
Then either star, or *bird*, should be
Shining, or singing still to thee.

4

I would I had in my best part
Fit rooms for thee! or that my heart   20
    Were so clean as
    Thy manger was!
But I am all filth, and obscene,
Yet, if thou wilt, thou canst make clean.

5

Sweet Jesu! will then; let no more
This leper haunt and soil thy door,
    Cure him, ease him,
    O release him!
And let once more by mystic birth°
The Lord of life be born in earth.   30

II

How kind is heav'n to man! If here°
    One sinner doth amend
Straight there is joy, and ev'ry sphere
    In music doth contend;
And shall we then no voices lift?
    Are mercy and salvation
Not worth our thanks? Is life a gift

Of no more acceptation?
Shall he that did come down from thence,
    And here for us was slain,   40
Shall he be now cast off? no sense
    Of all his woes remain?
Can neither love, nor suff'rings bind?
    Are we all stone and earth?
Neither his bloody passions mind,°
    Nor one day bless his birth?
    Alas, my God! Thy birth now here
    Must not be numbered in the year.

The Check

Peace, peace! I blush to hear thee; when thou art
    A dusty story,
A speechless heap, and in the midst my heart
    In the same livery dressed
    Lies tame as all the rest;
When six years thence digged up, some youthful eye
    Seeks there for symmetry
But finding none, shall leave thee to the wind,
    Or the next foot to crush,
    Scatt'ring thy kind°   10
    And humble dust, tell then dear flesh°
    Where is thy glory?

2

As he that in the midst of day expects
    The hideous night,
Sleeps not, but shaking off sloth and neglects,
    Works with the sun, and sets,
    Paying the day its debts;
That (for repose and darkness bound) he might
    Rest from the fears i' th' night;
So should we too. All things teach us to die   20
    And point us out the way
    While we pass by
    And mind it not; play not away°
    Thy glimpse of light.

3

View thy fore-runners: creatures giv'n to be°
     Thy youth's companions,
Take their leave, and die; birds, beasts, each tree,
     All that have growth, or breath
     Have one large language, *Death*.
O then play not! but strive to him, who can   30
     Make these sad shades pure sun,
Turning their mists to beams, their damps to day,
     Whose pow'r doth so excel
        As to make clay
     A spirit, and true glory dwell
        In dust and stones.

4

Hark, how he doth invite thee! with what voice
     Of love and sorrow
He begs and calls; *O that in these thy days*
     Thou knew'st but thy own good!   40
     Shall not the cries of blood,
Of God's own blood awake thee? He bids beware
     Of drunkness surfeits, care,
But thou sleep'st on; where's now thy protestation,
     Thy lines, thy love? Away,
        Redeem the day,
     The day that gives no observation,
        Perhaps tomorrow.

Disorder and Frailty

When first thou didst even from the grave
And womb of darkness beckon out
My brutish soul, and to thy slave
Becam'st thyself, both guide and scout;
     Even from that hour
Thou gotst my heart; and though here tossed
     By winds, and bit with frost
     I pine, and shrink
     Breaking the link
'Twixt thee and me; and oft-times creep   10

Into th' old silence and dead sleep,
      Quitting thy way
      All the long day,
Yet, sure, my God! I love thee most.
    Alas, thy love!

2

I threaten heaven, and from my cell°
Of clay and frailty break and bud
Touched by thy fire and breath; thy blood
Too, is my dew, and springing well.
      But while I grow°   20
And stretch to thee, aiming at all
    Thy stars and spangled hall,
      Each fly doth taste,
      Poison, and blast
My yielding leaves; sometimes a show'r
Beats them quite off, and in an hour
      Not one poor shoot
      But the bare root
Hid under ground survives the fall.
    Alas, frail weed!   30

3

Thus like some sleeping exhalation°
(Which waked by heat and beams, makes up
Unto that comforter, the sun,
And soars and shines; but ere we sup
      And walk two steps,
Cooled by the damps of night, descends,
    And, whence it sprung, there ends)
      Doth my weak fire
      Pine and retire,
And (after all my height of flames)   40
In sickly expirations tames
      Leaving me dead
      On my first bed
Until thy Sun again ascends.
    Poor, falling star!

4

O, yes! but give wings to my fire,°
And hatch my soul, until it fly
Up where thou art, amongst thy tire°
Of stars, above infirmity;
      Let not perverse   50
And foolish thoughts add to my bill
      Of forward sins, and kill
         That seed, which thou
         In me didst sow,
But dress and water with thy grace,
Together with the seed, the place;
      And for his sake
      Who died to stake
His life for mine, tune to thy will
      My heart, my verse.   60

Hosea Cap. 6. ver. 4°

*O Ephraim what shall I do unto thee? O Judah how shall I intreat
thee? for thy goodness is as a morning cloud, and as the early dew it goeth
away.*

Idle Verse

Go, go, quaint follies, sugared sin,
      Shadow no more my door;
I will no longer cobwebs spin,
      I'm too much on the score.°

For since amidst my youth and night,°
      My great preserver smiles,
We'll make a match, my only light,°
      And join against their wiles;

Blind, desp'rate *fits*, that study how°
      To dress and trim our shame,   10
That gild rank poison, and allow
      Vice in a fairer name;

The *purls* of youthful blood and bowls,°
    Lust in the robes of love,
The idle talk of fev'rish souls
    Sick with a scarf, or glove;°

Let it suffice my warmer days
    Simpered and shined on you,°
Twist not my cypress with your bays,°
    Or roses with my yew;°   20

Go, go, seek out some greener thing,
    It snows, and freezeth here;
Let nightingales attend the spring,°
    Winter is all my year.

Son-days°

Bright shadows of true rest! some shoots of bliss,
    Heaven once a week;
The next world's gladness prepossessed in this;
    A day to seek
Eternity in time; the steps by which
We climb above all ages; lamps that light
Man through his heap of dark days; and the rich
And full redemption of the whole week's flight.

2

The pulleys unto headlong man; time's bower;°
    The narrow way;   10
Transplanted Paradise; God's walking hour;°
    The cool o' th' day;
The Creatures' *jubilee*; God's parle with dust;°
Heaven here; man on those hills of myrrh and flowers;
Angels descending; the returns of trust;
A gleam of glory, after six-days-showers.

3

The Church's love-feasts; time's prerogative
            And interest
Deducted from the whole; the combs and hive,
            And home of rest.   20
The milky way chalked out with suns; a clue
That guides through erring hours; and in full story
A taste of Heav'n on earth; the pledge and cue
Of a full feast; and the out-courts of glory.

Repentance

Lord, since thou didst in this vile clay
    That sacred ray
Thy spirit plant, quick'ning the whole
With that one grain's infusèd wealth,
My forward flesh creeped on, and subtly stole
Both growth and power; checking the health
And heat of thine: that little gate°
And narrow way, by which to thee
The passage is, he termed a grate
And entrance to captivity;   10
Thy laws but nets, where some small birds
(And those but seldom too) were caught,
Thy Promises but empty words
Which none but children heard, or taught.
This I believed: and though a friend
Came oft from far, and whispered, *No*;
Yet that not sorting to my end°
I wholly listened to my foe.
Wherefore, pierced through with grief, my sad
Seducèd soul sighs up to thee,   20
To thee who with true light art clad
And seest all things just as they be.
Look from thy throne upon this roll
Of heavy sins, my high transgressions,
Which I confess with all my soul,
My God, accept of my confession.
        It was last day

(Touched with the guilt of my own way)
I sate alone, and taking up
   The bitter cup,   30
Through all thy fair and various store
Sought out what might outvie my score.
  The blades of grass, thy Creatures feeding,
  The trees, their leafs; the flowers, their seeding;
  The dust, of which I am a part,
  The stones much softer than my heart,
  The drops of rain, the sighs of wind,
  The stars to which I am stark blind,
  The dew thy herbs drink up by night,
  The beams they warm them at i' th' light,   40
  All that have signature or life,°
  I summoned to decide this strife,
  And lest I should lack for arrears,
  A spring ran by, I told her tears,°
  But when these came unto the scale,
  My sins alone outweighed them all.
O my dear God! my life, my love!
Most blessèd lamb! and mildest dove!
Forgive your penitent offender,
And no more his sins remember,   50
Scatter these shades of death, and give
Light to my soul, that it may live;
Cut me not off for my transgressions,°
Wilful rebellions, and suppressions,
But give them in those streams a part
Whose spring is in my Saviour's heart.
Lord, I confess the heinous score,
And pray, I may do so no more;
Though then all sinners I exceed
O think on this; *Thy Son did bleed*;   60
O call to mind his wounds, his woes,
His Agony, and bloody throes;
Then look on all that thou hast made,
And mark how they do fail and fade,
The heavens themselves, though fair and bright,°
Are dark and unclean in thy sight,
How then, with thee, can man be holy°
Who dost thine angels charge with folly?

O what am I, that I should breed
Figs on a thorn, flowers on a weed!°   70
I am the gourd of sin and sorrow°
Growing o'er night, and gone tomorrow;
In all this *round* of life and death
Nothing's more vile than is my breath,
Profaneness on my tongue doth rest,°
Defects and darkness in my breast,
Pollutions all my body wed,
And even my soul to thee is dead,
Only in him, on whom I feast,°
Both soul and body are well dressed,   80
        His pure perfection quits all score,°
        And fills the boxes of his poor;
He is the Centre of long life and light,
I am but finite, He is Infinite.
O let thy *Justice* then in him confine,
And through his merits, make thy mercy mine!

The Burial of an Infant

Blest infant bud, whose blossom-life
Did only look about, and fall,
Wearied out in a harmless strife
Of tears and milk, the food of all;

Sweetly didst thou expire: thy soul
Flew home unstained by his new kin,
For ere thou knew'st how to be foul,
Death *weaned* thee from the world and sin.

Softly rest all thy virgin-crumbs!
Lapped in the sweets of thy young breath,   10
Expecting till thy Saviour comes°
To *dress* them, and *unswaddle* death.

Faith

Bright and blest beam! whose strong projection
    Equal to all,
Reacheth as well things of dejection
    As th' high and tall;
How hath my God by raying thee°
    Inlarged his spouse,°
And of a private family
    Made open house!
All may be now co-heirs; no noise°
    Of *bond*, or *free*°   10
Can interdict us from those joys
    That wait on thee,
The Law and Ceremonies made
    A glorious night,
Where stars and clouds, both light and shade
    Had equal right;
But, as in nature, when the day
    Breaks, night adjourns,
Stars shut up shop, mists pack away,
    And the moon mourns;   20
So when the Sun of righteousness
    Did once appear,
That scene was changed, and a new dress
    Left for us here;
Veils became useless, altars fell,
    Fires smoking die;
And all that sacred pomp and shell
    Of things did fly;
Then did he shine forth, whose sad fall
    And bitter fights   30
Were figured in those mystical°
    And cloudy rites;
And as i' th' natural sun, these three,
    Light, motion, heat,
So are now *Faith, Hope, Charity*
    Through him complete;
Faith spans up bliss; what sin and death°
    Put us quite from,

Lest we should run for't out of breath,
    Faith brings us home;   40
So that I need no more, but say
    I do believe,
And my most loving Lord straightway
    Doth answer, *Live.*

The Dawning°

Ah! what time wilt thou come? when shall that cry
  The Bridegroom's coming! fill the sky?°
    Shall it in the evening run
    When our words and works are done?
    Or will thy all-surprising light
      Break at midnight?
When either sleep, or some dark pleasure
Possesseth mad man without measure;
Or shall these early, fragrant hours
    Unlock thy bowers?   10
And with their blush of light descry
Thy locks crowned with eternity;
Indeed, it is the only time
That with thy glory doth best chime,
All now are stirring, ev'ry field
    Full hymns doth yield,
The whole Creation shakes off night,
And for thy shadow looks the light,
Stars now vanish without number,
Sleepy planets set and slumber,   20
The pursy clouds disband and scatter,
All expect some sudden matter,
Not one beam triumphs, but from far
    That morning-star;°

O at what time soever thou
(Unknown to us) the heavens wilt bow,
And, with thy angels in the *van*,
Descend to judge poor careless man,
Grant, I may not like puddle lie°

In a corrupt security,
Where, if a traveller water crave,
He finds it dead, and in a grave;
But as this restless, vocal *spring*
All day and night doth run and sing,
And though here born, yet is acquainted
Elsewhere, and flowing keeps untainted;
So let me all my busy age
In thy free services engage,
And though (while here) of force I must
Have commerce sometimes with poor dust,   40
And in my flesh, though vile and low,
As this doth in her channel flow,
Yet let my course, my aim, my love,
And chief acquaintance be above;
So when that day and hour shall come
In which thyself will be the Sun,
Thou'lt find me dressed and on my way,
Watching the break of thy great day.

Admission

How shrill are silent tears! when sin got head°
    And all my bowels turned°
To brass and iron; when my stock lay dead,°
    And all my powers mourned;
  Then did these drops (for marble sweats,
      And rocks have tears)
  As rain here at our windows beats,
      Chide in thine ears;

2

No quiet couldst thou have: nor didst thou wink,°
    And let thy beggar lie,°   10
But ere my eyes could overflow their brink
    Didst to each drop reply;
  Bowels of love! at what low rate,°
      And slight a price
  Dost thou relieve us at thy gate,
      And still our cries!

3

We are thy infants, and suck thee; if thou°
    But hide, or turn thy face,
Because where thou art, yet, we cannot go,
    We send tears to the place,   20
    These find thee out, and though our sins
        Drove thee away,
    Yet with thy love that absence wins
        Us double pay.

4

O give me then a thankful heart! a heart
    After thy own, not mine;
So after thine, that all and ev'ry part
    Of mine, may wait on thine;
    O hear! yet not my tears alone,°
        Hear now a flood,   30
    A flood that drowns both tears and groans,
        My Saviour's blood.

Praise°

    King of comforts! King of life!°
        Thou hast cheered me,
    And when fears and doubts were rife,
        Thou hast cleared me!

    Not a nook in all my breast
        But thou fill'st it,
    Not a thought, that breaks my rest,
        But thou kill'st it;

    Wherefore with my utmost strength°
        I will praise thee,
    And as thou giv'st line and length,   10
        I will raise thee;

    Day and night, not once a day°
        I will bless thee,
    And my soul in new array
        I will dress thee;

Not one minute in the year
    But I'll mind thee,
As my seal and bracelet here°
    I will bind thee;   20

In thy word, as if in heaven
    I will rest me,
And thy promise till made even
    There shall feast me.

Then, thy sayings all my life
    They shall please me,
And thy bloody wounds and strife
    They will ease me;

With thy groans my daily breath
    I will measure,   30
And my life hid in thy death
    I will treasure.

    Though then thou art
    Past thought of heart
All perfect fullness,
    And canst no whit
    Access admit
From dust and dullness;

    Yet to thy name
    (As not the same   40
With thy bright Essence)
    Our foul, clay hands
    At thy commands
Bring praise and incense;

    If then, dread Lord,
    When to thy board°
Thy wretch comes begging,
    He hath a flower
    Or (to his pow'r)°
Some such poor off'ring;   50

When thou hast made
Thy beggar glad,
And filled his bosom,
Let him (though poor)
Strow at thy door
That one poor blossom.

Dressing°

O thou that lovest a pure and whitened soul!
That feed'st among the lilies, till the day°
Break, and the shadows flee; touch with one coal°
My frozen heart; and with thy secret key°

Open my desolate rooms; my gloomy breast
With thy clear fire refine, burning to dust°
These dark confusions, that within me nest,
And soil thy Temple with a sinful rust.

Thou holy, harmless, undefiled high-priest!
The perfect, full oblation for all sin,   10
Whose glorious conquest nothing can resist,
But even in babes dost triumph still and win;°

Give to thy wretched one
Thy mystical *Communion*,
That, absent, he may see,
Live, die, and rise with thee;
Let him so follow here, that in the end
He may take thee, as thou dost him intend.
Give him thy private seal,°
Earnest, and sign; thy gifts so deal   20
That these forerunners here
May make the future clear;
Whatever thou dost bid, let faith make good,
Bread for thy body, and wine for thy blood.
Give him (with pity) love,
Two flowers that grew with thee above;
Love that shall not admit

Anger for one short fit,
And pity of such a divine extent
That may thy members, more than mine, resent.°   30

Give me, my God! thy grace,
The beams and brightness of thy face,
That never like a beast
I take thy sacred feast,
Or the dread mysteries of thy blest blood°
Use, with like custom, as my kitchen food.
Some sit to thee, and eat
Thy body as their common meat,
O let not me do so!
Poor dust should lie still low,   40
Then kneel my soul and body; kneel and bow;
If *Saints* and *Angels* fall down, much more thou.

Easter-day°

Thou, whose sad heart and weeping head lies low,
Whose cloudy breast cold damps invade,
Who never feel'st the Sun, nor smooth'st thy brow,
But sitt'st oppressèd in the shade,
Awake, awake,
And in his Resurrection partake,
Who on this day (that thou might'st rise as he)
Rose up, and cancelled two deaths due to thee.°

Awake, awake; and, like the Sun, disperse
All mists that would usurp this day;   10
Where are thy palms, thy branches, and thy verse?
Hosanna! hark, why dost thou stay?
Arise, arise,
And with his healing blood anoint thine eyes,
Thy inward eyes; his blood will cure thy mind,
Whose spittle only could restore the blind.°

Easter Hymn

Death and darkness get you packing,
Nothing now to man is lacking,
All your triumphs now are ended,
And what Adam marred is mended;
Graves are beds now for the weary,
Death a nap, to wake more merry;
Youth now, full of pious duty,
Seeks in thee for perfect beauty,
The weak and agèd, tired with length
Of days, from thee look for new strength,   10
And infants with thy pangs contest
As pleasant, as if with the breast;
    Then, unto him, who thus hath thrown
Even to contempt thy kingdom down,
And by his blood did us advance
Unto his own inheritance,
To him be glory, power, praise,
From this, unto the last of days.

The Holy Communion

Welcome sweet and sacred feast; welcome life!°
    Dead I was, and deep in trouble;
But grace and blessings came with thee so rife,
That they have quickened even dry stubble;°
    Thus souls their bodies animate,
    And thus, at first, when things were rude,°
       Dark, void, and crude,
They, by thy Word, their beauty had, and date;
      All were by thee,
      And still must be,   10
       Nothing that is, or lives,
    But hath his quick'nings and reprieves
      As thy hand opes, or shuts;
       Healings and cuts,
Darkness and daylight, life and death

Are but mere leaves turned by thy breath.
      Spirits without thee die,
      And blackness sits
      On the divinest wits,
As on the sun eclipses lie.   20
But that great darkness at thy death°
When the veil broke with thy last breath,
      Did make us see
      The way to thee;
And now by these sure, sacred ties,
      After thy blood
      (Our sov'reign good)
      Had cleared our eyes,
      And given us sight;
Thou dost unto thyself betroth   30
      Our souls and bodies both
      In everlasting light.

Was't not enough that thou hadst paid the price°
      And given us eyes
When we had none, but thou must also take°
      Us by the hand
      And keep us still awake,
      When we would sleep,
      Or from thee creep,
Who without thee cannot stand?   40

Was't not enough to lose thy breath
And blood by an accursèd death,
      But thou must also leave
      To us that did bereave
Thee of them both, these seals the means
      That should both cleanse
      And keep us so,
      Who wrought thy woe?
O rose of Sharon! O the lily°
      Of the valley!   50
How art thou now, thy flock to keep,
Become both *food* and *Shepherd* to thy sheep.

Psalm 121°

Up to those bright and gladsome hills
    Whence flows my weal and mirth,
I look and sigh for him, who fills
    (Unseen) both heaven and earth.

He is alone my help and hope,
    That I shall not be moved,
His watchful eye is ever ope,
    And guardeth his beloved;

The glorious God is my sole stay,
    He is my sun and shade,   10
The cold by night, the heat by day,
    Neither shall me invade.

He keeps me from the spite of foes,
    Doth all their plots control,
And is a shield (not reckoning those)
    Unto my very soul.

Whether abroad, amidst the crowd,
    Or else within my door,
He is my pillar and my cloud,°
    Now, and for evermore.   20

Affliction°

Peace, peace; it is not so. Thou dost miscall
    Thy physic; pills that change°
Thy sick accessions into settled health,°
This is the great *Elixir* that turns gall°
To wine and sweetness; poverty to wealth,
  And brings man home, when he doth range.
  Did not he, who ordained the day,
      Ordain night too?
  And in the greater world display

What in the lesser he would do?   10
All flesh is clay, thou know'st; and but that God
        Doth use his rod,
And by a fruitful change of frosts and showers
    Cherish and bind thy *pow'rs*,
Thou wouldst to weeds and thistles quite disperse,
    And be more wild than is thy verse;
Sickness is wholesome, and crosses are but curbs
    To check the mule, unruly man,
They are heaven's husbandry, the famous fan°
    Purging the floor which chaff disturbs.   20
Were all the year one constant sunshine, we
        Should have no flowers,
All would be drought and leanness; not a tree
        Would make us bowers;
Beauty consists in colours; and that's best
    Which is not fixed, but flies and flows;
The settled *red* is dull, and *whites* that rest
    Something of sickness would disclose.
    Vicissitude plays all the game,°
        Nothing that stirs,   30
        Or hath a name,
    But waits upon this wheel,
Kingdoms too have their physic, and for steel,
    Exchange their peace and furs.
Thus doth God *key* disordered man°
    (Which none else can)
Tuning his breast to rise or fall;°
And by a sacred, needful art,
Like strings, stretch ev'ry part
Making the whole most musical.   40

The Tempest

How is man parcelled out! how ev'ry hour°
    Shows him himself, or something he should see!
    This late, long heat may his instruction be,
And tempests have more in them than a shower.

When nature on her bosom saw°
     Her infants die,
And all her flowers withered to straw,
     Her breasts grown dry;
She made the Earth, their nurse and tomb,
     Sigh to the sky,   10
Till to those sighs fetched from her womb
     Rain did reply,
So in the midst of all her fears
     And faint requests
Her earnest sighs procured her tears
     And filled her breasts.

O that man could do so! that he would hear
    The world read to him! all the vast expense
    In the Creation shed and slaved to sense
Makes up but lectures for his eye and ear.   20

Sure, mighty love foreseeing the descent
    Of this poor Creature, by a gracious art
    Hid in these low things snares to gain his heart,
And laid surprises in each element.

All things here show him heaven; *waters* that fall
    Chide and fly up; *mists* of corruptest foam
    Quit their first beds and mount; trees, herbs, flowers, all
Strive upwards still, and point him the way home.

How do they cast off grossness? only *earth*
    And *man* (like Issachar) in loads delight,°   30
    Water's refined to *motion*, air to *light*,
Fire to all three, but man hath no such mirth.°

Plants in the *root* with earth do most comply,°
    Their *leafs* with water and humidity,
    The *flowers* to air draw near, and subtlety,°
And *seeds* a kinred fire have with the sky.°

All have their *keys* and set *ascents*; but man°
    Though he knows these, and hath more of his own,
    Sleeps at the ladder's foot; alas! what can°
These new discoveries do, except they drown?   40

Thus grovelling in the shade and darkness, he
    Sinks to a dead oblivion; and though all
    He sees (like *Pyramids*) shoot from this ball
And less'ning still grow up invisibly,

Yet hugs he still his dirt; the *stuff* he wears°
    And painted trimming takes down both his eyes,
    Heaven hath less beauty than the dust he spies,
And money better music than the *spheres*.

Life's but a blast, he knows it; what? shall straw°
    And bulrush-fetters temper his short hour?   50
    Must he nor sip, nor sing? grows ne'er a flower
To crown his temples? shall dreams be his law?

O foolish man! how hast thou lost thy sight?°
    How is it that the sun to thee alone
    Is grown thick darkness, and thy bread, a stone?°
Hath flesh no softness now? mid-day no light?

Lord! thou didst put a soul here; if I must
    Be broke again, for flints will give no fire°
    Without a steel, O let thy power clear
Thy gift once more, and grind this flint to dust!   60

Retirement

Who on yon throne of azure sits,
    Keeping close house
Above the morning-star,
    Whose meaner shows,
And outward utensils these glories are
    That shine and share
Part of his mansion; he one day
    When I went quite astray
Out of mere love
    By his mild Dove   10
Did show me home, and put me in the way.

2

Let it suffice at length thy fits
    And lusts (said he)
  Have had their wish and way;°
    Press not to be
Still thy own foe and mine; for to this day
    I did delay,
And would not see, but chose to wink,
    Nay, at the very brink
    And edge of all
    When thou wouldst fall
My *love-twist* held thee up, my *unseen link*.°

20

3

I know thee well; for I have framed
    And hate thee not,
  Thy spirit too is mine;
    I know thy lot,
Extent, and end, for my hands drew the line
    Assignèd thine;
If then thou would'st unto my seat,
  'Tis not th' applause and feat
    Of dust and clay
    Leads to that way,
But from those follies a resolved Retreat.

30

4

Now here below where yet untamed
    Thou dost thus rove
  I have a house as well°
    As there above,
In it my *Name* and *honour* both do dwell
    And shall until
I make all new; there nothing gay°
    In perfumes or array,
    Dust lies with dust
    And hath but just
The same respect and room, with ev'ry clay.

40

5

A faithful school where thou mayst see°
In heraldry
Of stones and speechless earth
Thy true descent;
Where dead men preach, who can turn feasts and mirth
To funerals and *Lent*.   50
There dust that out of doors might fill°
Thy eyes, and blind thee still,
Is fast asleep;
Up then, and keep
Within those doors (my doors), dost hear? *I will*.

Love and Discipline

Since in a land not barren still
(Because thou dost thy grace distil)
My lot is fall'n, blest be thy will!°

And since these biting frosts but kill
Some tares in me which choke, or spill°
That seed thou sow'st, blest be thy skill!

Blest be thy dew, and blest thy frost,
And happy I to be so crossed,
And cured by crosses at thy cost.

The dew doth cheer what is distressed,   10
The frosts ill weeds nip and molest,
In both thou work'st unto the best.

Thus while thy sev'ral mercies plot,
And work on me now cold, now hot,
The work goes on, and slacketh not,

For as thy hand the weather steers,
So thrive I best, 'twixt joys and tears,°
And all the year have some green ears.

The Pilgrimage

As travellers when the twilight's come,
And in the sky the stars appear,
The past day's accidents do sum°
With, *Thus we saw there, and thus here*;

Then Jacob-like lodge in a place°
(A place, and no more, is set down)
Where till the day restore the race
They rest and dream homes of their own:

So for this night I linger here,
And full of tossings to and fro,   10
Expect still when thou wilt appear
That I may get me up, and go.

I long, and groan, and grieve for thee,
For thee my words, my tears do gush,
O that I were but where I see!
Is all the note within my bush.

As birds robbed of their native wood,
Although their diet may be fine,
Yet neither sing, nor like their food,
But with the thought of home do pine: 20

So do I mourn, and hang my head,
And though thou dost me fullness give,
Yet look I for far better bread°
Because by this man cannot live.

O feed me then! and since I may
Have yet more days, more nights to count,
So strengthen me, Lord, all the way,
That I may travel to thy Mount.

Heb. Cap. xi. ver. 13
And they confessed, that they were strangers and pilgrims on the earth.

The Law and the Gospel

Lord, when thou didst on Sinai pitch°
And shine from Paran, when a fiery Law°
Pronounced with thunder, and thy threats did thaw
Thy people's hearts, when all thy weeds were rich°
    And inaccessible for light;
        Terror and might,
How did poor flesh (which after thou didst wear)
        Then faint and fear!
Thy chosen flock, like leafs in a high wind,
Whispered obedience, and their heads inclined.   10

2

    But now since we to Sion came,
And through thy blood thy glory see,
With filial confidence we touch ev'n thee;
And where the other mount all clad in flame
    And threat'ning clouds would not so much
        As bide the touch,
We climb up this, and have too all the way
        Thy hand our stay,
Nay, thou tak'st ours, and (which full comfort brings)
Thy Dove too bears us on her sacred wings.   20

3

    Yet since man is a very brute
And after all thy Acts of grace doth kick,
Slighting that health thou gav'st, when he was sick,
Be not displeased, if I, who have a suit
    To thee each hour, beg at thy door
        For this one more;
O plant in me thy *Gospel* and thy *Law*,
        Both *Faith* and *Awe*;
So twist them in my heart, that ever there
I may as well as *love*, find too thy *fear*!   30

4

Let me not spill, but drink thy blood,
Not break thy fence, and by a black excess
Force down a just curse, when thy hands would bless;
Let me not scatter and despise my food,
    Or nail those blessèd limbs again
      Which bore my pain;
So shall thy mercies flow: for while I fear,
      I know, thou'lt bear,
But should thy mild injunction nothing move me,
I would both think and judge I did not love thee.   40

John Cap. 14. ver. 15
If ye love me, keep my commandments.

The World

I saw Eternity the other night°
Like a great *Ring* of pure and endless light,
    All calm, as it was bright,
And round beneath it, Time in hours, days, years
      Driv'n by the spheres
Like a vast shadow moved, in which the world
      And all her train were hurled;
The doting lover in his quaintest strain°
      Did there complain,
Near him, his lute, his fancy, and his flights,   10
      Wit's sour delights,
With gloves and knots, the silly snares of pleasure,
      Yet his dear treasure
All scattered lay, while he his eyes did pore°
      Upon a flower.

2

The darksome statesman hung with weights and woe
Like a thick midnight-fog moved there so slow
    He did not stay, nor go;
Condemning thoughts (like sad eclipses) scowl
      Upon his soul,   20

And clouds of crying witnesses without
    Pursued him with one shout.
Yet digged the mole, and lest his ways be found°
    Worked under ground,
Where he did clutch his prey, but one did see
    That policy,
Churches and altars fed him, perjuries
    Were gnats and flies,
It rained about him blood and tears, but he
    Drank them as free.   30

3

The fearful miser on a heap of rust
Sate pining all his life there, did scarce trust
    His own hands with the dust,
Yet would not place one piece above, but lives
    In fear of thieves.
Thousands there were as frantic as himself
    And hugged each one his pelf,
The downright epicure placed heav'n in sense
    And scorned pretence
While others slipped into a wide excess   40
    Said little less;
The weaker sort slight, trivial wares inslave
    Who think them brave,
And poor, despisèd truth sate counting by°
    Their victory.

4

Yet some, who all this while did weep and sing,°
And sing and weep, soared up into the *Ring*,
    But most would use no wing.
O fools (said I) thus to prefer dark night
    Before true light,   50
To live in grots and caves, and hate the day
    Because it shows the way,
The way which from this dead and dark abode
    Leads up to God,
A way where you might tread the sun, and be
    More bright than he.

But as I did their madness so discuss
       One whispered thus,
This Ring the Bridegroom did for none provide°
       But for his bride.   60

[I] John Cap. 2. ver. 16, 17
All that is in the world, the lust of the flesh, the lust of the eyes, and the
pride of life, is not of the father, but is of the world.
   And the world passeth away, and the lusts thereof, but he that doth the
will of God abideth for ever.

The Mutiny

Weary of this same clay and straw, I laid°
Me down to breathe, and casting in my heart
The after-burthens and griefs yet to come,
       The heavy sum
So shook my breast, that (sick and sore dismayed)
My thoughts, like water which some stone doth start,°
Did quit their troubled channel, and retire
Unto the banks, where, storming at those bounds,
They murmured sore; but I, who felt them boil
       And knew their coil,°   10
Turning to him, who made poor sand to tire°
And tame proud waves, If yet these barren grounds
       And thirsty brick must be (said I)
       My task and destiny,

2

Let me so strive and struggle with thy foes
(Not thine alone, but mine too) that when all
Their arts and force are built unto the height
       That Babel-weight°
May prove thy glory and their shame; so close
And knit me to thee, that though in this vale   20
Of sin and death I sojourn, yet one eye
May look to thee, to thee the finisher°
And Author of my faith; so show me home
       That all this foam

And frothy noise which up and down doth fly
May find no lodging in mine eye or ear,
  O seal them up! that these may fly
   Like other tempests by.

3

Not but I know thou hast a shorter cut
To bring me home, than through a wilderness,°   30
A sea, or sands and serpents; yet since thou
  (As thy words show)
Though in this desert I were wholly shut,
Canst light and lead me there with such redress
That no decay shall touch me; O be pleased
To fix my steps, and whatsoever path
Thy sacred and eternal will decreed
  For thy bruised reed°
O give it full obedience, that so seized°
Of all I have, I may nor move thy wrath   40
  Nor grieve thy *Dove*, but soft and mild
   Both live and die thy Child.

Revel. Cap. 2. ver. 17
*To him that overcometh will I give to eat of the hidden manna, and I
will give him a white stone, and in the stone a new name written, which
no man knoweth, saving he that receiveth it.*

The Constellation

Fair, ordered lights (whose motion without noise
  Resembles those true joys
Whose spring is on that hill where you do grow
  And we here taste sometimes below)

With what exact obedience do you move
  Now beneath and now above,
And in your vast progressions overlook
  The darkest night and closest nook!

Some nights I see you in the gladsome East,
    Some others near the West,   10
And when I cannot see, yet do you shine
    And beat about your endless line.

Silence, and light, and watchfulness with you
    Attend and wind the clue,°
No sleep, nor sloth assails you, but poor man
    Still either sleeps, or slips his span.°

He gropes beneath here, and with restless care
    First makes, then hugs a snare,
Adores dead dust, sets heart on corn and grass,
    But seldom doth make heav'n his glass.   20

Music and mirth (if there be music here)°
    Take up and tune his year,
These things are kin to him, and must be had,
    Who kneels, or sighs a life is mad.

Perhaps some nights he'll watch with you, and peep
    When it were best to sleep,
Dares know effects, and judge them long before,°
    When th' herb he treads knows much, much more.

But seeks he your *obedience, order, light*,
    Your calm and well-trained flight,   30
Where, though the glory differ in each star,°
    Yet is there peace still, and no war?

Since placed by him who calls you by your names°
    And fixed there all your flames,
Without command you never acted ought
    And then you in your courses fought.°

But here commissioned by a black self-will°
    The sons the father kill,
The children chase the mother, and would heal
    The wounds they give, by crying, zeal;   40

Then cast her blood and tears upon thy book
    Where they for fashion look,
And like that lamb which had the dragon's voice°
    Seem mild, but are known by their noise.

Thus by our lusts disordered into wars
    Our guides prove wand'ring stars,
Which for these mists and black days were reserved,
    What time we from our first love swerved.

Yet O for his sake who sits now by thee
    All crowned with victory,   50
So guide us through this darkness, that we may
    Be more and more in love with day;

Settle and fix our hearts, that we may move
    In order, peace, and love,
And taught obedience by thy whole Creation,
    Become an humble, holy nation.

Give to thy spouse her perfect and pure dress,
    Beauty and *holiness*,
And so repair these rents, that men may see°
    And say, *Where God is, all agree.*   60

The Shepherds

Sweet, harmless lives! (on whose holy leisure°
    Waits innocence and pleasure)
Whose leaders to those pastures and clear springs,
    Were Patriarchs, Saints, and Kings,
How happened it that in the dead of night°
    You only saw true light,
While Palestine was fast asleep, and lay
    Without one thought of day?
Was it because those first and blessed swains°
    Were pilgrims on those plains   10
When they received the promise, for which now
    'Twas there first shown to you?
'Tis true, he loves that dust whereon they go
    That serve him here below,

And therefore might for memory of those
    His love there first disclose;
But wretched Salem, once his love, must now°
    No voice, nor vision know,
Her stately piles with all their height and pride
    Now languishèd and died,   20
And Bethlem's humble cots above them stept°
    While all her seers slept;
Her cedar, fir, hewed stones and gold were all°
    Polluted through their fall,
And those once sacred mansions were now
    Mere emptiness and show;
This made the Angel call at reeds and thatch,
    Yet where the shepherds watch,
And God's own lodging (though he could not lack)
    To be a common *rack*;°   30
No costly pride, no soft-clothed luxury
    In those thin cells could lie,
Each stirring wind and storm blew through their cots
    Which never harboured plots,
Only content, and love, and humble joys
    Lived there without all noise,
Perhaps some harmless cares for the next day
    Did in their bosoms play,
As where to lead their sheep, what silent nook,
    What springs or shades to look,   40
But that was all; and now with gladsome care
    They for the town prepare,
They leave their flock, and in a busy talk
    All towards Bethlem walk
To see their souls' great shepherd, who was come
    To bring all stragglers home,
Where now they find him out, and taught before
    That Lamb of God adore,
That Lamb whose days great Kings and Prophets wished
    And longed to see, but missed.   50
The first light they beheld was bright and gay
    And turned their night to day,
But to this later light they saw in him,°
    Their day was dark and dim.

Misery

Lord, bind me up, and let me lie
A pris'ner to my liberty,
If such a state at all can be
As an impris'ment serving thee;
The wind, though gathered in thy fist,°
Yet doth it blow still where it list,°
And yet shouldst thou let go thy hold
Those gusts might quarrel and grow bold.
   As waters here, headlong and loose
The lower grounds still chase and choose,   10
Where spreading all the way they seek
And search out ev'ry hole and creek;
So my spilt thoughts winding from thee
Take the down-road to vanity,
Where they all stray and strive, which shall
Find out the first and steepest fall;
I cheer their flow, giving supply
To what's already grown too high,
And having thus performed that part
Feed on those vomits of my heart.   20
I break the fence my own hands made
Then lay that trespass in the shade,
Some fig-leafs still I do devise°
As if thou hadst nor ears nor eyes.
Excess of friends, of words, and wine
Take up my day, while thou dost shine
All unregarded, and thy book
Hath not so much as one poor look.
If thou steal in amidst the mirth
And kindly tell me, *I am earth*,   30
I shut thee out, and let that slip,
Such music spoils good fellowship.
Thus wretched I, and most unkind,
Exclude my dear God from my mind,
Exclude him thence, who of that cell
Would make a court, should he there dwell.°
He goes, he yields; and troubled sore
His holy spirit grieves therefore,°

The mighty God, th' eternal King
Doth grieve for dust, and dust doth sing.   40
But I go on, haste to devest°
Myself of reason, till oppressed
And buried in my surfeits I
Prove my own shame and misery.
Next day I call and cry for thee
Who shouldst not then come near to me,
But now it is thy servant's pleasure
Thou must (and dost) give him his measure.
Thou dost, thou com'st, and in a shower
Of healing sweets thyself dost pour   50
Into my wounds, and now thy grace
(I know it well) fills all the place;
I sit with thee by this new light,
And for that hour th'art my delight,
No man can more the world despise
Or thy great mercies better prize.
I school my eyes, and strictly dwell°
Within the circle of my cell,
That calm and silence are my joys
Which to thy peace are but mere noise.   60
At length I feel my head to ache,
My fingers itch and burn to take
Some new employment, I begin
To swell and foam and fret within.
    '*The Age, the present times, are not*
    To snudge in, and embrace a cot,°
    Action and blood now get the game,
    Disdain treads on the peaceful name,
    Who sits at home too bears a load
    Greater than those that gad abroad.'   70
Thus do I make thy gifts giv'n me
The only quarrellers with thee,
I'd loose those knots thy hands did tie,
Then would go travel, fight or die.°
Thousands of wild and waste infusions
Like waves beat on my resolutions,
As flames about their fuel run°
And work and wind till all be done,
So my fierce soul bustles about

And never rests till all be out.   80
Thus wilded by a peevish heart
Which in thy music bears no part
I storm at thee, calling my peace
A lethargy and mere disease,
Nay, those bright beams shot from thy eyes
To calm me in these mutinies
I style mere tempers, which take place°
At some set times, but are thy grace.
    Such is man's life, and such is mine,
The worst of men, and yet still thine,   90
Still thine thou know'st, and if not so
Then give me over 'to my foe.
Yet since as easy 'tis for thee
To make man good, as bid him be,
And with one glance (could he that gain)
To look him out of all his pain,°
O send me from thy holy hill
So much of strength, as may fulfil
All thy delight (whate'er they be)
And sacred institutes in me;   100
Open my rocky heart, and fill
It with obedience to thy will,
Then seal it up, that as none see,
So none may enter there but thee.
    O hear my God! hear him, whose blood
Speaks more and better for my good!
O let my cry come to thy throne!
My cry not poured with tears alone,
(For tears alone are often foul)
But with the blood of all my soul,   110
With spirit-sighs and earnest groans,
Faithful and most repenting moans,
With these I cry, and crying pine
Till thou both mend and make me thine.°

The Sap°

Come sapless blossom, creep not still on Earth
　　Forgetting thy first birth;
'Tis not from dust, or if so, why dost thou
　　Thus call and thirst for dew?
It tends not thither, if it doth, why then
　　This growth and stretch for heav'n?
Thy root sucks but diseases, worms there seat°
　　And claim it for their meat.
Who placed thee here, did something then infuse
　　Which now can tell thee news.　　　　　　　　10
There is beyond the stars an hill of myrrh°
　　From which some drops fall here,
On it the Prince of Salem sits, who deals°
　　To thee thy secret meals,
There is thy country, and he is the way
　　And hath withal the key.
Yet lived he here sometimes, and bore for thee
　　A world of misery,
For thee, who in the first man's loins didst fall
　　From that hill to this vale,　　　　　　　　20
And had not he so done, it is most true
　　Two deaths had been thy due;°
But going hence, and knowing well what woes
　　Might his friends discompose,
To show what strange love he had to our good°
　　He gave his sacred blood°
By will our sap and cordial; now in this
　　Lies such a heav'n of bliss,
That, who but truly tastes it, no decay°
　　Can touch him any way,　　　　　　　　　　30
Such secret life and virtue in it lies
　　It will exalt and rise
And actuate such spirits as are shed
　　Or ready to be dead,
And bring new too. Get then this sap, and get
　　Good store of it, but let
The vessel where you put it be for sure
　　To all your pow'r most pure;

There is at all times (though shut up) in you
    A powerful, rare dew,°   40
Which only grief and love extract; with this
    Be sure, and never miss,
To wash your vessel well: then humbly take
    This balm for souls that ache,
And one who drank it thus, assures that you°
    Shall find a joy so true,
Such perfect ease, and such a lively sense
    Of grace against all sins,
That you'll confess the comfort such, as even
    Brings to, and comes from Heaven.   50

Mount of Olives (II)°

When first I saw true beauty, and thy joys°
Active as light, and calm without all noise
Shined on my soul, I felt through all my powers
Such a rich air of sweets, as evening showers°
Fanned by a gentle gale convey and breathe
On some parched bank, crowned with a flow'ry wreath;
Odours, and myrrh, and balm in one rich flood
O'er-ran my heart, and spirited my blood,
My thoughts did swim in comforts, and mine eye
Confessed, *The world did only paint and lie.*   10
And where before I did no safe course steer
But wandered under tempests all the year,°
Went bleak and bare in body as in mind,
And was blown through by ev'ry storm and wind,°
I am so warmed now by this glance on me,
That, midst all storms I feel a ray of thee;
So have I known some beauteous *paisage* rise
In sudden flowers and arbours to my eyes,
And in the depth and dead of winter bring
To my cold thoughts a lively sense of spring.   20
   Thus fed by thee, who dost all beings nourish,
My withered leafs again look green and flourish,
I shine and shelter underneath thy wing
Where sick with love I strive thy name to sing,
Thy glorious name! which grant I may so do
That these may be thy *praise*, and my *joy* too.

Man

Weighing the steadfastness and state
Of some mean things which here below reside,
Where birds like watchful clocks the noiseless date
　　And intercourse of times divide,
Where bees at night get home and hive, and flowers
　　　　Early, as well as late,
Rise with the sun, and set in the same bowers;

2

I would (said I) my God would give
The staidness of these things to man! for these
To his divine appointments ever cleave,　　　　　　　10
　　And no new business breaks their peace;
The birds nor sow, nor reap, yet sup and dine,
　　　　The flowers without clothes live,
Yet Solomon was never dressed so fine.

3

Man hath still either toys or care,
He hath no root, nor to one place is tied,
But ever restless and irregular
　　About this Earth doth run and ride,
He knows he hath a home, but scarce knows where,
　　　　He says it is so far　　　　　　　　　　　　20
That he hath quite forgot how to go there.

4

He knocks at all doors, strays and roams,
Nay hath not so much wit as some stones have°
Which in the darkest nights point to their homes,
　　By some hid sense their Maker gave;
Man is the shuttle, to whose winding quest
　　　　And passage through these looms
God ordered motion, but ordained no rest.

¶

I walked the other day (to spend my hour)°
    Into a field
Where I sometimes had seen the soil to yield
    A gallant flower,°
But winter now had ruffled all the bower°
    And curious store
    I knew there heretofore.

2

Yet I whose search loved not to peep and peer
    I' th' face of things
Thought with myself, there might be other springs   10
    Besides this here
Which, like cold friends, sees us but once a year,
    And so the flower
    Might have some other bower.

3

Then taking up what I could nearest spy
    I digged about
That place where I had seen him to grow out,
    And by and by
I saw the warm Recluse alone to lie°
    Where fresh and green   20
    He lived of us unseen.

4

Many a question intricate and rare
    Did I there strow,
But all I could extort was, that he now
    Did there repair
Such losses as befell him in this air
    And would ere long
    Come forth most fair and young.

5

This past, I threw the clothes quite o'er his head,
    And stung with fear 30
Of my own frailty dropped down many a tear
    Upon his bed,
Then sighing whispered, *Happy are the dead!*
    What peace doth now
    Rock him asleep below!

6

And yet, how few believe such doctrine springs
    From a poor root
Which all the winter sleeps here under foot
    And hath no wings
To raise it to the truth and light of things, 40
    But is still trod
    By ev'ry wand'ring clod.

7

O thou! whose spirit did at first inflame
    And warm the dead,
And by a sacred incubation fed
    With life this frame°
Which once had neither being, form, nor name,
    Grant I may so
    Thy steps track here below,°

8

That in these masques and shadows I may see 50
    Thy sacred way,
And by those hid ascents climb to that day
    Which breaks from thee
Who art in all things, though invisibly;
    Show me thy peace,
    Thy mercy, love, and ease,

9

And from this care, where dreams and sorrows reign,
  Lead me above
Where light, joy, leisure, and true comforts move°
  Without all pain,   60
There, hid in thee, show me his life again°
  At whose dumb urn
 Thus all the year I mourn.

Begging (I)

 King of Mercy, King of Love,°
 In whom I live, in whom I move,°
 Perfect what thou hast begun,
 Let no night put out this Sun;
 Grant I may, my chief desire!
 Long for thee, to thee aspire,
 Let my youth, my bloom of days
 Be my comfort and thy praise,
 That hereafter, when I look
 O'er the sullied, sinful book,   10
 I may find thy hand therein
 Wiping out my shame and sin.
 O it is thy only Art°
 To reduce a stubborn heart,
 And since thine is victory,
 Strongholds should belong to thee;
 Lord then take it, leave it not
 Unto my dispose or lot,
 But since I would not have it mine,
 O my God, let it be thine!   20

Jude ver. 24, 25

*Now unto him that is able to keep us from falling, and to present us
 faultless before the presence of his glory with exceeding joy,*
*To the only wise God, our Saviour, be glory and majesty, dominion and
 power, now and ever, Amen.*

FINIS

Silex Scintillans:

SACRED

POEMS

And private

EJACULATIONS.

The second Edition, In two Books;
By *Henry Vaughan,* Silurist.

Job chap 35. ver. 10, 11.

Where is God my Maker, who giveth Songs in
  the night ?
Who teacheth us more then the beasts of the
  earth, and maketh us wiser then the fowls
  of heaven ?

London, Printed for *Henry Crips,* and *Lodo-*
wick Lloyd, next to the Castle in *Cornhil,*
and in *Popes-head Alley.* 1655.

SILEX SCINTILLANS

The Author's Preface to the Following Hymns

THAT this Kingdom hath abounded with those ingenious persons, which in the late notion are termed *Wits*, is too well known. Many of them having cast away all their fair portion of time in no better employments than a deliberate search, or excogitation of *idle words*,° and a most vain, insatiable desire to be reputed *Poets*; leaving behind them no other monuments of those excellent abilities conferred upon them, but such as they may (with a predecessor of theirs) term *parricides*,° and a soul-killing issue; for that is the *Brabeion*,° and laureate crown, which idle poems will certainly bring to their unrelenting authors.

And well it were for them, if those willingly-studied and wilfully-published vanities could defile no spirits, but their own; but the case is far worse. These vipers survive their parents, and for many ages after (like epidemic diseases) infect whole generations, corrupting always and unhallowing the best-gifted souls, and the most capable vessels; for whose sanctification and welfare, the glorious Son of God laid down his life, and suffered the precious blood of his blessed and innocent heart to be poured out. In the mean time it cannot be denied, but these men are had in remembrance, though we cannot say with any comfort, *Their memorial is blessed*; for, that I may speak no more than the truth (let their passionate worshippers say what they please) all the commendations that can be justly given them, will amount to no more, than what Prudentius the Christian-sacred poet bestowed upon Symmachus:°

> Os dignum aeterno tinctum quod fulgeat auro
> Si mallet laudare deum: cui sordida monstra
> Praetulit, et liquidam temeravit crimine vocem;
> Haud aliter, quam cum rastris qui tentat eburnis
> Caenosum versare solum, etc.

In English thus,

> A wit most worthy in tried gold to shine,
> Immortal gold! had he sung the divine
> Praise of his Maker: to whom he preferred
> Obscene, vile fancies, and profanely marred
> A rich, rare style with sinful, lewd contents;
> No otherwise, than if with instruments
> Of polished ivory, some drudge should stir
> A dirty sink, etc.

This comparison is nothing odious, and it is as true as it is appo-site; for a good wit in a bad subject, is (as Solomon said of the *fair* and *foolish woman*) *Like a jewel of gold in a swine's snout*, Prov. 11: 22. Nay, the more acute the author is, there is so much the more danger and death in the work. Where the sun is busy upon a dung-hill, the issue is always some unclean vermin. Divers persons of eminent piety and learning (I meddle not with the seditious and schismatical) have, long before my time, taken notice of this malady; for the com-plaint against vicious verse, even by peaceful and obedient spirits, is of some antiquity in this Kingdom. And yet, as if the evil con-sequence attending this inveterate error were but a small thing, there is sprung very lately another prosperous device to assist it in the subversion of souls. Those that want the genius of verse, fall to translating; and the people are (every term) plentifully furnished with various foreign vanities; so that the most lascivious compositions of France and Italy are here naturalized and made English: and this (as it is sadly observed) with so much favour and success, that nothing *takes* (as they rightly phrase it) like a Romance. And very frequently (if that character be not an ivy-bush) the buyer receives this lewd ware from persons of honour:° who want not reason to forbear, much private misfortune having sprung from no other seed at first, than some infectious and dissolving legend.

To continue (after years of discretion) in this vanity is an inexcus-able desertion of pious sobriety: and to persist so to the end is a wilful despising of God's sacred exhortations, by a constant, sensual volutation or wallowing in impure thoughts and scurrilous conceits, which both defile their authors, and as many more, as they are com-municated to. If *every idle word shall be accounted for*, and if *no corrupt communication should proceed out of our mouths*,° how desperate (I be-seech you) is their condition, who all their lifetime, and out of mere design,° study lascivious fictions; then carefully record and publish them, that instead of *grace* and *life*, they *may minister sin and death* unto their readers? It was wisely considered, and piously said by one, *That he would read no idle books; both in regard of love to his own soul, and pity unto his that made them, for* (said he) *if I be corrupted by them, their composer is immediately a cause of my ill: and at the day of reckoning (though now dead) must give an account for it, because I am corrupted by his bad example, which he left behind him. I will write none, lest I hurt them that come after me; I will read none, lest I augment his punishment that is gone before me. I will neither write, nor read, lest I prove a foe to my own soul: while I live, I sin too much; let me not continue longer in wickedness, than I do in life.*° It is a sentence of sacred authority, that *he that is dead, is freed from sin;*° because he cannot in that state, which is without the body, sin any more; but he that writes idle books makes for himself another body, in which he always lives, and sins (after death) as fast and as foul, as ever he did in his life; which very consideration, deserves to be a sufficient antidote against this evil disease.

And here, because I would prevent° a just censure by my free confession, I must remember, that I myself have, for many years together, languished of this very sickness; and it is no long time since I have recovered. But (blessed be God for it!) I have by his saving assistance suppressed my greatest follies, and those which escaped from me, are (I think) as innoxious, as most of that vein use to be; besides, they are interlined with many virtuous, and some pious mixtures. What I speak of them is truth; but let no man mistake it for an extenuation of faults, as if I intended an Apology for them, or myself, who am conscious of so much guilt in both, as can never be expiated without special sorrows, and that cleansing and precious effusion of my Almighty Redeemer: and if the world will be so charitable, as to grant my request, I do here most humbly and earnestly beg that none would read them.

But an idle or sensual subject is not all the poison in these pamphlets. Certain authors have been so irreverendly bold, as to dash Scriptures and the sacred Relatives of God with their impious conceits;° and (which I cannot speak without grief of heart) some of those desperate adventurers may (I think) be reckoned amongst the principal or most learned writers of English verse.

Others of a later date, being corrupted (it may be) by that evil genius which came in with the public distractions, have stuffed their books with oaths, horrid execrations, and a most gross and studied filthiness. But the hurt that ensues by the publication of pieces so notoriously ill, lies heavily upon the stationer's° account, who ought in conscience to refuse them, when they are put into his hands. No loss is so doleful as that gain, that will endamage the soul; he that prints lewdness and impieties is that mad man in the Proverbs, who *casteth firebrands, arrows and death*.°

The suppression of this pleasing and prevailing evil lies not altogether in the power of the Magistrate; for it will fly abroad in manuscripts, when it fails of entertainment at the press. The true remedy lies wholly in their bosoms, who are the gifted persons, by a wise exchange of vain and vicious subjects, for divine themes and celestial praise. The performance is easy, and were it the most difficult in the world, the reward is so glorious, that it infinitely transcends it: for *they that turn many to righteousness, shall shine like the stars for ever and ever*:° whence follows this undeniable inference, that the corrupting of many, being a contrary work, the recompense must be so too; and then I know nothing reserved for them, but the blackness of darkness for ever; from which (O God!) deliver all penitent and reformed spirits!

The first, that with any effectual success attempted a diversion of this foul and overflowing stream, was the blessed man, Mr. George Herbert, whose holy life and verse gained many pious converts (of whom I am the least) and gave the first check to a most flourishing and admired *wit*° of his time. After him followed diverse,—*Sed non passibus aequis*;° they had more of fashion than force. And the reason of their so vast distance from him, besides differing spirits and qualifications (for his measure was eminent) I suspect to be, because they aimed more at verse than perfection;° as may be easily gathered by their frequent impressions, and numerous pages. Hence sprang those wide, those weak, and lean conceptions, which in the most inclinable reader will scarce give any nourishment or help to devotion; for not flowing from a true, practic° piety, it was impossible they should effect those things abroad, which they never had acquaintance with at home; being only the productions of a common spirit, and the obvious ebullitions of that light humour, which takes the pen in hand, out of no other consideration, than to be seen in print. It is true indeed, that to give up our thoughts to pious themes and contemplations (if it be done for piety's sake) is a great step towards perfection; because it will refine and dispose to devotion and sanctity. And further, it will procure for us (so easily communicable is that loving spirit) some small prelibation° of those heavenly refreshments, which descend but seldom, and then very sparingly, upon men of an ordinary or indifferent holiness; but he that desires to excel in this kind of hagiography, or holy writing, must strive (by all means) for perfection and true holiness, that *a door may be opened to him in heaven*, Rev. 4: 1, and then he will be able to write (with Hierotheus° and holy Herbert) *A true Hymn.*°

To effect this in some measure, I have begged leave to communicate this my poor talent to the Church, under the protection and conduct of her glorious Head: who (if he will vouchsafe to own it, and go along with it) can make it as useful now in the public as it hath been to me in private. In the perusal of it, you will (peradventure) observe some passages, whose history or reason may seem something remote; but were they brought nearer, and plainly exposed to your view (though that perhaps might quiet your curiosity), yet would it not conduce much to your greater advantage. And therefore I must desire you to accept of them in that latitude, which is already allowed them. By the last poems in the book (were not that mistake here prevented) you would judge all to be fatherless, and the edition posthume; for (indeed) *I was nigh unto death,*° and am still at no great distance from it; which was the necessary reason for that solemn and accomplished dress,° you will now find this impression in.

But *the God of the spirits of all flesh*° hath granted me a further use of mine, than I did look for in the body; and when I expected, and had (by his assistance) prepared for a message of death, then did he answer me with life; I hope to his glory, and my great advantage: that I may flourish not with leaf only, but with some fruit also; which hope and earnest desire of his poor creature, I humbly beseech him to perfect and fulfil for his dear Son's sake, unto whom, with him and the most holy and loving Spirit, be ascribed by angels, by men, and by all his works, all glory, and wisdom, and dominion, in this the temporal and in the Eternal Being. *Amen.*

*Newton by Usk, near
Sketh-rock, Septem. 30. 1654.*

O Lord, the hope of Israel, all they that forsake thee shall be ashamed; and they that depart from thee, shall be written in the earth, because they have forsaken the Lord, the fountain of living waters.

Heal me, O Lord, and I shall be healed; save me, and I shall be saved, for thou art my health, and my great deliverer.

I said in the cutting off of my days, I shall go to the gates of the grave; I have deprived myself of the residue of my years.

I said, I shall not see the Lord, even the Lord in the land of the living: I shall behold man no more with the inhabitants of the world.   10

O Lord! by thee doth man live, and from thee is the life of my spirit: therefore wilt thou recover me, and make me to live.

Thou hast in love to my soul delivered it from the pit of corruption; for thou hast cast all my sins behind thy back.

For thy name's sake hast thou put off thine anger; for thy praise hast thou refrained from me, that I should not be cut off.

For the grave cannot praise thee, death cannot celebrate thee: they that go down into the pit, cannot hope for thy truth.

The living, the living, he shall praise thee, as I do this day: the father to the children shall make known thy truth.   20

O Lord! thou hast been merciful, thou hast brought back my life from corruption: thou hast redeemed me from my sin.

They that follow after lying vanities, forsake their own mercy.

Therefore shall thy songs be with me, and my prayer unto the God of my life.

I will go unto the altar of my God, unto God, the joy of my youth; and in thy fear will I worship towards thy holy temple.

I will sacrifice unto thee with the voice of thanksgiving; I will pay that which I have vowed: salvation is of the Lord.

The Dedication

To my most merciful, my most
loving, and dearly loved Redeemer, the ever blessed,
the only Holy and
JUST ONE,

JESUS CHRIST,

The Son of the living

G   O   D,

And the sacred

Virgin Mary.

I

My God! thou that didst die for me,
These thy death's fruits I offer thee;
Death that to me was life and light,
But dark and deep pangs to thy sight.
Some drops of thy all-quick'ning blood
Fell on my heart; those made it bud
And put forth thus, though Lord, before
The ground was cursed, and void of store.
Indeed I had some here to hire
Which long resisted thy desire,   10
That stoned thy servants, and did move
To have thee murthered for thy love;
But Lord, I have expelled them, and so bent,
Beg, thou wouldst take thy tenant's rent.

II

Dear Lord, 'tis finished! and now he
That copied it, presents it thee.
'Twas thine first, and to thee returns,
From thee it shined, though here it burns;
If the sun rise on rocks, is't right,
To call it their inherent light?   20
No, nor can I say, this is mine,
For, dearest Jesus, 'tis all thine.
As thy clothes (when thou with clothes wert clad)°
Both light from thee, and virtue had,
And now (as then within this place)
Thou to poor rags dost still give grace.
This is the earnest thy love sheds,°
The *Candle* shining on some heads,°
Till at thy charges they shall be,
Clothed all with immortality.   30

  My dear Redeemer, the world's light,
And life too, and my heart's delight!
For all thy mercies and thy truth
Showed to me in my sinful youth,
For my sad failings and my wild
Murmurings at thee, when most mild:

For all my secret faults, and each
Frequent relapse and wilful breach,
For all designs meant against thee,
And ev'ry published vanity   40
Which thou divinely hast forgiven,
While thy blood washed me white as heaven:
I nothing have to give to thee,
But this thy own gift, given to me;
Refuse it not! for now thy *Token*°
Can tell thee where a heart is broken.

Revel. Cap. 1. ver. 5, 6, 7

Unto him that loved us, and washed us from our sins in his own blood.
And hath made us Kings and Priests unto God and his Father; to him
be glory and dominion, for ever and ever. Amen.
Behold, he cometh with clouds, and every eye shall see him, and they
also which pierced him; and all kinreds of the earth shall wail because of
him: even so. Amen.

¶

Vain wits and eyes
Leave, and be wise:
Abuse not, shun not holy fire,
But with true tears wash off your mire.
Tears and these flames will soon grow kind,
And mix an eye-salve for the blind.
Tears cleanse and supple without fail,
And fire will purge your callous veil.
Then comes the light! which when you spy,
And see your nakedness thereby,   10
Praise him, who dealt his gifts so free
In tears to you, in fire to me.

SILEX SCINTILLANS

Ascension-day°

Lord Jesus! with what sweetness and delights,
Sure, holy hopes, high joys and quick'ning flights
Dost thou feed thine! O thou! the hand that lifts
To him, who gives all good and perfect gifts.°
Thy glorious, bright Ascension (though removed
So many Ages from me) is so proved
And by thy Spirit sealed to me, that I
Feel me a sharer in thy victory.
       I soar and rise
       Up to the skies,   10
          Leaving the world their day,
       And in my flight,
       For the true light
          Go seeking all the way;
I greet thy sepulchre, salute thy grave,
That blest inclosure, where the angels gave°
The first glad tidings of thy early light,
And resurrection from the earth and night.
I see that morning in thy Convert's tears,°
Fresh as the dew, which but this dawning wears!   20
I smell her spices, and her ointment yields°
As rich a scent as the now primrosed fields:
The day-star smiles, and light with thee deceased,
Now shines in all the chambers of the East.
What stirs, what posting intercourse and mirth°
Of saints and angels glorify the earth?
What sighs, what whispers, busy stops and stays,
Private and holy talk fill all the ways?
They pass as at the last great day, and run
In their white robes to seek the risen Sun;   30
I see them, hear them, mark their haste, and move
Amongst them, with them, winged with faith and love.
Thy forty days more secret commerce here,°
After thy death and funeral, so clear
And indisputable shows to my sight
As the Sun doth, which to those days gave light.

I walk the fields of Bethany which shine°
All now as fresh as Eden, and as fine.
Such was the bright world, on the first seventh day,
Before man brought forth sin, and sin decay;　　　　　40
When like a virgin clad in *flowers* and *green*
The pure earth sat, and the fair woods had seen
No frost, but flourished in that youthful vest,°
With which their great Creator had them dressed:
When Heav'n above them shined like molten glass,°
While all the planets did unclouded pass;
And springs, like dissolved pearls their streams did pour,
Ne'er marred with floods, nor angered with a shower.
With these fair thoughts I move in this fair place,
And the last steps of my mild Master trace;　　　　　50
I see him leading out his chosen train,°
All sad with tears, which like warm summer-rain
In silent drops steal from their holy eyes,
Fixed lately on the Cross, now on the skies.
And now (eternal Jesus!) thou dost heave
Thy blessèd hands to bless these thou dost leave;
The cloud doth now receive thee, and their sight°
Having lost thee, behold two men in white!
Two and no more: *what two attest, is true,*
Was thine own answer to the stubborn Jew.°　　　　　60
Come then thou faithful witness! come dear Lord
Upon the clouds again to judge this world!

Ascension Hymn

　　　　Dust and clay
　　　　Man's ancient wear!
　　　　Here you must stay,
　　　　But I elsewhere;
　　Souls sojourn here, but may not rest;
　　Who will ascend, must be undressed.

　　　　And yet some°
　　　　That know to die
　　　　Before death come,
　　　　Walk to the sky　　　　　10
　　Even in this life; but all such can
　　Leave behind them the old Man.°

                If a star
            Should leave the sphere,
            She must first mar
            Her flaming wear,
And after fall, for in her dress
Of glory, she cannot transgress.

                Man of old
            Within the line   20
            Of Eden could
            Like the sun shine
All naked, innocent and bright,
And intimate with Heav'n, as light;

                But since he
            That brightness soiled,
            His garments be
            All dark and spoiled,
And here are left as nothing worth,
Till the Refiner's fire breaks forth.°   30

                Then comes he!
            Whose mighty light
            Made his clothes be°
            Like Heav'n, all bright;
The Fuller, whose pure blood did flow
To make stained man more white than snow.°

                He alone
            And none else can
            Bring bone to bone°
            And rebuild man,   40
And by his all-subduing might°
Make clay ascend more quick than light.

                        ¶

Elect
They are all gone into the world of light!
        And I alone sit ling'ring here;
    Their very memory is fair and bright,
            And my sad thoughts doth clear.

It glows and glitters in my cloudy breast
    Like stars upon some gloomy grove,
Or those faint beams in which this hill is dressed,
    After the sun's remove.

I see them walking in an air of glory,
    Whose light doth trample on my days:
My days, which are at best but dull and hoary,
    Mere glimmering and decays.

O holy hope! and high humility,
    High as the Heavens above!
These are your walks, and you have showed them me
    To kindle my cold love.

Dear, beauteous death! the jewel of the Just,
    Shining nowhere, but in the dark;
What mysteries do lie beyond thy dust;
    Could man outlook that mark!

He that hath found some fledged bird's nest may know
    At first sight, if the bird be flown;
But what fair well, or grove he sings in now,
    That is to him unknown.

And yet, as angels in some brighter dreams
    Call to the soul, when man doth sleep:
So some strange thoughts transcend our wonted themes,
    And into glory peep.

If a star were confined into a tomb
    Her captive flames must needs burn there;
But when the hand that locked her up gives room,
    She'll shine through all the sphere.

O Father of eternal life, and all
    Created glories under thee!
Resume thy spirit from this world of thrall°
    Into true liberty.

Either disperse these mists, which blot and fill
   My perspective (still) as they pass,°
Or else remove me hence unto that hill,
   Where I shall need no glass.°   40

White Sunday°

Welcome white day! a thousand suns,
   Though seen at once, were black to thee;
For after their light, darkness comes,
   But thine shines to eternity.

Those flames which on the Apostles rushed°
   At this great feast, and in a tire°
Of cloven tongues their heads all brushed,
   And crowned them with prophetic fire:

Can these new lights be like to those,
   These lights of Serpents like the Dove?   10
Thou hadst no *gall*, ev'n for thy foes,°
   And thy two wings were *grief* and *love*.

Though then some boast that fire each day,
   And on Christ's coat pin all their shreds;
Not sparing openly to say,
   His candle shines upon their heads:°

Yet while some rays of that great light
   Shine here below within thy Book,
They never shall so blind my sight
   But I will know which way to look.   20

For though thou dost that great light lock,
   And by this lesser commerce keep:
Yet by these glances of the flock
   I can discern wolves from the sheep.°

Not, but that I have wishes too,
And pray, *These last may be as first*,°
Or better; but thou long ago
Hast said, *These last should be the worst*.°

Besides, thy method with thy own,°
Thy own dear people pens our times,   30
Our stories are in theirs set down
And penalties spread to our crimes.

Again, if worst and worst implies
A state that no redress admits,
Then from thy Cross unto these days
The *rule* without *exception* fits.

And yet, as in night's gloomy page
One silent star may interline:
So in this last and lewdest age,
Thy ancient love on some may shine.   40

For, though we hourly breathe decays,
And our best *note* and highest *ease*
Is but mere changing of the *keys*,
And a *consumption* that doth please;

Yet thou the great eternal Rock°
Whose height above all ages shines,
Art still the same, and canst unlock
Thy waters to a soul that pines.

Since then thou art the same this day
And ever, as thou wert of old,   50
And nothing doth thy love allay
But our hearts' dead and sinful cold:

As thou long since wert pleased to buy
Our drowned estate, taking the Curse°
Upon thyself, so to destroy
The knots we tied upon thy purse,

So let thy grace now make the way
Even for thy love; for by that means
We, who are nothing but foul clay,
Shall be fine gold, which thou didst cleanse.   60

O come! refine us with thy fire!
Refine us! we are at a loss.
Let not thy stars for Balaam's hire°
Dissolve into the common dross!

The Proffer°

Be still black parasites,
    Flutter no more;
Were it still winter, as it was before,
    You'd make no flights;
But now the dew and Sun have warmed my bowers,
  You fly and flock to suck the flowers.

But you would honey make:
    These buds will wither,
And what you now extract, in harder weather
    Will serve to take;°   10
Wise husband will (you say) there wants prevent,°
  Who do not so, too late repent.

O pois'nous, subtle fowls!
    The flies of hell
That buzz in every ear, and blow on souls
    Until they smell
And rot, descend not here, nor think to stay,
  I've read, who 'twas, drove you away.°

Think you these longing eyes,
    Though sick and spent,   20
And almost famished, ever will consent
    To leave those skies,
That glass of souls and spirits, where well dressed
  They shine in white (like stars) and rest.

Shall my short hour, my inch,°
　　　My one poor sand,
And crumb of life, now ready to disband,
　　　Revolt and flinch,
And having born the burthen all the day,
　Now cast at night my crown away?　　　　　　30

No, No; I am not he,
　　　Go seek elsewhere.
I skill not your fine tinsel and false hair,°
　　　Your sorcery
And smooth seducements: I'll not stuff my story
　With your Commonwealth and glory.

There are, that will sow tares°
　　　And scatter death
Amongst the quick, selling their souls and breath
　　　For any wares;　　　　　　　　　　　　40
But when thy Master comes, they'll find and see
　There's a reward for them and thee.

Then keep the ancient way!
　　　Spit out their phlegm°
And fill thy breast with home; think on thy dream:°
　　　A calm, bright day!
A land of flowers and spices! the word given,
　If these be fair, O what is Heaven!

darting. eye of Rooster
Divine immanation

Cock-crowing°

Father of lights! what sunny seed,°
What glance of day hast thou confined
Into this bird? To all the breed
This busy ray thou hast assigned;
　　　Their magnetism works all night,
　　　And dreams of Paradise and light.

antithesis
Heaven & chicken house

Their eyes watch for the morning hue,
Their little grain expelling night
So shines and sings, as if it knew
The path unto the house of light.   10
    It seems their candle, howe'er done,
    Was tinned and lighted at the sun.°

If such a tincture, such a touch,°
So firm a longing can impower
Shall thy own image think it much
To watch for thy appearing hour?
    If a mere blast so fill the sail,
    Shall not the breath of God prevail?

O thou immortal light and heat!
Whose hand so shines through all this frame,°   20
That by the beauty of the seat,
We plainly see, who made the same,
    Seeing thy seed abides in me,
    Dwell thou in it, and I in thee.

To sleep without thee, is to die;
Yea, 'tis a death partakes of hell:
For where thou dost not close the eye
It never opens, I can tell.
    In such a dark, Egyptian border,°
    The shades of death dwell and disorder.   30

If joys, and hopes, and earnest throes,
And hearts, whose pulse beats still for light
Are given to birds; who, but thee, knows
A love-sick soul's exalted flight?
    Can souls be tracked by any eye
    But his, who gave them wings to fly?

Only this veil which thou hast broke,°
And must be broken yet in me,
This veil, I say, is all the cloak
And cloud which shadows thee from me.   40
    This veil thy full-eyed love denies,
    And only gleams and fractions spies.

O take it off! make no delay,
But brush me with thy light, that I
May shine unto a perfect day,
And warm me at thy glorious Eye!
    O take it off! or till it flee,
    Though with no lily, stay with me!

The Star°

Whatever 'tis, whose beauty here below
Attracts thee thus and makes thee stream and flow,
    And wind and curl, and wink and smile,
    Shifting thy gait and guile:

Though thy close commerce nought at all imbars°
My present search, for eagles eye not stars,°
    And still the lesser by the best°
    And highest good is blest:

Yet, seeing all things that subsist and be,
Have their commissions from Divinity,
    And teach us duty, I will see
    What man may learn from thee.

First, I am sure, the subject so respected°
Is well disposed, for bodies once infected,°
    Depraved or dead, can have with thee
    No hold, nor sympathy.

Next, there's in it a restless, pure desire
And longing for thy bright and vital fire,
    Desire that never will be quenched,
    Nor can be writhed, nor wrenched.

These are the magnets which so strongly move
And work all night upon thy light and love,
    As beauteous shapes, we know not why,
    Command and guide the eye.

10

20

For where desire, celestial, pure desire
Hath taken root, and grows, and doth not tire,
    There God a commerce states, and sheds°
      His secret on their heads.

This is the heart he craves; and whoso will
But give it him, and grudge not; he shall feel   30
    That God is true, as herbs unseen
      Put on their youth and green.

The Palm-tree°

Dear friend sit down, and bear awhile this shade
As I have yours long since; this plant, you see
So pressed and bowed, before sin did degrade
Both you and it, had equal liberty

With other trees: but now shut from the breath
And air of Eden, like a malcontent
It thrives nowhere. This makes these weights (like death°
And sin) hang at him; for the more he's bent

The more he grows. Celestial natures still
Aspire for home; this Solomon of old   10
By flowers and carvings and mysterious skill°
Of wings, and cherubims, and palms foretold.

This is the life which hid above with Christ°
In God, doth always (hidden) multiply,
And spring, and grow, a tree ne'er to be priced,
A tree, whose fruit is immortality.

Here spirits that have run their race and fought°
And won the fight, and have not feared the frowns
Nor loved the smiles of greatness, but have wrought
Their master's will, meet to receive their crowns.   20

Here is the patience of the saints: this tree°
Is watered by their tears, as flowers are fed
With dew by night; but One you cannot see
Sits here and numbers all the tears they shed.

Here is their faith too, which if you will keep°
When we two part, I will a journey make
To pluck a garland hence, while you do sleep,
And weave it for your head against you wake.°

Joy

Be dumb, coarse measures, jar no more; to me
There is no discord, but your harmony.
False, juggling sounds; a groan well dressed, where care
Moves in disguise, and sighs afflict the air:
Sorrows in white; griefs tuned; a sugared dosis°
Of wormwood, and a Death's-head crowned with Roses.
He weighs not your forced accents, who can have
A lesson played him by a wind or wave.
Such numbers tell their days, whose spirits be
Lulled by those charmers to a lethargy.   10
  But as for thee, whose faults long since require
More eyes than stars; whose breath, could it aspire
To equal winds, would prove too short: thou hast
Another mirth, a mirth though overcast
With clouds and rain, yet full as calm and fine
As those *clear heights* which above tempests shine.
      Therefore while the various showers
      Kill and cure the tender flowers,
      While the winds refresh the year
      Now with clouds, now making clear,   20
      Be sure under pains of death°
      To ply both thine eyes and breath.
            As leafs in bowers
            Whisper their hours,
            And hermit-wells
            Drop in their cells:
      So in sighs and unseen tears
      Pass thy solitary years,
And going hence, leave written on some tree,°
Sighs make joy sure, and shaking fastens thee.   30

The Favour

O thy bright looks! thy glance of love
Shown, and but shown me from above!
Rare looks! that can dispense such joy
As without wooing wins the coy,
And makes him mourn, and pine and die
Like a starved eaglet, for thine eye.
Some kind herbs here, though low and far,°
Watch for, and know their loving star.
O let no star compare with thee!
Nor any herb out-duty me!   10
So shall my nights and mornings be
Thy time to shine, and mine to see.

The Garland

Thou, who dost flow and flourish here below,
To whom a falling star and nine-days' glory,
Or some frail beauty makes the bravest show,
Hark, and make use of this ensuing story.

    When first my youthful, sinful age
        Grew master of my ways,
    Appointing error for my page,
        And darkness for my days;
    I flung away, and with full cry°
        Of wild affections, rid°   10
    In post for pleasures, bent to try°
        All gamesters that would bid.
    I played with fire, did counsel spurn,
        Made life my common stake;
    But never thought that fire would burn,
        Or that a soul could ache.
    Glorious deceptions, gilded mists,
        False joys, phantastic flights,
    Pieces of sackcloth with silk-lists,°
        These were my prime delights.   20
    I sought choice bowers, haunted the spring,

    Culled flowers and made me posies:
Gave my fond humours their full wing,
    And crowned my head with roses.
But at the height of this career°
    I met with a dead man,
Who noting well my vain abear,°
    Thus unto me began:
Desist fond fool, be not undone,
    What thou hast cut today   30
Will fade at night, and with this sun
    Quite vanish and decay.

Flowers gathered in this world, die here; if thou
Wouldst have a wreath that fades not, let them grow,
And grow for thee; who spares them here, shall find
A garland, where comes neither rain, nor wind.

Love-sick°

Jesus, my life! how shall I truly love thee?
O that thy Spirit would so strongly move me,
That thou wert pleased to shed thy grace so far
As to make man all pure love, flesh a star!
A star that would ne'er set, but ever rise,
So rise and run, as to out-run these skies,
These narrow skies (narrow to me) that bar,
So bar me in, that I am still at war,
At constant war with them. O come and rend,°
Or bow the heavens! Lord bow them and descend,   10
And at thy presence make these mountains flow,
These mountains of cold ice in me! Thou art
Refining fire, O then refine my heart,°
My foul, foul heart! Thou art immortal heat,
Heat motion gives; then warm it, till it beat,
So beat for thee, till thou in mercy hear,
So hear that thou must open: open to°
A sinful wretch, a wretch that caused thy woe,
Thy woe, who caused his weal; so far his weal
That thou forgott'st thine own, for thou didst seal   20
Mine with thy blood, thy blood which makes thee mine,
Mine ever, ever; and me ever thine.

Trinity Sunday°

O holy, blessed, glorious three,
Eternal witnesses that be
In heaven, one God in trinity!

As here on earth (when men withstood)
The Spirit, Water, and the Blood,
Made my Lord's Incarnation good:

So let the *antitypes* in me
Elected, bought and sealed for free,
Be owned, saved, *sainted* by you three!

Psalm 104°

Up, O my soul, and bless the Lord. O God,
    My God, how great, how very great art thou!
Honour and majesty have their abode
    With thee, and crown thy brow.

Thou cloth'st thyself with light, as with a robe,
    And the high, glorious heav'ns thy mighty hand
Doth spread like curtains round about this globe
    Of air, and sea, and land.

The beams of thy bright chambers thou dost lay
    In the deep waters, which no eye can find;   10
The clouds thy chariots are, and thy pathway
    The wings of the swift wind.

In thy celestial, gladsome messages
    Dispatched to holy souls, sick with desire
And love of thee, each willing angel is
    Thy minister in fire.

Thy arm unmovable forever laid
    And founded the firm earth; then with the deep
As with a veil thou hidst it, thy floods played
    Above the mountains steep.   20

At thy rebuke they fled, at the known voice
    Of their Lord's thunder they retired apace:
Some up the mountains passed by secret ways,
    Some downwards to their place.

For thou to them a bound hast set, a bound
    Which (though but sand) keeps in and curbs whole seas:
There all their fury, foam and hideous sound
    Must languish and decrease.

And as thy care bounds these, so thy rich love
    Doth broach the earth, and lesser brooks lets forth,   30
Which run from hills to valleys, and improve
    Their pleasure and their worth.

These to the beasts of every field give drink;
    There the wild asses swallow the cool spring:
And birds amongst the branches on their brink
    Their dwellings have and sing.

Thou from thy upper springs above, from those
    Chambers of rain, where Heav'n's large bottles lie,
Dost water the parched hills, whose breaches close
    Healed by the showers from high.   40

Grass for the cattle, and herbs for man's use
    Thou mak'st to grow; these (blest by thee) the earth
Brings forth, with wine, oil, bread: all which infuse
    To man's heart strength and mirth.

Thou giv'st the trees their greenness, ev'n to those
    Cedars in Lebanon, in whose thick boughs
The birds their nests build; though the stork doth choose
    The fir-trees for her house.

To the wild goats the high hills serve for folds,
  The rocks give conies a retiring place: 50
Above them the cool moon her known course holds,
   And the sun runs his race.

Thou makest darkness, and then comes the night;
  In whose thick shades and silence each wild beast
Creeps forth, and pinched for food, with scent and sight
   Hunts in an eager quest.

The lion's whelps impatient of delay
  Roar in the covert of the woods, and seek
Their meat from thee, who dost appoint the prey
   And feed'st them all the week.   60

This past, the sun shines on the earth, and they
  Retire into their dens; man goes abroad
Unto his work, and at the close of day
   Returns home with his load.

O Lord my God, how many and how rare
  Are thy great works! In wisdom hast thou made
Them all, and this the earth, and every blade
   Of grass we tread, declare.

So doth the deep and wide sea, wherein are
  Innumerable, creeping things both small   70
And great: there ships go, and the shipmen's fear,
   The comely spacious whale.

These all upon thee wait, that thou mayst feed
  Them in due season: what thou giv'st, they take;
Thy bounteous open hand helps them at need,
   And plenteous meals they make.

When thou dost hide thy face (thy face which keeps
  All things in being) they consume and mourn:
When thou withdraw'st their breath, their vigour sleeps,
   And they to dust return.   80

Thou send'st thy spirit forth, and they revive,
    The frozen earth's dead face thou dost renew.
Thus thou thy glory through the world dost drive,
    And to thy works art true.

Thine eyes behold the earth, and the whole stage
    Is moved and trembles, the hills melt and smoke
With thy least touch: lightnings and winds that rage
    At thy rebuke are broke.

Therefore as long as thou wilt give me breath
    I will in songs to thy great name employ   90
That gift of thine, and to my day of death
    Thou shalt be all my joy.

I'll *spice* my thoughts with thee, and from thy word
    Gather true comforts; but the wicked liver
Shall be consumed. O my soul, bless thy Lord!
    Yea, bless thou him for ever!

The Bird

Hither thou com'st: the busy wind all night
Blew through thy lodging, where thy own warm wing
Thy pillow was. Many a sullen storm
(For which course man seems much the fitter born)
        Rained on thy bed
        And harmless head.

And now as fresh and cheerful as the light
Thy little heart in early hymns doth sing
Unto that *Providence*, whose unseen arm
Curbed them, and clothed thee well and warm.   10
        All things that be, praise him; and had
        Their lesson taught them, when first made.

So hills and valleys into singing break,
And though poor stones have neither speech nor tongue,
While active winds and streams both run and speak,
Yet stones are deep in admiration.
Thus praise and prayer here beneath the sun
Make lesser mornings, when the great are done.

For each inclosèd spirit is a star
    Inlight'ning his own little sphere,   20
Whose light, though fetched and borrowèd from far,
    Both mornings makes, and evenings there.

But as these birds of light make a land glad,
Chirping their solemn matins on each tree:
So in the shades of night some dark fowls be,
Whose heavy notes make all that hear them, sad.°

    The turtle then in palm-trees mourns,°
        While owls and satyrs howl;°
    The pleasant land to brimstone turns°
        And all her streams grow foul.   30

Brightness and mirth, and love and faith, all fly,
Till the day-spring breaks forth again from high.°

The Timber

Sure thou didst flourish once! and many springs,
Many bright mornings, much dew, many showers
Passed o'er thy head: many light *hearts* and *wings*
Which now are dead, lodged in thy living bowers.

And still a new succession sings and flies;
Fresh groves grow up, and their green branches shoot
Towards the old and still enduring skies,
While the low *violet* thrives at their root.

But thou beneath the sad and heavy *line*
Of death, dost waste all senseless, cold and dark;   10
Where not so much as dreams of light may shine,
Nor any thought of greenness, leaf or bark.

And yet (as if some deep hate and dissent,
Bred in thy growth betwixt high winds and thee,
Were still alive) thou dost great storms resent°
Before they come, and know'st how near they be.

Else all at rest thou liest, and the fierce breath
Of tempests can no more disturb thy ease;
But this thy strange resentment after death°
Means only those, who broke (in life) thy peace.   20

So murthered man, when lovely life is done,
And his blood freezed, keeps in the centre still
Some secret sense, which makes the dead blood run
At his approach, that did the body kill.

And is there any murth'rer worse than sin?
Or any storms more foul than a lewd life?
Or what *resentient* can work more within,°
Than true remorse, when with past sins at strife?

He that hath left life's vain joys and vain care,
And truly hates to be detained on earth,   30
Hath got an house where many mansions are,°
And keeps his soul unto eternal mirth.

But though thus dead unto the world, and ceased
From sin, he walks a narrow, private way;
Yet grief and old wounds make him sore displeased,
And all his life a rainy, weeping day.

For though he should forsake the world, and live
As mere a stranger, as men long since dead,
Yet joy itself will make a right soul grieve
To think, he should be so long vainly led.   40

But as shades set off light, so tears and grief
(Though of themselves but a sad blubbered story)
By showing the sin great, show the relief
Far greater, and so speak my Saviour's glory.

If my way lies through deserts and wild woods,°
Where all the land with scorching heat is cursed,
Better, the pools should flow with rain and floods
To fill my bottle, than I die with thirst.

Blest showers they are, and streams sent from above
Begetting *virgins* where they use to flow;   50
And trees of life no other waters love,°
These upper springs and none else make them grow.

But these chaste fountains flow not till we die;
Some drops may fall before, but a clear spring
And ever running, till we leave to fling
Dirt in her way, will keep above the sky.

Rom. Cap. 6. ver. 7
He that is dead is freed from sin.

The Jews°

When the fair year
Of your deliverer comes,
And that long frost which now benumbs
Your hearts shall thaw; when angels here
Shall yet to man appear,
And familiarly confer
Beneath the oak and juniper:°
When the bright *Dove*
Which now these many, many springs
Hath kept above,   10
Shall with spread wings
Descend, and living waters flow
To make dry dust, and dead trees grow;

O then that I
Might live, and see the olive bear°
Her proper branches! which now lie
Scattered each where,
And without root and sap decay
Cast by the husbandman away.°
And sure it is not far!   20
For as your fast and foul decays
Forerunning the bright morning-star,°
Did sadly note his healing rays

Would shine elsewhere, since you were blind,
And would be cross, when God was kind:
       So by all signs
Our fullness too is now come in,
And the same Sun which here declines
And sets, will few hours hence begin
To rise on you again, and look
Towards old Mamre and Eshcol's brook.°   30
       For surely he
Who loved the world so, as to give°
His only Son to make it free,
Whose spirit too doth mourn and grieve
To see man lost, will for old love
From your dark hearts this veil remove.°

Faith sojourned first on earth in you,
You were the dear and chosen stock:
The Arm of God, glorious and true,   40
Was first revealed to be your rock.

You were the *eldest* child, and when
Your stony hearts despisèd love,
The *youngest*, ev'n the Gentiles then
Were cheered, your jealousy to move.

Thus, righteous Father! dost thou deal
With brutish men; thy gifts go round
By turns, and timely, and so heal
The lost son by the newly found.°

Begging (II)°

O, do not go! thou know'st, I'll die!
My *Spring* and *Fall* are in thy book!
Or, if thou goest, do not deny
To lend me, though from far, one look!

My sins long since have made thee strange,
A very stranger unto me;
No morning-meetings since this change,
Nor evening-walks have I with thee.

Why is my God thus slow and cold,
When I am most, most sick and sad?   10
Well fare those blessèd days of old
When thou didst hear the *weeping lad*!°

O do not thou do as I did,
Do not despise a love-sick heart!
What though some clouds defiance bid
Thy Sun must shine in every part.

Though I have spoiled, O spoil not thou!
Hate not thine own dear gift and token!
Poor birds sing best, and prettiest show,
When their nest is fall'n and broken.   20

Dear Lord! restore thy ancient peace,
Thy quick'ning friendship, man's bright wealth!
And if thou wilt not give me ease
From sickness, give my spirit health!

Palm Sunday°

Come, drop your branches, strow the way,
      Plants of the day!
Whom sufferings make most green and gay.°

The King of grief, the man of sorrow°
Weeping still, like the wet morrow,
Your shades and freshness comes to borrow.

Put on, put on your best array;
Let the joyed road make holy-day,
And flowers that into fields do stray,
Or secret groves, keep the highway.   10

Trees, flowers and herbs, birds, beasts and stones,
That since man fell, expect with groans°
To see the Lamb, which all at ones,°
Lift up your heads and leave your moans!

For here comes he
Whose death will be
Man's life, and your full liberty.

Hark! how the children shrill and high
            Hosanna cry,
Their joys provoke the distant sky,   20
Where thrones and seraphins reply,°
And their own angels shine and sing
            In a bright ring:
            Such young, sweet mirth
            Makes heaven and earth
Join in a joyful symphony.

The harmless, young and happy ass,
Seen long before this came to pass,°
Is in these joys an high partaker
Ordained, and made to bear his Maker.   30

Dear feast of palms, of flowers and dew!
Whose fruitful dawn sheds hopes and lights;
Thy bright solemnities did shew
The third glad day through two sad nights.

I'll get me up before the sun,°
I'll cut me boughs off many a tree,
And all alone full early run
To gather flowers to welcome thee.

Then like the *palm*, though wrong, I'll bear,°
I will be still a child, still meek   40
As the poor ass, which the proud jeer,
And only my dear Jesus seek.

If I lose all, and must endure
The proverbed griefs of holy Job,
I care not, so I may secure
But one *green branch* and a *white robe*.°

Jesus Weeping (I)°

S. Luke 19. ver. 41

Blessed, unhappy city! dearly loved
But still unkind! art this day nothing moved?
    Art senseless still? O can'st thou sleep
    When God himself for thee doth weep!
    Stiff-neckèd Jews! your fathers' breed
    That served the calf, not Abr'am's seed,
    Had not the babes *Hosanna* cried,
    The stones had spoke, what you denied.°

Dear Jesus weep on! pour this latter
Soul-quick'ning rain, this living water°   10
    On their dead hearts; but (O my fears!)
    They will drink blood, that despise tears.
    My dear, bright Lord! my Morning-star!
    Shed this live-dew on fields which far
    From hence long for it! shed it there,
    Where the starved earth groans for one tear!

This land, though with thy heart's blest extract fed,°
Will nothing yield but thorns to wound thy head.

The Daughter of Herodias°

St. Matth. chap. 14. ver. 6 etc.

Vain, sinful art! who first did fit
    Thy lewd loathed *motions* unto *sounds*,
And made grave *music* like wild *wit*
    Err in loose airs beyond her bounds?

What fires hath he heaped on his head?
    Since to his sins (as needs it must)
His *art* adds still (though he be dead)
    New fresh accounts of blood and lust.

Leave then young sorceress; the *ice*°
Will those coy spirits cast asleep,   10
Which teach thee now to please his eyes°
Who doth thy loathsome mother keep.

But thou hast pleased so well, he swears,
And gratifies thy sin with vows:
His shameless lust in public wears,
And to thy soft arts strongly bows.

Skilful enchantress and true bred!
Who out of evil can bring forth good?
Thy mother's nets in thee were spread,
She tempts to *incest*, thou to *blood*.°   20

Jesus Weeping (II)°

St. John, chap. 11. ver. 35

My dear, Almighty Lord! why dost thou weep?
    Why dost thou groan and groan again,°
        And with such deep,
    Repeated sighs thy kind heart pain,
    Since the same sacred breath which thus
        Doth mourn for us,
    Can make man's dead and scattered bones
Unite, and raise up all that died, at once?

    O holy groans! groans of the Dove!
    O healing tears! the tears of love!   10
    Dew of the dead! which makes dust move
And spring, how is't that you so sadly grieve,
        Who can relieve?

    Should not thy sighs refrain thy store°
    Of tears, and not provoke to more?
    Since two afflictions may not reign
    In one at one time, as some feign.
    Those blasts, which o'er our heads here stray,
    If showers then fall, will showers allay,
    As those poor pilgrims oft have tried,°   20
    Who in this windy world abide.

Dear Lord! thou art all grief and love,
But which thou art most, none can prove.
Thou griev'st, man should himself undo,
And lov'st him, though he works thy woe.

'Twas not that vast, almighty measure
Which is required to make up life,
(Though purchased with thy heart's dear treasure)
   Did breed this strife
Of grief and pity in thy breast,   30
The throne where peace and power rest:
But 'twas thy love that (without leave)°
Made thine eyes melt, and thy heart heave;
For though death cannot so undo
What thou hast done (but though man too
Should help to spoil) thou canst restore
All better far than 'twas before;
Yet, thou so full of pity art
(Pity which overflows thy heart!)
That, though the cure of all man's harm   40
Is nothing to thy glorious arm,
Yet canst not thou that free cure do,
But thou must sorrow for him too.

   Then farewell joys! for while I live,
My business here shall be to grieve:
A grief that shall outshine all joys
For mirth and life, yet without noise.
A grief, whose silent dew shall breed
Lilies and myrrh, where the cursed seed°
Did sometimes rule. A grief so bright   50
'Twill make the land of darkness light;
And while too many sadly roam,
Shall send me (*swan-like*) singing home.°

Psal. 73. ver. 25
*Whom have I in heaven but thee? and there is none upon earth that I
desire besides thee.*

Providence

Sacred and secret hand!
By whose assisting, swift command
The angel showed that holy well,°
Which freed poor Hagar from her fears,
And turned to smiles the begging tears
Of young, distressèd Ishmael.

How in a mystic cloud
(Which doth thy strange sure mercies shroud)
Dost thou convey man food and money
Unseen by him, till they arrive   10
Just at his mouth, that thankless hive
Which kills thy bees, and eats thy honey!

If I thy servant be
(Whose service makes ev'n captives free)
A fish shall all my tribute pay,°
The swift-winged raven shall bring me meat,°
And I, like flowers shall still go neat,
As if I knew no month but May.

I will not fear what man,
With all his plots and power can;   20
Bags that wax old may plundered be,°
But none can sequester or let
A state that with the sun doth set
And comes next morning fresh as he.

Poor birds this doctrine sing,
And herbs which on dry hills do spring
Or in the howling wilderness
Do know thy dewy morning-hours,
And watch all night for mists or showers,
Then drink and praise thy bounteousness.   30

May he for ever die
Who trusts not thee! but wretchedly
Hunts gold and wealth, and will not lend

Thy service, nor his soul one day:
May his crown, like his hopes, be clay,
And what he saves, may his foes spend!

    If all my portion here,
The measure given by thee each year
Were by my causeless enemies
Usurped; it never should me grieve   40
Who know, how well thou canst relieve,
Whose hands are open as thine eyes.

    Great King of love and truth!
Who would'st not hate my froward youth,
And wilt not leave me, when grown old;
Gladly will I, like Pontic sheep,°
Unto their wormwood-diet keep
Since thou hast made thy Arm my fold.

The Knot°

Bright Queen of Heaven! God's Virgin Spouse!
    The glad world's blessed maid!
Whose beauty tied life to thy house,
    And brought us saving aid.

Thou art the true Loves-knot; by thee
    God is made our ally,
And man's inferior essence he
    With his did dignify.

For coalescent by that band
    We are his body grown,   10
Nourished with favours from his hand
    Whom for our head we own.

And such a Knot, what arm dares loose,
    What life, what death can sever?
Which us in him, and him in us
    United keeps for ever.

The Ornament

The lucky world showed me one day
Her gorgeous mart and glittering store,
Where with proud haste the rich made way
To buy, the poor came to adore.

Serious they seemed and bought up all
The latest modes of pride and lust,
Although the first must surely fall,
And the last is most loathsome dust.

But while each gay, alluring wear
With idle hearts and busy looks   10
They viewed (for idleness hath there
Laid up all her archives and books)

Quite through their proud and pompous file
Blushing, and in meek weeds arrayed,°
With native looks, which knew no guile,
Came the sheep-keeping Syrian maid.°

Whom straight the shining row all faced,
Forced by her artless looks and dress,
While one cried out, We are disgraced
For she is bravest, you confess.°   20

St. Mary Magdalen°

Dear, beauteous Saint! more white than day,
When in his naked, pure array,
Fresher than morning-flowers which shew
As thou in tears dost, best in dew.
How art thou changed! how lively-fair,
Pleasing and innocent an air,
Not tutored by thy glass, but free,
Native and pure shines now in thee!
But since thy beauty doth still keep

Bloomy and fresh, why dost thou weep?   10
This dusky state of sighs and tears
Durst not look on those smiling years,
When Magdal-castle was thy seat,°
Where all was sumptuous, rare and neat.
Why lies this *hair* despisèd now
Which once thy care and art did show?
Who then did dress the much loved toy,
In *spires*, *globes*, angry *curls* and coy,
Which with skilled negligence seemed shed
About thy curious, wild, young head?   20
Why is this rich, this pistic nard°
Spilt, and the box quite broke and marred?
What pretty sullenness did haste
Thy easy hands to do this waste?
Why art thou humbled thus, and low
As earth, thy lovely head dost bow?
Dear *soul*! thou knew'st, flowers here on earth°
At their Lord's foot-stool have their birth;
Therefore thy withered self in haste
Beneath his blest feet thou didst cast,   30
That at the root of this green tree
Thy great decays restored might be.
Thy curious vanities and rare;
Odorous ointments kept with care,
And dearly bought (when thou didst see
They could not cure, nor comfort thee)
Like a wise, early Penitent°
Thou sadly didst to him present,
Whose interceding, meek and calm
Blood, is the world's all-healing *Balm*.   40
This, this Divine Restorative
Called forth thy tears, which ran in live
And hasty drops, as if they had
(Their Lord so near) sense to be glad.
Learn, *Ladies*, here the faithful cure
Makes beauty lasting, fresh and pure;
Learn Mary's art of tears, and then
Say, *You have got the day from men.*
Cheap, mighty Art! her Art of love,°
Who loved much and much more could move;°   50

Her Art! whose memory must last
Till truth through all the world be past,
Till his abused, despisèd flame
Return to Heaven, from whence it came,
And send a fire down, that shall bring
Destruction on his ruddy wing.

Her Art! whose pensive, weeping eyes,
Were once sin's loose and tempting spies,
But now are fixèd stars, whose light
Helps such dark stragglers to their sight.   60

Self-boasting Pharisee! how blind
A judge wert thou, and how unkind!
It was impossible, that thou
Who wert all false, should'st true grief know;
Is't just to judge her faithful tears
By that foul rheum thy false eye wears?

This woman (say'st thou) *is a sinner*:
And sate there none such at thy dinner?
Go leper, go; wash till thy flesh°
Comes like a child's, spotless and fresh;   70
He is still leprous, that still paints:
Who saint themselves, they are no *saints*.°

The Rainbow

Still young and fine! but what is still in view
We slight as old and soiled, though fresh and new.
How bright wert thou, when Shem's admiring eye°
Thy burnished, flaming *Arch* did first descry!
When Terah, Nahor, Haran, Abram, Lot,°
The youthful world's gray fathers in one knot,
Did with intentive looks watch every hour
For thy new light, and trembled at each shower!
When thou dost shine darkness looks white and fair,
Storms turn to music, clouds to smiles and air: 10
Rain gently spends his honey-drops, and pours°

Balm on the cleft earth, milk on grass and flowers.
Bright pledge of peace and sunshine! the sure tie
Of thy Lord's hand, the object of his eye.°
When I behold thee, though my light be dim,
Distant and low, I can in thine see him,
Who looks upon thee from his glorious throne
And minds the Covenant 'twixt *All* and *One*.
O foul, deceitful men! my God doth keep
His promise still, but we break ours and sleep.   20
After the *Fall*, the first sin was in *blood*,°
And *drunkenness* quickly did succeed the flood;°
But since Christ died (as if we did devise
To lose him too, as well as Paradise)
These two grand sins we join and act together,
Though blood and drunkenness make but foul, foul weather.
Water (though both Heaven's windows and the deep,°
Full forty days o'er the drowned world did weep)
Could not reform us, and blood (in despite)
Yea God's own blood we tread upon and slight.   30
So those bad daughters, which God saved from fire,°
While Sodom yet did smoke, lay with their sire.

Then peaceful, signal bow, but in a cloud
Still lodged, where all thy unseen arrows shroud,
I will on thee, as on a comet look,
A comet, the sad world's ill-boding book;
Thy light as luctual and stained with woes°
I'll judge, where penal flames sit mixed and close.
For though some think, thou shin'st but to restrain
Bold storms, and simply dost attend on rain,   40
Yet I know well, and so our sins require,
Thou dost but court cold rain, till *rain* turns *fire*°

The Seed Growing Secretly°

S. Mark 4. 26

If this world's friends might see but once
What some poor man may often feel,
Glory, and gold, and crowns and thrones
They would soon quit and learn to kneel.

My dew, my dew! my early love,
My soul's bright food, thy absence kills!
Hover not long, eternal Dove!
Life without thee is loose and spills.

Something I had, which long ago
Did learn to suck, and sip, and taste,   10
But now grown sickly, sad and slow,
Doth fret and wrangle, pine and waste.

O spread thy sacred wings and shake°
One living drop! one drop life keeps!
If pious griefs Heaven's joys awake,
O fill his bottle! Thy child weeps!°

Slowly and sadly doth he grow,
And soon as left, shrinks back to ill;
O feed that life, which makes him blow°
And spread and open to thy will!   20

For thy eternal, living wells
None stained or withered shall come near:
A fresh, immortal *green* there dwells,
And spotless *white* is all the wear.

Dear, secret *greenness*! nursed below°
Tempests and winds, and winter-nights,
Vex not, that but one sees thee grow,°
That *One* made all these lesser lights.

If those bright joys he singly sheds
On thee, were all met in one crown,°   30
Both sun and stars would hide their heads;
And moons, though full, would get them down.

Let glory be their bait, whose minds°
Are all too high for a low cell:
Though hawks can prey through storms and winds,
The poor bee in her hive must dwell.

Glory, the crowd's cheap tinsel, still
To what most takes them, is a drudge;
And they too oft take good for ill,
And thriving vice for virtue judge.   40

What needs a conscience calm and bright
Within itself an outward test?
Who breaks his glass to take more light,
Makes way for storms into his rest.

Then bless thy secret growth, nor catch°
At noise, but thrive unseen and dumb;
Keep clean, bear fruit, earn life and watch°
Till the white-wingèd Reapers come!

¶

As time one day by me did pass°
    Through a large dusky glass
    He held, I chanced to look
    And spied his curious book°
Of past days, where sad Heav'n did shed
A mourning light upon the dead.

Many disordered lives I saw
    And foul records which thaw
    My kind eyes still, but in°
    A fair, white page of thin   10
And ev'n, smooth lines, like the sun's rays,
Thy name was writ, and all thy days.

O bright and happy calendar!°
    Where youth shines like a star
    All pearled with tears, and may
    Teach age, *The Holy way*;°
Where through thick pangs, high agonies,
Faith into life breaks, and death dies.

As some meek *night-piece* which day quails,°
    To candle-light unveils: 20
    So by one beamy line
    From thy bright lamp did shine,
In the same page thy humble grave
Set with green herbs, glad hopes and brave.

Here slept my thoughts' dear mark! which dust°
    Seemed to devour, like rust;
    But dust (I did observe)
    By hiding doth preserve,
As we for long and sure recruits,°
Candy with sugar our choice fruits.   30

O calm and sacred bed where lies
    In death's dark mysteries
    A beauty far more bright
    Than the noon's cloudless light
For whose dry dust green branches bud°
And robes are bleached in the *Lamb's* blood.°

Sleep happy ashes! (blessed sleep!)
    While hapless I still weep;
    Weep that I have out-lived
    My life, and unrelieved   40
Must (soul-less shadow!) so live on,
Though life be dead, and my joys gone.

¶

Fair and young light! my guide to holy
Grief and soul-curing melancholy;
Whom living here I did still shun
As sullen night-ravens do the sun,
And led by my own foolish fire
Wandered through darkness, dens and mire:
How am I now in love with all
That I termed then mere bonds and thrall,
And to thy name, which still I keep,

Like the surviving turtle, weep!°   10
O bitter cursed delights of men!
Our souls' diseases first, and then
Our bodies'; poisons that entreat
With fatal sweetness, till we eat;
How artfully do you destroy,
That kill with smiles and seeming joy?
If all the subtleties of vice
Stood bare before unpracticed eyes,
And every act she doth commence
Had writ down its sad consequence,   20
Yet would not men grant their ill fate
Lodged in those false looks, till too late.
O holy, happy, healthy Heaven,
Where all is pure, where all is even,
Plain, harmless, faithful, fair and bright,
But what Earth breathes against thy light!
How blest had men been, had their *sire*
Lived still in league with thy chaste fire,
Nor made life through her long descents
A slave to lustful elements!   30
I did once read in an old book
Soiled with many a weeping look,
That the seeds of foul sorrows be
The finest things that are, to see.
So that famed fruit which made all die
Seemed fair unto the woman's eye.
If these supplanters in the shade°
Of Paradise could make man fade,
How in this world should they deter
This world, their fellow-murtherer!   40
And why then grieve we to be sent
Home by our first fair punishment,
Without addition to our woes
And ling'ring wounds from weaker foes?
Since that doth quickly freedom win,
For he that's dead, is freed from sin.°

O that I were wingèd and free
And quite undressed just now with thee,
Where freed souls dwell by living fountains

On everlasting, spicy mountains!°   50
   Alas! my God! take home thy sheep;
   This world but laughs at those that weep.

The Stone°

Josh. chap. 24. ver. 27

     I have it now:
But where to act, that none shall know,
Where I shall have no cause to fear
    An eye or ear,
      What man will show?
If nights, and shades, and secret rooms,
    Silent as tombs,
Will nor conceal nor assent to
My dark designs, what shall I do?
Man I can bribe, and woman will   10
Consent to any gainful ill,
But these dumb creatures are so true,
No gold nor gifts can them subdue.
Hedges have ears, said the old *sooth*,
And ev'ry bush is something's booth;
This cautious fools mistake, and fear
Nothing but man, when ambushed there.

    But I (alas!)
Was shown one day in a strange glass
That busy commerce kept between   20
God and his Creatures, though unseen.

    They hear, see, speak,
And into loud discoveries break,
As loud as blood. Not that God needs°
Intelligence, whose spirit feeds
All things with life, before whose eyes,
Hell and all hearts stark naked lies.
But he that judgeth as he hears,°
He that accuseth none, so steers

His righteous course, that though he knows 30
All that man doth, conceals or shows,
Yet will not he by his own light
(Though both all-seeing and all right)
Condemn men; but will try them by
A process, which ev'n man's own eye
Must needs acknowledge to be just.
      Hence sand and dust
Are shaked for witnesses, and stones
Which some think dead, shall all at once
With one attesting voice detect 40
Those secret sins we least suspect.
For know, wild men, that when you err
Each thing turns Scribe and Register,
And in obedience to his Lord,
Doth your most private sins record.

      The *Law* delivered to the Jews,
Who promised much, but did refuse
Performance, will for that same deed
Against them by a *stone* proceed;
Whose substance, though 'tis hard enough, 50
Will prove their hearts more stiff and tough.
But now, since God on himself took
What all mankind could never brook,
If any (for he all invites)
His easy yoke rejects or slights,
The *Gospel* then (for 'tis his word°
And not himself shall judge the world)
Will by loose *dust* that man arraign,
As one than dust more vile and vain.

The Dwelling-place°

S. John, chap. 1. ver. 38, 39
    What happy, secret fountain,
      Fair shade, or mountain,
  Whose undiscovered virgin glory
  Boasts it this day, though not in story,°

Was then thy dwelling? did some cloud
Fixed to a tent, descend and shroud
My distressed Lord? or did a star
Beckoned by thee, though high and far,
In sparkling smiles haste gladly down
To lodge light, and increase her own?   10
My dear, dear God! I do not know
What lodged thee then, nor where, nor how;
But I am sure, thou dost now come
Oft to a narrow, homely room,
Where thou too hast but the least part,
My God, I mean *my sinful heart.*°

The Men of War°

S. Luke, chap. 23. ver. 11

If any have an ear
Saith holy John, then let him hear.°
He that into captivity
Leads others, shall a captive be.
Who with the sword doth others kill,
A sword shall his blood likewise spill.
Here is the patience of the saints,
And the true faith, which never faints.

Were not thy word (dear Lord!) my light,
How would I run to endless night,   10
And persecuting thee and thine,
Enact for *saints* myself and mine.°
But now enlightened thus by thee,
I dare not think such villainy;
Nor for a temporal self-end
Successful wickedness commend.
For in this bright, instructing verse
Thy saints are not the conquerors;°
But patient, meek, and overcome
Like thee, when set at naught and dumb.   20
Armies thou hast in Heaven, which fight,°
And follow thee all clothed in white,

But here on earth (though thou hast need)
Thou wouldst no legions, but wouldst bleed.
The sword wherewith thou dost command°
Is in thy mouth, not in thy hand,
And all thy saints do overcome°
By thy blood, and their martyrdom.
But seeing soldiers long ago°
Did spit on thee, and smote thee too;   30
Crowned thee with thorns, and bowed the knee,
But in contempt, as still we see,
I'll marvel not at ought they do,
Because they used my Saviour so;
Since of my *Lord* they had their will,
The servant must not take it ill.

   Dear Jesus give me patience here,
And faith to see my crown as near
And almost reached, because 'tis sure
If I hold fast and slight the *lure*.   40
Give me humility and peace,
Contented thoughts, innoxious ease,°
A sweet, revengeless, quiet mind,
And to my greatest haters kind.
Give me, my God! a heart as mild
And plain, as when I was a child;
That when *thy throne is set*, and all°
These *conquerors* before it fall,
I may be found (preserved by thee)
Amongst that chosen company,   50
Who by no blood (here) overcame
But the blood of the *blessed Lamb*.

The Ass

St. Matt. 21

Thou! who didst place me in this busy street
Of flesh and blood, where two ways meet:
The *One* of goodness, peace and life,
The *other* of death, sin and strife;

Where frail visibles rule the mind,
And present things find men most kind:°
Where obscure cares the *mean* defeat,
And splendid vice destroys the *great*;
As thou didst set no law for me,° 10
But that of perfect liberty,
Which neither tires, nor doth corrode,
But is a *pillow*, not a *load*:
So give me grace ever to rest,
And build on it, because the best;
Teach both mine eyes and feet to move
Within those bounds set by thy love;
Grant I may soft and lowly be,
And mind those things I cannot see;
Tie me to faith, though above reason,
Who question power, they speak treason: 20
Let me thy Ass be only wise
To carry, not search mysteries;
Who carries thee, is by thee led,
Who argues, follows his own head.
To check bad motions, keep me still
Amongst the dead, where thriving ill
Without his brags and conquests lies,
And truth (oppressed here) gets the prize.
At all times, whatsoe'er I do,
Let me not fail to question, who 30
Shares in the *act*, and puts me to't?
And if not thou, let not me do't.
Above all, make me love the poor,
Those burthens to the rich man's door,
Let me admire those, and be kind
To low estates, and a low mind.
If the world offers to me ought,
That by thy book must not be sought,
Or though it should be lawful, may°
Prove not expedient for thy way; 40
To shun that peril, let thy grace
Prevail with me to shun the place.
Let me be wise to please thee still,
And let men call me what they will.
    When thus thy mild, instructing hand

Finds thy poor *foal* at thy command,
When he from wild is become wise,
And slights that most, which men most prize;
When all things here to thistles turn
Pricking his lips, till he doth mourn   50
And hang the head, sighing for those
Pastures of life, where the Lamb goes:
O then, just then! break or untie
These bonds, this sad captivity,
This leaden state, which men miscall
Being and life, but is dead thrall.
And when (O God!) the Ass is free,
In a state known to none but thee;
O let him by his *Lord* be led,
To living springs, and there be fed   60
Where light, joy, health and perfect peace
Shut out all pain and each disease;
Where death and frailty are forgotten,
And bones rejoice, which once were broken!°

The Hidden Treasure

S. Matt. 13. 44

What can the man do that succeeds the King?°
Even what was done before, and no new thing.
Who shows me but one grain of sincere light?
False stars and fire-drakes, the deceits of night°
Set forth to fool and foil thee, do not boast;
Such coal-flames show but kitchen-rooms at most.
And those I saw searched through; yea those and all
That these three thousand years time did let fall
To blind the eyes of lookers-back, and I
Now all is done, find all is vanity.   10
Those secret searches, which afflict the wise,
Paths that are hidden from the *vulture's* eyes°
I saw at distance, and where grows that fruit
Which others only grope for and dispute.
    The world's loved wisdom (for the world's friends think
There is none else), did not the dreadful brink

And precipice it leads to, bid me fly,
None could with more advantage use, than I.
   Man's favourite sins, those tainting appetites
Which nature breeds, and some fine clay invites,   20
With all their soft, kind arts and easy strains
Which strongly operate, though without pains,
Did not a greater beauty rule mine eyes,
None would more dote on, nor so soon entice.
But since these sweets are sour and poisoned here
Where the impure seeds flourish all the year,
And private tapers will but help to stray
Ev'n those, who *by them* would find out the day,
I'll seal my eyes up, and to thy commands
Submit my wild heart, and restrain my hands;   30
I will do nothing, nothing know, nor see
But what thou bidst, and showst, and teachest me.
Look what thou gav'st; all that I do restore
But for one thing, though purchased once before.

Child-hood°

I cannot reach it; and my striving eye
Dazzles at it, as at eternity.
      Were now that Chronicle alive,
Those white designs which children drive,
And the thoughts of each harmless hour,
With their content too in my pow'r,
Quickly would I make my path even,°
And by mere playing go to Heaven.
      Why should men love
A Wolf, more than a Lamb or Dove?   10
Or choose hell-fire and brimstone streams
Before bright stars, and God's own beams?
Who kisseth thorns, will hurt his face,
But flowers do both refresh and grace,°
And sweetly living (*fie on men!*)
Are when dead, medicinal then.
If seeing much should make staid eyes,
And long experience should make wise;

Since all that age doth teach, is ill,
Why should I not love child-hood still?   20
Why if I see a rock or shelf,
Shall I from thence cast down myself,
Or by complying with the world,
From the same precipice be hurled?
Those observations are but foul
Which make me wise to lose my soul.

And yet the *practice* worldlings call°
Business and weighty action all,
Checking the poor child for his play,
But gravely cast themselves away.   30

   Dear, harmless age! the short, swift span,
Where weeping virtue parts with man;
Where love without lust dwells, and bends
What way we please, without self-ends.

An age of mysteries! which he°
Must live twice, that would God's face see;
Which *angels* guard, and with it play,
Angels! which foul men drive away.

How do I study now, and scan
Thee, more than e'er I studied man,   40
And only see through a long night
Thy edges, and thy bordering light!
O for thy Centre and mid-day!
For sure that is the *narrow way*.°

The Night *of the Agnostic Soul*

John 3. 2°

Through that pure *Virgin-shrine*,°
That sacred <u>veil</u> drawn o'er thy glorious noon
That men might look and live as glow-worms shine,
    And face the moon:
  Wise Nicodemus saw such light
  As made him know his God by night.

Most blest believer he!   *but he is not*
Who in that land of darkness and blind eyes
Thy long expected healing wings could see,°
    When thou didst rise,   10
  And what can never more be done,
  Did at mid-night speak with the S<u>un</u>!   *pun*

    O who will tell me, where
He found thee at that dead and silent hour!
What hallowed solitary ground did bear   *contains the Deity*
    So rare a flower,   *pantheistic*
  Within whose sacred leafs did lie
  The fullness of the Deity.

    No mercy-seat of gold,°
No dead and dusty *cherub*, nor carved stone,   20
But his own living works did my Lord hold
    And lodge alone;
  Where *trees* and *herbs* did watch and peep
  And wonder, while the Jews did sleep.   *Change of direction*

apost. night   Dear night! this world's defeat;   *Night itself*
The stop to busy fools; care's check and curb;
The day of spirits; my soul's calm retreat
    Which none disturb!
  Christ's progress, and his prayer time;°
  The hours to which high Heaven doth chime.   30

    God's silent, searching flight:
When my Lord's head is filled with dew, and all°
His locks are wet with the clear drops of night;
    His still, soft call;°
  His knocking time; the soul's dumb watch,°
  When spirits their fair kinred catch.°

    Were all my loud, evil days
Calm and unhaunted as is thy dark tent,
Whose peace but by some *angel's* wing or voice
    Is seldom rent;   40
  Then I in Heaven all the long year
  Would keep, and never wander here.

wrldofshade

      But living where the sun
Doth all things wake, and where all mix and tire
Themselves and others, I consent and run
        To ev'ry mire,
    And by this world's ill-guiding light,
    Err more than I can do by night.

      There is in God (some say)
A deep, but dazzling darkness; as men here°   50
Say it is late and dusky, because they
        See not all clear;
    O for that night! where I in him
    Might live invisible and dim.

Abel's Blood

    Sad, purple well! whose bubbling eye
    Did first against a murth'rer cry;°
    Whose streams still vocal, still complain
        Of bloody Cain,
    And now at evening are as red
    As in the morning when first shed.
        If single thou
    (Though single voices are but low)
    Could'st such a shrill and long cry rear
    As speaks still in thy maker's ear,   10
    What thunders shall those men arraign
    Who cannot count those they have slain,
    Who bathe not in a shallow flood,
    But in a deep, wide sea of blood?
    A sea, whose loud waves cannot sleep,
    But *deep* still calleth upon *deep*:°
    Whose urgent *sound* like unto that
    Of many waters, beateth at°
    The everlasting doors above,
    Where souls behind the altar move,   20
    And with one strong, incessant cry
    Inquire *How long?* of the most high.°
        Almighty Judge!

At whose just laws no just men grudge;
Whose blessed, sweet commands do pour
Comforts and joys, and hopes each hour
On those that keep them; O accept
Of his vowed heart, whom thou hast kept
From bloody men! and grant, I may
That sworn memorial duly pay   30
To thy bright arm, which was my light
And leader through thick death and night!
　　　　　Aye, may that flood,
That proudly spilt and despised blood,
Speechless and calm, as infants sleep!
Or if it watch, forgive and weep
For those that spilt it! May no cries
From the low earth to high Heaven rise,
But what (like his, whose blood peace brings)
Shall (when they rise) *speak better things*,°   40
Than Abel's doth! may Abel be
Still single heard, while these agree
With his mild blood in voice and will,
Who prayed for those that did him kill!

Righteousness°

Fair, solitary path! whose blessed shades
The old, white prophets planted first and dressed:
Leaving for us (whose goodness quickly fades)
A shelter all the way, and bowers to rest.

Who is the man that walks in thee? who loves
Heav'n's secret solitude, those fair abodes
Where turtles build, and careless sparrows move°
Without tomorrow's evils and future loads?

Who hath the upright heart, the single eye,
The clean, pure hand, which never meddled pitch?°   10
Who sees *Invisibles*, and doth comply
With hidden treasures that make truly rich?

He that doth seek and love
　　The things above,
Whose spirit ever poor, is meek and low;
　　Who simple still and wise,
　　Still homewards flies,
Quick to advance, and to retreat most slow.

　　Whose acts, words and pretence°
　　Have all one sense,   20
One aim and end; who walks not by his sight:
　　Whose eyes are both put out,
　　And goes about
Guided by faith, not by exterior light.

　　Who spills no blood, nor spreads
　　Thorns in the beds
Of the distressed, hasting their overthrow;
　　Making the time they had
　　Bitter and sad
Like *chronic* pains, which surely kill, though slow.°   30

　　Who knows earth nothing hath
　　Worth love or wrath,
But in his *hope* and *Rock* is ever glad.°
　　Who seeks and follows peace,
　　When with the ease
And health of conscience it is to be had.

　　Who bears his cross with joy
　　And doth employ
His heart and tongue in prayers for his foes;
　　Who lends, not to be paid,   40
　　And gives full aid
Without that bribe which usurers impose.

　　Who never looks on man
　　Fearful and wan,
But firmly trusts in God; the great man's measure
　　Though high and haughty must
　　Be ta'en in dust,
But the good man is God's peculiar treasure.°

Who doth thus, and doth not
These good deeds blot   50
With bad, or with neglect; and heaps not wrath
By secret filth, nor feeds
Some snake, or weeds,
Cheating himself; that man walks in this path.

Anguish

My God and King! to thee
I bow my knee,
I bow my troubled soul, and greet
With my foul heart thy holy feet.
Cast it, or tread it! It shall do
Even what thou wilt, and praise thee too.

My God, could I weep blood,
Gladly I would;
Or if thou wilt give me that art,
Which through the eyes pours out the heart,   10
I will exhaust it all, and make
Myself all tears, a weeping lake.

O! 'tis an easy thing
To write and sing;
But to write true, unfeignèd verse
Is very hard! O God, disperse
These weights, and give my spirit leave
To act as well as to conceive!

O my God, hear my cry;
Or let me die!—   20

Tears

O when my God, my glory brings
His white and holy train,
Unto those clear and living *springs*,
Where comes no *stain*!

Where all is *light*; and *flowers*, and *fruit*,
　　　And *joy*, and *rest*,
Make me amongst them ('tis my suit!)
　　　The last one, and the least.

And when they all are fed, and have
　　　Drunk of thy living stream,   10
Bid thy poor Ass (with tears I crave!)°
　　　Drink after them.

Thy love claims highest thanks, my sin
　　　The lowest pitch:°
Buf if he pays, who *loves much*, then°
　　　Thou hast made beggars rich.

Jacob's Pillow and Pillar°

I see the Temple in thy Pillar reared,°
And that dread glory, which thy children feared,
In mild, clear visions, without a frown,°
Unto thy solitary self is shown.
'Tis number makes a schism: throngs are rude,
And God himself died by the multitude.
This made him put on clouds, and fire and smoke,°
Hence he in thunder to thy offspring spoke;
The small, still voice, at some low cottage knocks,
But a strong wind must break thy lofty rocks.   10

　　The first true worship of the world's great King
From private and selected hearts did spring,
But he most willing to save all mankind,
Enlarged that light, and to the bad was kind.
Hence Catholic or Universal came
A most fair notion, but a very name.
For this rich Pearl, like some more common stone,
When once made public, is esteemed by none.
Man slights his Maker, when familiar grown,
And sets up laws, to pull his honour down.   20
This God foresaw: and when slain by the crowd
(Under that stately and mysterious cloud°
Which his death scattered) he foretold the place,°

And form to serve him in, should be true grace
And the meek heart, not in a Mount, nor at
Jerusalem, with blood of beasts and fat.°
A heart is that dread place, that awful cell,
That secret Ark, where the mild Dove doth dwell
When the proud waters rage: when heathens rule°
By God's permission, and man turns a mule.   30
This little Goshen, in the midst of night°
And Satan's seat, in all her coasts hath light,
Yea Bethel shall have tithes (saith Israel's stone)°
And vows and visions, though her foes cry, None.
Thus is the solemn temple sunk again
Into a Pillar, and concealed from men.
And glory be to his eternal Name!
Who is contented, that this holy flame
Shall lodge in such a narrow pit, till he
With his strong arm turns our captivity.°   40

        But blessèd Jacob, though thy sad distress
Was just the same with ours, and nothing less;
For thou a brother, and blood-thirsty too°
Didst fly, whose children wrought thy children's woe:
Yet thou in all thy solitude and grief,
On stones didst sleep and found'st but cold relief;
Thou from the Day-star a long way didst stand
And all that distance was Law and command.
But we a healing Sun by day and night,
Have our sure Guardian, and our leading light;   50
What thou didst hope for and believe, we find
And feel a friend most ready, sure and kind.
Thy pillow was but type and shade at best,°
But we the substance have, and on him rest.

The Agreement

        I wrote it down. But one that saw
        And envied that record, did since
        Such a mist over my mind draw,
        It quite forgot that purposed glimpse.
                I read it sadly oft, but still
                Simply believed, 'twas not my quill;

At length, my life's kind angel came,
And with his bright and busy wing
Scatt'ring that cloud, showed me the flame
Which straight, like morning-stars did sing,°   10
    And shine, and point me to a place,
    Which all the year sees the Sun's face.

O beamy book! O my mid-day
Exterminating fears and night!
The mount, whose white ascendents may°
Be in conjunction with true light!
    My thoughts, when towards thee they move,
    Glitter and kindle with thy love.

Thou art the oil and the wine-house:
Thine are the present healing leaves,   20
Blown from the tree of life to us
By his breath whom my dead heart heaves.
    Each page of thine hath true life in't,
    And God's bright mind expressed in print.

Most modern books are blots on thee,
Their doctrine chaff and windy fits:
Darkened along, as their scribes be,
With those foul storms, when they were writ;
    While the man's zeal lays out and blends
    Only self-worship and self-ends.   30

Thou art the faithful, pearly rock,
The hive of beamy, living lights,
Ever the same, whose diffused stock
Entire still, wears out blackest nights.
    Thy lines are rays, the true Sun sheds;
    Thy leaves are healing wings he spreads.°

For until thou didst comfort me,
I had not one poor word to say:
Thick busy clouds did multiply,
And said, I was no child of day;   40
    They said, my own hands did remove
    That candle given me from above.

O God! I know and do confess
My sins are great and still prevail,
Most heinous sins and numberless!
But thy *compassions* cannot fail.
    If thy sure mercies can be broken,
    Then all is true, my foes have spoken.

But while time runs, and after it
Eternity, which never ends,   50
Quite through them both, still infinite
Thy Covenant by Christ extends;°
    No sins of frailty, nor of youth
    Can foil his merits, and thy truth.

And this I hourly find, for thou
Dost still renew, and purge and heal:
Thy care and love, which jointly flow
New cordials, new *cathartics* deal.°
    But were I once cast off by thee
    I know (my God!) this would not be.   60

Wherefore with tears (tears by thee sent)
I beg, my faith may never fail!
And when in death my speech is spent,
O let that silence then prevail!
    O chase in that *cold calm* my foes,
    And hear my heart's last private throes!

So thou, who didst the work begin
(For *I till drawn came not to thee*)°
Wilt finish it, and by no sin
Will thy free mercies hindered be.   70
    For which, O God, I only can
    Bless thee, and blame unthankful man.

The Day of Judgement

O day of life, of light, of love!
The only day dealt from above!
A day so fresh, so bright, so brave
'Twill show us each forgotten grave,
And make the dead, like flowers, arise
Youthful and fair to see new skies.
All other days, compared to thee,
Are but light's weak minority,
They are but veils and ciphers drawn
Like clouds, before thy glorious dawn.   10
O come, arise, shine, do not stay
          Dearly loved day!
The fields are long since white, and I°
With earnest groans for freedom cry,
My fellow-creatures too say, *Come!*
And stones, though speechless, are not dumb.
When shall we hear that glorious voice
          Of life and joys?
That voice, which to each secret bed
          Of my Lord's dead,   20
Shall bring true day, and make dust see
The way to immortality.
When shall those first white pilgrims rise,
Whose holy, happy Histories
(Because they sleep so long) some men
Count but the blots of a vain pen?
          Dear Lord! make haste,
Sin every day commits more waste,
And thy old enemy, which knows°
His time is short, more raging grows.   30
Nor moan I only (though profuse)
Thy Creatures' bondage and abuse;
But what is highest sin and shame,
The vile despite done to thy name;
The forgeries, which impious wit
And power force on Holy Writ,
With all detestable designs
That may dishonour those pure lines.

O God! though mercy be in thee
The greatest attribute we see,   40
And the most needful for our sins;
Yet, when thy mercy nothing wins
But mere disdain, let not man say
Thy arm doth sleep; but write this day°
Thy judging one: Descend, descend!
Make all things new! and without end!°

Psalm 65°

Sion's true, glorious God! on thee
Praise waits in all humility.
All flesh shall unto thee repair,
To thee, O thou that hearest prayer!
But sinful words and works still spread
And overrun my heart and head;
Transgressions make me foul each day,
O purge them, purge them all away!

Happy is he! whom thou wilt choose
To serve thee in thy blessed house!   10
Who in thy holy Temple dwells,
And filled with joy, thy goodness tells!
King of Salvation! by strange things
And terrible, Thy Justice brings
Man to his duty. Thou alone
Art the world's hope, and but thee, none.
Sailors that float on flowing seas
Stand firm by thee, and have sure peace.
Thou still'st the loud waves, when most wild
And mak'st the raging people mild.   20
Thy arm did first the mountains lay
And girds their rocky heads this day.
The most remote, who know not thee,
At thy great works astonished be.

The *outgoings* of the *even* and *dawn*,
In *antiphones* sing to thy Name.
Thou visit'st the low earth, and then
Water'st it for the sons of men,
Thy upper river, which abounds

With fertile streams, makes rich all grounds,   30
And by thy mercies still supplied
The sower doth his bread provide.
Thou water'st every ridge of land
And settlest with thy secret hand
The furrows of it; then thy warm
And opening showers (restrained from harm)
Soften the mould, while all unseen
The blade grows up alive and green.
The year is with thy goodness crowned,
And all thy paths drop fatness round,   40
They drop upon the wilderness,
For thou dost even the deserts bless,
And hills full of springing pride,
Wear fresh adornments on each side.
The fruitful flocks fill every dale,
And purling corn doth clothe the vale;°
They shout for joy, and jointly sing,
Glory to the eternal King!

The Throne°

Revel. chap. 20. ver. 11

When with these eyes closed now by thee,
      But then restored,
The great and white throne I shall see
      Of my dread Lord:
And lowly kneeling (for the most
      Stiff then must kneel)
Shall look on him, at whose high cost
      (Unseen) such joys I feel.

Whatever arguments, or skill
      Wise heads shall use,   10
Tears only and my blushes still
      I will produce.
And should those speechless beggars fail,
      Which oft have won;
Then taught by thee, I will prevail,
      And say, *Thy will be done!*

Death

Though since thy first sad entrance by
            Just Abel's blood,
'Tis now six thousand years well nigh,°
And still thy sov'reignty holds good:
Yet by none art thou understood.

We talk and name thee with much ease
            As a tried thing,
And everyone can slight his lease
As if it ended in a Spring,
Which shades and bowers doth rent-free bring.   10

To thy dark land these heedless go:
            But there was *One*,°
Who searched it quite through to and fro,
And then returning, like the Sun,
Discovered all, that there is done.°

And since his death, we throughly see
            All thy dark way;
Thy shades but thin and narrow be,
Which his first looks will quickly fray:°
Mists make but triumphs for the day.   20

As harmless violets, which give
            Their virtues here°
For salves and syrups, while they live,
Do after calmly disappear,
And neither grieve, repine, nor fear:

So die his servants; and as sure
            Shall they revive.
Then let not dust your eyes obscure,
But lift them up, where still alive,
Though fled from you, their spirits hive.   30

The Feast

O come away,°
Make no delay,
    Come while my heart is clean and steady!
While Faith and Grace
Adorn the place,
    Making dust and ashes ready.

No bliss here lent
Is permanent,
    Such triumphs poor flesh cannot merit;
Short sips and sights
Endear delights,   10
    Who seeks for more, he would inherit.

Come then true bread,°
Quick'ning the dead,
    Whose eater shall not, cannot die,
Come, antedate
On me that state
    Which brings poor dust the victory.

Aye victory°
Which from thine eye   20
    Breaks as the day doth from the east,
When the spilt dew,
Like tears doth shew
    The sad world wept to be released.

Spring up, O wine,
And springing shine
    With some glad message from his heart,
Who did, when slain,
These means ordain
    For me to have in him a part.   30

Such a sure part
In his blest heart,
    The well, where living waters spring,°
That with it fed
Poor dust though dead
    Shall rise again, and live and sing.

O drink and bread
Which strikes death dead,
    The food of man's immortal being!
Under veils here   40
Thou art my cheer,
    Present and sure without my seeing.

How dost thou fly
And search and pry
    Through all my parts, and like a quick
And knowing lamp
Hunt out each damp,
    Whose shadow makes me sad or sick?

O what high joys!
The turtle's voice°   50
    And songs I hear! O quick'ning showers
Of my Lord's blood,
You make rocks bud
    And crown dry hills with wells and flowers!

For this true ease,
This healing peace,
    For this taste of living glory,
My soul and all,
Kneel down and fall
    And sing his sad victorious story.   60

O thorny crown
More soft than down!
    O painful Cross, my bed of rest!
O spear, the key
Opening the way!
    O thy worst state, my only best!

Oh! all thy griefs
Are my reliefs,
    And all my sins, thy sorrows were!
And what can I,   70
To this reply;
    What (O God!) but a silent tear?

Some toil and sow,
That wealth may flow,
    And dress this earth for next year's meat:
But let me heed,
Why thou didst bleed,
    And what in the next world to eat.

Revel. chap. 19. ver. 9
Blessed are they which are called unto the marriage supper of the Lamb!

The Obsequies

Since dying for me, thou didst crave no more
        Than common pay,
Some few true tears, and those shed for
        My own ill way;
With a cheap, plain remembrance still
        Of thy sad death,
Because forgetfulness would kill
        Even life's own breath:
I were most foolish and unkind
        In my own sense,   10
Should I not ever bear in mind,
If not thy mighty love, my own defence.
Therefore, those loose delights and lusts, which here
        Men call good cheer,
    I will close girt and tied
For mourning sack-cloth wear, all mortified.
Not but that mourners too, can have
        Rich weeds and shrouds;
For some wore *white* ev'n in thy grave,°
And joy, like light, shines oft in clouds: 20

But thou, who didst man's whole life earn,
Dost so invite and woo me still,
That to be merry I want skill,
             And time to learn.
Besides, those kerchiefs sometimes shed°
           To make me brave,
I cannot find, but where thy head
Was once laid for me in thy grave.
Thy grave! To which my thoughts shall move
Like bees in storms unto their hive,   30
That from the murd'ring world's false love
Thy death may keep my soul alive.

The Waterfall

With what deep murmurs through time's silent stealth
Doth thy transparent, cool and wat'ry wealth
         Here flowing fall,
         And chide, and call,
As if his liquid, loose retinue stayed
Ling'ring, and were of this steep place afraid,
         The common pass
         Where, clear as glass,
         All must descend
         Not to an end: 10
But quickened by this deep and rocky grave,
Rise to a longer course more bright and brave.

       Dear stream! dear bank, where often I
       Have sate, and pleased my pensive eye,
       Why, since each drop of thy quick store
       Runs thither, whence it flowed before,
       Should poor souls fear a shade or night,
       Who came (sure) from a sea of light?
       Or since those drops are all sent back
       So sure to thee, that none doth lack,   20
       Why should frail flesh doubt any more
       That what God takes, he'll not restore?

O useful element and clear!
My sacred wash and cleanser here,
My first consigner unto those
Fountains of life, where the Lamb goes!°
What sublime truths, and wholesome themes,
Lodge in thy mystical, deep streams!
Such as dull man can never find
Unless that Spirit lead his mind,°   30
Which first upon thy face did move,
And hatched all with his quick'ning love.
As this loud brook's incessant fall
In streaming rings restagnates all,
Which reach by course the bank, and then
Are no more seen, just so pass men.
O my invisible estate,
My glorious liberty, still late!°
Thou art the channel my soul seeks,
Not this with cataracts and creeks.

Quickness°

False life! a foil and no more, when°
           Wilt thou be gone?
Thou foul deception of all men
That would not have the true come on.

Thou art a moon-like toil; a blind°
           Self-posing state;°
A dark contest of waves and wind;
A mere tempestuous debate.

Life is a fixed, discerning light,
           A knowing joy;   10
No chance, or fit: but ever bright,
And calm and full, yet doth not cloy.

'Tis such a blissful thing, that still
           Doth vivify,
And shine and smile, and hath the skill
To please without Eternity.°

Thou art a toilsome mole, or less,
          A moving mist,
But life is, what none can express,
A quickness, which my God hath kissed.   20

The Wreath

Since I in storms used most to be
     And seldom yielded flowers,
How shall I get a wreath for thee
     From those rude, barren hours?

The softer dressings of the Spring,
     Or Summer's later store
I will not for thy temples bring,
     Which *thorns*, not *roses* wore.

But a twined wreath of *grief* and *praise*,
Praise soiled with tears, and tears again   10
Shining with joy, like dewy days,
This day I bring for all thy pain,
Thy causeless pain! and sad as death,
Which sadness breeds in the most vain,
(O not in vain!) now beg thy breath;
Thy quick'ning breath, which gladly bears
Through saddest clouds to that glad place,
Where cloudless choirs sing without tears,
Sing thy just praise, and see thy face.

The Queer°

O tell me whence that joy doth spring
Whose diet is divine and fair,
Which wears heaven, like a bridal ring,
And tramples on doubts and despair?

Whose eastern traffic deals in bright
And boundless empyrean themes,
Mountains of spice, day-stars and light,
Green trees of life, and living streams?

Tell me, O tell who did thee bring
And here, without my knowledge, placed,   10
Till thou didst grow and get a wing,
A wing with eyes, and eyes that taste?°

Sure, *holiness* the *magnet* is,
And *love* the *lure*, that woos thee down;
Which makes the high transcendent bliss
Of knowing thee, so rarely known.

The Book

Eternal God! maker of all
That have lived here, since the man's fall;
The Rock of ages! in whose shade
They live unseen, when here they fade.

Thou knew'st this *paper*, when it was
Mere *seed*, and after that but *grass*;
Before 'twas *dressed* or *spun*, and when
Made *linen*, who did *wear* it then:
What were their lives, their thoughts and deeds
Whether good *corn*, or fruitless *weeds*.   10

Thou knew'st this *tree*, when a green *shade*
Covered it, since a *cover* made,°
And where it flourished, grew and spread,
As if it never should be dead.

Thou knew'st this harmless *beast*, when he
Did live and feed by thy decree
On each green thing; then slept (well fed)
Clothed with this *skin*, which now lies spread
A *covering* o'er this aged book,

Which makes me wisely weep and look   20
On my own dust; mere dust it is,
But not so dry and clean as this.
Thou knew'st and saw'st them all and though
Now scattered thus, dost know them so.

O knowing, glorious spirit! when
Thou shalt restore trees, beasts and men,
When thou shalt make all new again,
Destroying only death and pain,
Give him amongst thy works a place,
Who in them loved and sought thy face!   30

To the Holy Bible

O book! life's guide! how shall we part,
And thou so long seized of my heart!°
Take this last kiss, and let me weep
True thanks to thee, before I sleep.

Thou wert the first put in my hand,
When yet I could not understand,
And daily didst my young eyes lead
To letters, till I learnt to read.
But as rash youths, when once grown strong
Fly from their nurses to the throng,   10
Where they new consorts choose, and stick
To those, till either hurt or sick:
So with that first light gained from thee
Ran I in chase of vanity,
Cried dross for gold, and never thought°
My first cheap Book had all I sought.
Long reigned this vogue; and thou cast by
With meek, dumb looks didst woo mine eye,
And oft left open would'st convey
A sudden and most searching ray   20
Into my soul, with whose quick touch
Refining still, I struggled much.
By this mild art of love at length

Thou overcam'st my sinful strength,
And having brought me home, didst there
Show me that pearl I sought elsewhere.°
Gladness, and peace, and hope, and love,
The secret favours of the Dove,
Her quick'ning kindness, smiles and kisses,
Exalted pleasures, crowning blisses,   30
Fruition, union, glory, life
Thou didst lead to, and still all strife.
Living, thou wert my soul's sure ease,
And dying mak'st me go in peace:
Thy next *effects* no tongue can tell;
Farewell O book of God! farewell!

> S. Luke, chap. 2. ver. 14
> *Glory be to God in the highest, and on*
> *Earth peace, good will towards men.*

L'Envoy°

O the new world's new, quick'ning Sun!
Ever the same, and never done!
The seers of whose sacred light
Shall all be dressed in shining white,°
And made conformable to his
Immortal shape, who wrought their bliss,
   Arise, arise!
And like old clothes fold up these skies,°
This long worn veil: then shine and spread
Thy own bright self over each head,   10
And through thy creatures pierce and pass
Till all becomes thy cloudless glass,
Transparent as the purest day
And without blemish or decay,
Fixed by thy spirit to a state
For evermore immaculate.
A state fit for the sight of thy
Immediate, pure and unveiled eye,
A state agreeing with thy mind,

A state thy birth and death designed: 20
A state for which thy creatures all°
Travail and groan, and look and call.
O seeing thou hast paid our score,
Why should the curse reign any more?
But since thy number is as yet
Unfinished, we shall gladly sit
Till all be ready, that the train
May fully fit thy glorious reign.
Only, let not our haters brag,
Thy seamless coat is grown a rag,°   30
Or that thy truth was not here known,
Because we forced thy judgements down.
Dry up their arms, who vex thy spouse,
And take the glory of thy house
To deck their own; then give thy saints
That faithful zeal, which neither faints
Nor wildly burns, but meekly still
Dares own the truth, and show the ill.
Frustrate those cancerous, close arts
Which cause solution in all parts,°   40
And strike them dumb, who for mere words
Wound thy belovèd, more than swords.
Dear Lord, do this! and then let grace
Descend, and hallow all the place.
Incline each hard heart to do good,
And cement us with thy son's blood,
That like true sheep, all in one fold
We may be fed, and one mind hold.
Give watchful spirits to our guides!
For sin (like water) hourly glides   50
By each man's door, and quickly will
Turn in, if not obstructed still.
Therefore write in their hearts thy law,
And let these long, sharp judgements awe
Their very thoughts, that by their clear
And holy lives, mercy may here
Sit regent yet, and blessings flow
As fast, as persecutions now.
So shall we know in war and peace
Thy service to be our sole ease,   60

With prostrate souls adoring thee,
Who turned our sad captivity!°

S. Clemens apud Basil:°
Ζῆ ὁ Θεὸς, καὶ ὁ κύριος Ἰησοῦς Χριστὸς,
καὶ τὸ πνεῦμα τὸ ἅγιον.

FINIS

from POEMS, WITH THE TENTH SATIRE
OF JUVENAL ENGLISHED, 1646

To my Ingenuous Friend, R.W.°

When we are dead, and now, no more
Our harmless mirth, our wit, and score°
Distracts the town; when all is spent
That the base niggard world hath lent
Thy purse, or mine; when the loathed noise
Of drawers, 'prentices and boys°
Hath left us, and the clam'rous bar
Items no pints i' th' Moon or Star;°
When no calm whisp'rers wait the doors,
To fright us with forgotten scores;   10
And such agèd long bills carry,°
As might start an antiquary;
When the sad tumults of the Maze,°
Arrests, suits, and the dreadful face
Of sergeants are not seen, and we°
No lawyers' ruffs, or gowns must fee:
When all these mulcts are paid, and I
From thee, dear wit, must part, and die;
We'll beg the world would be so kind,
To give's one grave as we'd one mind;   20
There, as the wiser few suspect,
That spirits after death affect,°
Our souls shall meet, and thence will they,
Freed from the tyranny of clay,
With equal wings, and ancient love
Into the Elysian fields remove,
Where in those blessed walks they'll find
More of thy genius, and my mind.
  First, in the shade of his own bays,°
Great BEN they'll see, whose sacred lays°   30
The learnèd ghosts admire, and throng
To catch the subject of his song.

Then Randolph in those holy meads,°
His *Lovers* and *Amyntas* reads,
Whilst his Nightingale, close by,
Sings his and her own elegy.
From thence dismissed, by subtle roads,
Through airy paths and sad abodes,
They'll come into the drowsy fields
Of Lethe, which such virtue yields,°   40
That, if what poets sing be true,
The streams all sorrow can subdue.
Here, on a silent, shady green,
The souls of lovers oft are seen,
Who, in their life's unhappy space,
Were murthered by some perjured face.
All these th' enchanted streams frequent,
To drown their cares and discontent,
That th' inconstant, cruel sex
Might not in death their spirits vex.   50
    And here our souls, big with delight
Of their new state, will cease their flight:
And now the last thoughts will appear,
They'll have of us, or any here;°
But on those flow'ry banks will stay,
And drink all sense and cares away.
    So they that did of these discuss,°
    Shall find their fables true in us.

Les Amours

Tyrant, farewell! this heart, the prize
And triumph of thy scornful eyes,
I sacrifice to Heaven, and give
To quit my sins, that durst believe
A woman's easy faith, and place
True joys in a changing face.
    Yet ere I go: by all those tears
And sighs I spent 'twixt hopes and fears;
By thy own glories, and that hour
Which first enslaved me to thy power;   10

I beg, fair one, by this last breath,
This tribute from thee after death.
If, when I'm gone, you chance to see
That cold bed where I lodgèd be,
Let not your hate in death appear,
But bless my ashes with a tear:
This influx from that quick'ning eye,°
By secret pow'r, which none can spy,
The cold dust shall inform, and make°
Those flames, though dead, new life partake,   20
Whose warmth, helped by your tears, shall bring
O'er all the tomb a sudden spring
Of crimson flowers, whose drooping heads
Shall curtain o'er their mournful beds:
And on each leaf, by Heaven's command,
These emblems to the life shall stand:
   Two hearts, the first a shaft withstood;
The second, shot and washed in blood;
And on this heart a dew shall stay,
Which no heat can court away;   30
But fixed forever, witness bears
That hearty sorrow feeds on tears.
Thus Heaven can make it known, and true
That you killed me, 'cause I loved you.

To Amoret

The Sigh

Nimble sigh, on thy warm wings,
   Take this message and depart;
Tell Amoret, that smiles and sings,
At what thy airy voyage brings,
   That thou cam'st lately from my heart.

Tell my lovely foe that I
Have no more such spies to send,
But one or two that I intend,
Some few minutes ere I die,
   To her white bosom to commend.   10

Then whisper by that holy spring,
   Where for her sake I would have died,
Whilst those water-nymphs did bring
   Flowers to cure what she had tried;°
And of my faith and love did sing.

That if my Amoret, if she
   In after-times would have it read,
How her beauty murthered me,
With all my heart I will agree,
   If she'll but love me, being dead.   20

To His Friend Being in Love

Ask, lover, ere thou diest; let one poor breath
Steal from thy lips, to tell her of thy death;
Doting idolater! can silence bring
Thy saint propitious? or will Cupid fling
One arrow for thy paleness? leave to try
This silent courtship of a sickly eye.
Witty to tyranny, she too well knows°
This but the incense of thy private vows,
That breaks forth at thine eyes, and doth betray
The sacrifice thy wounded heart would pay;   10
Ask her, fool, ask her; if words cannot move,
The language of thy tears may make her love.
   Flow nimbly from me then; and when you fall
On her breast's warmer snow, O may you all,
By some strange fate fixed there, distinctly lie,
The much loved volume of my tragedy.
   Where, if you win her not, may this be read,
The cold that freezed you so, did strike me dead.

Song

   Amyntas go, thou art undone,
      Thy faithful heart is crossed by fate;
   That love is better not begun,
      Where love is come to love too late.

Had she professèd hidden fires,
   Or showed one knot that tied her heart,
I could have quenched my first desires,
   And we had only met to part.

But, tyrant, thus to murther men,
   And shed a lover's harmless blood,   10
And burn him in those flames again,
   Which he at first might have withstood.

Yet, who that saw fair Chloris weep
   Such sacred dew, with such pure grace,
Durst think them feignèd tears, or seek
   For treason in an angel's face?

This is her art, though this be true,
   Men's joys are killed with griefs and fears,
Yet she, like flowers oppressed with dew,
   Doth thrive and flourish in her tears.   20

This, cruel, thou hast done, and thus
   That face hath many servants slain,
Though th' end be not to ruin us,
   But to seek glory by our pain.

To Amoret,

Walking in a Starry Evening

If, Amoret, that glorious eye,°
   In the first birth of light,
     And death of night,
Had with those elder fires you spy
     Scattered so high,
     Receivèd form and sight,

We might suspect in the vast ring,°
    Amidst these golden glories,
     And fiery stories,°
Whether the sun had been the king   10
    And guide of day,
Or your brighter eye should sway.

But, Amoret, such is my fate,
  That if thy face a star
    Had shined from far,
I am persuaded in that state,
    'Twixt thee and me,
Of some predestined sympathy.°

For sure such two conspiring minds,°
  Which no accident, or sight,   20
    Did thus unite,
Whom no distance can confine,
    Start, or decline,°
One for another were designed.

To Amoret Gone from Him

Fancy and I, last evening, walked,°
And Amoret, of thee we talked;
The West just then had stolen the sun,
And his last blushes were begun:
We sate, and marked how every thing
Did mourn his absence; how the spring
That smiled and curled about his beams,
Whilst he was here, now checked her streams:
The wanton eddies of her face
Were taught less noise, and smoother grace;   10
And in a slow, sad channel went,
Whisp'ring the banks their discontent:
The careless ranks of flowers that spread
Their perfumed bosoms to his head,
And with an open, free embrace,
Did entertain his beamy face,
Like absent friends point to the West,
And on that weak reflection feast.
If creatures then that have no sense,
But the loose tie of influence,°   20
Though fate and time each day remove°
Those things that element their love,
At such vast distance can agree,
Why, Amoret, why should not we?

A Song to Amoret

If I were dead, and in my place
  Some fresher youth designed
To warm thee with new fires, and grace
  Those arms I left behind;

Were he as faithful as the sun,
  That's wedded to the sphere;
His blood as chaste and temp'rate run,
  As April's mildest tear;

Or were he rich, and with his heaps
  And spacious share of Earth,   10
Could make divine affection cheap,
  And court his golden birth:

For all these arts I'd not believe
  (No, though he should be thine)
The mighty amorist could give
  So rich a heart as mine.

Fortune and beauty thou might'st find,
  And greater men than I:
But my true resolvèd mind
  They never shall come nigh.   20

For I not for an hour did love,
  Or for a day desire,
But with my soul had from above
  This endless, holy fire.

An Elegy

'Tis true, I am undone: yet, ere I die,
I'll leave these sighs and tears a legacy
To after-lovers: that, rememb'ring me,
Those sickly flames which now benighted be,

Fanned by their warmer sighs, may love, and prove
In them the metempsychosis of love.°
'Twas I (when others scorned) vowed you were fair,
And sware that breath enriched the coarser air,
Lent roses to your cheeks, made Flora bring°
Her nymphs with all the glories of the Spring   10
To wait upon thy face, and gave my heart
A pledge to Cupid for a quicker dart,°
To arm those eyes against myself; to me
Thou ow'st that tongue's bewitching harmony.
I courted angels from those upper joys,
And made them leave their spheres to hear thy voice.
I made the Indian curse the hours he spent
To seek his pearls, and wisely to repent
His former folly, and confess a sin,
Charmed by the brighter lustre of thy skin.   20
I borrowed from the winds the gentler wing
Of Zephyrus, and soft souls of the Spring,°
And made (to air those cheeks with fresher grace)
The warm inspirers dwell upon thy face.°
                    Oh! jam satis—°

A Rhapsody°

*Occasionally written upon a meeting° with some of his friends at the Globe
Tavern, in a chamber painted overhead with a cloudy sky and some
few dispersed stars, and on the sides with landscapes, hills, shepherds
and sheep.*

Darkness, and stars i' th' mid-day! They invite
Our active fancies to believe it night:
For taverns need no sun, but for a sign,
Where rich tobacco and quick tapers shine;
And royal, witty sack, the poet's soul,°
With brighter suns than he doth gild the bowl;
As though the pot and poet did agree,
Sack should to both illuminator be.
That artificial cloud, with its curled brow,
Tells us 'tis late; and that blue space below   10

Is fired with many stars; mark, how they break
In silent glances o'er the hills, and speak
The evening to the plains, where, shot from far,
They meet in dumb salutes, as one great star.
   The room (methinks) grows darker; and the air
Contracts a sadder colour, and less fair.
Or is't the drawer's skill? hath he no arts°
To blind us so we can't know pints from quarts?
No, no, 'tis night: look where the jolly clown°
Musters his bleating herd and quits the down.   20
Hark! how his rude pipe frets the quiet air,
Whilst ev'ry hill proclaims Lycoris fair.
Rich, happy man! that canst thus watch and sleep,
Free from all cares, but thy wench, pipe and sheep.
But see, the moon is up; view where she stands
Sentinel o'er the door, drawn by the hands
Of some base painter, that for gain hath made
Her face the landmark to the tippling trade.
This cup to her, that to Endymion give;°
'Twas wit at first, and wine that made them live.   30
Choke may the painter! and his box disclose
No other colours than his fiery nose;
And may we no more of his pencil see°
Than two churchwardens, and mortality.
   Should we go now a-wand'ring, we should meet
With catchpoles, whores and carts in ev'ry street:°
Now when each narrow lane, each nook and cave,
Sign-posts and shop-doors, pimp for ev'ry knave,
When riotous sinful plush, and tell-tale spurs
Walk Fleet Street and the Strand, when the soft stirs   40
Of bawdy, ruffled silks turn night to day;
And the loud whip and coach scolds all the way;
When lust of all sorts, and each itchy blood
From the Tower-wharf to Cymbeline and Lud,°
Hunts for a mate, and the tired footman reels
'Twixt chairmen, torches, and the hackney wheels.
   Come, take the other dish; it is to him°
That made his horse a senator: each brim
Look big as mine; the gallant, jolly beast
Of all the herd (you'll say) was not the least.   50
   Now crown the second bowl, rich as his worth

I'll drink it to; he! that like fire broke forth°
Into the Senate's face, crossed Rubicon,
And the State's pillars, with their laws thereon,
And made the dull grey beards and furred gowns fly°
Into Brundusium to consult and lie.
    This, to brave Sylla! why should it be said°
We drink more to the living than the dead?
Flatt'rers and fools do use it: let us laugh
At our own honest mirth; for they that quaff   60
To honour others, do like those that sent
Their gold and plate to strangers to be spent.
    Drink deep; this cup be pregnant, and the wine
Spirit of wit, to make us all divine,
That big with sack and mirth we may retire
Possessors of more souls, and nobler fire;
And by the influx of this painted sky,°
And laboured forms, to higher matters fly;
So, if a nap shall take us, we shall all,
After full cups, have dreams poetical.   70

Let's laugh now, and the pressed grape drink,
Till the drowsy day-star wink;
And in our merry, mad mirth run
Faster and further than the sun;
And let none his cup forsake,
Till that star again doth wake;
So we men below shall move
Equally with the gods above.

To Amoret, of the Difference 'Twixt Him and Other Lovers, and What True Love is

Mark, when the evening's cooler wings
  Fan the afflicted air, how the faint sun,
      Leaving undone,
      What he begun,
Those spurious flames sucked up from slime and earth
      To their first, low birth,
      Resigns and brings.

They shoot their tinsel beams and vanities,
    Threading with those false fires their way;
        But as you stay   10
        And see them stray,
You lose the flaming track, and subtly they
        Languish away,
        And cheat your eyes.

Just so base, sublunary lovers' hearts°
    Fed on loose profane desires,
        May for an eye
        Or face comply:
But those removed, they will as soon depart,
        And show their art,   20
        And painted fires.

Whilst I by pow'rful love, so much refined,
    That my absent soul the same is,
        Careless to miss
        A glance or kiss,
Can with those elements of lust and sense
        Freely dispense,
        And court the mind.

Thus to the North the loadstones move,°
    And thus to them th' enamoured steel aspires: 30
        Thus, Amoret,
        I do affect;°
And thus by wingèd beams, and mutual fire,
        Spirits and stars conspire:
        And this is LOVE.

To Amoret Weeping

Leave, Amoret, melt not away so fast°
Thy eyes' fair treasure; Fortune's wealthiest cast
Deserves not one such pearl; for these, well spent,
Can purchase stars, and buy a tenement
For us in heaven; though here the pious streams

Avail us not; who from that clue of sunbeams°
Could ever steal one thread? or with a kind
Persuasive accent charm the wild loud wind?
    Fate cuts us all in marble, and the Book°
Forestalls our glass of minutes; we may look   10
But seldom meet a change; think you a tear
Can blot the flinty volume? shall our fear
Or grief add to their triumphs? and must we°
Give an advantage to adversity?
Dear, idle prodigal! is it not just
We bear our stars? What though I had not dust
Enough to cabinet a worm? nor stand
Enslaved unto a little dirt, or sand?
I boast a better purchase, and can show
The glories of a soul that's simply true.   20
    But grant some richer planet at my birth
Had spied me out, and measured so much earth
Or gold unto my share: I should have been
Slave to these lower elements, and seen
My high-born soul flag with their dross, and lie
A pris'ner to base mud and alchemy.
I should perhaps eat orphans, and suck up
A dozen distressed widows in one cup;
Nay, further, I should by that lawful stealth,
Damned usury, undo the commonwealth;   30
Or patent it in soap, and coals, and so°
Have the smiths curse me, and my laundress too;
Geld wine, or his friend tobacco; and so bring°
The incensed subject rebel to his king;
And after all (as those first sinners fell)
Sink lower than my gold, and lie in hell.
    Thanks then for this deliv'rance! blessed pow'rs,
You that dispense man's fortune and his hours,
How am I to you all engaged! that thus
By such strange means, almost miraculous,   40
You should preserve me; you have gone the way
To make me rich by taking all away.
For I (had I been rich) as sure as fate,
Would have been meddling with the King, or State,
Or something to undo me; and 'tis fit,
(We know) that who hath wealth should have no wit.

But, above all, thanks to that Providence
That armed me with a gallant soul, and sense,
'Gainst all misfortunes, that hath breathed so much
Of Heav'n into me, that I scorn the touch   50
Of these low things; and can with courage dare
Whatever fate or malice can prepare:
I envy no man's purse or mines; I know
That, losing them, I've lost their curses too;
And Amoret (although our share in these
Is not contemptible, nor doth much please)
Yet whilst content and love we jointly vie,°
We have a blessing which no gold can buy.

Upon The Priory Grove, His Usual Retirement°

Hail, sacred shades! cool, leavy house!
Chaste treasurer of all my vows
And wealth! on whose soft bosom laid
My love's fair steps I first betrayed:°
    Henceforth no melancholy flight,
No sad wing, or hoarse bird of night,
Disturb this air, no fatal throat
Of raven, or owl, awake the note
Of our laid echo, no voice dwell°
Within these leaves, but Philomel.°   10
The poisonous ivy here no more
His false twists on the oak shall score;
Only the woodbine here may twine,
As th' emblem of her love, and mine;
The amorous sun shall here convey
His best beams, in thy shades to play;
The active air the gentlest show'rs
Shall from his wings rain on thy flowers;
And the moon from her dewy locks
Shall deck thee with her brightest drops.   20
Whatever can a fancy move,
Or feed the eye, be on this grove;
    And when at last the winds and tears
Of heaven, with the consuming years,

Shall these green curls bring to decay,
And clothe thee in an agèd grey
(If ought a lover can foresee,
Or if we poets, prophets be)
From hence transplanted, thou shalt stand
A fresh grove in th' Elysian land;   30
Where (most blest pair!) as here on Earth
Thou first didst eye our growth and birth;
So there again, thou'lt see us move
In our first innocence and love;
And in thy shades, as now, so then,
We'll kiss, and smile, and walk again.

NOTES

ABBREVIATIONS

B	The Bodleian manuscript of Herbert's *Temple*.
BCP	The Book of Common Prayer.
Geneva	The Geneva version of the Bible.
Hutchinson	Herbert's *Works*, edited by F. E. Hutchinson.
KJ	The King James (Authorized) version of the Bible.
OED	*The Oxford English Dictionary.*
Martin	Vaughan's *Works* (2nd edn.), edited by L. C. Martin.
Rudrum	Vaughan's *Complete Poems*, edited by Alan Rudrum.
W	The early manuscript of Herbert's *Temple*, in Dr William's Library, Gordon Square, London.
1633	The first edition of Herbert's *Temple*.

For other works identified in the notes by author or short title, a full reference is given in 'Further Reading.'

GEORGE HERBERT

THE TEMPLE

4   *The Printers to the Reader*. This preface was written by Nicholas Ferrar, founder of the community at Little Gidding; he received the manuscript of *The Temple* after Herbert's death and supervised its publication. See Walton, pp. 314–15. There is no evidence that Herbert was responsible for the title *The Temple*, or for the epigraph from Psalm 29: 8 (*BCP*) that appears on the title-page of *1633*. They do not appear in *W*; and in *B* they are added in what seems to be Ferrar's hand (see Charles, *Life of Herbert*, p. 185).

5   *an ecclesiastical dignity*. The office of prebend of Leighton Ecclesia, which had its church at Leighton Bromswold, in Huntingdonshire. Herbert attempted to transfer the office to Nicholas Ferrar, but, not succeeding in this, he undertook an elaborate restoration of the ruined church. See Walton, pp. 278–9.

    The Dedication. l. 6. *refrain*: stop, prevent.

6   *The Church-porch. Perirrhanterium*: instrument used for sprinkling holy water.

    l. 15. *afford*: give, grant.

    l. 16. *stays*: restraints.

    ll. 19–20. *common ... th' incloser*. The imagery is drawn from the practice of enclosing public grazing land (the 'common') for private use.

l. 21. *impaled*: fenced in.

l. 24. *cross*: perverse, contrary.

7   l. 27. *list*: desire, like, choose.

l. 30. *keep the round*: i.e., drink at each pass of the bottle.

l. 35. *devest*: annul, in legal usage; abandon.

l. 37. *wine-sprung*: drunk.

l. 39. *can*: drinking vessel. Hutchinson paraphrases 38–40, 'I may not drink what the hardened drinker allows himself; need I humour him to my own undoing?'

l. 44. *several*: separate.

l. 50. Philippians 3: 19, 'Whose end is destruction, whose God is their belly, and whose glory is in their shame, who mind earthly things.'

l. 53. *flat*: unconditional, outright.

8   l. 60. *Epicure*: a follower of the philosophy of Epicurus; 'one who recognizes no religious motives for conduct' (*OED*). *bate*: omit.

l. 80. An echo of Donne's 'To Mr. Tilman': 'As if their day were only to be spent / In dressing, mistressing and compliment' (29–30).

l. 83. *brave*: splendid, grand.

9   l. 92. *phlegm*. The phlegmatic humour was thought to cause sloth when it was in preponderance over the other three humours (blood, black and yellow bile); thus the modern 'phlegmatic'.

l. 99. *mark*: note the place where the game bird has hidden after having been flushed out. *fashion*: behaviour, but also with the sense of 'fashioning' or education.

l. 100. *ship them over*: i.e., send them abroad.

l. 102. Hutchinson paraphrases, 'If thou art not moved by thy child being in God's image (see l. 379 and Genesis 1: 26), be careful of him as being in thine own image.'

10   l. 117. *stour*: strong, stout.

l. 118. *thrall*: thraldom.

l. 120. Nature makes man a ship, but man makes himself into a reef ('shelf') on which he himself founders.

ll. 123–4. *Simp'ring ... clue undoes*. Difficult lines. A simper is a weak, unmanly disguise, a *lay-hypocrisy* perhaps in the sense that it is an unlearned form of hypocrisy, as well as a layman's (courtier's) form of hypocrisy, with an agreeable appearance covering corruption. It is the sort of 'mask' worn by one 'who fears to do well' (l. 126). Give it any part whatsoever—any *corner*—in your makeup, and you are sure to be found out: a *clue* is a ball of thread or yarn that *undoes*.

l. 128. *sconces*: forts, earthworks.

l. 132. *withal*: in addition. The second half of the line is a quotation from the Burial Office in the Book of Common Prayer.

l. 137. *ecliptic line*: orbit of the sun in the Ptolemaic system.

l. 142. *parcel*: part. *underwrites*: confirms by signing.

11   l. 145. *use*: habitually practise.

l. 146. *Salute*: 'Greet with some gesture . . . of respect or courteous recognition' (*OED*).

ll. 157–60. 'Youth can afford to spend all the year's income, but age must make provision for the declining years' (Hutchinson).

l. 169. *What skills it*: What does it matter, what good is it?

l. 171. *told*: counted. See Luke 12:33, 'provide yourselves bags which wax not old, a treasure in the heavens that faileth not.'

12   l. 179. *curious*: fastidious, particular (about fashions). *unthrift*: spendthrift.

l. 187. *bear the bell*: win first prize.

l. 190. *brave*: elegant, fine.

l. 191. *curiousness*: fastidiousness in dressing.

ll. 197–8. 'When a man's very name was passing out of local memory, a herald, making his official Visitation every thirty years or so, after some search ('at length') finds it in a cracked church-window' (Hutchinson).

l. 204. *increase*: profits, but also children.

13   l. 205. *conversation*: 'manner of conducting oneself in the world or in society' (*OED*).

l. 207. *assay*: try, attempt.

l. 208. *bravery*. Often used in the sense of 'an act of bravado'—swaggering; but this shades into the modern meaning, as in l. 222.

l. 211. *complexion*: temperament.

l. 212. *allay*: alloy.

l. 217. *Catch at*: snatch at; be eager to enter quarrels.

l. 218. *home*: 'to the point', 'close to the mark'.

l. 223. *posed*: questioned.

l. 227. *plays*: manages.

l. 228. *toy*: trivial thing.

l. 232. *conceit*: witticism. 'Conceit' is the object of 'advance'.

14   l. 240. *vein*: aptitude, disposition.

l. 244. *want*: lack.

l. 247. *sad*: serious, solemn.

l. 248. *van*: front-line of an attacking army.

l. 250. *fired beacon*: a warning of danger. *ditties*: words for songs.

l. 252. *cock*: victor.

l. 253. *respective*: respectful.

l. 254. *temper*: disposition, temperament.

l. 256. *rateably*: proportionately.

l. 258. *parcel-devil*: part-devil, joint-devil.

15   ll. 265–6. *bate . . . honour*. Diminish the honour due the place.

l. 272. *still*: always.

l. 276. *David . . . Jonathan*. See I Samuel 18.

ll. 287–8. 'Even love cannot make more than *one man* of me, and to attempt more would only make my inability run up a score against me' (Hutchinson).

16   l. 297. *rest*: in primero (a card game), the stakes held in reserve.

17   l. 327. *parts*: abilities, talents. *great places*: high or important positions.

ll. 329–30. *go less / To*: fall short of.

l. 334. *means*: aims at.

l. 341. *spirits live alone*: such spirits alone truly live.

l. 348. *quit*: pay, pay off.

l. 352. *sling*. Alludes to story of David and Goliath, I Samuel 17: 20 ff.

18   l. 365. *fit*: activity, inclination.

l. 367. *Affect*: be drawn to, have affection for (cleanliness).

l. 368. *board*: come close to, approach.

19   l. 391. *Twice . . . understood*. It is our duty to attend service twice on Sunday.

l. 393. *cheer*: food; also comfort ('mended' by spiritual quality). *bate of*: reduce the amount of.

l. 395. *cross*: perverse.

l. 396. *Fast . . . loss*. 'Fasting may be *gain* any day *but then*.' (Hutchinson)

l. 397. *brave*: excellent, splendid.

l. 401. *six and seven*. A phrase from gambling with dice, 'denoting the hazard of one's whole fortune, or carelessness as to the consequences of one's actions' (*OED*).

l. 403. *bare*: bare-headed.

l. 407. *quit thy state*: give up your high position or stately manner.

l. 409. *Resort to*: go to frequently.

20   l. 422. *plots*: plans, not necessarily evil ones.

l. 428. *conceiv'st him not*: do not understand him.

l. 429. See I Corinthians 1: 21, 'it pleased God by the foolishness of preaching to save them that believe.'

l. 430. See II Corinthians 4: 7, 'But we have this treasure in earthen vessels.'

l. 443. *condition*: character, nature, state of being.

21   l. 449. *refusèd thunder*. Referring to the Law set forth with thunder on Mt. Sinai (Exodus 19: 16), and to I Corinthians 1: 18, 'For the preaching of the cross is to them that perish foolishness.'

l. 450. See Job 3: 23, 'Why is light given to a man whose way is hid, and whom God hath hedged in?'

l. 460. *ell*: a unit of measure (45 inches).

Superliminare: lintel above the entrance.

l. 4. *mystical*: 'Having a certain spiritual character or import by virtue of a connexion or union with God ... said esp. with reference to the Church as the Body of Christ, and to sacramental ordinances' (*OED*).

l. 5. *Avoid*. A command: 'withdraw'.

22   *The Church. The Altar.* A long tradition lies behind Herbert's use of the shaped poem (see also *Easter-wings*); notable examples may be found in the Greek Anthology.

ll. 1–2. *broken ... heart.* See Psalm 51: 17, 'The sacrifices of God are a broken spirit: a broken and a contrite heart, O God, thou wilt not despise.'

l. 3. *frame*: form, shape.

l. 4. Exodus 20: 25, 'And if thou wilt make me an altar of stone, thou shalt not build it of hewn stone: for if thou lift up thy tool upon it, thou hast polluted it.'

l. 5. The poem implicitly alludes to II Corinthians 3: 2–3, 'Ye are our epistle written in our hearts ... Forasmuch as ye are manifestly declared to be the epistle of Christ ministered by us, written not with ink, but with the Spirit of the living God; not in tables of stone, but in fleshy tables of the heart.'

l. 11. *frame*: structure, including the body, this poem, and 'The Church'.

ll. 13–14. Luke 19:40, 'I tell you that, if these [the disciples] should hold their peace, the stones would immediately cry out.'

The Sacrifice. Spoken by Christ from the Cross, in a tradition deriving from the medieval liturgy for Holy Week, especially the 'Reproaches' spoken on Good Friday; see Rosemond Tuve, *A Reading of George Herbert*, pp. 24 ff. The poem coalesces the story of the Passion as recorded in Matthew 26–7, Mark 14–15, Luke 22–3, and John 18–19.

l. 1. See Lamentations 1: 12, 'Is it nothing to you, all ye that pass by? behold, and see if there be any sorrow like unto my sorrow.'

l. 4. *grief*: along with its modern meaning, in Herbert's day the word retained its older meaning of physical pain, bodily injury, wound.

l. 5. *make a head*: advance against.

l. 7. *except*: unless.

l. 9. *brave*: treat insolently.

23   l. 13. *apostle*. Judas, who was the treasurer for the disciples, 'had the bag' (John 12: 6).

l. 18. *at three hundred*. When Mary Magdalene anointed Christ's feet with oil, Judas said, 'Why was not this ointment sold for three hundred pence, and given to the poor?' (John 12: 5).

l. 22. *the only beads*. An allusion to counting beads while saying the rosary.

l. 23. The prayer of Jesus in Gethsemane: 'O my Father, if it be possible, let this cup pass from me: nevertheless not as I will, but as thou wilt' (Matthew 26: 39).

l. 25. *tempered*: mixed.

l. 38. *Way and Truth*. John 14: 6, 'I am the way, the truth, and the life.'

24   l. 47. *loosed their bands*. See Ezekiel 34: 27, 'they shall be safe in their land, and shall know that I am the Lord, when I have broken the bands of their yoke.' *bands*: anything that binds the limbs or body.

l. 59. *Paschal Lamb*: the lamb slain at Passover; a term traditionally applied to Christ.

l. 63. *any robbery*. Philippians 2: 6, 'Who, being in the form of God, thought it not robbery to be equal with God.'

ll. 65–6. See John 2: 19–21, where the words of Jesus are applied to 'the temple of his body'.

l. 71. Adam took his first breath from God, and now his descendants return the breath by condemning God.

25   l. 77. *set me light*: despise me.

l. 85. *despitefulness*: contemptuousness.

l. 89. *prove*: test, try.

ll. 94–5. A reference to the story of Noah's ark. See especially Genesis 8: 8–9.

l. 107. Matthew 27: 25, 'Then answered all the people, and said, His blood be on us, and on our children.'

26   l. 113. *a murderer*. Barabbas. See Matthew 27: 15–26.

ll. 118–19. *peace ... understanding*. Philippians 4: 7, 'the peace of God, which passeth all understanding.' *doth glass*: i.e., surpasses glass (see I Corinthians 13: 12).

l. 122. This is spoken ironically. It was God, through Moses, who brought water from a rock (Exodus 17: 6, Numbers 20: 11, Psalm 78: 16).

l. 127. *mysteriousness*: a 'mystery' in the theological sense: 'a doctrine of the faith involving difficulties which human reason is incapable of solving' (*OED*).

l. 129. *list*: wish.

l. 134. John 9: 6, 'he [Jesus] spat on the ground, and made clay of the spittle, and he anointed the eyes of the blind man with the clay.'

l. 138. Exodus 34: 33, ''till Moses had done speaking with them, he put a vail on his face.'

27   l. 141. *abjects*: outcast or degraded people.

l. 142. *ditty*: words (for a song or chant); see Matthew 26: 68; Luke 22: 64.

ll. 149–50. With allusion to Christ's bloody sweat in the garden of Gethsemane, Luke 22: 44.

ll. 161–3. For the imagery of this passage, see Isaiah 5: 1–7.

ll. 165–7. Hutchinson paraphrases, 'The *curse in Adam's fall* brought thorns upon the earth (Genesis 3: 18), and now a crown of thorns is put *unto my brows*.' *thrall*: thraldom, servitude.

l. 170. *my head, the rock*. I Corinthians 10: 4, 'for they drank of that spiritual Rock that followed them: and that Rock was Christ.' This passage is a typological interpretation of the rock of Horeb (Exodus 17: 6). See the note to l. 122.

28   l. 175. *sink*: cesspool.

l. 178. *weeds*: clothing, but with a pun on the modern sense.

l. 185. *rout*: mob.

l. 193. *engross*: concentrate.

l. 199. *The decreed burden*. Matthew 16: 24, 'Then said Jesus unto his disciples, If any man will come after me, let him deny himself, and take up his cross, and follow me.'

l. 203. *but*: except.

29   ll. 205–7. 'The natural world came into being by mere divine Fiat,

but *a world of sin* can only be redeemed at greater cost than by words' (Hutchinson).

ll. 213–15. See Matthew 27: 46; Mark 15: 34, 'My God, my God, why hast thou forsaken me?' The cry echoes Psalm 22: 1.

l. 221. See Luke 4: 23; Matthew 27: 40; Mark 15: 30.

l. 233. *prefixed on high.* With double meaning: first, with reference to the sign 'set up over his head', reading 'This is Jesus the King of the Jews' (Matthew 27: 37; Luke 23: 38); and secondly, with the implication that this fate was decreed 'on high' by God long beforehand.

30   l. 239. *manna.* See Exodus 16: 14–15. *Angels' food.* Psalm 78: 25, 'Man did eat angels' food.'

ll. 242–3. *My coat . . . help.* Matthew 14: 35–6, 'they sent out into all that country round about, and brought unto him all that were diseased; And besought him that they might only touch the hem of his garment: and as many as touched were made perfectly whole.'

l. 250. *weal*: welfare, happiness.

The Thanksgiving. l. 1. *grief.* See note on *The Sacrifice*, l. 4.

l. 4. *preventest*: comes before; also, surpasses.

ll. 5–6. With allusion to Christ in the garden of Gethsemane, Luke 22: 44, 'and his sweat was as it were great drops of blood falling down.' *store*: abundance.

l. 9. See note on *The Sacrifice*, ll. 213–15.

l. 14. *posy*: a bouquet; also, a collection of poems.

l. 16. *hand*: handwriting.

31   l. 33. *spittle*: hospital; poorhouse. *common ways*: public highways.

l. 43. *wit*: intelligence.

l. 47. *art of love.* With ironic allusion to Ovid's *Ars Amatoria.*

The Reprisal. The title includes the sense of 'reprise': a renewal of an action or theme previously attempted. In *W* this poem is entitled *The Second Thanksgiving.*

32   l. 6. *disentangled*: debt-free.

l. 8. *by thy death.* i.e. through the redemptive power of your death I have the strength to die for you.

The Agony. The title is the traditional name for the scene of Christ's anguish and bloody sweat in the garden of Gethsemane, or the Mount of Olives: Luke 22: 39–44; Matthew 26: 36–9.

l. 1. *Philosophers*: thinkers in all areas of 'philosophy', especially 'natural philosophy', science.

l. 3. *staff*: a surveyor's instrument for measuring heights and distances; also, a 'divining rod' for finding water.

l. 5. *doth more behove*: is more necessary.

l. 7. *repair*: go.

l. 11. *press*: the wine-press, traditional eucharistic image.

l. 13. *assay*: test the nature of.

33 *The Sinner*. l. 1. *ague*: an acute fever, especially a malarial fever.

l. 7. *cross*: perverse, contrary.

l. 9. *quintessence*. This word is stressed on the first and last syllables.

l. 11. *the many hundred part*: i.e., one part in many hundreds.

l. 14. *write in stone*. Exodus 31: 18, 'two tables of testimony, tables of stone, written with the finger of God.'

Good Friday. In *W* ll. 21–32 are entitled *The Passion* and placed after *The Second Thanksgiving* (*The Reprisal*). In *B*, on the other hand, the lines follow *Good Friday*, untitled, but beginning a new page. Herbert may, therefore, have intended these lines to stand as a separate poem.

l. 4. *tell*: count up, reckon the value of; also, narrate.

ll. 11–12. *fruit ... true vine*. John 15: 1–2, 'I am the true vine, and my Father is the husbandman. . . . and every branch that beareth fruit, he purgeth it, that it may bring forth more fruit.'

34 l. 18. *several*: individual.

Redemption. In *W* this poem is entitled *The Passion*.

l. 9. *straight*: straightway, immediately.

l. 10. *resorts*: places where people are accustomed to gather.

35 *Sepulchre*. l. 5. *good store*: in good measure (phrase used adverbially).

l. 7. *toys*: trivialities.

l. 13. *took up stones*. John 10: 31, 'Then the Jews took up stones again to stone him.'

l. 18. *writ in stone*. See note on *The Sinner*, l. 14.

l. 19. *no fit heart*. See note on *The Altar*, l. 5.

36 *Easter*. l. 13. *Consort*: harmonize. *twist*: interlace musical parts.

l. 15. *three parts*: the three tones of a chord. *vied*: placed in competition.

ll. 19–30. *W* gives an earlier version of these lines as a separate poem entitled *Easter*. As printed, however, the lines make up the song promised in l. 13. *straw*: strew.

l. 22. *sweets*: fragrancies.

l. 29. *miss*: miscount; err.

Easter-wings. l. 1. *store*: abundance.

l. 10. This line refers to the 'fortunate fall', the view that Adam's fall was fortunate since it occasioned Christ's incarnation and man's redemption.

37 l. 19. *imp*: engraft an injured wing with feathers.

H. Baptism (I). l. 7. *prevent*: come before, anticipate (along with modern sense).

l. 13. *miscall*: misname, but also with the sense of 'malign' or 'abuse'.

H. Baptism (II). l. 2. *A narrow way and little gate*. Matthew 7: 14, 'strait is the gate, and narrow is the way, which leadeth unto life.'

38 l. 10. *behither*: short of, barring.

Nature. ll. 5–6. II Corinthians 10: 4, 'For the weapons of our warfare are not carnal, but mighty through God to the pulling down of strong holds.'

l. 9. *straight*: immediately.

l. 10. *by kind*: according to nature.

ll. 13–14. Jeremiah 31: 33, 'I will put my law in their inward parts, and write it in their hearts.'

39 *Sin* (I). l. 6. *sorted*: assorted, varied.

l. 14. *bosom-sin*: a deeply cherished sin, close to the heart.

Affliction (I). l. 2. *brave*: splendid, elegant.

l. 7. *furniture*: furnishings.

l. 12. *mirth*: joy, happiness, pleasure.

40 l. 21. *strawed*: strewn.

l. 24. *party*: side in a contest.

l. 25. *began*: i.e., began to complain, as Hutchinson notes. The complaints of the flesh are recorded in the next three lines.

l. 47. *where*. The reading of *W*; *B* and *1633* have 'neere', although in *B* 'where' is written above it, apparently as a correction.

l. 53. *cross-bias*: give an inclination counter to. The metaphor is from the game of bowls; a 'bias' altered the course of the ball.

41 l. 60. *just*: 'Adapted to something else, or to an end or purpose; appropriate; suitable' (*OED*).

ll. 65–6. 'Although it may seem that I have been completely forgotten by you (or: although I have completely forgotten what I owe to you), I love you, and if I should not love you, I deserve the penalty of being denied the power of loving you.'

Repentance. l. 3. *quick*: living, but also, briefly flowering.

l. 14. *compassionate*: a verb, to treat with compassion.

42 l. 21. *wormwood*. Jeremiah 9: 15, 'thus saith the Lord of hosts . . . Behold, I will feed them, even this people, with wormwood.'

l. 22. *stay*: delay, stay away.

ll. 25–6. Psalm 39: 11, 'When thou with rebukes dost correct man for iniquity, thou makest his beauty to consume away like a moth.'

l. 26. *waxeth*: becomes, turns. *woe*: woeful, sorrowful.

l. 32. Psalm 51: 8, 'Make me to hear joy and gladness; that the bones which thou hast broken may rejoice.'

Faith. l. 6. *conceit*: imagine.

l. 9. *outlandish*: foreign.

l. 11. A reference to Genesis 3: 15, 'And I will put enmity between thee and the woman, and between thy seed and her seed; it shall bruise thy head, and thou shalt bruise his heel.'

43   l. 30. *clerk*: clergyman.

l. 35. *allow*: accept as.

l. 37. *clean*: entirely.

44   *Prayer* (I). l. 1. *banquet*. The modern meaning may be present, but in Herbert's day the word also indicated 'a course of sweetmeats, fruit, and wine, served either as a separate entertainment, or as a continuation of the principal meal' (*OED*). See *The Banquet*, where the title is closely associated with 'sweetness'. *angels' age*. 'Prayer acquaints man with the blessed timeless existence of the angels' (Hutchinson).

l. 2. Genesis 2: 7, 'And the Lord God formed man of the dust of the ground, and breathed into his nostrils the breath of life.'

l. 3. *soul in paraphrase*. 'In prayer the soul opens out and more fully discovers itself' (Hutchinson).

l. 5. *Engine*. Any machine used against fortifications, such as a battering-ram or catapult.

l. 7. *transposing*: putting into a different musical key (see 'tune' below); the *six-days' world* of the Creation may be regarded in musical terms as a hexachord.

l. 10. *manna*. See Exodus 16: 14–15.

l. 11. *in ordinary*. A common phrase indicating something that occurs 'in the ordinary course, as a regular custom or practice' (*OED*). An *ordinary* was also 'a regular daily meal', a meal provided at an eating-house, or the eating-house itself (*OED*); hence here a means or place of spiritual refreshment.

l. 12. *bird of Paradise*. In Herbert's day the bird was thought to live continually in the air, never touching the earth.

The H. Communion. W has only the second part of this poem (ll. 25–40), which it entitles *Prayer. W* also includes another poem called *The H. Communion*, not printed in the 1633 edition. See below, p. 181–2.

ll. 1–2. For the story of the punishment of Achan, who coveted 'a goodly Babylonish garment' and 'a wedge of gold,' see Joshua 7: 19–26. *furniture*: furnishings.

l. 3. *for*. The reading of *B*; *1633* prints 'from'.

l. 5. *without*: outside.

l. 13. *these*: the physical 'elements' of the service, the bread and wine.

l. 16. *outworks*: outer defences.

45   l. 21. *privy*: private, secret.

l. 23. *those*: the elements (l. 19), i.e., the bread and wine, changed into vapours ('spirits') rising from the blood.

l. 24. *friend*: Christ.

Antiphon (I). An antiphon is normally a hymn sung responsively by two choirs; here the abbreviation 'Vers.' indicates the 'versicle' spoken or sung by the priest or minister leading the service, after which the congregation responds as a chorus.

46   *Love* I. l. 1. *this great frame*: the universe.

l. 6. *invention*: inventiveness, creativity.

Love II. l. 6. *pant*: pant after.

47   l. 12. *disseizèd*: dispossessed.

l. 13. *All knees shall bow*. Isaiah 45: 23, 'That unto me every knee shall bow.'

The Temper (I). The word 'temper' means 'the due or proportionate mixture of elements or qualities' (*OED*). While the primary meaning here and in the next poem refers to a well-proportioned soul, Herbert plays with the sense of 'tempering' steel to harden it, and with the sense of 'tempering' or tuning a musical instrument.

l. 5. *some forty*. This number seems arbitrarily chosen to indicate an indefinite large number. *W* has 'a hundred'.

l. 13. *meet*. With a pun on 'mete' (measure), referring to the measuring of swords before a duel (Hutchinson).

l. 16. *spell*: 'consider, contemplate, scan intently' (*OED*).

48   *The Temper* (II). l. 4. *that*: the 'mighty joy' of l. 1.

l. 7. *race*: raze.

l. 9. *chair of grace*. Perhaps a reference to the 'mercy seat' carried in the Ark of the Covenant (Exodus 25: 17) that Solomon 'fixed' in the Temple of Jerusalem (I Chronicles 28: 11). The mercy seat came to signify the throne of God in heaven.

Jordan (I). Since the Jordan was the river in which Christ was baptized, the primary implication seems to be the 'baptism' of Herbert's muse: the Jordan replaces the springs of the Muses on Mount Helicon as a source of poetic inspiration. At the same time the Jordan was regarded as dividing the Holy Land from the lands to the East: thus the title may also suggest a division between the sacred and the secular.

l. 5. *painted chair*. This phrase may suggest a reference to *Republic* x. i–viii, where Socrates, as part of his attack on 'mimetic poetry', argues that a painting of a couch is at two removes from reality, in that it imitates a couch, which itself imitates the 'idea' of a couch.

49 l. 7. *sudden arbours*: 'that appear unexpectedly, it being an aim of the designer of a garden that it should have surprises' (Hutchinson). *shadow*: provide shade for, but also, sketch or paint.

l. 12. *who list*: whoever wishes. *pull for prime.* In the card game primero, 'to draw for a card or cards which will make the player *prime*' (*OED*), i.e., give him the winning hand.

Employment (I). l. 8. *doom.* Judgement Day.

50 l. 23. *consort*: a group of musicians.

l. 24. *reed*: a wood-wind instrument, but see also Isaiah 42: 3, 'A bruised reed shall he not break.'

The H. Scriptures (I). ll. 1–2. Psalm 119: 103, 'How sweet are thy words unto my taste! yea, sweeter than honey to my mouth!' Also, Ezekiel 2: 9, 3: 3, 'and, lo, a roll of a book was therein . . . Then did I eat it; and it was in my mouth as honey for sweetness.'

l. 8. *thankful*: worthy of thanks.

l. 11. *lidger*: ledger, or lieger: a resident ambassador.

l. 13. *handsel*: a token or gift implying good to come.

The H. Scriptures (II). l. 2. *configurations*: the relative positions of the stars and planets.

l. 7. *watch a potion*: watch for opportunities to make up a medicine (with allusion to the current belief in a live relation between the stars and the growth of vegetation).

51 *Whitsunday*: the seventh Sunday after Easter, the festival of Pentecost, which commemorates the coming of the Holy Spirit to the Apostles. See Acts 2.

l. 17. *pipes of gold.* Zechariah 4: 12, 14, 'What be these two olive branches which through the two golden pipes empty the golden oil out of themselves? . . . These are the two anointed ones, that stand by the Lord of the whole earth.' Herbert thus represents the Apostles as the conduits of God's grace.

l. 23. *braves*: insolent challenges.

52 *Grace.* l. 1. *stock*: a tree-trunk with branches cut off, a stump. See Job 14: 7–8, 'For there is hope of a tree, if it be cut down, that it will

sprout again ... Though the root thereof wax old in the earth, and the stock thereof die in the ground.' But the meaning of 'estate' or 'property' is also present.

53   *Praise* (I). l. 11. *sling.* A reference to the sling with which David killed Goliath (I Samuel 17: 23–51).

ll. 13–16. The poor, who can ascend to God, may outstrip the 'herb', which ascends only to the head.

Affliction (II). l. 4. *broken pay*: payment by instalments.

l. 5. *Methusalem's stay.* Genesis 5: 27, 'And all the days of Methuselah were nine hundred sixty and nine years.'

l. 10. *discolour*: take the colour from. *bloody sweat.* Another allusion to the Agony (see note on poem by that title).

l. 15. *imprest*: advance payment.

54   *Mattens*: matins, morning prayer.

Sin (II). ll. 4–5. Evil was commonly thought to lack real substance, to be only a privation of good.

l. 10. *in perspective.* As in a drawing or painting done according to principles of perspective (see 'paint', line 2).

56   *Church-monuments.* The text here follows *B* and *W* in not dividing the poem into six-line stanzas, as implied by the rhyme-scheme and so divided in *1633*. The effect of 'death's incessant motion' may be enhanced by the way in which the poem's movement overrides the expected formal divisions. The intimate colloquy with the flesh is emphasized by the indentation of line 17 in *W*.

l. 8. *elements*: letters of the alphabet, with a pun on the material elements, earth, air, fire, and water.

l. 24. *fit thyself against*: prepare yourself for (death); also, prepare to meet the consequences of (the fall of man).

Church-music. l. 1. *Sweetest of sweets.* The phrase, together with 'sweetly' in l. 7, provides a striking example of Herbert's rich and varied uses of 'sweet' and its derivatives. Here 'sweets' means primarily 'pleasures', 'delights'. But the adjective 'sweet' could also mean 'pleasing to the ear; having or giving a pleasant sound; musical, melodious, harmonious: said of a sound, a voice, an instrument, a singer or performer on an instrument' (*OED*): thus church music is the sweetest of all music. Furthermore, l. 7, 'We both together sweetly live and love', brings in the connotations retained in 'sweetheart', with 'sweetly' implying a relationship of deep affection.

57   l. 9. *post*: hurry.

58   *The Church-floor.* l. 10. *one sure band.* Colossians 3: 14, 'And above all these things put on charity, which is the bond of perfectness.'

l. 14. *curious*: fine, delicate.

The Windows. l. 2. *crazy*: full of flaws and cracks.

l. 6. *anneal in glass*: fix the painting on the glass by a process of heating.

Trinity Sunday: the Sunday following Whitsunday; that is, the eighth Sunday after Easter: a Sunday dedicated to the celebration of the Trinity.

59   *Content.* l. 15. *let loose to*: aim at (the image is from archery).

60   l. 28. *rent*: rend; i.e., be rent.

l. 33. *discoursing*: 'busily thinking, passing rapidly from one thought to another' (*OED*).

The Quiddity. In *W* this poem is entitled *Poetry*. A 'quiddity' (Latin, *quidditas*), in Scholastic philosophy, is the real nature or essence of a thing.

l. 8. *my great. 1633* reads 'a great'. The possessive adjective found in both *B* and *W* is justified by the implied dramatic context of this monologue and by the first person pronoun in ll. 11–12. *demesne*: landed estate (a legal term).

l. 10. *Hall*: probably a guild hall, a place where merchants or tradesmen meet.

l. 12. *most*: i.e., the most, the greatest amount. The phrase sounds as though it were an expression used in playing some game.

61   *Humility.* l. 10. *Mansuetude*: gentleness. Each beast, representing one of man's passions, gives a gift to the corresponding but opposed virtue, which can better use that gift.

l. 13. *coral-chain*: the wattle of the turkey; here, an emblem of the flesh.

l. 27. *train*: tail-feather.

l. 29. *bandying*: banding together.

l. 31. *amerced*: fined.

l. 32. *Session-day*: a day for 'the sitting together of a number of persons (esp. of a court, a legislative, administrative, or deliberative body) for conference or the transaction of business' (*OED*).

62   *Frailty.* l. 9. *Regiments*: methods or systems of governing; but with military overtones fulfilled in l. 23.

l. 11. *sad*: solemn, serious.

l. 13. *weeds*: clothing.

l. 14. *Brave*: showy, ostentatious.

l. 16. *prick*: irritate, inflame.

l. 19. *Affront*: confront, attack.

Constancy. l. 2. *still*: always.

63   l. 22. *tentations*: temptations.

l. 33. *To writhe his limbs*. The image of a bowler who contorts his body to control the ball even after he has released it.

l. 34. *mark-man*: marksman.

64   *Affliction* (III). l. 8. *tallies*: reckonings, accounts.

ll. 10–12. A sigh was apparently believed to shorten life.

The Star. l. 14. *quickness*: life.

65   *Sunday.* l. 11. *worky-days*: working-days.

l. 19. *still*: always.

66   ll. 26–8. *W*'s version of these lines makes the image clearer: 'They are the rows of fruitful trees / Parted with alleys or with grass / In God's rich Paradise.'

l. 40. *took in*: enclosed.

ll. 43–6. Matthew 27: 51, 'and the earth did quake, and the rocks rent.'

l. 47. *Sampson.* Judges 16: 3, 'And Samson . . . took the doors of the gate of the city [Gaza], and the two posts, and went away with them.'

l. 49. *did unhinge that day*. By removing the day of rest from its position as the seventh day (Genesis 2: 2–3) to its present position as the first day, in commemoration of the Resurrection.

ll. 52–6. Revelation 7: 14, 'These are they which came out of great tribulation, and have washed their robes, and made them white in the blood of the Lamb.'

67   *Avarice.* l. 7. *fain*: willing (under the circumstances); necessitated, obliged.

To All Angels and Saints. l. 1. *after all your bands*. As Hutchinson points out, if 'glorious spirits' refers to the 'angels' of the title, then this phrase means 'according to your various ranks'; if, however, the 'glorious spirits' are the redeemed of heaven, the phrase means 'after you have been released from earthly *bonds*'.

l. 5. *yet in his hands*. Isaiah 62: 3, 'Thou shalt also be a crown of glory in the hand of the Lord, and a royal diadem in the hand of thy God.'

68   l. 12. *restorative*. Gold was often used in drugs.

ll. 16–25. Herbert sums up here the Protestant reasons for refusing to engage in prayer to angels and saints for 'special aid' (l. 7): first, because the Bible 'bids no such thing'; and secondly, because 'all worship is [the] prerogative' of God, the ultimate 'power'.

l. 25. *posy*: a bouquet.

Employment (II). l. 5. *complexions*. A complexion is 'the combination of the four "humours" of the body in a certain proportion, or the bodily habit attributed to such combination' (*OED*).

69   l. 6. *quick*: live.

ll. 11–15. Earth was considered the lowest of the four elements because least active, fire the highest.

l. 20. *Watch*: watch for.

l. 22. *busy plant*. An orange-tree blossoms and bears fruit at the same time.

l. 25. *dressèd*. Used here with special reference to the image of the tree: tended, pruned, cultivated.

l. 26. *still too young or old*. We always excuse ourselves as too young or too old to begin.

l. 27. *the Man*. The capitalization in *B* and *W* stresses the general meaning: manhood, maturity, the time when a man might best perform his employment.

70   *Denial*. l. 10. *alarms*: calls to battle.

Christmas. l. 3. *full cry*: full pursuit: a term from hunting; *cry* refers to 'the yelping of hounds in the chase' or to 'a pack of hounds' (*OED*). Hence the pun on 'dear' (l. 5).

l. 6. *expecting*: waiting.

71   l. 8. *passengers*: passers-by, travellers.

l. 14. *rack*: frame to hold fodder.

l. 26. See Proverbs 20: 27, 'The spirit of man is the candle of the Lord.'

Ungratefulness. l. 5. *brave*: splendid.

l. 6. Matthew 13: 43, 'Then shall the righteous shine forth as the sun in the kingdom of their Father.'

72   l. 19. *sweets*. See note on *Church-music*.

Sighs and Groans. l. 2. *After*: according to, proportionate to. See Psalm 103: 10, 'He hath not dealt with us after our sins; nor rewarded us according to our iniquities.'

l. 5. *silly*: weak, feeble, pitiable, lowly, lacking in good sense.

73   l. 10. *magazines*: storehouses.

ll. 14–15. *Egyptian night ... thicken*. Exodus 10: 22, 'and there was a thick darkness in all the land of Egypt three days.'

l. 16. *sewed fig-leaves*. After the Fall, Adam and Eve 'knew that they were naked; and they sewed fig leaves together, and made themselves aprons' (Genesis 3: 7). The spelling 'sow'd' in *1633* suggests a possible pun.

l. 20. Revelation 16: 1, 'And I heard a great voice out of the temple saying to the seven angels, Go your ways, and pour out the vials of the wrath of God upon the earth.'

l. 28. *Corrosive*: a medical substance that destroys organic tissue.

The World. l. 7. *Balconies*. Accented *Balcónies*.

74   l. 11. *Sycamore*. 'A species of fig-tree, *Ficus Sycomorus*, common in Egypt, Syria, and other countries.' (*OED*)

l. 14. *sommers*: supporting beams.

Coloss. 3. 3. The full verse from Colossians reads, 'For ye are dead, and your life is hid with Christ in God.'

l. 2. *double motion*. Herbert refers to the 'two motions' of the sun in the Ptolemaic system: its daily ('diurnal', l. 3) route around the earth, and its 'oblique' (l. 4) yearly shifts in the sky.

l. 7. *still*: always.

l. 9. *Quitting*: paying for, paying up.

Vanity (I). l. 2. *spheres*. In the Ptolemaic system, the planets (including the sun and moon) were thought to move around the earth in nine concentric spheres.

l. 3. *stations*: the points at the extreme limits of a planet's movement where it seems to be standing still.

l. 7. *aspects*: the relative positions of the planets and stars as seen from earth, but also with a pun on the meaning 'face', 'countenance'.

75   l. 15. *chymick*: an alchemist. *devest*: unclothe.

Lent. For Herbert's views on fasting, see *The Country Parson*, ch. X.

l. 6. *Corporation*: a legal body 'having authority to preserve certain rights in perpetual succession' (*OED*).

76   l. 23. *dishonest*: ugly, unseemly; also, shameful, disgraceful.

l. 31. *Christ's fortieth day*. Matthew 4: 1–2, 'Then was Jesus led up of the Spirit into the wilderness to be tempted of the devil. And when he had fasted forty days and forty nights, he was afterward an hungred.'

l. 35. *Be holy ev'n as he.* I Peter 1: 16, 'Be ye holy; for I am holy.'

77   *Virtue.* l. 1. *Sweet*. Again, as in *Church-music*, the poem works with the varied meanings of *sweet*, beginning with the old meaning current in Herbert's day: 'having a pleasant smell or odour; fragrant'. (See also Herbert's poem *The Odour*.) Thus the 'box where sweets compacted lie' of l. 10 implies a box of crushed petals from which fragrant odours arise ('sweets'). Beyond this basic sense the implications move out to include 'agreeable, delightful, charming, lovely' and 'dearly loved or prized, precious, beloved' and from these on to the application of 'sweet' to the soul in l. 13: 'free from offensive or

disagreeable taste or smell; not corrupt, putrid, sour, or stale; free from taint or noxious matter; in a sound and wholesome condition' (*OED*).

l. 2. *bridal*: wedding.

l. 5. *angry*. *OED* suggests: 'having the colour of an angry face: red.' *brave*: splendid, handsome; but also, in this context, implying a bold and challenging manner.

l. 11. *closes*. With a play on the musical meaning of *close*: a cadence, phrase, or movement—part of a larger composition.

l. 15. *coal*: cinder.

The Pearl. Matth. 13. 45. Matthew 13: 45–6, 'Again, the kingdom of heaven is like unto a merchant man, seeking goodly pearls: Who, when he had found one pearl of great price, went and sold all that he had, and bought it.'

ll. 1–2. See note on *Whitsunday*, l. 17. Here Herbert associates the olive press with the printing press.

l. 4. *huswife*: housewife. The old form indicates the pronunciation: 'huzwif' or 'huzzif'.

l. 5. *conspire*: unite to produce (by supposed influence upon earthly things).

l. 6. *forced by fire*: i.e., as if compelled by torture (in scientific experiments).

l. 12. *wit*: cleverness in repartee.

ll. 13–17. *vies*: contests. *whether party*: which of two parties. Hutchinson quotes H. C. Beeching's paraphrase of these lines: 'I know how to gauge by the rules of courtesy who wins in a contest of doing favours; when each party is urged by ambition to do all he can by look or deed to win the world and bind it on his back.'

78 l. 18. *spirit*: alcoholic liquor.

l. 22. *relishes*: pleasures; also, in musical sense, ornaments, embellishments.

l. 26. *unbridled store*: uncontrolled abundance.

l. 32. *sealed*. *W* has *seeled*; the verb 'to seel' means to sew up a hawk's eyelids. See *The Church-porch*, l. 415.

l. 34. *commodities*: material advantages.

l. 37. *labyrinths*: evoking the story of Ariadne. *wit*: intellect.

l. 38. *silk twist*. This image stems ultimately from the golden chain with which Zeus joins heaven and earth (*Iliad* 8. 19–27).

Affliction (IV). l. 4. *wonder*. Psalm 71: 7, 'I am as a wonder unto many; but thou art my strong refuge.'

79 l. 12. *pink*: stab, prick, pierce (a fencing term).

Man. l. 5. *to*: compared to.

80   l. 8. *more fruit.* The reading of *W*; *B* and *1633* have *no fruit.*

l. 12. *go upon the score*: appear on the account; i.e., they are indebted.

l. 21. *dismount*: bring down.

l. 22. *in little all the sphere*: the entire universe in miniature, the microcosm.

l. 34. *kind*: related, but also with the modern meaning.

l. 39. *Distinguishèd*: divided. God's separation of the waters produced dry land, man's 'habitation' (Genesis 1: 9–10).

l. 40. *above*. Above, since rain is necessary to produce food ('meat').

l. 42. *neat*: well-ordered, skilfully made.

81   l. 50. *brave*: splendid.

l. 52. *wit*: wisdom.

Antiphon (II). See note on *Antiphon* (I).

l. 15. *take*. In the elements of Communion.

l. 18. *crouch*: bow down deferentially.

82   *Unkindness.* The title has both its modern meaning and that of 'unnatural behaviour'.

l. 1. *coy*: reserved, reluctant.

l. 11. *curious*: elegant, finely made.

l. 14. *thou within them.* Matthew 25: 34–46, especially verse 40, 'Inasmuch as ye have done it unto one of the least of these my brethren, ye have done it unto me.'

l. 16. *pretendeth to a place*: aspires to a political position.

83   *Life.* l. 1. *posy*: bouquet, but also poetry.

ll. 2–3. A parenthetical address to the self, explaining the poem's aim.

l. 3. *band*: the string or other material by which the 'posy' is bound.

Submission. l. 4. *design*: i.e., goal in life.

l. 8. *degree*: rank, status.

l. 10. *resume my sight*: 'take back the aims that I had given up'.

l. 12. *Disseize*: dispossess.

84   *Justice* (I). l. 1. *skill of*: understand.

l. 9. *mean*: aim at.

l. 10. *the hand*: i.e., the upper hand.

Charms and Knots. Knots: 'knotty' sayings.

l. 6. *told*: counted.

85   ll. 15–16. The tithe (one-tenth) paid by the parishioner is repaid by the sermons he hears.

Affliction (V). l. 2. *planted Paradise*. Genesis 2: 8, 'And the Lord God planted a garden eastward in Eden.'

l. 3. *thy floating Ark*. 'The allusion is to the Christian traditional use of the word *Ark*, as in the Baptismal Office, for "the Arke of Christs Church"' (Hutchinson).

l. 15. *Some angels*. Alluding to the angel who brought the 'good tidings of great joy' at the birth of Christ (Luke 2: 10); and perhaps also to Luke 15: 10, 'there is joy in the presence of the angels of God over one sinner that repenteth'.

l. 17. *sev'ral*: different. *baits*. Along with the modern sense, *baits* is also used in the old general sense of 'food', while referring specifically to a brief meal served to travellers. *in either kind*. In the context of 'thy [the Lord's] table' in the next line, this phrase is bound to evoke implications of the two 'kinds' or species of the Communion, that is, the bread and the wine, especially in view of the strong controversy in Herbert's day over whether or not Communion should be served in 'both kinds'. Thus 'our relief' in l. 15 comes to have overtones of reference to Christ, who 'took up' grief in order to accomplish the salvation represented in the Lord's Supper.

86   l. 22. *curious knots*: intricate flower-beds. *store*: abundance.

l. 24. *bow*. Both the instrument of God's vengeance and Noah's rainbow (Genesis 9: 11–17), announcing God's covenant.

Mortification. The title indicates the process of decaying, along with the practice of 'mortifying the flesh' by meditating on death and human weakness.

l. 2. *sweets*: perfumes.

l. 5. *clouts*: swaddling-clothes. *winding sheets*: cloths in which to wrap the dead.

l. 13. *frank*: free from obligation or worry (the phrase *frank and free* is common).

l. 17. *knell*. As Hutchinson notes, the passing-bell was rung not just after someone had died, but also while he was dying.

l. 18. *befriend him*. By encouraging others to offer prayers for the dying.

l. 24. *attends*: awaits.

87   l. 32. *solemnity*: a solemn ceremony.

l. 33. *dressed*: prepared. *hearse*: a framework placed over a coffin onto which decorations or verses could be attached.

Decay. l. 1. *Lot*. See Genesis 19: 1–26.

l. 2. *Jacob*. See Genesis 32: 24–30. *Gideon*. See Judges 6: 11–23.

l. 3. *Abraham*. See Genesis 17: 1–22.

ll. 4–5. See Exodus 32: 7–14, especially verses 9–10, 'And the Lord said unto Moses, I have seen this people, and, behold, it is a stiff-necked people: Now therefore let me alone, that my wrath may wax hot against them.' *could not / Encounter*. could not go counter to, oppose (Moses' complaint): 'And the Lord repented of the evil which he thought to do unto his people' (Exodus 32: 14).

l. 6. *presently*: at once.

l. 7. God or his messenger appeared to Gideon at an oak (Judges 6: 11), to Moses in a burning bush (Exodus 3: 2–4), to Elijah in a cave (I Kings 19: 9), and to the Samaritan woman at a well (John 4: 6–7).

l. 10. *Aaron's bell*. Directions for the making of Aaron's breastplate and robe include the detail, 'a golden bell and a pomegranate, upon the hem of the robe round about' (Exodus 28: 34).

l. 14. *straiten*: confine.

l. 15. *thirds*: a legal term; a widow was entitled to inherit a third of her husband's property at his death.

l. 16. *whenas*: inasmuch as.

88   *Misery*. l. 5. *Man is but grass*. Isaiah 40: 6, 'All flesh is grass.'

l. 16. *curtains*: i.e., bed-curtains.

ll. 17–18. Ironical, with allusion to various biblical texts that warn against the 'eating' of the moth: Isaiah 50: 9, 51: 8; Matthew 6: 19.

l. 25. *quarrel*: find fault with.

89   l. 39. *crouch*: bow reverently.

l. 51. *rug*: blanket, coverlet.

l. 62. *winks*: i.e., closes the eyes to something he wishes to ignore. *humours*: the four bodily fluids of the old physiology: blood, phlegm, choler (yellow bile), and melancholy (black bile); without the control of 'knowledge,' these physical influences run riot.

90   l. 69. *posy*: motto, line of poetry. A posy-ring was a ring with an inscription on the inside.

l. 73. *fooled him*: made a fool out of him.

l. 77. *shelf*: reef.

Jordan (II). See the note on *Jordan* (I) for the meaning of the title; the poem is entitled *Invention* in *W*.

l. 3. *quaint*: artful, elaborate. *invention*: in rhetorical theory, the stage of composition devoted to discovering and developing the subject-matter.

l. 4. *burnish*: spread out, swell.

l. 8. *sped*: successful.

l. 10. *quick*: alive, lively.

l. 15. *a friend*. This is an appropriate place to point out that Herbert's frequent references to Christ as 'friend' are based on the words of Christ in John 15: 12–15, where the term 'friend' derives from 'love': 'This is my commandment, That ye love one another, as I have loved you. Greater love hath no man than this, that a man lay down his life for his friends. Ye are my friends, if ye do whatsoever I command you. Henceforth I call you not servants; for the servant knoweth not what his lord doeth: but I have called you friends; for all things that I have heard of my Father I have made known unto you.' (I am grateful to Mr Eric Smith for pointing out to me the strong emphasis on 'friends' in this passage.)

l. 16. *wide*: wide of the mark. *pretence*: ambitious effort.

ll. 16–18. These lines (and, in fact, the poem as a whole) echo the first sonnet of Sidney's *Astrophil and Stella*, especially its final line: 'Fool, said my muse to me, look in thy heart and write.' But since this is a recurring theme in Sidney's sequence, other sonnets are also deeply involved. See Sonnet 3, where Sidney scorns the attempts of 'dainty wits' with 'phrases fine' and 'strange similes', and concludes: 'in Stella's face I read / What Love and Beauty be; then all my deed / But copying is, what in her Nature writes.' Also Sonnet 28, which, after denying any attempt to create allegory, concludes: 'But know that I in pure simplicity / Breathe out the flames which burn within my heart, / Love only reading unto me this art.' Or Sonnet 55, where Sidney tells how he has often called upon the Muses to help him with their 'choicest flowers'; but now he has given up such efforts at 'sugaring of my speech': 'For let me but name her whom I do love, / So sweet sounds straight mine ear and heart do hit, / That I well find no eloquence like it.' Perhaps closest of all to Herbert's ending is the conclusion of Sonnet 90: 'For nothing from my wit or will doth flow, / Since all my words thy beauty doth indite, / And love doth hold my hand, and makes me write.'

91   *Prayer* (II). l. 4. *state*: high rank, powerful position.

l. 9. God joins the earth ('centre') to the outermost sphere of the universe.

l. 15. *fain*: glad.

l. 24. *ell*: a unit of measure (45 inches).

Obedience. l. 2. *Convey a Lordship*: transfer legal title to a lord's estate.

92   l. 8. *pass*: convey, transfer legally.

l. 13. *reservation*: a clause in a deed reserving certain rights to the property from being conveyed.

l. 21. *what is man to thee*. Psalm 8: 4, 'What is man, that thou art mindful of him?'

l. 22. *a rotten tree*. Luke 6: 43, 'For a good tree bringeth not forth corrupt fruit; neither doth a corrupt tree bring forth good fruit.'

l. 28. *in earnest*. With a play on the legal meaning of 'earnest': money paid to secure a contract; Christ's sorrows are given 'by way of earnest', as a pledge of salvation to come.

93   l. 42. *kind*: of kindred spirit, along with modern meaning.

l. 43. *Court of Rolls*. The Court of the Master of the Rolls had custody of legal records.

Conscience. l. 12. *physic*: medicine.

l. 13. *receipt*: prescription (for the medicine).

l. 14. *board*: the Communion table, 'God's board', in the ancient phrase preserved in the Prayer Book of Herbert's time.

l. 21. *bill*: a halberd.

94   *Sion*. l. 2. For the building of Solomon's temple on Mount Zion, see I Kings 5-7.

l. 5. *mystical*: with a secret significance.

ll. 11-12. See Acts 7: 47-8, 'Solomon built him an house. Howbeit the most High dwelleth not in temples made with hands'; and I Corinthians 3: 16, 'Know ye not that ye are the temple of God?'

l. 21. *quick*: full of life.

Home. l. 2. *stay*: stay where you are, delay coming, stay away.

95   l. 15. *without*: outside.

l. 37. *meat*: food.

ll. 39-40. *wink / Into*. The primary meaning of 'wink' is 'to close the eyes': one can shut the temptations of the flesh into 'blackness' merely by closing the eyes.

96   l. 56. *corn*: grain, in British usage.

l. 73. *pass not*: do not disregard.

l. 76. *The word is, Stay*. To rhyme with 'pray' (l. 74).

97   *The British Church*. It is significant that Herbert does not say 'Anglican', 'English', or even 'Church of England'. *OED* does not record the term 'Anglican' before 1635; it was evidently not in common use in Herbert's day. Several reasons for the phrase 'British Church' may have been at work here. James I was of course also King of Scotland, and perhaps the title glances at some hope for a union of the two national churches. Still, a *Scot* was not usually regarded as a *Briton*; but the Welsh were, and Herbert came from a Welsh family. Furthermore, the church in Wales was regarded by Welshmen as retaining, in its mountainous stronghold, the pure, true Christianity held by the ancient Britons, before the coming of missionaries from

Rome. According to the ancient legend, British Christianity derived directly from Joseph of Arimathea, who came to Britain after Christ's death and established a centre of devotion at Glastonbury. Thus Herbert's title implies a 'British' root for his church, independent of Rome from the beginning.

l. 5. *dates her letters*. Letters were often dated according to holy days; Lady Day (Feast of the Annunciation, 25 March) marked the beginning of the new year, according to the old calendar.

l. 8. *mean*: paltry, shabby.

l. 10. *Outlandish*: foreign.

l. 13. *She on the hills*. Roman Catholicism (on the hills of Rome).

l. 15. *preferred*: advanced (either politically or to heaven).

l. 19. *She in the valley*. Calvinism (Geneva lies in a valley).

l. 26. *The mean*: the middle, moderate way.

98   *The Quip*. l. 2. *train-bands*: the citizen soldiery of London, the 'trained bands'.

l. 8. The refrain is based on Psalm 38: 15 (*BCP*): 'thou shalt answer for me, O Lord my God.'

l. 11. *skill*. Izaak Walton tells us that Herbert was 'a most excellent Master' of music: *Life*, pp. 269, 303.

l. 15. *half an eye*: i.e., a glance.

l. 19. *Oration*. Perhaps a wry allusion to Herbert's post as Public Orator at Cambridge.

l. 23. *at large*: expansively.

l. 24. *home*: directly, thoroughly, going to the heart of the matter.

Vanity (II). l. 1. *silly*: simple, naïve.

99   l. 7. *betimes*: in good time, before it is too late.

l. 11. *mould*. In double sense: pattern, and soil.

The Dawning. Christ's followers came to the tomb on Easter Day 'as it began to dawn' (Matthew 28: 1).

l. 14. *burial-linen*. For the 'linen clothes' and 'napkin' left by Christ in the sepulchre, see Luke 24: 12 and John 20: 5–7.

100   *Jesu*. l. 7. *parcels*: parts, fragments.

l. 9. *I ease you*. I and J were in Herbert's day used interchangeably to indicate both vowel and consonant. In l. 5 'J' must be pronounced as 'I', to rhyme with 'instantly', as Hutchinson notes.

Business. Title: in the basic sense of 'busy-ness'. Such busy activity, forgetting sin, is really idleness. Mankind's true 'business' lies in repentance and remembering Christ's sacrifice.

l. 22. *two deaths*. One of the body, the other of the soul in hell; see

Revelation 20: 14, 'And death and hell were cast into the lake of fire. This is the second death.' *fee*: reward, payment.

101   l. 28. *Two lives*. The second 'life' may refer either to a condemned man's second existence in hell, or to Christ's existence without the crucifixion, which would have meant eternal damnation for all men.

l. 32. *cross*: misfortune, adversity.

Dialogue. l. 4. *waving*. The old spelling allows two meanings: the old sense of 'wavering' (in one's faith), and the modern 'waiving' (Christ's offer of salvation).

l. 9. *balance*: pair of scales.

l. 10. *poise*: a weight used in balancing scales.

102   l. 20. *savour*: understanding, comprehension.

l. 30. *desert*. Pronounced 'desàrt'.

Dullness. l. 3. *quickness*: liveliness.

l. 5. *curious*: elaborate, intricate.

l. 7. *quaint*: elegant, ingenious.

l. 12. *red and white*. The colours of ladies' beautiful complexions in courtly love poetry; Herbert had a precedent for an allegorical application to Christ in Song of Solomon 5: 10, 'My beloved is white and ruddy.'

103   l. 18. *window-songs*: serenades.

l. 19. *pretending*: courting, wooing.

Love-joy. l. 3. *Annealed*: fixed on (technically, to glass) by a burning process.

l. 8. *JESUS CHRIST*. See John 15: 1, 'I am the true vine.'

Providence. The poem makes repeated allusions to Psalm 104.

ll. 1–2. Wisdom of Solomon 8: 1, 'Wisdom reacheth from one end to another mightily: and sweetly doth she order all things.'

104   l. 9. *fain would*: would like to (this phrase governs 'ditty' as well as 'sing'). *ditty*. compose words for music.

l. 39. *temper'st*: tunes.

105   l. 45. *Tempests are calm to thee*. Matthew 8: 26, 'Then he arose, and rebuked the winds and the sea; and there was a great calm.'

ll. 47–8. Jeremiah 5: 22, 'Will ye not tremble at my presence, which have placed the sand for the bound of the sea . . . and though the waves thereof toss themselves, yet can they not prevail.'

l. 48. *proud sea*. Job 38: 11, 'and here shall thy proud waves be stayed.'

l. 49. *meat*: food.

l. 51. *their net*. I.e., their mouths.

l. 53. *prevent*: anticipate, come before.

l. 56. *cheer*: provisions, food.

l. 60. *bowls*: bowling-balls (in the English sport), made not quite round, or weighted, so as to run on the 'bias'.

l. 64. *fledge*: feathered.

106 l. 73. *virtue*: power. *express*: press out, extract; also, describe.

l. 74. *virtues*: inherent powers, especially healing qualities (of herbs) or supposed occult influences (of stones).

l. 85. *Ev'n poisons praise thee*. Poisons often have medicinal qualities.

l. 94. *curious*: involved, complex.

l. 97. *good cheap*: at a low price.

107 l. 126. *The Indian nut*: the coconut.

l. 130. *fruits*. Probably the object of 'help', but may be possessive (*fruits'*).

l. 133. *Thy creatures leap not*. I.e., there are no gaps in the chain of being; the gradations between species and kinds are smooth and regular.

108 l. 144. *owes*: owns.

l. 145. *sev'ral*: different.

l. 146. *advice*: judgement, opinion.

l. 148. *twice*. Both for himself as poet and for the world as its 'high priest' (l. 13).

Hope. See Hebrews 6: 19, 'Which hope we have as an anchor of the soul.' Hutchinson offers this explanation: 'The *watch* given to Hope suggests the giver's notion that the time for fulfilment of hopes is nearly due, but the *anchor*, given in return, shows that the soul will need to hold on for some time yet; the *old prayer-book* tells of prayers long used, but the *optick*, or telescope, shows that their fulfilment can only be descried afar off; *tears* receive in return only *a few green eares*, which will need time to ripen for harvest; and then the donor's patience gives out.' The *ring* that the speaker has expected is perhaps a wedding-ring for the bride of Christ (the redeemed soul) at 'the marriage supper of the Lamb' in heaven (Revelation 19: 7–9). The poem may have some relation to the 'figure of the Body of Christ extended upon an Anchor' which, Izaak Walton reports, John Donne had engraved in small stones, set in gold, and sent to his close friends (including George Herbert) 'to be used as seals or rings' (*Life of Donne*, pp. 63–5). For Donne's and Herbert's Latin poems upon the gift, see Hutchinson, pp. 438–9, and Dame Helen Gardner's edition of Donne's *Divine Poems*, especially Appendix G.

Sin's Round. l. 2. *course it*: run or gallop about.

l. 4. *cockatrice*. See Isaiah 59: 5, where the wicked 'hatch cockatrice'

eggs, and weave the spider's web: he that eateth of their eggs dieth.'
The cockatrice, or basilisk, is a mythological serpent-like creature
that could kill by its glance alone, or by its breath.

109　　l. 8. *the Sicilian Hill*. Mt. Etna.

l. 9. *vent*: expel, but also sell, vend.

l. 10. *ventilate*: increase by blowing; also, make public.

l. 11. *lewd*: bad, evil (but not necessarily lascivious).

l. 15. *As Babel grew*. See Genesis 11: 1–9.

110　　*Time*. l. 23. *wants*: lacks.

111　　*Gratefulness*. l. 23. *country-airs*: folk-songs.

112　　*Peace*. ll. 22–3. *a Prince of old / At Salem dwelt*. See Genesis 14: 18,
'And Melchizedek king of Salem brought forth bread and wine'—a
passage interpreted as foreshadowing the elements of the Communion. See also Hebrews 6: 20 and 7: 1–2, where Melchizedek is
interpreted as the 'type' of Jesus, 'made an high priest for ever after
the order of Melchisedec', whose title 'King of Salem' means 'King
of peace'.

l. 28. *twelve stalks*. The twelve Apostles.

l. 33. *rehearse*: relate, declare.

l. 34. *virtue*: power, especially 'the power or operative influence inherent in a supernatural or divine being' (*OED*). As the final stanza
shows, allusion is made to the Communion service.

113　　*Confession*. l. 12. *rheums*: 'watery matter secreted by the mucous
glands or membranes' (*OED*).

l. 30. *to*: compared to.

Giddiness. l. 3. *sev'ral*: different, separate.

114　　l. 11. *snudge*. Herbert seems to draw on two meanings of this word.
The first, 'to remain snug and quiet', accords well with the preceding line; the other, 'to be miserly, stingy, or saving' (*OED*), leads to
the next line. *scorns increase*: i.e., scorns to grow in wealth (spends
recklessly).

ll. 19–20. As Hutchinson points out, Herbert refers here not to the
mammal, but to the mackerel-like fish whose colour changes rapidly
when it is removed from the water.

The Bunch of Grapes. The speaker of the poem parallels his own
spiritual situation with the wanderings of the children of Israel in the
wilderness: Exodus 13–17. The 'bunch of grapes' refers to the fruit
brought back from the Promised Land of Canaan by Moses' spies to
demonstrate the land's fertility: Numbers 13: 17–25.

l. 4. *vogue*: general course.

l. 5. *air*: manner, mood.

l. 10. *spanned*: measured.

115   l. 15. *guardian fires and clouds*. Exodus 13: 21, 'And the Lord went before them by day in a pillar of a cloud, to lead them the way; and by night in a pillar of fire, to give them light.'

l. 16. *Our Scripture-dew*. Manna fell with the dew (Exodus 16: 14–15).

l. 17. *shrouds*: temporary shelters, tents.

l. 18. *murmurings*: bitter complaints against God: e.g. Exodus 16: 2–12.

l. 23. *I have their fruit*. See Christ's words in John 15: 1, 'I am the true vine.'

l. 24. *Noah's vine*. Genesis 9: 20, 'And Noah began to be an husbandman, and he planted a vineyard.'

l. 25. *good store*: abundantly.

ll. 27–8. Another allusion to the wine of the Communion, and to its sacramental origin in Christ's blood. See *The Agony*, stanza 2, and Isaiah 63: 3, 'I have trodden the winepress alone.'

Love Unknown. This poem depends heavily on a tradition, common to emblem books, of representing the heart as undergoing various afflictions and purifications. See Rosemary Freeman, *English Emblem Books*, pp. 132–40, 164–6. The use of the word 'Friend' in the opening line, and again in l. 43, may alert us to the meaning of the dramatic situation: the naïve speaker, it gradually appears, is really talking with his other self—the 'friend' who lives within him, that is, Christ: see note to *Jordan* (II). Christ of course is also the 'Lord' and 'servant' (l. 9) of the poem: the suffering of the 'servant' in Isaiah 53 was interpreted as a prophecy of Christ's passion.

l. 5. *two lives*. A legal mode of land-tenure; the speaker's life in this world and the next.

ll. 12–15. The *fruit* (good works) is of no help toward salvation; only the sacrifice of Christ (the 'rock') has made redemption possible, beginning with baptism (the 'font'); see Herbert's *H. Baptism* (I).

116   ll. 26–8. *furnace ... AFFLICTION*. See Isaiah 48: 10, 'Behold, I have refined thee, but not with silver; I have chosen thee in the furnace of affliction.'

l. 42. *board*: 'God's board', the Communion table. See Herbert's *Conscience*, ll. 13–15.

117   l. 63. *wot*: know.

l. 66. *quicken*: make lively.

Man's Medley. A 'medley' is any mixture or combination. Herbert calls on two specific senses of the word: a cloth made up of various colours, and 'a musical composition consisting of parts or subjects of a diversified or incongruous character' (*OED*).

l. 8. *pretence*: claim.

l. 15. *stuff*: material, cloth.

l. 17. *take place*: assume his rank or station.

l. 18. *After*: according to, in accordance with. *ground*: 'a piece of cloth used as a basis for embroidery or decoration' (*OED*).

118   *The Storm*. l. 6. *Amuse*: bewilder, puzzle. This is the reading of *B*; *1633* reads *Amaze*. *object*: place before; i.e., set their crimes before them.

l. 7. *storms*: meteor-showers.

119   *The Method*. l. 3. *rub*: in the game of bowls, an obstacle that stopped or diverted the ball.

l. 6. *move*: request, entreat for.

l. 8. *he is Love*. I John 4: 8, 'For God is love.'

l. 10. *turn thy book*. I.e., turn the pages, look through the 'book' of your soul.

120   l. 19. *motions*: pleas.

l. 23. *motion*: impulse, inclination.

Divinity. l. 2. *spheres*: the concentric globes in which the stars and planets were supposed to move; and 'a globe or other construction illustrating the place and motions of the celestial bodies' (*OED*).

l. 3. *clod*: clodhopper? i.e., a farm labourer?

121   l. 11. *jagged*: slashed by way of decoration.

ll. 17–18. Matthew 22: 37–9 and 26: 41; Luke 6: 31.

l. 25. *Epicycles*. In the Ptolemaic system, each planet was thought to move in a small orbit ('epicycle') which had its centre in the circumference of its larger orbit.

Ephes. 4. 30. Grieve not the Holy Spirit, etc. The entire verse reads, 'And grieve not the holy Spirit of God, whereby ye are sealed unto the day of redemption.'

122   l. 16. *sense*: capability of feeling, emotional consciousness.

l. 24. *bowels*. In the Bible, the bowels are considered the seat of emotions; see, for instance, Genesis 43: 30, 'And Joseph made haste; for his bowels did yearn upon his brother.' Herbert plays on the fact that lute strings are made of animal gut.

l. 31. *still*: always.

l. 36. *store*: abundance.

123   *The Family*. l. 14. *Expecting*: awaiting.

The Size. For the title, compare *The Rose*, l. 4: 'my strict, yet welcome size'. More specifically, a *size* could also mean 'a quantity or portion of bread, ale, etc.', a usage current at Cambridge (*OED*).

l. 4. *passing brave*: surpassingly splendid.

l. 7. *fraught*: freight, cargo.

124   l. 16. *Exact*: demand, insist upon. This is the reading of *B*; *1633* reads *Enact.*

l. 22. *on score*: on credit.

l. 31. *case*: physical condition, perhaps with a pun on the sense of 'container'.

l. 36. *pretender*: suitor.

l. 39. The stanza form indicates that a short line is missing here.

l. 46. *meridian*: 'a graduated ring (sometimes a semi-circle only) of brass in which an artificial globe is suspended and revolves concentrically' (*OED*).

125   *Artillery*. l. 2. *Me thoughts*: it seemed to me.

l. 6. *usest*: are accustomed to do.

l. 7. *motions*: impulses, inclinations.

ll. 11–12. Psalm 104: 4, 'Who maketh his angels spirits; his ministers a flaming fire.'

l. 17. *shooters*: shooting stars.

l. 31. *articling*: arranging by treaty.

126   *Church-rents and Schisms*. l. 1. *rose*. The Church, the 'rose of Sharon' in the traditional interpretation of Song of Solomon 2: 1.

l. 21. *start*: break away from their place.

127   *Justice* (II). l. 9. *beam*: the cross-piece from which the dishes of a balance hang. *scape*: the upright piece of a balance on which the beam is fixed.

l. 10. *engine*: device, machine.

l. 13. *Christ's pure veil*. See Hebrews 10: 20, 'the veil, that is to say, his flesh'. This new veil of the Incarnation replaces the veil of the Temple which was rent at the Crucifixion (Matthew 27: 51).

128   *The Pilgrimage*. l. 7. *Fancy's meadow*. A place of worldly delights—in poetry, music, or love. *Fancy*, a contracted form of *fantasy*, is a rich word suggesting works of the creative imagination, a musical *fantasia* (improvization), or amorous attraction. *strowed*: strewn.

l. 10. *quickened by my hour*. I.e., spurred to action by the consciousness of life's brevity.

ll. 13–15. *wild of Passion . . . sometimes rich*. A passage from the *Imitation of Christ* will help to explain these lines: 'all this mortal life is full of miseries, and is all beset about and marked with crosses, and the more highly that a man profiteth in spirit, the more painful crosses shall he find . . . nevertheless, a man thus vexed with pain is not left wholly without all comfort, for he seeth well that great fruit

and high reward shall grow unto him by the bearing of his cross . . .
when tribulations come, take them as special consolations, saying
with the apostle thus: The passions of this world be not worthy of
themselves to bring us to the glory that is ordained for us in the life
to come' (bk. 2, chap. 12, in the translation by Richard Whitford).
Passion in l. 13 seems to mean primarily *suffering*, with special allusion to Christ and to what Whitford translates as 'the passions of
this world' (Romans 8: 18, 'the sufferings of this present time'). But
the modern meanings of 'passion' are also present, enforced by
'wild', which means 'wilderness', though the adjectival overtones can
hardly be avoided. The change to 'wold' recalls localities in England
known as 'The Wold', or 'The Wild', or 'The Weald'; the three
words or forms were all used to describe what the *OED* defines
(under 'wild') as a 'waste place'—that is, a region or tract of land at
one time not under cultivation.

l. 17. *Angel*: a gold coin bearing the device of the angel Michael;
also, a guardian angel.

l. 36. *chair*: litter, sedan chair.

129   *The Holdfast.* The title and the basic meaning of the poem may be
explained by the occurrence of the phrase 'hold fast' in Hebrews 4:
14–16, 'Seeing then that we have a great high priest, that is passed
into the heavens, Jesus the Son of God, let us hold fast our profession. For we have not an high priest which cannot be touched
with the feeling of our infirmities; but was in all points tempted like
as we are, yet without sin. Let us therefore come boldly unto the
throne of grace, that we may obtain mercy, and find grace to help in
time of need.' As Hutchinson notes, the title may also echo Psalm
73: 28 (*BCP*), 'But it is good for me to hold me fast by God.' One
may also recall I Thessalonians 5: 21, 'Prove all things: hold fast
that which is good.' The word 'holdfast' was a common workman's
term (like 'The Pulley'); it meant anything that 'binds, supports, or
keeps together; *spec.* a staple, hook, clamp, or bolt securing a part of
a building or other structure' (*OED*).

ll. 3–10. It is significant that the 'one' who offers all the stern advice in
these lines does not appear to be the same as the 'friend' (l. 11) who
offers the final consolation.

130   *The Discharge.* A *discharge* is a release from legal obligation.

l. 3. *lickerous*: 'fond of choice or delicious food'; 'having a keen relish
or desire for something pleasant'; 'lecherous, lustful, wanton'
(*OED*).

l. 8. *with the whole depart*: part with the whole, give it up; also, take
leave of, go away from.

l. 21. *fee*: wage, portion.

131   l. 31. *provide*: look into the future.

l. 32. *breaks the square*. I.e., upsets the correct order.

l. 45. *bottom*: a ball of thread or yarn. *an end*: continuously.

l. 46. *wilt*: wilt thou.

132 *Praise* (II). l. 26. *enrol*: 'record with honour, celebrate' (*OED*).

133 *An Offering*. ll. 11–12. See I Chronicles 21: 17, 'And David said unto God . . . let thine hand, I pray thee, O Lord my God, be on me, and on my father's house, but not on thy people, that they should be plagued.'

l. 22. *All-heal*. A name commonly applied to various plants, because of their supposed medicinal qualities.

134 *Longing*. ll. 8–9. *ground . . . curse*. See God's words to Adam, 'cursed is the ground for thy sake; in sorrow shalt thou eat of it all the days of thy life' (Genesis 3: 17).

l. 19. *Bowels of pity*. See Herbert's poem *Ephes. 4. 30. Grieve not the Holy Spirit*, note on l. 24.

l. 21. Psalm 86: 1, 'Bow down thine ear, O Lord, hear me.'

135 l. 26. *furnace*. See note on *Love Unknown*, ll. 26–8.

ll. 35–6. Psalm 94: 9, 'He that planted the ear, shall he not hear?'

l. 53. *board*: table; again with the connotation of 'God's board'.

ll. 59–60. *styled / Thy child*. E.g. Romans 8: 16, 'we are the children of God.'

136 *The Bag*. As ll. 31–2 indicate, the image is that of a bag for letters or dispatches; the stanza-form resembles a bag with handles: a typical piece of Herbertian wit. The image may be related to Job 14: 17, 'My transgression is sealed up in a bag.' The opening line makes clear that the poem is a direct reply to the laments of *Longing*, especially to the prayer of its last stanza. The irregularity of the line-lengths in *Longing* contrasts significantly with the stable stanza-form of *The Bag*.

ll. 2–6. See the story of Christ's calming the tempest, which begins, 'there arose a great tempest in the sea, insomuch that the ship was covered with the waves: but he was asleep' (Matthew 8: 24–7).

137 l. 11. *light*: alight.

l. 13. *tire*: head-dress.

l. 14. *fire*: lightning.

l. 38. *kind*: manner. *door*. See John 10: 9, 'I am the door: by me if any man enter in, he shall be saved.'

138 *The Jews*. l. 2. *scions*: slips of a plant used for grafting; shoots, twigs.

l. 5. *debtor*. See Galatians 5: 3, where St Paul says the Jew, by rejecting Christ, 'is a debtor to do the whole law' – an impossible obligation.

l. 6. *by keeping lose the letter*. This line depends on St Paul's distinction between spirit and letter; see Romans 7: 6, 'But now we are delivered from the law, that being dead wherein we were held; that we should serve in newness of spirit, and not in the oldness of the letter.' By attempting to observe the *letter* of the Old Testament law, the Jews lose the New Testament message.

l. 8. *trumpet*. See Joel 2: 1, which was taken to refer to the Last Judgement, 'Blow ye the trumpet in Zion, and sound an alarm in my holy mountain.' It was commonly believed that the conversion of the Jews would take place shortly before the Second Coming.

The Collar. The title contains a pun on 'collar' as an emblem of discipline, and 'choler', yellow bile, the 'humour' causing anger, irascibility. The 'choler' (sometimes spelled 'collar' in Herbert's day) was regarded as a disease; here it implies 'a fit of anger'.

l. 1. *board*. Readers of Herbert's time, and anyone reading *The Temple* in sequence, could hardly avoid the implication that the speaker is striking 'God's board', threatening to leave the Communion table (see *Conscience*, l. 14, *Love Unknown*, l. 42, and *Longing*, l. 53). Hence the ironic echoes of the Communion in ll. 7–12.

l. 6. *still in suit*: always waiting on another, asking favours from another.

l. 9. *cordial*: restorative.

l. 11. *corn*: grain.

l. 14. *bays*: laurels.

139   l. 26. *wink*: close the eyes.

ll. 27–9. See Appendix II.

l. 35. *Me thoughts*: it seemed to me.

The Glimpse. l. 6. *Me thinks*: it seems to me.

l. 13. *Lime*. I.e., quicklime, which reacts caustically with water.

140   l. 27. *so that thy stay be short*: 'so that your absence may seem short', or, 'provided that your absence is not greatly prolonged'.

ll. 29–30. 'Do not by thy absence give grief and sin an occasion to jeer at me, whereas *thy coming* would transform my heart into *a court*' (Hutchinson).

Assurance. l. 17. *devils*. Treated as one syllable.

141   l. 25. *desert*: merit, deserving; what makes me worthy. The whole stanza alludes to the doctrine that salvation comes only from the 'merits' of Christ, demonstrated in the Crucifixion, and 'imputed' as 'righteousness' to human beings. This is the *league* that Christ has made, 'indited'.

l. 26. *league*. Herbert plays upon the political and military meaning: a 'covenant or compact made between parties for their mutual protection and assistance against a common enemy, the prosecution or safeguarding of joint interests' (*OED*).

l. 29. *indite*: compose, write; perhaps with overtones of *indict*: for by the 'league' Christ condemned himself to death.

l. 35. *my rock and tower*. Psalm 18: 2, 'The Lord is my rock ... and my high tower.'

The Call. l. 1. John 14: 6, 'I am the way, the truth, and the life.'

l. 7. *mends in length*: improves as it progresses.

142 l. 10. *move*: remove. See John 16: 22, 'and your joy no man taketh from you.'

143 *Praise* (III). l. 17. *Pharaoh's wheels*. Exodus 14: 24–5, 'the Lord ... took off their chariot wheels, that they drave them heavily; so that the Egyptians said, Let us flee from the face of Israel.'

l. 23. *stint*: boundary, limitation.

l. 27. *bottle*. Psalm 56: 8, 'put thou my tears into thy bottle.'

l. 33. *streamers*: flags hung after a victory.

l. 40. *at use*: at interest. *good store*: abundance.

144 *Joseph's Coat.* For the title, see Genesis 37: 3, 'Now Israel loved Joseph more than all his children ... and he made him a coat of many colours.' The 'many colours' of the speaker's life are a sign of God's love.

l. 1. *indite*: compose, write.

l. 8. *both.* I.e., 'grief and smart' (one concept) and 'my heart'.

l. 9. *both.* I.e., 'my heart' and 'the body'. *due*: owed.

l. 11. *ticing*: enticing.

The Pulley. The poem represents a reworking of the myth of Pandora's box. In one version, she opened the box containing all mankind's troubles, which thus made their way into the world, with only Hope remaining in the box; in another version, the box contained all the gods' blessings, which evaporated when she rashly opened it.

l. 5. *span*: the width of an extended hand.

145 *The Priesthood.* ll. 1–3. Refers to the 'power of the keys', which Christ granted to Peter and then to all the disciples; see Matthew 16: 19, 'And I will give unto thee the keys of the kingdom of heaven: and whatsoever thou shalt bind on earth shall be bound in heaven: and whatsoever thou shalt loose on earth shall be loosed in heaven.'

l. 9. *habit*: clothing.

l. 10. *compositions*: 'states of the body, or of body and mind combined' (Hutchinson).

l. 13. *cunning*: skilful.

l. 20. *vessels*. The image of man as a vessel fashioned by God is a biblical commonplace. See, for instance, Jeremiah 18: 6 and Romans 9: 20–3.

146   ll. 25–30. Hutchinson notes, citing the Latin, how closely this stanza seems to echo a passage from the fourth book of the *Imitation of Christ*, the book dealing with the sacrament of Communion: 'O how great and how honourable is the office of priests, to whom is given power to consecrate with the holy words of consecration the Lord of all majesty, to bless him with their lips, to hold him in their hands, to receive him into their mouths, and to minister him to other! O how clean should those hands be, how pure a mouth, how holy a body, and how undefouled should be the heart of a priest, to whom so oft entereth the author of cleanness!' (bk. 4, chap. 11, translated by Richard Whitford).

ll. 31–2. See II Samuel 6: 6–7, 'Uzzah put forth his hand to the ark of God, and took hold of it; for the oxen shook it. And the anger of the Lord was kindled against Uzzah; and God smote him.' *Ark.* The Ark of the Covenant, the wooden chest containing the tables of the law in the Old Testament.

l. 35. *meet*: suitable.

l. 37 *there will I lie*. Walton reports that at Herbert's induction into the priesthood, 'his friend Mr. Woodnot looked in at the church window, and saw him lie prostrate on the ground before the altar' (*Life*, p. 289).

The Search. l. 4. *prove*: prosper, succeed.

l. 7. *centre*: the earth.

147   l. 14. *Simper*: twinkle.

l. 31. *covert*: covering.

l. 33. 'If anything keeps me from you, don't let it be your will that does so.'

148   l. 47. *charge*: burden.

l. 59. *bear the bell*: win first prize.

Grief. l. 10. *a less world*. I.e., man, the microcosm.

149   *The Cross*. A *cross* is any adversity or thwarting of one's aims: the poem's self-irony stems from such biblical texts as Christ's words in Matthew 10: 38, 'And he that taketh not his cross, and followeth after me, is not worthy of me.'

l. 1. *uncouth*: unknown, hard to understand.

l. 12. *threat'nings*: vows.

l. 16. *allowed for*: accepted as; judged to be.

ll. 17–18. 'I am altogether weak except when I contemplate the cross; but its strength spurs me to action' (Hutchinson).

l. 23. *sped*: successfully accomplished.

l. 29. *delicates*: luxuries, delicacies.

150   *The Flower.* l. 3. *demean.* Both demeanour and demesne, estate.

l. 11. *blown*: blossomed, bloomed.

l. 16. *quick'ning*: giving life.

l. 18. *chiming*: a harmonious blending of notes. *passing-bell*: bell rung when someone was dying; as Hutchinson notes, it was a *single* bell and therefore could not *chime.*

151   *Dotage.* l. 2. *Foolish night-fires.* Herbert translates the Latin *ignis fatuus*, the will o' the wisp.

l. 3. *Chases in arras*: representations of hunts (*chases*) on a tapestry (*arras*).

l. 4. *in a career.* I.e., in full career, at full speed.

l. 8. *in grain*: dyed permanently. *blown*: already blossomed.

152   *The Son.* l. 3. *coast*: region.

153   *A True Hymn.* l. 14. *behind*: lacking.

l. 15. *in kind.* I.e., properly (a true hymn).

The Answer. l. 8. *exhalation*: vapour rising from the ground, regarded as source of a meteor.

l. 9. *means*: aims at.

ll. 13–14. The enigmatic 'answer' or 'reply' seems to depend upon some biblical text such as 'the answer of a good conscience toward God' advised in I Peter 3: 14–21, when people 'speak evil of you': 'But sanctify the Lord God in your hearts: and be ready always to give an answer to every man that asketh you a reason of the hope that is in you with meekness and fear: Having a good conscience.' The 'reason' of course is Christ, and 'the rest' is ultimately Heaven, where those who have come there 'know more than' the speaker can know on earth. (See the 'rest to the people of God' in Hebrews 4.)

A Dialogue-Anthem. An *anthem* is a hymn sung antiphonally.

ll. 1–2. I Corinthians 15: 55, 'O death, where is thy sting? O grave, where is thy victory?'

l. 3. *void of story*: ignorant of history.

154   l. 6. *Thy curse.* Galatians 3: 13, 'Christ hath redeemed us from the curse of the law, being made a curse for us.'

The Water-course. l. 8. *sov'reign.* Used of medicine to indicate a pre-eminent curative power.

l. 10. *Salvation. Damnation.* The terms are bound to evoke the controversial Calvinist doctrine of 'double predestination'; but Herbert deals with the issue in a characteristically guarded and subtle way. God here gives to man either salvation or damnation 'as he [God] sees fit', not 'according to His Will', as the strict Calvinist would say; 'fit' means 'suitable', 'appropriate'—to what? To what is in God's mind, including, perhaps, consideration of a person's efforts toward virtue and the love of God (aided of course by grace). See Herbert's use of the same words ('as he sees fit') at the beginning of chapter XXX of *The Country Parson*.

Self-condemnation. l. 2. *choosing Barabbas*. See Mark 15: 6–11.

l. 6. *That choice*. I.e., of Barabbas.

155   l. 19. *prevent*: anticipate.

l. 22. *snuffs*. A *snuff* is the portion of a candle-wick that is partly burned away and thus must be removed from time to time.

The Glance. l. 6. *Passing*: surpassing. *cordials*: restoratives.

l. 7. *embalm*: anoint, with fragrant oil or spices.

156   *The 23d Psalm*. Herbert's version mingles phrasing from three translations of his time: the King James version, the Coverdale version contained in the Book of Common Prayer, and the versified version of Sternhold and Hopkins, whose metre he adopts. He adds the stress on 'love' (ll. 1 and 21), 'And all this not for my desert' (l. 11), 'wine' (l. 19), and the echo of the Song of Solomon in l. 3: 'My beloved is mine, and I am his' (2: 16).

l. 10. *in frame*: into the proper disposition.

157   l. 24. *thy*. The reading of *B*; *1633* reads *my*.

Mary Magdalene. For the details of this poem, see Luke 7: 37–50. The identification of this unnamed woman with Mary Magdalene was traditional.

l. 14. *dash*: splash.

Aaron. l. 1–4. For the description of Aaron's garments, see Exodus 28: 4–43.

l. 2. *Light and perfections*. Urim and Thummim, the stones on Aaron's breastplate (Exodus 28: 30).

l. 5. *drest*. The old spelling has here been kept, because of the visual 'rhyme'.

158   ll. 19–20. *old man . . . new drest*. The 'old man' of sin is covered over by the 'imputed righteousness' of Christ.

The Odour. 2. *Cor*. 2. 15. 'For we are unto God a sweet savour of Christ, in them that are saved, and in them that perish.' As Herbert's title indicates, 'savour' is the equivalent of the Greek word for 'smell'; 'savour', like 'sweet', refers here to 'fragrancy' (for Herbert's plays upon the various meanings of 'sweet', see the notes to *Church-music* and *Virtue*).

l. 2. *ambergris*: a secretion of the sperm-whale, used both for cooking and for making perfume.

159 l. 16. *Pomander*: a ball of aromatic substances that gives off its scent when squeezed or warmed in the hand (see l. 20).

l. 27. *traffic*: have dealings or relations with one another.

The Foil. A *foil* is a thin leaf of metal placed beneath a gem in order to accentuate its brightness.

160 *The Forerunners*. l. 1. *harbingers . . . mark*. Harbingers were those sent in advance to procure lodgings or places for an army or a royal party; they chalked the doors of buildings set aside for royal or military use.

l. 3. *dispark*: turn out of a park (country estate), with a pun on *spark*.

l. 6. *Thou art still my God*. Psalm 31: 14, 'But I trusted in thee, O Lord: I said, Thou art my God.'

l. 9. *pass*: care (again in l. 31).

l. 11. *ditty*: words for music.

l. 21. *fond*: infatuated; also, foolish. *ticed*: enticed.

l. 26. *arras*: tapestries.

161 *The Rose*. l. 18. *it purgeth*. The flower was used as a laxative.

162 l. 29. *physic*: medicine.

163 *Discipline*. l. 22. *a man of war*. Exodus 15: 3, 'The Lord is a man of war.' Cupid, of course, also carried a bow.

The Invitation. The speaker (apparently a priest) invites 'all' to partake of the Communion 'Banquet'.

ll. 1–3. These lines, as Hutchinson notes, are reminiscent of Isaiah 55: 1–2, 'Ho, every one that thirsteth, come ye to the waters, and he that hath no money; come ye, buy, and eat; yea, come, buy wine and milk without money and without price. Wherefore do ye spend money for that which is not bread?'

l. 4. *dressed*: made ready (for the service).

l. 8. *define*: characterize.

l. 17. *cheer*: food and drink; also gladness, source of joy.

164 l. 24. *lower grounds*. Fields were flooded as a means of fertilization.

The Banquet. For the title see note to *Prayer* (I), l. 1.

l. 1. *cheer*. See above, note on *The Invitation*, l. 17.

l. 4. *neatness*: 'elegance of form or arrangement, with freedom from all unnecessary additions or embellishments' (see *OED*, 'neat').

l. 7. *sweetness*. For Herbert's plays upon the various meanings of 'sweet,' see notes to *Church-music* and *Virtue*.

165 l. 14. *Made a head*: set up a resistance (literally, raised troops).

l. 25. *pomanders*. See *The Odour*, l. 16 and note.

166   l. 49. *his*. The reading of *B*; *1633* prints *this*.

l. 50. *ditty*: words for music; also, theme.

The Posy. A *posy* is a motto.

ll. 3–4. This was Herbert's personal motto, which alludes to Genesis 32: 10, 'I am not worthy of the least of all the mercies, and of all the truth, which thou hast shewed unto thy servant'; and to Ephesians 3: 8, 'Unto me, who am less than the least of all saints, is this grace given.'

A Parody. The term *parody* here is derived from the Greek *parodia* ('alongside a song'), a term that had emerged in the late 16th century to describe a common practice of imitation in Renaissance music, especially the transmutation of secular music into sacred music. 'The essential feature of parody technique is that ... the whole substance of the source—its themes, rhythms, chords and chord progressions—is absorbed into the new piece and subjected to free variation in such a way that a fusion of old and new elements is achieved' (see the article on 'Parody' in *The New Grove Dictionary of Music and Musicians*). Herbert has performed here a sacred parody by adapting the rhythms, stanzaic form, theme, and some of the words in the following love-song, once attributed to John Donne, but now generally attributed to William Herbert, the 3rd Earl of Pembroke:

> Soul's joy, now I am gone,
>   And you alone,
>   Which cannot be,
> Since I must leave myself with thee,
>   And carry thee with me;
>
> Yet when unto our eyes
>   Absence denies
>   Each other's sight,
> And makes to us a constant night,
>   When others change to light,
>
> O give no way to grief,
>   But let belief
>   Of mutual love
> This wonder to the vulgar prove:
>   Our bodies, not we move.
>
> Let not thy wit beweep
>   Wounds but sense-deep,
>   For when we miss
> By distance our lip-joining bliss,
>   Even then our souls shall kiss.

> Fools have no means to meet,
> But by their feet.
> Why should our clay
> Over our spirits so much sway,
> To tie us to that way?
>
> O give no way to grief,
> But let belief
> Of mutual love
> This wonder to the vulgar prove:
> Our bodies, not we move.

(Spacing is here arranged to fit Herbert's parody; we do not know what manuscript of the love-song Herbert used. He may also have been following music to which the song was set. The text here is based on H. J. C. Grierson's revised edition of Donne's *Poetical Works*, 1933; Grierson notes that one MS reads 'when I am gone' in the opening line.)

167   *The Elixir.* The early version of this poem, in *W*, is entitled *Perfection*. The present title refers to the philosopher's stone, which believers in alchemy thought could turn base metals into gold (see ll. 21–2).

l. 7. *still to make thee prepossessed*: always to place thy claim first.

l. 8. *his*: its (as in l. 15).

168   l. 15. *tincture*: in alchemy, 'a supposed spiritual principle or immaterial substance whose character or quality may be infused into material things' (*OED*).

l. 23. *touch*: prove genuine by rubbing with a touchstone.

l. 24. *told*: counted.

Death. l. 1. *uncouth*: strange, not really known; also, with modern sense.

169   l. 11. *fledge*: i.e., fledged; fully-feathered, able to fly.

Doomsday. l. 12. *tarantula's raging pains.* 'Tarantism, an hysterical malady, was supposed to be caused by the bite of the wolf-spider or tarantula and to be cured by music and wild dancing' (Hutchinson).

170   l. 29. *consort*: a group of musicians playing or singing together.

Judgement. l. 5. *peculiar book*: individual story or book of accounts.

171   *Heaven.* There is a long tradition of 'echo' poems, including famous examples by Sir Philip Sidney and by Herbert's brother, Lord Herbert of Cherbury.

l. 19. *persever.* The old spelling indicates the accent: *persèver.*

Love (III). l. 12. See Psalm 94: 9, 'he that formed the eye, shall he not see?'

172   l. 16. *then I will serve.* But the human speaker is no longer a servant: he is the friend of Love; see note on *Jordan* (II).

ll. 17–18. See Luke 12: 37, 'Blessed are those servants, whom the Lord when he cometh shall find watching: verily I say unto you, that he shall gird himself, and make them to sit down to meat, and will come forth and serve them.' With this text and the preceding poem in the background, the poem evokes the reception of the redeemed at 'the marriage supper of the Lamb' (Revelation 19: 9) as well as the administration of the Communion service.

At the conclusion of *The Church* Herbert has chosen to include poems that deal with only three out of the traditional 'Four Last Things': Death, Judgement, Hell, and Heaven. He has, characteristically, substituted Love for Hell, making Love the culmination of his personal sequence, the climax of his effort to 'copy out only that'.

173 *The Church Militant*: 'The Church on earth considered as warring against the powers of evil' (*OED*).

l. 5. *Commonweals*: commonwealths.

l. 15. *Noah's shady vine.* See Genesis 9: 20, 'And Noah began to be an husbandman, and he planted a vineyard.'

l. 20. *the other Ark.* The Ark of the Covenant, which the Israelites carried through the wilderness and which Solomon placed in the newly built temple in Jerusalem (II Chronicles 5: 5).

l. 26. *the partition-wall.* At Christ's death an earthquake tore in half the veil separating the inner sanctum from the remainder of the temple (Matthew 27: 51); see also Ephesians 2: 14, 'he is our peace, who hath made both one, and hath broken down the middle wall of partition between us.'

174 ll. 41–6. Macarius and Anthony (4th century AD) were Christian hermits in Egypt. Herbert plays on the belief that Nile mud could spontaneously generate creatures, associating this phenomenon with the 'second birth' of Baptism.

ll. 47–8. Herbert draws his refrain from Psalm 139: 17 (*BCP*), and from Psalm 89: 6.

l. 51. *posed*: examined, tested; also, nonplussed, befuddled. *set*: puzzled, at a loss.

l. 54. *Christ-Cross*: 'or criss-cross-row, was a name for the alphabet, because a cross was prefixed to it in the horn-books' (Hutchinson).

l. 56. *Ergo*: therefore; the word usually introduces the third term of a syllogism.

l. 63. *resounds*: vaunts, boasts of.

l. 72. Refers to the replacement of pagan festivals with Christian holy days; 'numbers' may refer to Pope Gregory XIII's reform (1582) of the Julian calendar.

l. 73. *th' empire dwelt in Greece.* Constantine moved his capital from Rome to Byzantium in AD 330.

l. 76. *against*: in preparation for (the time when).

175　ll. 89–91. Spain and Germany were parts of the Holy Roman Empire, but England shared the more spiritual link of the Reformation with Germany, by making the monarch head of the Church.

l. 93–8. Herbert argues that the uniting of Church and State under Henry VIII had an English precedent, since Constantine, the first Christian emperor of Rome, was crowned at York in 306 (his mother, Helena, was believed to be British). Herbert therefore accepts as legitimate the Donation of Constantine ('this mystery ... Within a sheet of paper'), which gave temporal power to the Pope and which, in fact, Lorenzo Valla had already proved to be a forgery.

l. 110. *sallet*: salad.

l. 112. *garlic*. See the complaint of the children of Israel: 'We remember the fish which we did eat in Egypt freely ... and the onions and the garlic' (Numbers 11: 5).

176　l. 131. *poet*. Oracles were often delivered in verse.

l. 132. *sublimate*. 'The poison of the *sublimate* (mercuric chloride) in the medicinal *conserve* is concealed by the sugar coating of the pill' (Hutchinson).

l. 134. *pull*: draw a card or lot.

l. 147. *Disparking*: turning out of a park; i.e., the gods of the oracles were driven out of their sanctuaries.

l. 149. *rogue*. Mohammed.

l. 150. *coy*: apparently, reserved, not demonstrative.

l. 152. *curious*: subtle, complicated.

177　l. 174. *three offices*. Prophet, priest, and king.

l. 182. *Babylon*. A common epithet for Rome among the Protestants.

l. 184. *that name*. Babel, the building of which caused the different languages of various 'nations' (Genesis 11: 1–9).

l. 186. *vizards*: masks.

l. 187. *anchorism*: the way of life practised by religious hermits (anchorites). *retiredness*: withdrawal from the world.

l. 192. *captivate*: capture.

l. 195. *post*: ride; hurry, hasten.

l. 200. *without doors*: outside.

178　l. 204. *mule*. I.e., a beast of burden bearing the load of popery; with a pun on *mule* as 'slipper'. Kissing the Pope's 'public foot' (l. 196) was a traditional act of reverence.

l. 219. *crest*: coat of arms.

ll. 232–4. The Church must shrink to the size of its beginning in Judea before the Last Coming.

ll. 235–6. According to Walton, when the Vice-Chancellor of Cambridge received the manuscript of *The Temple* from Nicholas Ferrar, he considered refusing the book a license on the basis of these two lines, but Ferrar insisted on their inclusion (*Life*, p. 315).

179   l. 260. *instantly*: persistently.

      l. 268. *sound*: inlet, bay.

180   *L'Envoy*. l. 2. *make war to cease*. Psalm 46: 9, 'He maketh wars to cease unto the end of the earth.'

POEMS NOT INCLUDED IN THE TEMPLE

181   *The H. Communion*. ll. 4–6. These lines allude to the Roman Catholic doctrine of transubstantiation: that at the consecration of the bread and wine, the whole *substance* of these elements is replaced by the body and blood of Christ, with only the *appearance* of the physical elements remaining.

      l. 6. *thy poor creature*. The bread of the Eucharist.

      ll. 13–18. Herbert here ponders the central issue raised by extreme Protestant theologians, who argued that the elements of bread and wine are only tokens and that there is no Real Presence of Christ in them: the Presence of Christ is wholly spiritual and comes directly to mankind ('thy foes'). Possibly so, Herbert says, but then if Christ chooses to reach mankind in two stages ('stations') the way is longer, but still aimed at reaching 'me'.

      l. 25. *Impanation*. A eucharistic doctrine based on an analogy with Christ's Incarnation. *OED* cites a definition of 1548: 'such a presence of Christ's body in the bread wherewith they both . . . have all their conditions and properties'.

      l. 26. *At the rate of*: in proportion to, by analogy with.

182   l. 41. *meres*: marker or boundary lines.

183   *Love*. ll. 13–14. As Christ slept during the storm on the Sea of Galilee (Mark 4: 36–41).

184   *Evensong*. The stanza form reverses the metric of *Mattens*, which it immediately follows in *W*.

      The Knell. l. 3. *wishly*: longingly, intently.

      l. 5. *offers . . . makes a stand*. I.e., offers battle . . . takes a defensive position.

185   l. 17. *Juleps*: sweet, medicated drinks.

      Perseverance. The title evokes one of the most controversial points of strict Calvinist doctrine, 'perseverance of the saints', the doctrine that those who are 'elected' to salvation by the will of God can never permanently fall from grace. Herbert seems not to accept the full implications of the doctrine, for in the third stanza he implies that his sins (not the will of God) may operate to effect his damnation. His perseverance is one of faith and hope.

l. 12. *banns*: announcement of intended marriage, with allusion to participation in 'the marriage supper of the Lamb' (Revelation 19: 9).

l. 13. *Only my soul hangs*: i.e., my soul hangs only.

l. 16. *Thou art my rock*. Psalm 18: 2, 'The Lord is my rock.'

186   *Poems from Walton's Life*. Walton says the two sonnets were sent to Herbert's mother 'in the first year of his going to Cambridge . . . for a New-year's gift', along with a letter from which Walton quotes a portion in which Herbert writes: 'my meaning (dear Mother) is in these sonnets, to declare my resolution to be, that my poor abilities in poetry shall be all and ever consecrated to God's glory' (*Life*, pp. 267–9). Since we do not know whether Walton here takes the New Year as beginning on 1 January 1610 or on 25 March, we cannot date the occasion exactly; Herbert would have reached his seventeenth birthday on 3 April 1610.

Walton says that Herbert had 'To my Successor' engraved on the mantle of his rectory at Bemerton (*Life*, p. 293).

Sonnet II. l. 14. *discovery*: uncovering, revealing.

A PRIEST TO THE TEMPLE

Published in *Herbert's Remains* (1652), nineteen years after Herbert's death. The main title may be an editorial addition, alluding to the earlier publication of Herbert's poetry. The subtitle seems more appropriate.

190   *The Author to the Reader. The argument of a pastor's love.* See John 21: 15–17, where Christ tells Peter: 'Feed my sheep.'

pastoral: a treatise dealing with the duties of a pastor.

191   *Chap. I. reducing*: leading back.

revoking: calling back.

the beginning of his Epistles. See, for example, Romans 1: 1–7.

fills up . . . the Church. Colossians 1: 24.

Chap. II. cures. I.e., the parishes in their care.

192   *schoolmen*: the medieval scholars and theologians.

Psalm 50.16. The version of *BCP*.

seasonably: at a proper time.

193   *Chap. III. luxury*: indulgence in bodily pleasures.

fellowship with . . . reprove them. Ephesians 5: 11.

I sat daily . . . Temple. Matthew 26: 55.

keeping his word . . . hindrance. See Psalm 15: 5 (*BCP*), 'He that sweareth unto his neighbour, and disappointeth him not: though it were to his own hindrance.'

conversation: ordinary relationships.

194   *Chap. IIII.*   *severally*: separately.

well is deep . . . draw with. See John 4: 11.

open mine eyes . . . of thy Law. Psalm 119: 18 (*BCP*).

scope: aim, intention.

Comment: commentary.

195   *Chap. V.*   *bane*: poison.

196   *Chap. VI.*   *treatable*: 'deliberate; distinct, clear, intelligible' (*OED*).

clerk's: i.e., the parish clerk, who leads the responses.

pausably: deliberately.

a reasonable service. Romans 12: 1, 'I beseech you therefore, brethren, by the mercies of God, that ye present your bodies a living sacrifice, holy, acceptable unto God, which is your reasonable service.'

a piece of state: a part of their rank or privilege.

197   *causes them to be presented.* I.e., reports them to the archdeacon or bishop.

churchwardens: laymen who assist in the administration of the parish.

Chap. VII.   *against some great festival.* I.e., in preparation for some important feast-day of the Church, such as Easter.

two or three witnesses . . . established. II Corinthians 13: 1, 'In the mouth of two or three witnesses shall every word be established.'

198   *Hermogenes.* A rhetorician from Tarsus (2nd century AD) who wrote a treatise on the art of speaking.

affecting: feeling.

cordially: from the heart.

Oh Lord . . . in himself. Jeremiah 10: 23.

199   *affection*: feeling, tendency, disposition.

Chap. VIII.   *presently:* at once, immediately.

use to: are accustomed to.

200   *induce*: introduce.

Thou art the man. The words of Nathan to David: II Samuel 12: 7.

privy purse: private or personal treasury.

like hinds' feet. Psalm 18: 33, 'He maketh my feet like hinds' feet, and setteth me upon high places.'

Chap. IX.   *temper*: disposition. See I Corinthians 7.

meat dressed: food prepared (throughout this work *meat* means food in general).

201   *sojourn*: live as a lodger.

ghostly: spiritual.

armour of God . . . shield of faith. Ephesians 6: 13–16.

pestilence . . . noonday. Psalm 91: 6 (*BCP*).

202   *accommodation.* I.e., supplying desirable circumstances of living.

spiritual wickednesses in high places. See Ephesians 6: 12.

experiment: experience.

203   *Chap. X. sustentation*: sustenance.

haply . . . not able to do. I.e., perhaps he is not able to afford the cost of educating his other children for the ministry.

prentices: apprentices.

the Chamber of London: 'the City Chamberlain's office or treasury . . . regarded as specially good security' (Hutchinson).

expressed in a fair table: i.e., written out in a well-designed drawing.

204   *straitly*: strictly.

boards: comes close to (the state of a child).

back-side: the premises or out-buildings at the back of his property.

corn: grain of any kind.

205   *exinanition*: exhausted condition.

206   *Chap. XI. conceits*: conceptions.

207   *Chap. XII. that excellent statute.* The Poor Law Act of 1601.

disseized: dispossessed.

charged: burdened with responsibilities or liabilities.

208   *Chap. XIII. strawed.* Strewn with rushes or straw on the floor.

antics: grotesque drawings (of animals, monsters, etc.).

209   *Chap. XIV. in frame*: in good order, with proper behaviour.

receipts: formulas, prescriptions.

carking: anxious thought or toil.

210   *as Nathan did.* The prophet Nathan made David recognize his sin with Bathsheba by telling him a parable about another man's act of injustice (II Samuel 12: 1–14).

our Saviour's rule. Matthew 18: 15, 'if thy brother shall trespass against thee, go and tell him his fault between thee and him alone.'

more comfortable: giving more comfort.

211   *Chap. XV. even to lilies.* 'Consider the lilies of the field', Matthew 6: 28–30.

disaffected: emotionally or mentally troubled.

212   *Chap. XVII. outlandish*: foreign. See the collection attributed to Herbert: *Outlandish Proverbs*, Hutchinson, pp. 321–55.

seasonably: at an appropriate time.

213   *Chap. XIX. in Reference*: in relation to others.

set at: assessed to provide (for military purposes).

country-duty. national duty.

respectively: respectfully.

Diocesan: the head of his diocese; his bishop.

Visitations: meetings concerned with the condition of a parish or diocese (a *visitation* is normally a visit of examination by the bishop or archdeacon).

214   *correspondence*: relationship.

neighbourhood: neighbourliness.

we should do . . . any praise. Philippians 4: 8 (condensed).

expects no brief: i.e., does not wait for a formal authorization.

Chap. XX. tester: half a shilling.

216   *Chap. XXI. silly*: simple, uneducated.

in virtue: i.e., virtually.

218   *Chap. XXII. complemental*: merely ceremonious or formal.

puts up to an Apostle: raises himself up to (acts as though he were) an apostle.

219   *Chap. XXIII. Dalton's Justice of Peace*. Michael Dalton, *The Country Justice* (1618).

220   *tickle cases*: ticklish cases, difficult to diagnose.

seeing one anatomy: observing a dissection of a body, or perhaps examining a model of a body.

Fernelius. Jean François Fernel, author of *Universa Medicina* (1586).

simples: medicinal herbs.

bolearmena: 'an astringent earth from Armenia' (Hutchinson).

221   *premise*: place before, say before.

Chap. XXIV. reduce. lead back.

scandal. Some practice or belief that the dissenter finds to be an offence against his own religion.

223   *Chap. XXVI. undecently to the station*: in a way inappropriate to the position in life.

baned: spoiled.

224   *school rules*: rules derived from medieval scholars and theologians.

licorous: greedily desirous.

225   *disgest*: old form of *digest*.

Gerson. Jean Charlier de Gerson (1363–1429), mystic, chancellor of the University of Paris; in Herbert's day often regarded as the author of the *Imitation of Christ*.

when the people hungered . . . made food miraculously. See Matthew 14: 15–21 and 15: 32–8.

226   *Chap. XXVIII. the Apostle's rule.* I Timothy 4: 12, 'Let no man despise thy youth.'

bootless: useless.

227   *Chap. XXIX. as David says . . . house of God.* Psalm 84: 10.

Canons: rules of the Church, specifically, '"The Constitutions and Canons Ecclesiastical" agreed upon by Convocation, and ratified by King James I . . . in 1603' (*OED*).

Visitation Articles. Rules to be observed in making visitations (see note on Chap. XIX).

228   *Chap. XXX. soil*: manure.

the sun stood still, the fire burned not. See Joshua 10: 12–13; Exodus 3: 2.

utter: send to market.

229   *Chap. XXXI. emergent*: unexpected; pressing, urgent.

exigent: critical occasion.

230   *resent*: feel regret for.

passing: very great, surpassing.

doubt: fear.

231   *Chap. XXXII. our Saviour's precept.* Mark 10: 21.

232   *drowning*: flooding of land to increase fertility.

graff: old form of *graft*.

233   *Sessions and Sizes.* A *session* (or a *sessions*) was a 'sitting' of the Justice of the Peace or other magistrate for the hearing of legal cases; the *size* (or, more properly, *assize*) was a county court convened by a judge.

law is practice: i.e., works according to customary procedures and by precedents.

great horse: a charger, a war-horse.

234   *Chap. XXXIII. the Kingdom of God . . . shall be added.* Matthew 6: 33; Luke 12: 31.

the original: i.e. the derivation of the word, from *paenitere*, 'to be sorry'.

235   *as Saint Paul implies.* Romans 2: 21, 'Thou therefore which teachest another, teachest thou not thyself?'

Chap. XXXIV.   the Devil for a time . . . their own food. As in Christ's Temptation in the wilderness: Matthew 4: 11; Luke 4: 10-13.

236   *earing*: ploughing.

Joseph might meet. Might provide: as in Genesis 41.

238   *witnesses . . . established.* See note on Chap. VII.

Chap. XXXV.   Condescending. Far from having its modern implications, the word here implies a gracious and willing way of 'coming down' to acceptance of popular customs, perhaps with some thought of Romans 12: 16, 'Mind not high things, but condescend to men of low estate.'

Procession. A popular ceremony consisting of walking around the bounds of the parish (see 'perambulation' below).

239   *Chap. XXXVI.   niceness*: excessive concern for style.

not proper to: not the exclusive quality or right of.

ministration of condemnation . . . blessing. II Corinthians 3: 9, 'For if the ministration of condemnation be glory, much more doth the ministration of righteousness exceed in glory.'

240   *Commination*: 'A recital of Divine threatenings against sinners; in the Anglican Liturgy, forming part of an office appointed to be read after the Litany on Ash Wednesday and at other times' (*OED*).

HENRY VAUGHAN

SILEX SCINTILLANS (1650)

The emblematic title page (with its living faces visible within and along the edges of the heart), the Latin explanation of that emblem's meaning, and the 14-line *Dedication*: these were all that preceded *Regeneration* in Vaughan's volume of 1650. But in 1655, when the unsold sheets of 1650 were bound up with additional poems, Vaughan removed the emblematic title page (along with the explanatory Latin poem), replaced it with the printed title page, added the prose preface and the group of biblical texts, greatly expanded the dedication with an elaborate title and 32 additional lines, and added also the short poem 'Vain wits and eyes'. For these new prefatory materials see pp. 343-50.

248   *The Author's Emblem.* l. 10. *Caro . . . Lapis.* Ezekiel 36: 26, 'I will take away the stony heart out of your flesh, and I will give you an heart of flesh.'

l. 13. *undantes Petras.* An allusion to Moses' bringing water out of the rock: Exodus 17: 6.

249   *The Dedication.* l. 8. *void of store*: empty of any produce.

ll. 9–11. The lines allude to the parable of the evil 'husbandmen', Matthew 21: 33–41.

l. 14. *tenant's rent.* See Herbert, *Redemption.*

Regeneration. Compare Herbert's *The Pilgrimage* for stanza-form and a similar journey.

l. 1. *A ward, and still in bonds.* The first three stanzas narrate the speaker's troubles under the bondage of sin and the Old Testament Law; but the term *ward* indicates that he is in someone's care.

250   ll. 25–6. These lines appear to allegorize the doctrinal view of 'calling' and grace contained in the passage on 'predestination to life' in the 17th of the Articles of Religion of Vaughan's Church: 'Wherefore, they which be endued with so excellent a benefit of God be called according to God's purpose by his Spirit working in due season: they through Grace obey the calling . . .'

ll. 27–8. *Full East . . . Jacob's Bed.* Jacob made his journey 'into the land of the people of the east' (Genesis 29: 1). On his way 'he lighted upon a certain place, and tarried there all night, because the sun was set; and he took of the stones of that place, and put them for his pillows, and lay down in that place to sleep.' There he had the vision of the 'ladder' reaching to heaven and heard the voice of the Lord. See Genesis 28: 10–22.

l. 32. *friends of God.* 'In all ages entering into holy souls, she [Wisdom] maketh them friends of God, and Prophets' (Wisdom of Solomon 7: 27). See also James 2: 23, where Abraham is said to have been called 'the Friend of God'.

ll. 33–50. The state of grace is imaged through glancing allusions to the Song of Solomon 4: 12–15, 'A garden inclosed is my sister, my spouse; a spring shut up, a fountain sealed. Thy plants are an orchard of pomegranates, with pleasant fruits; camphire, with spikenard, Spikenard and saffron; calamus and cinnamon, with all trees of frankincense; myrrh and aloes, with all the chief spices: A fountain of gardens, a well of living waters, and streams from Lebanon.' Martin and Rudrum cite a number of striking parallels with this scene in the work of Vaughan's twin-brother Thomas, *Lumen de Lumine* (1651). The relationship is significant for the brothers' shared interest in occult, 'hermetic' studies.

l. 41. *unthrift*: spendthrift. *vital*: life-giving.

251   l. 55. *divers stones.* I Peter 2: 5, 'Ye also, as lively stones, are built up a spiritual house, an holy priesthood, to offer up spiritual sacrifices, acceptable to God by Jesus Christ.'

l. 60. *Centre*: earth.

l. 70. *rushing wind.* 'And suddenly there came a sound from heaven as of a rushing mighty wind, and it filled all the house where they [the apostles] were sitting' (Acts 2: 2: the day of Pentecost).

l. 80. *Where I please.* 'The wind bloweth where it listeth, and thou hearest the sound thereof, but canst not tell whence it cometh, and whither it goeth: so is every one that is born of the Spirit' (John 3: 8).

252   The biblical verse at the end combines two versions of Song of Solomon 4: 16, the Genevan, 'Arise, O North, and come O South, and blow on my garden', and the King James, 'Awake, O north wind; and come, thou south; blow upon my garden.'

253   *Resurrection and Immortality.* Vaughan's placement of this poem near the beginning of his book (linked with the preceding poem *Death*) sets up the contrast of light ('vital Ray') against darkness (clouds, mists, shadows) that runs throughout the volume of 1650 and continues in some of the finest poems of 1655. At the same time the poem introduces the terms and concepts of that occult 'Hermetic philosophy' developed in the treatises of Vaughan's twin brother Thomas, who wrote under the name Eugenius Philalethes. The recent edition of Thomas Vaughan's *Works* (1984), edited by Alan Rudrum, has fortunately made these easily available. A reading of the short (45-page) *Anthroposophia Theomagica* (1650) will show the basic affinities between many of Henry Vaughan's concepts and this eclectic philosophy based in part on the writings attributed to the mythical Hermes Trismegistus ('Thrice-great Hermes'), the Greek name given to the Egyptian god of wisdom, Thoth. The surviving 'Hermetic' writings (an amalgam of theology, astrology, medicine, alchemy, and magic) appear to date from Alexandrian culture of the first three centuries AD. Thomas Vaughan also draws heavily upon the works of Cornelius Agrippa (1486–1535), German physician and reputed magician, and Paracelsus (*c.*1490–1541), Swiss physician and alchemist. The following passages from the *Anthroposophia* will suggest some of the themes and images shared by the twin brothers:

'[The Aristotelians] look on God, as they do on carpenters, who build with stone and timber, without any infusion of life. But the world, which is God's building, is full of Spirit, quick and living. This Spirit is the cause of multiplication, of several perpetual productions of minerals, vegetables, and creatures ingendered by putrefaction: all which are manifest, infallible arguments of life. Besides, the texture of the universe clearly discovers its animation. The earth, which is the visible natural basis of it, represents the gross, carnal parts. The element of water answers to the blood, for in it the pulse of the great world beats ... The air is the outward refreshing spirit, where this vast creature breathes, though invisibly, yet not altogether insensibly. The interstellar skies are his vital, aethereal waters, and the stars his animal sensual fire' (*Works*, ed. Rudrum, pp. 52–3).

'As the great world consists of three parts, the elemental, the coelestial, and the spiritual, above all which God himself is seated in that infinite, inaccessible Light, which streams from his own Nature; even so man hath in him his earthly, elemental parts, together with the coelestial, and angelical natures, in the center of all which moves and shines the Divine Spirit. The sensual, coelestial, aethereal part of man is that whereby we do move, see, feel, taste, and smell, and have a commerce with all material objects whatsoever. It is the same in us as in beasts, and it is derived from Heaven, where it is predominant, to all the inferior earthly creatures. In plain terms it is part of *anima mundi*, commonly called *anima media*, because the influences of the Divine Nature are conveyed through *it* to the more material parts of the creature ... By means of this *anima media*, or the aethereal nature, man is made subject to the influence of stars, and is partly disposed of by the coelestial harmony. For this middle spirit ... is of a fruitful insinuating nature, and carried with a strong desire to multiply itself, so that the coelestial form stirs up and excites the elemental. For this Spirit is in man, in beasts, in vegetables, in minerals, and in every thing it is the mediate cause of composition and multiplication. Neither should any wonder that I affirm this spirit to be in minerals, because the operations of it are not discerned there ... For nature employs her gifts only where she finds a conveniency and fit disposition of organs, which being not in minerals, we may not expect so clear an expression of the natural powers in them. Notwithstanding in the flowers of several vegetables ... there is a more subtile, acute perception of heat and cold, and other coelestial influences than in any other part. This is manifest in those herbs which open at the rising, and shut towards the sun-set: which motion is caused by the Spirit being sensible of the approach and departure of the sun. For indeed the flowers are (as it were) the spring of the Spirit, where it breaks forth, and streams, as it appears by the odours that are more coelestial ...' (*ibid.* 76–8).

'[Man] must be united to the Divine Light from whence by disobedience he was separated. A flash, or tincture of this must come, or he can no more discern things spiritually, than he can distinguish colours naturally without the light of the sun. This light descends, and is united to him by the same means as his soul was at first ... The soul of man, whiles she is in the body, is like a candle shut up in a dark-lanthorn, or a fire that is almost stifled for want of air. Spirits (say the Platonics) when they are *in sua patria* [in their own country] are like the inhabitants of green fields, who live perpetually amongst flowers, in a spicy odorous air; but here below ... they mourn because of darkness and solitude, like people locked up in a pest-house.... This is it makes the soul subject to so many passions ... Now she flourishes, now she withers, now a smile, now a tear: and when she hath played out her stock, then comes a repetition of the same fancies, till at last she cries out with Seneca, *Quousque eadem?* [How long will this go on?] This is occasioned by her vast and infinite capacity, which is satisfied with nothing but God, from whom at first she descended ... In her are patterns and notions of all things in the world ... She makes an invisible voyage from one place to another, and presents to herself things absent, as if they were present. The dead live to her, there is no grave can hide them from her thoughts' (*ibid.* 81–2).

'We should therefore pray continually that God would open our eyes whereby we might see to employ that talent, which he hath bestowed upon us, but lies buried now in the ground, and doth not fructify at all . . . This influx from Him is the true, proper efficient of our Regeneration, that *sperma* of Saint John, the seed of God which remains in us' (*ibid.* 83).

Biblical motto. The heading from Hebrews follows the Geneva version, with minor differences.

l. 3. *Inspired*: breathed. *quick'ning*: life-giving.

l. 13. *Esteemed of*: estimated, regarded. *two whole elements*. Water and earth.

254   l. 14. *mean, and span-extents*: contemptible, limited things extending only a hand's-breadth.

l. 21. *recruits*: fresh supplies, means of renewal. The whole of section 2 represents Vaughan's version of the 'Hermetic philosophy' of nature's constant power of renewal. Martin and Rudrum cite relevant passages from the Hermetic writings.

l. 26. *Incorporates*: becomes a body, takes form.

l. 33. *resolve*: dissolve into some other form.

l. 38. *deprave*: corrupt.

255   l. 51. *saw darkly in a glass.* 'For now we see through a glass darkly; but then face to face' (I Corinthians 13: 12).

l. 59. *To read some star, or min'ral.* The reference is to astrological studies, by which it was thought one could ascertain a relationship between the stars and certain earthly things, including human beings.

l. 68. See Deuteronomy 28: 66–7, 'and thou shalt fear day and night, and shalt have none assurance of thy life: In the morning thou shalt say, Would God it were even! and at even, thou shalt say, Would God it were morning!'

256   *Day of Judgement.* l. 13. *like a scroll.* 'And the heaven departed as a scroll when it is rolled together; and every mountain and island were moved out of their places' (Revelation 6: 14).

l. 21. *the clouds thy seat.* 'And I looked, and behold a white cloud, and upon the cloud one sat like unto the Son of man' (Revelation 14: 14).

l. 23. *The quick and dead.* A common biblical phrase concerning Judgement Day: see Acts 10: 42; II Timothy 4: 1; I Peter 4: 5; and the Apostles' Creed: '[. . Jesus] shall come to judge the quick and the dead.' *quick*: alive. *small and great.* 'And I saw the dead, small and great, stand before God; and the books were opened' (Revelation 20: 12).

l. 32. *the man of sin.* See Romans 6: 6, 'Knowing this, that our old man is crucified with him, that the body of sin might be destroyed.' Also II Thessalonians 2: 3, 'for that day shall not come, except there come a falling away first, and that man of sin be revealed, the son of perdition.'

257   l. 41. *a HEART of flesh.* 'And I will give them one heart, and I will put a new spirit within you; and I will take the stony heart out of their flesh, and will give them an heart of flesh' (Ezekiel 11: 19).

The appended verse from I Peter is given in the Geneva version.

Religion. See Herbert's *Decay.*

l. 5. *juniper.* 'And as [Elijah] lay and slept under a juniper tree, behold, then an angel touched him, and said unto him, Arise and eat' (I Kings 19: 5).

l. 6. *myrtle's.* See Zechariah 1: 8–11 for the appearance of 'the angel of the Lord that stood among the myrtle trees'.

l. 7. *oak's.* 'And there came an angel of the Lord, and sat under an oak' (Judges 6: 11).

l. 8. *fountain's.* 'And the angel of the Lord found [Hagar] by a fountain of water in the wilderness' (Genesis 16: 7).

l. 9. *Jacob dreams and wrestles.* For Jacob's dream, see Genesis 28: 11–12. His wrestling with God is described in Genesis 32: 24–30.

l. 10. *Elias by a raven is fed.* 'And the ravens brought him bread and flesh in the morning, and bread and flesh in the evening; and he drank of the brook' (I Kings 17: 6).

l. 11. *Another time by th' Angel.* 'And he looked, and, behold, there was a cake baken on the coals, and a cruse of water at his head' (I Kings 19: 6).

ll. 13–16. *In Abr'ham's tent ... shady even.* Abraham entertained three 'men' (interpreted as angels in disguise) at the time that Sarah's son was foretold. See Genesis 18: 1–8.

l. 17. *in fire.* 'And the angel of the Lord appeared unto him in a flame of fire out of the midst of a bush' (Exodus 3: 2). See also Leviticus 9: 24 and Deuteronomy 4: 12, 5: 4.

l. 18. *Whirlwinds.* 'Then the Lord answered Job out of the whirlwind' (Job 38: 1 and 40: 6). *clouds.* 'And the Lord came down in a cloud, and spake unto him [Moses]' (Numbers 11: 25). See also Exodus 24: 16, 'and the seventh day he called unto Moses out of the midst of the cloud.' *the soft voice.* 'And after the earthquake a fire; but the Lord was not in the fire: and after the fire a still small voice' (I Kings 19: 12).

l. 19. *admire*: am amazed, wonder.

l. 20. *conf'rence*: conversation, discourse.

258   l. 32. *Cordials*: invigorating drinks.

l. 37. *drilling*: flowing in a small stream, dripping.

l. 43. *puddle*: foul, polluted water.

l. 44. *physic*: medicine.

l. 45. *sink*: sewer, cesspool.

l. 46. *Samaritan's dead well.* See John 4: 5–15: the water from Jacob's well is 'dead' in comparison to the 'living water' Christ offers to the Samaritan woman.

l. 50. *the springing rock.* See Exodus 17: 6. From the rock which Moses struck, water sprang forth for the Israelites in the desert. St Paul interpreted it thus: 'for they drank of that spiritual Rock that followed them: and that Rock was Christ' (I Corinthians 10: 4).

l. 52. *water into wine.* As at the marriage-feast in Cana: John 2: 1–10. The final biblical verse is given in the Geneva version.

259   *The Search.* Vaughan's poem represents a subtle and ironic variation upon the ancient practice of meditating upon the life of Christ and using the imagination and the senses to re-create the scenes of his life and death as though one were 'really present' at the event. (See Vaughan's example of this mode of meditation in his prose treatise, *Mount of Olives*, Martin, pp. 161–2.) The point is that, for this searcher, these old methods do not work: nor need they work, for the 'Pilgrim-Sun' of the opening lines is also the 'Lord' of the closing biblical verse: constantly present.

l. 4. *ecstasy.* A mystical state of rapture wherein the body becomes incapable of sensation, while the soul contemplates divine things; a trance-like prophetic state.

ll. 15–17. *Temple ... dust; town ... ashes.* Referring to the destruction of the temple at Jerusalem in AD 70, and the later destruction of the city itself.

l. 19. *beneath the pole*: under the pole-star, on the earth.

ll. 21–32. See John 4: 5–14, 'Then cometh he to a city of Samaria, which is called Sychar, near to the parcel of ground that Jacob gave to his son Joseph. Now Jacob's well was there. Jesus therefore, being wearied with his journey, sat thus on the well ... The woman saith unto him, Sir, thou hast nothing to draw with, and the well is deep: from whence then hast thou that living water? Art thou greater than our father Jacob, which gave us the well, and drank thereof himself, and his children, and his cattle? Jesus answered and said unto her, Whosoever drinketh of this water shall thirst again: But whosoever drinketh of the water that I shall give him shall never thirst, but the water that I shall give him shall be in him a well of water springing up into everlasting life.'

l. 38. *Ideas.* Vaughan's italic in the text may indicate the Greek meaning: 'the look or appearance of a thing, as opposed to its reality'. *Agony.* See notes on Herbert's poem by that title.

260   l. 44. *Balsam*: a healing balm, medicinal oil.

ll. 45–7. *But, O his grave . . . monument.* Matthew 27: 57–60, 'When the even was come, there came a rich man of Arimathea, named Joseph, who also himself was Jesus' disciple: He went to Pilate, and begged the body of Jesus . . . he wrapped it in a clean linen cloth, And laid it in his own new tomb which he had hewn out in the rock.'

l. 48. *corner-stone.* Christ: Acts 4: 11, 'This is the stone which was set at nought of you builders, which is become the head of the corner.' Also I Peter 2: 6, 'Behold, I lay in Sion a chief corner stone, elect, precious: and he that believeth on him shall not be confounded.'

ll. 53–62. For Christ's sojourn and temptation in the wilderness, see Matthew 4: 1–11; Mark 1: 12–13; Luke 4: 1–13.

l. 64. *his bride.* The Church, the Bride of Christ. See Revelation 12: 6, 'And the woman fled into the wilderness, where she hath a place prepared of God.'

l. 74. See Herbert, *The Collar*, l. 35: 'Me thoughts I heard one calling, *Child*!'

261   l. 78. *Still*: ever, always.

l. 95. *another world.* The world within, not 'out of doors'.

Acts Cap. 17. happily. A variant spelling of *haply* ('perhaps'), but *happily* also meant 'by good fortune, successfully'.

Isaac's Marriage. Two leaves (B2, B3) of the 1650 *Silex* were reset for the 1655 edition, in order to allow some revisions in this poem – the only poem in *1650* so revised. The substantive variants are listed below.

Gen. cap. 24. ver. 63. The KJ version, except that Vaughan chooses *pray* instead of *meditate*; *pray* is the reading of the Geneva version, and is an alternative reading in the margin of KJ. *lift*: lifted. For the story of Isaac's marriage to Rebekah, see Genesis 24.

l. 2. *monstrous*: unnatural.

l. 4. *degenerate*: 'To become or be altered in nature or character (without implying debasement)' (*OED*).

262   l. 10. *constellation*: disposition, character—as determined by one's 'stars'.

ll. 11–12. The 1650 reading makes the point more clearly (and more bluntly): 'But being for a bride, sure, prayer was / Very strange stuff wherewith to court thy lass.'

l. 14. *dull:* 'coarse' (*1650*).

l. 16. *sev'ral*: different.

l. 19. 'When sin, by sinning oft, had not lost sense' (*1650*).

l. 21. *antic*: 'Absurd from fantastic incongruity; grotesque' (*OED*).

l. 23. *Retinue*. Pronounced *retìnue*.

l. 28. *thy servant*. Abraham's 'eldest servant', sent to seek a wife for Isaac. See Genesis 24: 2–4.

ll. 35–6. 'But in a frighted, virgin-blush approached / Fresh as the morning, when 'tis newly coached' (*1650*).

l. 46. *fortunates*: makes fortunate.

263   l. 53. *Lahai-roi's well*. Vaughan provides here a marginal note: 'A well in the south country where Jacob dwelt, between Cadesh and Bered; Hebrew, the well of him that liveth and seeth me.' See Genesis 16: 13–14, 'And she [Hagar] called the name of the Lord that spake unto her, Thou God seest me: for she said, Have I also here looked after him that seeth me? Wherefore the well was called Beer-lahai-roi.'

l. 67. *timed*: matured, seasoned.

The British Church. The poem presents a marked contrast with Herbert's poem of the same title; for the use of 'British', see note on Herbert's poem. Here, in accord with traditional interpretation of the Song of Solomon, the Church as the bride and beloved of Christ laments the ravages of the English civil wars and the disruption of the established Church in the 1640s.

l. 4. *hills of myrrh and incense*. Song of Solomon 4: 6, 'Until the day break, and the shadows flee away, I will get me to the mountain of myrrh, and to the hill of frankincense.'

ll. 6–10. John 19: 23–4, 'Then the soldiers, when they had crucified Jesus, took his garments, and made four parts, to every soldier a part; and also his coat: now the coat was without seam, woven from the top throughout. They said therefore among themselves, Let us not rend it, but cast lots for it, whose it shall be.'

264   ll. 18–20. *And haste thee so . . . mounts of spices*. Song of Solomon 8: 14, 'Make haste, my beloved, and be thou like to a roe or to a young hart upon the mountains of spices.'

O rosa campi . . . aprorum. 'O rose of the field! O lily of the valleys! how have you now become the food of wild boars!' See Song of Solomon 2: 1, 'I am the rose of Sharon, and the lily of the valleys.' Also Psalm 80: 13, 'The boar out of the wood doth waste it, and the wild beast of the field doth devour it.' The heading for Psalm 80 in the Geneva Bible interprets the psalm as 'A lamentable prayer to God to help the miseries of his Church'.

The Lamp. l. 2. *stars nod and sleep*. See Herbert, *Divinity*, l. 1: 'for fear the stars should sleep and nod'.

265 *Man's Fall and Recovery*. l. 1. *everlasting hills*. See Genesis 49: 26 (the dying words of Jacob to his sons), 'The blessings of thy father have prevailed above the blessings of my progenitors unto the utmost bound of the everlasting hills.'

l. 13. *sullen beam*. Conscience.

l. 16. *Jeshurun's king*. Moses: Deuteronomy 33: 4–5, 'Moses commanded us a law, even the inheritance of the congregation of Jacob. And he was king in Jeshurun, when the heads of the people and the tribes of Israel were gathered together.' Jeshurun is one name for the Israelites. See Deuteronomy 32: 15, 'But Jeshurun waxed fat, and kicked.'

ll. 18–20. *These swelled my fears . . . from the Law*. Romans 7: 5, 7–8, 'For when we were in the flesh, the motions of sins, which were by the law, did work in our members to bring forth fruit unto death . . . What shall we say then? Is the law sin? God forbid. Nay, I had not known sin, but by the law: For I had not known lust, except the law had said, Thou shalt not covet. But sin, taking occasion by the commandment, wrought in me all manner of concupiscence. For without the law sin was dead.'

266 l. 32. *their Red Sea*. The Israelites laboured in their journey toward the Promised Land: they waded across the bed of the Red Sea (an image of the state of sin under the Old Testament Law). But now the speaker is washed in the blood of Christ.

Rom. Cap. 5. ver. 18. 1650 reads in error 'Cap. 18. ver. 19.' Vaughan gives the Geneva version of the verse, except that he substitutes 'righteousness' from KJ for 'justifying'.

The Shower. l. 9. *quick access*. See Herbert, *Prayer* (II), l. 1: 'Of what an easy quick access, / My blessed Lord, art thou!'

267 *Distraction*. l. 1. *crumbled dust*. See Herbert, *Church-monuments*, l. 22: 'crumbled into dust'; *The Temper* (I), l. 14: 'A crumb of dust'; and *Longing*, ll. 41–2: 'Thy pile of dust, wherein each crumb / Says, Come.'

l. 6. *a star, a pearl, or a rainbow*. See Herbert, *Mattens*, ll. 6–7: 'Silver, or gold, or precious stone, / Or star, or rainbow'.

l. 12. *Man is called and hurled*. See Herbert, *Doomsday*, ll. 27–8: 'Man is out of order hurled, / Parcelled out to all the world.'

l. 30. *Dust that would rise*. See Herbert, *Frailty*, ll. 15–16: 'That which was dust before, doth quickly rise, / And prick mine eyes.'

l. 34. *parcels*: parts, pieces.

268 *The Pursuit*. See Herbert, *The Pulley*.

l. 7. *commerce*. Perhaps a reference to man's preoccupation with studying the stars.

l. 11. *the lost son*. The prodigal son of Luke 15: 16–19.

Mount of Olives (I). Just as Herbert has two poems entitled *Jordan*, urging poets to write sacred verse, so Vaughan has two poems on this theme, entitled *Mount of Olives*. As ll. 18–19 make plain, Vaughan is replacing Mount Helicon and the fountain of the pagan Muses with the 'hill' which Christ made his place for retirement and prayer. See Matthew 24: 3; 26: 30; Mark 13: 3; 14: 26; Luke 21: 37; 22: 39; John 8: 1. See also Vaughan's prose treatise with this title.

l. 2. *My Saviour sate*. 'And as he sat upon the mount of Olives, the disciples came unto him privately' (Matthew 24: 3).

ll. 5–6. *wit, / Conceit*. Both terms here mean 'the faculty of conceiving, creating'.

l. 9. *Cotswold and Cooper's*. The Cotswolds were praised by Drayton, Jonson, Randolph, and others in *Annalia Dubrensia. Upon the yearly celebration of Mr. Robert Dover's Olympic Games upon Cotswold-Hills* (1636). Sir John Denham wrote *Cooper's Hill* (1642).

269   l. 16. *sheepward*: shepherd.

l. 21. *wept once*. Luke 19: 41, 'And when he was come near, he beheld the city [Jerusalem], and wept over it.' *walked whole nights on thee*. Luke 21: 37, 'And in the daytime he was teaching in the temple; and at night he went out, and abode in the mount that is called the mount of Olives.'

ll. 22–4. Christ ascended into heaven from the Mount of Olives; see Acts 1: 9–12.

l. 26. *narrow footstool*. Isaiah 66: 1, 'Thus saith the Lord, the heaven is my throne, and the earth is my footstool.'

l. 28. *Unsearchable*. Romans 11: 33, 'how unsearchable are his judgments, and his ways past finding out!'

l. 29. *comprise*: comprehend.

l. 32. *chair*. See the last line of Herbert's *Pilgrimage*, 'And but a chair.'

The Incarnation and Passion. ll. 1–4. See Herbert, *The Bag*, ll. 7–12.

l. 6. *the morning-star*. Revelation 22: 16, 'I am the root and the offspring of David, and the bright and morning star.'

270   ll. 19–20. *for Love . . . than death*. Song of Solomon 8: 6, 'for love is strong as death.'

The Call. l. 11. *sands*. The sands of an hour-glass.

271   l. 29. *Those beasts were clean, that chewed the cud*. Leviticus 11: 3, 'Whatsoever parteth the hoof, and is cloven-footed, and cheweth the cud, among the beasts, that shall ye eat.'

'Thou that know'st for whom I mourn.' There are six untitled poems in *Silex 1650*, all headed by the symbol ¶. With one possible exception, they appear to commemorate Vaughan's younger brother, William, who died in July 1648, at about the age of twenty.

ll. 22–3. *feather ... shell ... stick ... rod.* Perhaps suggesting the curious objects that people collect.

272 l. 32. *close*: private, secret.

l. 36. *The wise man's madness, laughter.* Ecclesiastes 2: 2, 'I said of laughter, It is mad.'

l. 44. *And tares had choked the corn.* See the parable of the wheat and tares, Matthew 13: 24–30. *corn*: grain.

ll. 49–52. *silent tear ... groan ... arted string.* A striking recension of Herbertian words and themes: see *The Family*, ll. 17–20: 'Joys oft are there, and griefs as oft as joys; / But griefs without a noise: / Yet speak they louder than distempered fears. / What is so shrill as silent tears?' and *Sion*, ll. 21–4: 'But groans are quick, and full of wings, / And all their motions upward be; / And ever as they mount, like larks they sing; / The note is sad, yet music for a King.'

l. 51. *airs*: melodies, music for voice or instruments.

l. 57. *know my end.* Psalm 39: 4, 'Lord, make me to know mine end, and the measure of my days, what it is; that I may know how frail I am.'

Vanity of Spirit. Ecclesiastes 1: 14, 'I have seen all the works that are done under the sun; and behold, all is vanity and vexation of spirit.'

273 l. 4. *brave*: grand, splendid.

ll. 9–14. *I summoned nature ... Creatures.* Vaughan is describing here the first stage in the traditional mode of Augustinian meditation, which begins with meditation on the Creation. His account suggests a pursuit of the occult, alchemical researches regarded as scientific in his day.

ll. 15–24. *To search myself ...* This is the second stage in the Augustinian mode of meditation: to find the 'traces' (*vestigia*) of God within the self, in the presence of the now defaced Image of God, man's soul, the 'piece of much antiquity' which the speaker here tries vainly to restore. He makes some progress, 'but this near done', he realizes that spiritual illumination in this life is transitory.

l. 17. *drills*: trickles, streams.

The Retreat. The title plays upon 'retreat' as backward movement and 'retreat' as an action of withdrawal from the world for religious devotion, or a place where such seclusion occurs.

l. 4. *my second race.* Hebrews 12: 1, 'let us run with patience the race that is set before us.' The poem alludes throughout to the platonic doctrine of the soul's pre-existence.

274   l. 8. *my first love.* Revelation 2: 4, 'Nevertheless, I have somewhat against thee, because thou hast left thy first love.'

l. 18. *sev'ral*: separate.

l. 20. *shoots of everlastingness.* Owen Felltham calls the soul 'a shoot of everlastingness' in *Resolves*, i. 64 (1620).

l. 26. *city of palm trees.* Deuteronomy 34: 1-4, 'And Moses went up from the plains of Moab unto the mountain of Nebo, to the top of Pisgah, that is over against Jericho. And the Lord showed him . . . the plain of the valley of Jericho, the city of palm trees.' Here an image of the Heavenly City.

ll. 27-8. *soul . . . is drunk, and staggers.* A parallel in Plato's *Phaedo* emphasizes the Christianized Platonism that inspires this poem: 'Were we not saying [asks Socrates] that the soul too is then dragged by the body into the region of the changeable, and wanders and is confused; the world spins round her, and she is like a drunkard, when she touches change? . . . But when returning into herself she reflects, then she passes into the other world, the region of purity, and eternity, and immortality, and unchangeableness, which are her kindred.' *Dialogues of Plato*, trans. by B. Jowett (3rd edn, 5 vols., Oxford University Press, 1892), ii. 222.

'Come, come, what do I here?' l. 2. *he is gone.* William, his brother; see 'Thou that know'st for whom I mourn'.

275   *Midnight.* l. 4. *Baruch* 3: 34, 'The stars shined in their watches, and rejoiced: when he calleth them, they say, Here we be; and so with cheerfulness they showed light unto him that made them.'

276   l. 19. *aye*: ever, always.

ll. 22-3. *Shine on this blood / And water in one beam.* I John 5: 6-8, 'This is he that came by water and blood, even Jesus Christ, not by water only, but by water and blood. And it is the Spirit that beareth witness, because the Spirit is truth. For there are three that bear record in heaven, the Father, the Word, and the Holy Ghost: and these three are one. And there are three that bear witness in earth, the spirit, and the water, and the blood: and these three agree in one.'

Content. l. 1. *brave*: splendid, fine, fashionable.

l. 4. *piece*: article of (fine) clothing.

l. 6. *wardrobes*: stock of clothing (with overtones of finery).

277   l. 17. *points.* A *point* is 'a tagged lace or cord, of twisted yarn, silk, or leather, for attaching the hose to the doublet, lacing a bodice, and fastening various parts where buttons are now used' (*OED*).

l. 18. *story.* Probably in the sense of a work of visual art that tells a 'story'.

l. 23. *cross to*: in opposition to.

'Joy of my life! while left me here'. l. 1. *Joy of my life!* Probably his brother, as in the other untitled poems of *1650*; but possibly his first wife, the date of whose death is uncertain.

278   l. 17. *Saints*. Vaughan is using the term in the reformed, Protestant sense: the chosen of God, or persons of extraordinary holiness of life.

l. 25. *pillar-fires*. The Lord in a pillar of fire led the Israelites by night through the wilderness: Exodus 13: 21.

ll. 27–8. *They are that City's shining spires / We travel to.* Hebrews 11: 10, 16, 'For he [Abraham] looked for a city which hath foundations, whose builder and maker is God ... But now they desire a better country, that is, an heavenly: wherefore God is not ashamed to be called their God: for he hath prepared for them a city.' For a description of the city of God or the heavenly Jerusalem, see Revelation 21.

ll. 29–31. *A swordlike gleam ... First Out.* Genesis 3: 24, 'So he drove out the man: and he placed at the east of the garden of Eden cherubims, and a flaming sword which turned every way, to keep the way of the tree of life.'

The Storm. See Herbert's poem by this title, also in three stanzas, with similar two-foot line.

l. 1. *use*: moral application; but see different implications of *use* in l. 23.

l. 11. *discuss*: debate.

279   l. 17. *round*: surround.

l. 21. *Recluse*. As usual, Vaughan's typographical emphasis suggests special meanings: the *recluse* (hermit devoted to religious life) is his inner self, secluded within the body; but *OED* also records the obsolete meaning of *recluse* as a 'reservoir for water'.

ll. 21–4. See Herbert's *The Storm*, 'If as the winds and waters here below / Do fly and flow, / My sighs and tears as busy were above ... / Poets have wronged poor storms: such days are best; / They purge the air without, within the breast' (ll. 1–3, 17–18).

l. 23. *to thy use*: for thy purpose.

The Morning-watch.   watch: devotional observance, prayer.

l. 1. *O joys! Infinite sweetness!* See Herbert, *The H. Scriptures* (I), l. 1: 'O book! infinite sweetness!'

l. 10. *quick*: alive, lively.

l. 16. *hurled*: whirled, rotated, spun (*hurl* was sometimes confused with *whirl*).

ll. 18–19. *Prayer is / The world in tune.* See Herbert, *Prayer* (I), l. 8: 'A kind of tune, which all things hear and fear'.

l. 22. *Echo is heav'n's bliss.* Prayer produces a distant response that intimates heavenly bliss.

280　*The Evening-watch.* l. 2. *the day-star.* Christ. II Peter 1: 19, 'Until the day dawn, and the day-star arise in your hearts'. Also Revelation 22: 16, 'I am the root and the offspring of David, and the bright and morning star.'

l. 8. *Writ in his book.* Revelation 20: 12, 'And I saw the dead, small and great, stand before God; and the books were opened: and another book was opened, which is the book of life: and the dead were judged out of those things which were written in the books, according to their works.'

l. 14. *blinds*: things which conceal the design. Though *OED* does not record such a usage before 1702, Vaughan may be using the word to indicate something that 'obstructs the light or sight'.

l. 16. *prime.* The first hour of the day in the ancient 'hours' of the Church; also the spring; the time of full strength and vigour.

'Silence, and stealth of days!' Once again, about his brother William's death.

l. 3. *Twelve hundred hours.* Since William died about 14 July 1648, this poem must have been composed around 1 September 1648.

l. 9. *sun.* The lamp of l. 7: the memory of his brother.

281　l. 19. *snuff*: burnt wick or candle-end.

l. 29. *one Pearl.* Matthew 13: 45–6, 'Again, the kingdom of heaven is like unto a merchant man, seeking goodly pearls: who when he had found one pearl of great price, went and sold all that he had, and bought it.' Vaughan's 'pearl' seems to be the presence of Christ within.

Church Service. ll. 4–6. *interceding ... stones.* Romans 8: 26, 'For we know not what we should pray for as we ought: but the Spirit itself maketh intercession for us with groanings which cannot be uttered.'

282　l. 24. *sighs and groans.* See Herbert's poem with these words as title.

Burial. l. 1. *the first fruits.* I Corinthians 15: 20, 'But now is Christ risen from the dead, and become the firstfruits of them that slept.'

l. 5. *wages of my sin.* Romans 6: 23, 'For the wages of sin is death; but the gift of God is eternal life through Jesus Christ our Lord.'

l. 10. *sometimes*: at one time.

283　ll. 39–40. *come ... quickly.* See Revelation 22: 20.

284　*Cheerfulness.* ll. 22–4. *And to ... here below.* See Herbert, *Doomsday*, ll. 29–30: 'Lord, thy broken consort raise, / And the music shall be praise.'

l. 23. *consort*: music created by several voices or instruments.

'Sure, there's a tie of bodies!' ll. 5–6. The italicized words suggest the technical vocabulary of the Hermetic or Paracelsian 'science' which underlies this poem and which deeply interested Vaughan and his brother Thomas. *centred*: fixed to the earth in death. *còntaction*: contact, touching.

l. 7. *these*. 'Beams and action'—capacity for contact.

l. 9. *Absents . . . sense*. Note the word-play. *Absents*: things distant from one another. *within the line*. Perhaps with allusion to the phrase 'line of life': 'the thread fabled to be spun by the Fates, determining the duration of a person's life' (*OED*). *conspire*: breathe together, work together. *sense*: physical sense-perception.

l. 13. *kind*: closely related.

285   l. 17. *Lazarus was carried out of town*. Inferred from the fact that his tomb was in a cave (John 11: 38).

l. 18. *foe's*. May be either singular or plural possessive.

l. 21. *Death's-head*: a skull kept as a reminder of mortality.

The Passion. l. 1. *O my chief good!* See Herbert, *Good Friday*, l. 1.

l. 4. *forced by the rod*. Christ was buffeted by hands and struck by a reed, but as Rudrum points out, Vaughan's use of 'rod' evokes Moses' smiting the rock in the wilderness, and bringing forth water; the incident was interpreted as a 'type' of the Crucifixion.

286   l. 15. *Most blessed Vine!* John 15: 5, 'I am the vine, ye are the branches.'

ll. 15–18. *Most . . . as blood*. See Herbert, *The Agony*, ll. 17–18: 'Love is that liquor sweet and most divine, / Which my God feels as blood; but I, as wine.'

ll. 19–20. *How wert thou pressed / To be my feast!* See Herbert, *The Bunch of Grapes*, ll. 27–8: 'Who of the law's sour juice sweet wine did make, / Ev'n God himself, being pressèd for my sake.'

l. 28. *When none would own thee*. An allusion to Peter's denial: Matthew 26: 69–75.

l. 40. *Father forgive*. See Luke 23: 34.

287   l. 51. *two small mites*. Mark 12: 42–4, 'And there came a certain poor widow, and she threw in two mites, which make a farthing. And he called unto him his disciples, and saith unto them, Verily I say unto you, that this poor widow hath cast more in, than all they which have cast into the treasury: For all they did cast in of their abundance; but she of her want did cast in all that she had, even all her living.'

'And do they so?' The scriptural text is Beza's Latin translation: 'For created things, watching with upraised head, await the revelation of the sons of God.'

l. 2. *influence*: astrological influence.

l. 3. *expect*: wait for; also, look forward to.

l. 4. *And groan too?* Romans 8: 22, 'For we know that the whole creation groaneth.'

ll. 9–14. *Go, go . . . to sing!* See Herbert, *Affliction* (I), ll. 55–60.

l. 16. *my date*: the day of his death.

288   ll. 39–40. *Sure, thou wilt joy.* See Herbert, *The Star*, l. 29.

The Relapse. ll. 9–12. Another combination of Herbertian words and themes: see Herbert, *Discipline*, ll. 1–4: 'Throw away thy rod, / Throw away thy wrath: / O my God / Take the gentle path'; and *The Thanksgiving*, l. 34: 'But mend mine own without delays.'

ll. 13–14. See Exodus 10: 22, 'and there was a thick darkness in all the land of Egypt three days.' Also Herbert, *Sighs and Groans*, ll. 14–15: 'I have deserved that an Egyptian night / Should thicken all my powers.'

289   l. 15. *mist*. As so often, Vaughan's italic indicates a biblical allusion: Acts 13: 11, the curse of Paul upon the false prophet, 'And now, behold, the hand of the Lord is upon thee, and thou shalt be blind, not seeing the sun for a season. And immediately there fell on him a mist and a darkness.' Also II Peter 2: 17, speaking of false prophets, 'These are wells without water, clouds that are carried with a tempest; to whom the mist of darkness is reserved for ever.'

l. 18. *yew*. The graveyard tree.

l. 22. *scores*: debts.

l. 23. *challenge*: lay claim to, demand.

ll. 23–4. *challenge . . . day*. See Herbert, *Confession*, l. 28: 'I challenge here the brightest day.'

l. 25. *lily-shades*. Again, Vaughan's italic hints at a biblical allusion: the 'lily' or 'lilies' of the Song of Solomon 2: 1, 16, etc., or the 'lilies of the field' in Matthew 6: 28.

The Resolve. l. 1. *I have considered it; and find*. The same line as in Herbert, *The Reprisal*, l. 1.

l. 3. *mind*: have in mind.

l. 10. *catch at the place*. See Herbert, *Affliction* (I), l. 17: 'Therefore my sudden soul caught at the place, / And made her youth and fierceness seek thy face.'

l. 12. *case*: (1) exterior covering. (2) a chance occurrence, as in Latin *casus*, which also means falling down, or an adverse event.

l. 13. *parcelled*: divided into parts.

l. 17. *powers*. Probably the 'powers of the soul', memory, understanding, and will.

l. 20. *span*. The italic seems to indicate a special sense: perhaps to 'span' (harness) horses? But the common sense of measuring with a hand's breadth is sufficient.

l. 21. *cry*. Another technical sense, this time from hunting. The 'cry' is the yelping of hounds, or the pack of hounds; hence, any crowd.

290   ll. 23–4. See Herbert, *Affliction* (I), ll. 21–2: 'My days were strawed with flow'rs and happiness; / There was no month but May.'

l. 28. *Prize*. I Corinthians 9: 24, 'one receiveth the prize'. Also Philippians 3: 14, 'I press toward the mark for the prize of the high calling of God in Christ Jesus.'

The Match. l. 1. *Dear friend*. The opening words of Herbert's *Love Unknown*. The 'friend' here is Herbert; the poem is a direct response to the wish expressed in the last two stanzas of Herbert's *Obedience*: 'He that will pass his land, / As I have mine, may set his hand / And heart unto this Deed, when he hath read; / ... How happy were my part, / If some kind man would thrust his heart / Into these lines.'

l. 8. *Deed*. The legal term *Deed* is used three times in *Obedience*, ll. 10, 33, 38.

l. 9. *duties*. In the old legal sense: debts or payments legally due.

ll. 10–11. *And if hereafter ... claim their share*. See *Obedience*, ll. 11–12: 'If that hereafter Pleasure / Cavil, and claim her part and measure'.

l. 19. *lifes*. Another legal term: a lease 'for two (or more) lives' is 'one which is to remain in force during the life of the longest liver of (two, three, etc.) specified persons' (*OED*). Herbert uses the same imagery in *Love Unknown*, ll. 4–5.

291   l. 28. *house*. In this Herbertian context, the italicized word seems bound to evoke Herbert's *The Family*, where 'house' occurs twice (ll. 5, 21) and 'Humble Obedience near the door doth stand' (l. 13).

ll. 31–2. *Lord Jesu! ... Upon a tree*. See Herbert, *Longing*, ll. 31–2: 'Lord Jesu, thou didst bow / Thy dying head upon the tree.'

l. 40. *grain*. Probably an allusion to the parable of the 'grain of mustard seed, which a man took, and sowed in his field' (Matthew 13: 31–2).

ll. 40–2. *grain ... tears ... increase*. A complex of biblical allusions: Matthew 13: 31–2, the parable of the 'grain of mustard seed'; Psalm 126: 5, 'They that sow in tears shall reap in joy'; I Corinthians 3: 7, 'So then neither is he that planteth anything, neither he that watereth; but God that giveth the increase.'

Rules and Lessons. The stanza-form and epigrammatic manner are modelled on Herbert's *Church-porch*; but whereas Herbert has composed a series of 77 stanzas (a 'perfect' number) leading up to the 'Church', Vaughan has composed a series of 24 stanzas giving directions for daily conduct of a religious life from sunrise to sunrise, and has placed them exactly in the centre of the *1650* volume.

ll. 9–10. *the manna . . . sun-rising.* Exodus 16: 21, 'And they gathered it every morning, every man according to his eating: and when the sun waxed hot, it melted.'

l. 11. *prevent*: anticipate. Wisdom of Solomon 16: 28, 'we must prevent the sun, to give thee thanks.'

l. 16. *I AM.* Exodus 3:14, 'and God said unto Moses, I AM THAT I AM: and he said, Thus shalt thou say unto the children of Israel, I AM hath sent me unto you.'

292   ll. 19–22. *let him not go . . . shine.* See Genesis 32: 24–30, where Jacob wrestles with the angel and finally receives the name of Israel, particularly verse 26: 'And he said, Let me go, for the day breaketh. And he [Jacob] said, I will not let thee go, except thou bless me.'

ll. 23–4. *Pour . . . heav'n.* When Jacob had finished his dream of the ladder he awoke and consecrated the spot: Genesis 28: 18, 'And Jacob rose up early in the morning, and took the stone that he had put for his pillows, and set it up for a pillar, and poured oil upon the top of it.'

l. 27. *Shroud in*: lie hid within.

l. 28. *their star, the stone, and hidden food.* Revelation 22: 16, 'I Jesus have sent mine angel to testify unto you these things in the churches. I am the root and offspring of David, and the bright and morning star.' Also Revelation 2: 17, 'To him that overcometh will I give to eat of the hidden manna, and will give him a white stone, and in the stone a new name written, which no man knoweth saving he that receiveth it.'

l. 32. *temper*: equanimity, balanced disposition.

l. 36. *choose the better part.* See Christ's admonition about temporal and spiritual activity, Luke 10: 41–2, 'Martha, Martha, thou art careful and troubled about many things: But one thing is needful: and Mary hath chosen that good part, which shall not be taken away from her.'

l. 45. *Judas Jew.* See Herbert, *Self-condemnation*, ll. 17–18: 'For he hath sold for money his dear Lord, / And is a Judas-Jew.'

ll. 50–2. *Sure trot . . . lag behind.* See Herbert, *Constancy*, ll. 9–10: 'Who rides his sure and even trot, / While the world now rides by, now lags behind.' *dust it on.* hurry on (raise a dust).

293   ll. 63–4. See Matthew 25: 31–46, especially verses 34–6: 'Then shall the King say unto them on his right hand, Come, ye blessed of my Father, inherit the kingdom prepared for you from the foundation of the world: For I was an hungered, and ye gave me meat: I was thirsty, and ye gave me drink: I was a stranger, and ye took me in: Naked, and ye clothed me.'

l. 64. *fence*: ward off, protect against.

ll. 65–6. *Though . . . day*. Ecclesiastes 11: 1, 'Cast thy bread upon the waters: for thou shalt find it after many days.'

l. 66. *fraughts*: shiploads, freight.

l. 71. *unbitted*: unbridled, unrestrained.

l. 75. *voids*: issues, empties out.

294 l. 108. *span*: the measure of an extended hand.

l. 110. *trim thy lamp, buy oil*. See the parable of the virgins, Matthew 25: 1–13, 'Then shall the kingdom of heaven be likened unto ten virgins, which took their lamps, and went forth to meet the bridegroom. . . . the wise took oil in their vessels with their lamps.'

l. 125. *conversation*: society, company.

l. 126. See Herbert, *Church-monuments*, ll. 2–3: 'Here I intomb my flesh, that it betimes / May take acquaintance of this heap of dust.'

295 l. 132. *That bush where God is, shall not burn*. Exodus 3: 2, 'And the angel of the Lord appeared unto him [Moses] in a flame of fire out of the midst of a bush: and he looked, and, behold, the bush burned with fire, and the bush was not consumed.'

l. 134. *dead age*. The phrase comes from Owen Felltham, who speaks of 'the dead age of night' in his meditation on death, *Resolves*, i. 47.

ll. 139–40. The same biblical verses are quoted in Herbert's *Divinity*, ll. 17–18; see notes to that poem.

Corruption. l. 9. *till*: the act of tilling or ploughing. (But *sweat* and *till* may also be read as verbs.)

l. 10. *a thorn, or weed*. Genesis 3: 17–19, 'cursed is the ground for thy sake; in sorrow shalt thou eat of it all the days of thy life; Thorns also and thistles shall it bring forth to thee . . . In the sweat of thy face shalt thou eat bread.'

l. 14. *felled*. *1650* reads *fel*. This seems to be a misprint for *fel'd*, in parallel with *foyl'd*.

296 l. 25. *leiger*: 'resident in the capacity of ambassador' (*OED*: 'ledger').

l. 25–8. *each bush . . . view them*. See Herbert, *Decay*, ll. 6–7: 'One might have sought and found thee presently / At some fair oak, or bush, or cave, or well.'

l. 30. *freezeth on*. See Herbert, *Employment* (II), l. 29.

ll. 33–4. *thy bow . . . cloud*. The rainbow of the Covenant: Genesis 9: 13.

l. 36. *Centre*. The earth.

l. 37. *thick darkness*. A frequent biblical phrase: see Exodus 10: 22 (the plagues of Egypt), and especially Joel 2: 1–2, the prophecy of the day of Judgement: 'Blow ye the trumpet in Zion . . . for the day of the Lord cometh, for it is nigh at hand; A day of darkness and of gloominess, a day of clouds and of thick darkness.'

l. 38. *hatcheth o'er.* closes over, forms a 'hatch' over. Perhaps also with the suggestion of bringing to maturity a hidden process.

ll. 39–40. See Revelation 14: 15, 'And another angel came out of the temple, crying with a loud voice to him that sat on the cloud, Thrust in thy sickle, and reap: for the time is come for thee to reap; for the harvest of the earth is ripe.'

H. Scriptures. l. 5. *the hidden stone, the manna.* See note to *Rules and Lessons*, l. 28.

l. 6. *elixir.* See Herbert, *The Elixir*, and note.

l. 8. *characters*: letters of the alphabet.

297   ll. 9–10. *O that . . . thee!* See Herbert, *The Altar*, ll. 5–12.

l. 12. *the Law and stones.* The Mosaic law was recorded on 'tables of stone, written with the finger of God' (Exodus 31: 18).

l. 13. *my faults are thine.* See Herbert, *Judgement*, l. 15: 'There thou shalt find my faults are thine.'

Unprofitableness. Luke 17: 10, 'when ye shall have done all those things which are commanded you, say, We are unprofitable servants: we have done that which was our duty to do'; and Matthew 25: 30, 'And cast ye the unprofitable servant into outer darkness.'

l. 1. *How rich . . . are!* See Herbert, *The Flower*, ll. 1–2: 'How fresh, O Lord, how sweet and clean / Are thy returns!' The whole poem constitutes a recension of themes and phrases from Herbert's *The Flower* and *The Glance*, with a closing echo of Herbert's *The Odour*.

l. 4. *share.* shear.

298   *Christ's Nativity.* l. 7. *hark . . . rings.* See Herbert, *Man's Medley*, ll. 1–2: 'Hark, how the birds do sing, / And woods do ring.'

l. 9. *consort*: harmonious combination of voices or instruments.

ll. 11–12. *Man . . . sacrifice.* See Herbert, *Providence*, ll. 13–14: 'Man is the world's high priest: he doth present / The sacrifice for all.'

l. 29. *mystic birth.* The spiritual renewal of the speaker himself.

ll. 31–3. *How kind . . . joy.* Luke 15: 7, 'likewise joy shall be in heaven over one sinner that repenteth, more than over ninety and nine just persons, which need no repentance.'

299   l. 45. *passions mind*: remember his sufferings.

ll. 45–8. These lines, and all of Part II, reflect Vaughan's bitter opposition to the act passed by Parliament on 23 December 1644, abolishing the observance of Good Friday and Christmas, along with other traditional holy days.

The Check. l. 10. *kind*: naturally related.

l. 11. *dear flesh*. See Herbert, *Church-monuments*, l. 17: 'Dear flesh, while I do pray'.

l. 23. *mind it not*: pay no attention, take no heed.

300   l. 25. *fore-runners*. See Herbert's poem by this title.

ll. 39–40. *these thy days . . . thy own good*. An allusion to Luke 19: 42, 'If thou hadst known, even thou, at least in this thy day, the things which belong unto thy peace!'

l. 47. *The day . . . observation*. Luke 17: 20, 'The Kingdom of God cometh not with observation.'

301   *Disorder and Frailty*. l. 16. *threaten*. attempt to achieve, seem about to achieve.

ll. 20–1. *grow and stretch*. See Herbert, *The Discharge*, l. 5: 'And in thy lookings stretch and grow'; and *The Flower*, ll. 29–30: 'But while I grow in a straight line, / Still upwards bent.' The whole of Vaughan's stanza 2 echoes words and themes from *The Flower*.

l. 31. *exhalation*: a body of vapour, a meteor: see Herbert's use of a similar image in *The Answer*, ll. 8–12.

302   l. 46. *yes. 1650* reads *is*, apparently a colloquial form of *yis* (*yes*).

ll. 46–8. *give wings . . . thou art*. See Herbert, *Whitsunday*, ll. 1–4.

l. 48. *tire*: attire, specifically, a head-dress.

The biblical motto blends the Genevan and the K J versions.

Idle Verse. l. 4. *on the score*: in debt.

l. 5. *amidst my youth and night*. See Herbert, *The Glance*, l. 2.

l. 7. *my only light*. See Herbert, *The Flower*, l. 39.

l. 9. *fits*. Besides spasms, or attacks of disease, there is a sense of *fit* as part of a poem, a canto.

303   l. 13. *purls*. Vaughan's italic indicates a complex pun: (1) whirling rills of water; (2) in the context of 'dress and trim' (l. 10), the loops of decorative edging used for fine garments ('robes', l. 14); (3) perhaps also, in view of 'bowls', a kind of liquor 'made by infusing . . . bitter herbs in ale or beer' (*OED*); also, perhaps, pearls, as ornament.

l. 16. *Sick with a scarf, or glove*. See Herbert, *Love* (I), ll. 13–14: 'only a scarf or glove / Doth warm our hands, and make them write of love.'

l. 18. *Simpered and shined*. See Herbert, *The Search*, l. 14.

l. 19. *cypress*. A tree planted in churchyards. *bays*: the laurel used to crown poets.

l. 20. *yew*. Another churchyard tree.

l. 23 *nightingales . . . spring*. See Herbert, *Jordan* (I), l. 13: 'I envy no man's nightingale or spring.'

Son-days. The whole poem is done in the Elizabethan mode of the definition-poem (a rapid sequence of analogies)—used by Southwell and Sidney, and by Herbert, in *Sin* (I), *Prayer* (I), and the first stanza of his own poem *Sunday*.

l. 9. *The pulleys.* See Herbert, *The Pulley*.

ll. 11–12. *God's ... day.* Genesis 3: 8, 'And they heard the voice of the Lord God walking in the garden in the cool of the day.'

l. 13. *Jubilee.* The jubilee year was celebrated every fifty years by the Jews as a time of restitution and emancipation. See Leviticus 25: 8–13.

304   *Repentance.* ll. 7–9. *little gate / And narrow way ... passage.* See Herbert, *H. Baptism* (II), ll. 1–3; Matthew 7: 14.

l. 17. *not sorting to my end*: not suiting my purpose.

305   l. 32. *outvie my score*: exceed my list (of sins).

l. 41. *signature.* As Martin and Rudrum point out, this technical term is explained by Vaughan in his treatise on *Hermetical Physic*: 'That thou mayst have some knowledge of those materials or ingredients which are requisite and proper to make such specifical medicaments, thou must diligently read the books of the Hermetists, *De signaturis rerum*, that is to say, Of those impressions and characters which God hath communicated to, and marked (as I may say) all his Creatures with.' (Martin, p. 583).

l. 44. *told*: counted.

l. 53. *Cut me not off for my transgressions.* See Herbert, *Repentance*, l. 15.

ll. 65–6. *The heavens ... thy sight.* Job 25: 4–5, 'How then can man be justified with God? or how can he be clean that is born of a woman? Behold even to the moon, and it shineth not; yea, the stars are not pure in his sight.'

ll. 67–8. *How then ... charge with folly?* Job 4: 17–18, 'Shall mortal man be more just than God? shall a man be more pure than his maker? Behold, he put no trust in his servants; and his angels he charged with folly.'

306   l. 70. *Figs ... weed!* Luke 6: 44, 'For of thorns men do not gather figs, nor of a bramble bush gather they grapes.'

ll. 71–2. *I am the gourd of sin ... tomorrow.* See Jonah 4: 6–10. A gourd grew over Jonah to give shade and it withered the next day by God's will.

ll. 75–6. *Profaneness ... Defects and darkness in my breast.* See Herbert, *Aaron*, ll. 6–7.

ll. 79–80. *Only in him ... well dressed.* See Herbert, *Aaron*, l. 15.

l. 81. *quits all score*: pays the debt, balances the books.

l. 82. *the boxes of his poor.* See Herbert, *Praise* (III), l. 28.

The Burial of an Infant. l. 11. *Expecting*: waiting.

307   *Faith.* l. 5. *raying*: emitting, sending forth.

l. 6. *his spouse.* The Church.

l. 9. *co-heirs.* Romans 8: 16–17, 'The Spirit itself beareth witness with our spirit, that we are the children of God: and if children, then heirs; heirs of God, and joint-heirs with Christ.'

l. 10. *Of bond, or free.* Galatians 3: 28, 'There is neither Jew nor Greek, there is neither bond nor free, there is neither male nor female: for ye are all one in Christ Jesus.'

l. 21. *Sun of righteousness.* Malachi 4: 2, 'But unto you that fear my name shall the Sun of righteousness arise with healing in his wings.'

ll. 31–2. *figured in . . . rites.* See Hebrews 9: St Paul's account of how the Hebrew ceremonies formed a 'figure' of imperfect 'gifts and sacrifices . . . imposed on them until the time of reformation.'

l. 37. *spans up*: reaches (as by a span or arch); encompasses.

308   *The Dawning.* Matthew 24: 36, 42, 'But of that day and hour knoweth no man, no, not the angels of heaven, but my Father only. . . . Watch therefore, for ye know not what hour your Lord doth come.'

l. 2. *The Bridegroom's coming.* Matthew 25: 6, 'And at midnight there was a cry made, Behold, the bridegroom cometh.'

l. 24. *That morning-star.* Revelation 22: 16, 'I am the root and the offspring of David, and the bright and morning star.'

l. 29. *puddle*: foul, dirty water.

309   *Admission.* l. 1. *How shrill are silent tears.* See Herbert, *The Family*, l. 20: 'What is so shrill as silent tears?' *got head*: gained power.

l. 2. *bowels*: feelings (centre of compassion).

l. 3. *when my stock lay dead.* See Herbert, *Grace*, l. 1: 'My stock lies dead.'

l. 9. *wink*: close the eyes.

l. 10. *thy beggar.* See Herbert, *Gratefulness*, ll. 3–4: 'See how thy beggar works on thee / By art.'

l. 13. *Bowels of love!* See Colossians 3: 12, 'bowels of mercies'; I John 3: 17, 'bowels of compassion'; and Herbert, *Longing*, l. 19: 'Bowels of pity, hear!'

ll. 13–14. *rate . . . price.* See Herbert, *The Pearl*, l. 35: 'And at what rate and price I have thy love.'

310   l. 17. *infants . . . suck thee.* See Herbert, *Longing*, l. 17: 'Their infants, them; and they suck thee / More free.'

ll. 29–32. *O hear! ... blood.* See Herbert, *Church-lock and Key*, ll. 9–12.

Praise. See Herbert, *Praise* (II) for the model of Vaughan's first thirty-two lines here. The second part of Herbert's *An Offering*, which follows *Praise* (II) in *The Temple*, has a stanza-form similar to ll. 33–56 of this poem.

l. 1. *King ... life!* See Herbert, *Praise* (II), l. 1: 'King of Glory, King of Peace.'

ll. 9–10. *Wherefore ... thee.* See Herbert, *Praise* (II), ll. 9–10: 'Wherefore with my utmost art / I will sing thee.'

l. 13. *Day ... day.* See Herbert, *Praise* (II), l. 17: 'Sev'n whole days, not one in seven.'

311   l. 19. *seal and bracelet.* Song of Solomon 8: 6, 'Set me as a seal upon thine heart, as a seal upon thine arm.'

l. 46. *board*: Communion table.

l. 49. *to his pow'r*: as he is able.

312   *Dressing.* Preparation for taking Communion.

ll. 2–3. *that feed'st ... shadows flee.* Song of Solomon 2: 16–17, 'My beloved is mine, and I am his: he feedeth among the lilies. Until the day break, and the shadows flee away, turn, my beloved.'

ll. 3–4. *touch with one coal / My frozen heart.* See Isaiah 6: 6–7, where a seraph touches the lips of the prophet with a 'live coal'.

ll. 4–5. *key ... rooms.* See Herbert, *The H. Communion*, ll. 21–2: 'And hath the privy key, / Op'ning the soul's most subtle rooms.'

l. 6. *thy clear fire.* Malachi 3: 2, 'For he is like a refiner's fire.'

l. 12. *even ... win.* Psalm 8: 2, 'Out of the mouth of babes and sucklings hast thou ordained strength because of thine enemies.'

ll. 19–20. *thy private ... sign.* II Corinthians 1: 21–2, 'Now he which stablisheth us with you in Christ, and hath anointed us, is God; who hath also sealed us, and given the earnest of the Spirit in our hearts.' *earnest*: pledge, foretaste.

313   l. 30. *resent*: 'to feel (something) as a cause of depression or sorrow; to feel deeply or sharply' (*OED*).

ll. 35–42. The more extreme Protestants chose to sit rather than kneel while receiving the Communion, in order to avoid the tradition of Roman Catholicism.

Easter-day. See Herbert's *The Dawning* for Vaughan's model here.

l. 8. *two deaths.* Temporal and spiritual deaths.

l. 16. *Whose spittle ... blind.* See Mark 8: 22–5 and John 9: 1–7 for the story of how Christ healed the blind man by putting spit, or spit (spittle) mixed with clay, upon his eyes.

314   *The Holy Communion.* l. 1. *Welcome ... life!* See Herbert, *The Banquet*, ll. 1–2: 'Welcome sweet and sacred cheer, / Welcome dear.'

l. 4. *quickened*: revived, enlivened. *dry stubble.* Job 13: 25, 'And wilt thou pursue the dry stubble?'

l. 6–8. *at first ... date.* See Genesis 1: 1–3.

315   ll. 21–2. *But ... last breath.* Matthew 27: 45, 50–1, 'Now from the sixth hour there was darkness over all the land unto the ninth hour.... Jesus, when he had cried again with a loud voice, yielded up the ghost. And, behold, the veil of the temple was rent in twain from the top to the bottom.'

l. 33. *paid the price.* I Corinthians 6: 20, 'for ye are bought with a price.'

ll. 35–6. *take / Us by the hand.* See Herbert, *Easter*, l. 3; *Lent*, l. 41; *Love* (III), l. 11.

ll. 49–50. *O rose ... valley.* See Song of Solomon 2: 1.

316   *Psalm 121.* A very free adaptation, in the ballad metre used by Herbert for his version of Psalm 23—which occurs in roughly the same position, near the close of *The Church*.

l. 19. *my pillar and my cloud.* See Exodus 13: 21; the allusion is added by Vaughan.

Affliction. The poem seems to imitate the irregular verse-form of Herbert's *The Collar*, with a similar effect of greater regularity in the last four lines.

l. 2. *physic*: medicine.

l. 3. *accessions*: attacks of bad health.

l. 4. *Elixir.* Both in the alchemical sense of a transforming substance that turns a base metal to gold, and in the medicinal sense of a drug to cure disease or to prolong life.

317   ll. 19–20. *the famous fan ... disturbs.* A winnowing fan. See Matthew 3: 12, 'Whose fan is in his hand, and he will thoroughly purge his floor, and gather his wheat into the garner; but he will burn up the chaff with unquenchable fire.'

l. 29. *plays all the game.* See Herbert, *Misery*, l. 3.

l. 35. *key*: tune.

ll. 37–40. *Tuning his breast ... musical.* See Herbert, *The Temper* (I), ll. 22–4: 'Stretch or contract me, thy poor debtor: / This is but tuning of my breast, / To make the music better.'

The Tempest. l. 1. *How is man parcelled out!* See Herbert, *Doomsday*, ll. 27–8: 'Man is out of order hurled, / Parcelled out to all the world.'

318   ll. 5–16. The italicized passage is a poetical 'emblem' from which the following commentary arises.

l. 30. *Issachar*. Genesis 49: 14, 'Issachar is a strong ass couching down between two burdens.'

l. 32. *all three*. A marginal note in *1650* explains: 'Light, motion, heat.'

ll. 33–6. Rudrum quotes a passage from the occult writings of Cornelius Agrippa that forms a close parallel with this stanza.

l. 35. *subtlety*: fineness of texture.

l. 36. *kinred*. Old form of *kindred*.

l. 37. *keys . . . ascents*. As in music.

l. 39. *Sleeps at the ladder's foot*. See Genesis 28: 12, Jacob's ladder.

319   l. 45. *Yet hugs he still his dirt*. See Herbert, *Misery*, l. 46: 'Give him his dirt to wallow in all night.'

l. 49. *Life's but a blast, he knows it*. See Herbert, *Misery*, ll. 5–6: 'Man is but grass, / He knows it.'

ll. 49–52. *what? . . . law?* See Herbert, *The Collar*, ll. 3, 13–15, 21–5.

l. 53. *O foolish man! . . . sight?* See Herbert, *Misery*, l. 49: 'Oh foolish man! where are thine eyes?'

l. 55. *thick darkness*. See note on l. 37 of *Corruption*. *thy bread, a stone*. Matthew 7: 9, 'Or what man is there of you, whom if his son ask bread, will he give him a stone?'

ll. 58–60. *flints . . . steel . . . flint to dust*. A reminder of the emblem which opened the volume of 1650.

320   *Retirement*. l. 14. *Have . . . way*. See Herbert, *Affliction* (I), l. 20: 'I had my wish and way.'

l. 22. *love-twist*. See Herbert, *The Pearl*, l. 38: 'thy silk twist let down from heav'n to me'.

ll. 36–8. *I have a house . . . dwell*. Psalm 26: 8, 'Lord, I have loved the habitation of thy house, and the place where thine honour dwelleth.'

l. 40. *I make all new*. Revelation 21: 5, 'And he that sat upon the throne said, Behold, I make all things new.'

321   ll. 45–8. *faithful school . . . true descent*. See Herbert, *Church-monuments*, ll. 6–9, 17–18.

ll. 51–2. *dust . . . eyes, and blind thee still*. See Herbert, *Love* (II), ll. 9–10, 'Our eyes shall see thee, which before saw dust; / Dust blown by wit, till that they both were blind.'

Love and Discipline. l. 3. *My lot is fall'n*. See Psalm 16: 6 (*BCP*), 'The lot is fallen unto me in a fair ground' (Rudrum).

ll. 5–6. *Some tares . . . sow'st*. See the parable of the wheat and tares. Matthew 13: 24–30.

ll. 17–18. *So thrive I . . . green ears*. See Herbert, *Hope*, ll. 5–6: 'With that I gave a vial full of tears: / But he a few green ears.'

322 *The Pilgrimage*. l. 3. *accidents*: events, incidents.

l. 5. *Jacob-like . . . place*. See Genesis 28: 11.

ll. 23–4. *bread . . . live*. Matthew 4: 4, 'Man shall not live by bread alone, but by every word that proceedeth out of the mouth of God.'

ll. 25–8. *O feed me then! . . . Mount*. I Kings 19: 8, 'And he [Elijah] arose, and did eat and drink, and went in the strength of that meat forty days and forty nights unto Horeb the mount of God.'

323 *The Law and the Gospel*. l. 1. *on Sinai pitch*. Exodus 19: 2, 'For they were departed from Rephidim, and were come to the desert of Sinai, and had pitched in the wilderness; and there Israel camped before the mount.'

l. 2. *And shine . . . fiery Law*. Deuteronomy 33: 2, 'And he [Moses] said, The Lord came from Sinai, and rose up from Seir unto them; he shined forth from mount Paran . . . from his right hand went a fiery law for them.'

ll. 2–10. *Law . . . inclined*. For the details, see Exodus 19: 16 and 20: 18–21.

ll. 4–5. *thy weeds . . . for light*. Exodus 24: 17, 'And the sight of the glory of the Lord was like devouring fire on the top of the mount in the eyes of the children of Israel.' *weeds*: garments.

324 *The World*. ll. 1–7. Rudrum cites a passage from Plato's *Timaeus* (37) that indicates the philosophic background for this conception of eternity and time.

l. 8. *doting lover . . . quaintest strain*. See Herbert, *Dullness*, l. 5: 'The wanton lover in a curious strain'. *quaintest*: most ingenious.

l. 14. *pore*: 'ruin one's sight by close reading or over-study' (*OED*).

325 ll. 23–5. *Yet digged . . . clutch his prey*. See Herbert, *Confession*, ll. 13–16: 'they, / Like moles within us, heave, and cast about: / And till they foot and clutch their prey, / They never cool.'

ll. 44–5. *And poor . . . victory*. See Herbert, *The Church Militant*, l. 190: 'While Truth sat by, counting his [Sin's] victories.'

ll. 46–7. *Yet some . . . sing and weep*. Revelation 7: 14, 17, 'These are they which came out of great tribulation, and have washed their robes, and made them white in the blood of the Lamb . . . and God shall wipe away all tears from their eyes'; Revelation 15: 3, 'And they sing the song of Moses the servant of God, and the song of the Lamb.'

326 ll. 59–60. *Bridegroom . . . bride*. Alluding both to the Song of Solomon and the 'marriage' of Revelation 19: 7–9.

The Mutiny. Stanza 1. The imagery of 'straw' and 'brick' is based on the labours of the Israelites in Egypt: Exodus 5.

l. 6. *start*: cause to break away.

l. 10. *coil*: tumult.

ll. 11–12. *who made . . . waves.* See Herbert, *Providence*, ll. 47–8: 'Thou hast made poor sand / Check the proud sea, ev'n when it swells and gathers.'

l. 18. *Babel-weight.* See Genesis 11: 1–9, for the tower of Babel.

ll. 22–3. *May look . . . faith.* Hebrews 12: 2, 'Looking unto Jesus the author and finisher of our faith'.

327 ll. 30–1. *than through . . . serpents.* Refers to the forty years of Exodus. For the serpents, see Numbers 21: 6.

l. 38. *bruised reed.* See Isaiah 42: 3 and Matthew 12: 20.

ll. 39–40. *seized / Of*: 'to be the legal possessor of' (*OED*).

328 *The Constellation.* l. 14. *clue*: a ball of thread or yarn.

l. 16. *slips his span*: wastes, idles away his time or life.

l. 21. *Music and mirth.* See Herbert, *The Pearl*, l. 24.

ll. 27–8. *effects . . . much more.* With allusion to the astrological theory of the close relation between stars and plants.

l. 31. *though . . . star.* I Corinthians 15: 41, 'one star differeth from another star in glory.'

l. 33. *Since . . . names.* Psalm 147: 4, 'He telleth the number of the stars; he calleth them all by their names.'

l. 36. *in your courses fought.* Judges 5: 20, 'the stars in their courses fought against Sisera.'

ll. 37–44. A bitter attack on those reformers whose reliance on biblical authority and 'zeal' had, as Vaughan sees it, caused the civil wars of the 1640s and the destruction of the established Church of England (their 'mother'). The 'father' may well be Charles I, executed on 30 Jan. 1649.

329 l. 43. *lamb . . . dragon's voice.* Revelation 13: 11, 'And I beheld another beast coming up out of the earth; and he had two horns like a lamb, and he spake as a dragon.'

ll. 59–60. *repair these rents . . . all agree.* I Corinthians 1: 10, 'Now I beseech you, brethren, by the name of our Lord Jesus Christ, that ye all speak the same thing, and that there be no divisions among you; but that ye be perfectly joined together in the same mind and in the same judgment.' See also I John 4.

The Shepherds. l. 1. *lives.* Sometimes emended to *livers*, for metrical reasons.

ll. 5–6. *How . . . true light.* See Luke 2: 8–9.

ll. 9–11. *first and blessed swains . . . promise.* Abraham and his family were shepherds when he was promised a chosen progeny in Genesis

12: 2–3, 'And I will make of thee a great nation, and I will bless thee, and make thy name great; and thou shalt be a blessing: And I will bless them that bless thee, and curse him that curseth thee: and in thee shall all families of the earth be blessed.'

330 l. 17. *Salem*: Jerusalem.

l. 21. *cots*: cottages.

l. 23. *cedar ... gold*. Used to build the temple at Jerusalem: II Chronicles 2–4.

l. 30. *rack*: manger (though Vaughan's italic may indicate a glance at *rack* as an instrument of torture, i.e. Christ's sufferings).

ll. 49–50. *kings and prophets ... missed*. See Matthew 13: 17.

l. 53. *to*: compared to.

331 *Misery*. l. 5. *The wind ... fist*. Proverbs 30: 4, 'who hath gathered the wind in his fists?'

l. 6. *blow still ... list*. John 3: 8, 'the wind bloweth where it listeth.' *where it list*: where it wishes.

l. 23. *fig-leafs*. See Genesis 3: 7.

l. 36. *Would make a court ... dwell*. See Herbert, *The Glimpse*, l. 30: 'Who by thy coming may be made a court.'

ll. 38–40. *spirit grieves ... dust*. See Herbert's poem on the text 'Ephes. 4. 30. Grieve not the Holy Spirit', ll. 1–10, 16.

332 l. 41. *devest*. Literally, unclothe: an old form of *divest*.

ll. 57–8. *I school ... cell*. See Herbert, *Mortification*, ll. 20–2: 'Getting a house and home, where he may move / Within the circle of his breath, / Schooling his eyes.'

l. 66. *snudge*: nestle, be snug and secure. See Herbert, *Giddiness*, l. 11: 'snudge in quiet'.

l. 74. *travel, fight or die*. See Herbert, *Nature*, ll. 1–2: 'Full of rebellion, I would die, / Or fight, or travel.'

ll. 77–81. *flames ... work and wind ... fierce soul bustles ... wilded by a peevish heart*. A complex of Herbertian echoes: see *Jordan* (II), ll. 13–15; *The Collar*, l. 33; and *Sion*, l. 13.

333 l. 87. *tempers*: passing feelings, humours, inclinations.

l. 96. *To look ... pain*. See Herbert, *The Glance*, l. 21: 'When thou shalt look us out of pain'.

l. 114. *mend and make*. See Herbert, *Love* (II), l. 14.

334 *The Sap*. The poem's theme is the spiritual nourishment gained from taking the Communion; hence it echoes many of Herbert's eucharistic poems and passages, and bears an especially close relation to Herbert's *Peace*, which closes with words that suggest the service of Communion.

ll. 7-8. *Thy root ... meat.* See Herbert, *Peace*, ll. 16-18: 'Peace at the root must dwell. / But when I digged, I saw a worm devour / What showed so well.'

l. 11. *an hill of myrrh.* Song of Solomon 4: 6, 'Until the day break, and the shadows flee away, I will get me to the mountain of myrrh, and to the hill of frankincense.'

l. 13. *Prince of Salem.* Christ and Melchizedek: see Herbert, *Peace*, ll. 22-3 and note.

l. 22. *two ... due.* See Herbert, *Business*, l. 22: 'And two deaths had been thy fee.' Death of the body and condemnation of the soul.

ll. 25-6. *strange love ... sacred blood.* See Herbert, *Obedience*, ll. 26-7: 'thy death and blood / Showed a strange love to all our good.' Also Donne, *Holy Sonnet* XI (Grierson's order), l. 9: 'Oh let me then his strange love still admire.'

ll. 26-9. *his sacred blood ... cordial ... decay.* See Herbert, *The Sacrifice*, ll. 158-9: 'Which shows my blood to be the only way / And cordial left to repair man's decay.'

ll. 29-31. *who but truly tastes it ... secret life and virtue.* See Herbert, *Peace*, ll. 33-6: 'For they that taste it do rehearse, / That virtue lies therein, / A secret virtue bringing peace and mirth / By flight of sin.' *virtue*: inherent power.

335   l. 40. *A powerful, rare dew.* Repentance, tears.

l. 45. *one who drank it thus.* An allusion to Herbert, as the following Herbertian echoes indicate: see *The H. Communion*, where the first poem under this title deals with the action of grace, and the second celebrates the 'ease' with which the soul here communicates with heaven; also *The Invitation*, stanza 4, concerned with 'joy', and *The Banquet*, which celebrates the 'sweet and sacred cheer' of the Communion and its power of raising the soul to 'the sky'.

Mount of Olives (II). See notes on preceding poem by this title.

l. 1. *When first ... thy joys.* Reminiscent of the opening line of Herbert's *Jordan* (II): 'When first my lines of heav'nly joys made mention'.

ll. 1-8. Reminiscent of the opening line and stanza of Herbert's *The Glance*: 'When first thy sweet and gracious eye / Vouchsafed ... / To look upon me ... / I felt a sugared strange delight ... / Bedew, embalm, and overrun my heart.'

l. 4. *sweets*: fragrances (which 'perfume' the whole being, as in Herbert's *The Odour*).

ll. 12-22. Reminiscent of Herbert's *The Flower*, in theme and occasional wording.

l. 14. *And was blown through by ev'ry storm and wind.* Almost identical with l. 36 of Herbert's *Affliction* (I).

l. 17. *paisage*: landscape (Vaughan's italic indicates both a foreign word and perhaps also a technical term in painting).

336   *Man.* A striking contrast, in theme and mood, with Herbert's poem *Man.*

ll. 12–14. *The birds ... fine.* Matthew 6: 26, 28–9, 'Behold the fowls of the air: for they sow not, neither do they reap, nor gather into barns; yet your heavenly Father feedeth them. . . . And why take ye thought for raiment? Consider the lilies of the field, how they grow; they toil not, neither do they spin: And yet I say unto you, that even Solomon in all his glory was not arrayed like one of these.'

l. 23. *wit*: intelligence. *stones*: loadstones—used as magnetic compasses.

337   'I walked the other day'. Another poem on the death of his brother William.

l. 1. *to spend my hour.* His usual hour of meditation.

l. 4. *a gallant flower.* The same phrase occurs in l. 14 of Herbert's *Peace.*

ll. 5–6. *ruffled ... bower ... curious store.* See Herbert, *Affliction* (V), ll. 21–2: 'While blust'ring winds destroy the wanton bowers, / And ruffle all their curious knots and store.' *curious store*: fine abundance.

ll. 19–21. *I saw ... unseen.* See Herbert, *The Flower*, ll. 8–14.

338   l. 46. *frame*: construction: (1) human body; (2) universe.

l. 49. *Thy steps.* The *vestigia*, the signs of God's presence and power that may be found by meditating on the creation.

339   l. 59. *light, joy, leisure.* See Herbert, *Heaven*, l. 19: 'Light, joy, and leisure.'

l. 61. *hid in thee, show me his life again.* Colossians 3: 3, 'For ye are dead, and your life is hid with Christ in God.'

Begging (I). l. 1. *King of Mercy, King of Love.* See Herbert, *L'Envoy*, l. 1: 'King of Glory, King of Peace'. Also *Praise* (II), l. 1.

l. 2. *In whom ... move.* Acts 17: 28, 'for in him we live, and move, and have our being.'

ll. 13–16. *O it is thy only Art ... to thee.* See Herbert, *Nature*, ll. 4–6: 'O tame my heart; / It is thy highest art / To captivate strongholds to thee.'

The verses from Jude follow KJ, with the substitution of *us* for *you.*

SILEX SCINTILLANS (1655)

343   *The Author's Preface. idle words.* Matthew 12: 36, 'But I say unto you, That every idle word that men shall speak, they shall give account thereof in the day of judgment.'

parricides. An allusion to Robert Greene's *Groatsworth of Wit* (1592): 'Ah Gentlemen, that live to read my broken and confused lines, look not I should (as I was wont) delight you with vain fantasies; but gather my follies all together, and as ye would deal with so many parricides, cast them into the fire.'

Brabeion: a prize in athletic contests.

Prudentius. b. AD 348. *Symmachus*. b. *c*. AD 340; famous orator and defender of pagan religion.

344   *character ... ivy-bush ... persons of honour.* I.e., if the description ('character') of the author as a person of high rank or title ('honour') is no more than a mere advertisement, as an ivy-bush or a picture of it is placed outside a tavern to show that wine is sold there.

idle word ... no corrupt communication. See Matthew 12: 36 and Ephesians 4: 29, 'Let no corrupt communication proceed out of your mouth, but that which is good to the use of edifying, that it may minister grace unto the hearers.'

mere design: deliberate intent.

345   The passage is a free quotation from Owen Felltham, *Resolves* (1628), Century II, i, 'Of Idle Books'.

he that is dead. Romans 6: 7.

prevent: anticipate.

conceits: conceptions, ingenious turns of thought.

stationer: bookseller, publisher.

346   *casteth firebrands.* Proverbs 26: 18.

they that turn many. Daniel 12: 3.

flourishing and admired wit. Sometimes taken to allude to Andrew Melville, a Scottish reformer whose attack on the rituals of the Church of England Herbert answered in his Latin poems (these had not been published at this time, but Vaughan may have known of them).

non passibus aequis. '[But] not with equal steps,' *Aeneid* 2. 724.

perfection. Christian perfection, holiness of life.

practic: pertaining to, shown in, practice or action.

prelibation: foretaste.

347   *Hierotheus.* 'A mythical first-century bishop of Athens, apparently invented by Dionysius the pseudo-Areopagite, who ... speaks of Hierotheus as his teacher and as a writer of hymns' (Martin).

A true Hymn. See Herbert's poem by that title.

nigh unto death. See Paul's words concerning his companion Epaphroditus: 'For indeed he was sick nigh unto death: but God had mercy on him' (Philippians 2: 27).

accomplished dress: completed appearance or presentation; see introduction.

God . . . flesh. Numbers 16: 22.

348   This *catena* (chain) of biblical verses follows an ancient tradition of creating a personal psalm out of an arrangement and adaptation of passages. The sequence runs as follows: Jeremiah 17: 13–14 (*thou art my health, and my great deliverer.* KJ: *thou art my praise*); Isaiah 38: 10 (*I have deprived myself.* KJ: *I am deprived*); Isaiah 38: 11; Isaiah 38: 16 (KJ: 'O Lord, by these things men live, and in all these things is the life of my spirit'); Isaiah 38: 17; Isaiah 48: 9 (KJ: 'For my name's sake will I defer mine anger, and for my praise will I refrain for thee, that I cut thee not off'); Isaiah 38: 18–19; Jonah 2: 6, 8 (freely treated); Psalms 42: 8; 43: 4; 5: 7; Jonah 2: 9.

349   *To my most merciful*. For section I, see notes to *The Dedication*, p. 484–5.

    ll. 23–4. The lines refer to the brightness of Christ's clothing at his Transfiguration (Matthew 17: 2) and to the *virtue* (healing power) of Christ demonstrated in the story of the woman who was healed by touching his clothes (Mark 5: 25–34).

    l. 27. *earnest*: 'A foretaste, instalment, pledge, of anything afterwards to be received in greater abundance' (*OED*).

    l. 28. *The Candle*. Job 29: 3, 'When his candle shined upon my head'.

350   l. 45. *Token*. Probably a reference to the 'token of the covenant' in Genesis 9: 12–17.

351   *Ascension-day*. The Thursday forty days after Easter.

    l. 4. *all good and perfect gifts*. James 1: 17, 'Every good gift and every perfect gift is from above.'

    ll. 16–18. *where the angels . . . night*. At the empty tomb angels stood watch to announce the absence of the resurrected Lord. See Matthew 28: 1–7; Luke 24: 1–8.

    l. 19. *thy Convert's tears. 1655* provides a footnote: 'St. Mary Magdalene.'

    l. 21. *I smell her spices, and her ointment*. Mark 16: 1, 'And when the sabbath was past, Mary Magdalene, and Mary the mother of James, and Salome, had bought sweet spices, that they might come and anoint him.' Also Matthew 26: 12, 'For in that she hath poured this ointment on my body, she did it for my burial.'

    l. 25. *posting*: swift.

    l. 33. *commerce*: relations, activities: see Acts 1: 3, 'To whom [the apostles] also he shewed himself alive after his passion by many infallible proofs, being seen of them forty days, and speaking of the things pertaining to the Kingdom of God.'

352   l. 37. *the fields of Bethany*. Luke 24: 50–1, 'And he led them out as

far as to Bethany, and he lifted up his hands, and blessed them. And it came to pass, while he blessed them, he was parted from them, and carried up into heaven.'

l. 43. *vest*: clothing, vesture.

l. 45. *Heaven . . . like molten glass*. Job 37: 18, 'Hast thou with him spread out the sky, which is strong, and as a molten looking glass?'

l. 51. *train*: followers.

ll. 57–8. *The cloud . . . behold two men in white*. Acts 1: 9–11, 'he was taken up; and a cloud received him out of their sight. And while they looked stedfastly toward heaven as he went up, behold, two men stood by them in white apparel; Which also said, Ye men of Galilee, why stand ye gazing up into heaven? this same Jesus, which is taken up from you into heaven, shall so come in like manner as ye have seen him go into heaven.'

ll. 59–60. *Two and no more . . . stubborn Jew*. John 8: 17, 'It is also written in your law, that the testimony of two men is true.'

Ascension Hymn. ll. 7–11. *some . . . life*. The 'death' of mystical experience.

l. 12. *Leave . . . old Man*. Colossians 3: 9, 'ye have put off the old man with his deeds.'

353   l. 30. *the Refiner's fire*. Malachi 3: 2, 'But who may abide the day of his coming? . . . for he is like a refiner's fire, and like fullers' soap.'

ll. 33–5. *clothes . . . The Fuller*. Mark 9: 3, 'And his raiment became shining, exceeding white as snow; so as no fuller on earth can white them.' A *fuller* is one who *fulls* cloth, that is, cleans and whitens it.

l. 36. *more white than snow*. Isaiah 1: 18, 'though your sins be as scarlet, they shall be as white as snow.'

l. 39. *Bring bone to bone*. Ezekiel 37: 7, 'and the bones came together, bone to his bone.'

l. 41. *all-subduing might*. Philippians 3: 20–1, 'according to the working whereby he is able even to subdue all things unto himself.'

354   'They are all gone into the world of light!' l. 35. *Resume*: take back.

355   l. 38. *perspective*: telescope.

l. 40. *no glass*. I Corinthians 13: 12, 'For now we see through a glass, darkly; but then face to face.'

White Sunday: Whitsunday; the seventh Sunday after Easter—commemorating the descent of the Holy Spirit on the day of Pentecost: Acts 2: 1–4.

ll. 5–8. *Those flames . . . fire*. Acts 2: 3, 'And there appeared unto them cloven tongues like as of fire, and it sat upon each of them.'

l. 6. *tire*: head-dress.

ll. 9–16. *new lights . . . candle shines*. Vaughan is attacking the extreme sects of his day whose members claimed to have special illumination from God which justified new religious doctrines and practices.

l. 11. *gall*. With allusion to the vinegar 'mingled with gall' given as a drink to Christ just before his Crucifixion: Matthew 27: 34.

l. 16. *His candle shines*. Job 29: 3, 'When his candle shined upon my head, and when by his light I walked through darkness.'

l. 24. *discern wolves from the sheep*. Matthew 7: 15, 'Beware of false prophets, which come to you in sheep's clothing, but inwardly they are ravening wolves.'

356   l. 26. *These last may be as first*. Matthew 19: 30, 'But many that are first shall be last; and the last shall be first.'

l. 28. *These last should be the worst*. II Timothy 3: 13, 'But evil men and seducers shall wax worse and worse.'

ll. 29–31. *Thy method . . . set down*. See Herbert, *The Bunch of Grapes*, l. 11: 'Their story pens and sets us down', that is, God's way of dealing with the Israelites foretells the present times.

ll. 45–8. *great eternal Rock . . . soul that pines*. See Exodus 17: 6 and I Corinthians 10: 4, 'for they drank of that spiritual Rock that followed them: and that Rock was Christ.'

ll. 54–6. *Curse . . . purse*. See Herbert, *Prayer* (II), ll. 15–18: 'Wert fain to take our flesh and curse, / . . . That by destroying that which tied thy purse, / Thou mightst make sure for liberality!'

357   l. 63. *Balaam's hire*. See Numbers 22 for Balak's offers to 'promote' Balaam 'unto very great honour' if he will disobey God.

The Proffer. The poem appears to reject an offer of some appointment to an office in the government of the 'Commonwealth' (l. 36) established by Cromwell and his associates after the execution of Charles I in 1649.

l. 10. *to take*. I.e., to take as food.

l. 11. *Wise husband will (you say) there wants prevent*. The line has a proverbial sound. *Good husband* was a common phrase for one who manages his household or business 'with skill and thrift' (*OED*). *there* refers to the time of 'harder weather' (l. 9). *prevent*: anticipate. The line is usually emended to read *husbands*, with *there* interpreted as *their*; but no emendation is needed.

l. 18. *I've read . . . away*. Exodus 8: 31, 'And the Lord did according to the word of Moses; and he removed the swarms of flies from Pharaoh, from his servants, and from his people; there remained not one.'

358   ll. 25–7. *Shall my short hour . . . crumb of life*. See Herbert, *Complaining*, ll. 16–18: 'Let not thy wrathful power / Afflict my hour, / My inch of life.'

l. 33. *skill not*: do not value.

ll. 37–42. *will sow tares . . . reward for them and thee*. See the parable of the wheat and tares, Matthew 13: 24–30, 37–42.

ll. 44–5. *Spit out . . . with home*. See Herbert, *The Church-porch*, l. 92: 'Spit out thy phlegm, and fill thy breast with glory.'

ll. 45–8. *think on thy dream . . . Heaven*. Patterned after the last four lines of Herbert's *The Size*. The similarity may serve as a reminder of a larger kinship between these two poems: both have eight stanzas; the stanza-forms are similar (though not identical); and the theme of both is renunciation of worldly prosperity.

Cock-crowing. Elizabeth Holmes (p. 37) has called attention to a passage in Thomas Vaughan's *Anima Magica Abscondita* (1650) which bears a close relation to this poem and shows how strongly it is influenced by the occult, Hermetic philosophy in which both brothers were interested: 'For she [*Anima*] is guided in her operations by a *Spiritual Metaphysical Grain*, a Seed or Glance of *Light*, simple, and without any mixture, descending from the *first Father of Lights*. For though his *full-eyed* Love shines on nothing but *Man*, yet everything in the world is in some measure directed for his preservation by a *spice* or *touch* of the *first Intellect*' (Rudrum edn., p. 111).

l. 1. *Father of lights*. James 1: 17, 'Every good gift and every perfect gift is from above, and cometh down from the Father of lights.'

359   l. 12. *tinned*: kindled.

l. 13. *tincture*. A term from alchemy: a spiritual principle—the essence or soul of a thing.

l. 14. *impower*: bestow power on.

ll. 20–2. *Whose hand . . . who made the same*. Romans 1: 20, 'For the invisible things of him from the creation of the world are clearly seen, being understood by the things that are made, even his eternal power and Godhead.'

l. 29. *dark Egyptian border*. See Exodus 10: 21.

ll. 37–40. *Only this veil . . . thee from me*. II Corinthians 3: 14, 'But their minds were blinded: for until this day remaineth the same vail untaken away in the reading of the old testament; which vail is done away in Christ.' Also, Hebrews 10: 20, 'By a new and living way, which he hath consecrated for us, through the veil, that is to say, his flesh.'

l. 41. *full-eyed love*. The phrase occurs in Herbert's *The Glance*, l. 20; also in the above passage from Thomas Vaughan.

360   l. 48. *Though with no lily*. Song of Solomon 2: 16, 'My beloved is mine, and I am his: he feedeth among the lilies.'

The Star. The guiding concept of this poem is the Hermetic and astrological theory that a close and active inter-relationship ('commerce', ll. 5 and 27) exists between creatures on earth and the celestial bodies.

l. 3. *And wind ... smile.* See Herbert, *The Star*, l. 26: 'Glitter, and curl, and wind as they.'

l. 5. *imbars*: impedes, prohibits.

l. 6. *eagles eye not stars.* Because, according to tradition, they look toward the sun.

ll. 7–8. *And still the lesser ... blest.* Hebrews 7: 7, 'And without all contradiction the less is blessed of the better.'

l. 13. *the subject.* Whatever on earth attracts the star—the object of the star's streaming and flowing. *respected*: regarded, looked upon (with esteem and close attention).

l. 14. *well disposed*: healthy.

361   *The Palm-tree.* In this poem the soul (representing the 'inward speaking' of Christ) is addressing the body on the verge of death (as in Vaughan's *The Evening-watch*). The palm-tree had become a symbol of the Church, through the traditional interpretation of Song of Solomon 7: 7–8, 'This thy stature is like to a palm tree ... I said, I will go up to the palm tree, I will take hold of the boughs thereof.' The opening lines seem to allude to the physical church or churchyard, where the speaker's body will endure the 'shade' of death. But the chief reference is to the spiritual Church on earth and in heaven.

l. 1. *Dear friend sit down.* The opening words of Herbert's *Love Unknown*.

ll. 7–9. *these weights ... grows.* Martin cites M. P. Tilley, *Proverbs in England* (p. 37): 'The straighter grows the palm the heavier the weight it bears.'

ll. 11–12. *By flowers ... and palms foretold.* Details of Solomon's Temple: see I Kings 6: 23–35. Also Herbert, *Sion*, ll. 4–5.

ll. 13–14. *This is the life ... God.* Colossians 3: 3, 'For ye are dead, and your life is hid with Christ in God.'

ll. 17–20. *Here spirits ... won the fight ... crowns.* II Timothy 4: 7–8, 'I have fought a good fight, I have finished my course, I have kept the faith: henceforth there is laid up for me a crown of righteousness'; Hebrews 12: 1, 'let us run with patience the race that is set before us'; I Corinthians 9: 24–5, 'Know ye not that they which run in a race run all, but one receiveth the prize? So run, that ye may obtain. ... Now they do it to obtain a corruptible crown; but we an incorruptible.'

362   ll. 21, 25. *Here is the patience of the saints ... Here is their faith too.* Revelation 14: 12, 'Here is the patience of the saints: here are they that keep the commandments of God, and the faith of Jesus.' Also

Revelation 13: 10, 'Here is the patience and the faith of the saints.'

l. 28. *against you wake*. In preparation for the Last Judgement.

Joy. l. 5. *dosis*: a prescribed quantity of medicine.

ll. 21–2. *pains of death . . . eyes and breath*. See Herbert, *The Banquet*, ll. 52–3: 'Hearken under pain of death, / Hands and breath.'

ll. 29–30. *leave written on some tree . . . fastens thee*. See Herbert, *Affliction* (V), l. 20: 'We are the trees, whom shaking fastens more.'

363   *The Favour*. l. 6. *starved eaglet*. See note on *The Star*, l. 6.

l. 7. *kind*: related to (the star).

The Garland. ll. 9–11. *I flung away . . . for pleasures*. See Herbert, *Christmas*, ll. 1–3 (and note): 'All after pleasures as I rid one day, / My horse and I, both tired, body and mind, / With full cry of affections, quite astray.' Also Herbert, *The Pilgrimage*, ll. 31–2: 'so I flung away, / Yet heard a cry.'

l. 10. *affections*: passions, emotions. *rid*: rode.

l. 11. *In post*: in haste.

l. 19. *silk-lists*: silk borders or trimming.

364   l. 25. *career*. A term associated with horsemanship: 'a short gallop at full speed' (*OED*); see ll. 9–11.

l. 27. *abear*: behaviour (*OED*); perhaps also associated with the verb *aberr*: to go astray (?).

Love-sick. For the repetitive technique of this poem, compare Herbert's *A Wreath*.

ll. 9–11. *O come and rend . . . mountains flow*. Isaiah 64: 1, 'Oh that thou wouldest rend the heavens, that thou wouldest come down, that the mountains might flow down at thy presence.'

ll. 12–13. *Thou art / Refining fire*. Malachi 3: 2, 'For he is like a refiner's fire.'

l. 17. *So hear that thou must open*. Matthew 7: 7, 'Knock, and it shall be opened unto you.'

365   *Trinity Sunday*. Patterned after Herbert's poem by this title.

l. 7. *antitypes*. *OED* defines an *antitype* as that which is shadowed forth or represented by the 'type' or symbol—Vaughan's own spirit and body (water and blood).

Psalm 104. A free paraphrase, greatly expanded; compare KJ version.

369   *The Bird*. l. 26. *heavy*: sad, melancholy.

l. 27. *turtle*: turtle-dove. See Song of Solomon 2: 12, 'the voice of the turtle'; and Isaiah 38: 14, 'I did mourn as a dove.'

l. 28. *satyrs*. 'In the English Bible the word is applied . . . to the hairy demons or monsters . . . supposed to inhabit deserts' (*OED*). See

Isaiah 34: 14, 'The wild beasts of the desert shall also meet with the wild beasts of the island, and the satyr shall cry to his fellow; the screech owl also shall rest there.'

l. 29. *the pleasant land ... turns.* Genesis 19: 24, 'The Lord rained upon Sodom and upon Gomorrah brimstone and fire.'

l. 32. *day-spring ... from high.* Luke 1: 78, 'Through the tender mercy of our God; whereby the dayspring from on high hath visited us.'

The Timber. l. 15. *resent*: perceive, feel sharply (with overtones of the modern meaning?).

370   l. 19. *resentment.* See note on line 15.

l. 20. *Means*: refers to, signifies.

l. 27. *resentient*: 'that which causes a change of feeling'—Vaughan's use is the only example in the *OED*.

l. 31. *an house where many mansions are.* John 14: 2, 'In my Father's house are many mansions.'

ll. 45–8. *If my way lies ... thirst.* See the account of the thirst of Hagar and Ishmael in the wilderness: Genesis 21: 14–19, 'And God opened her eyes, and she saw a well of water; and she went, and filled the bottle with water, and gave the lad drink.'

371   ll. 51–2. *trees of life ... make them grow.* See Revelation 22: 1–2.

The Jews. The poem is based on the tradition that the Jews would be converted shortly before the Last Judgement. To Vaughan (and many of his contemporaries) the troubled religious conditions of England seemed to point toward the Last Days.

l. 7. *Beneath the oak and juniper.* See *Religion*, ll. 5, 7 and notes.

l. 12. *and living waters flow.* Jeremiah 17: 13, 'the Lord, the fountain of living waters.'

ll. 15–18. *the olive ... decay.* Jeremiah 11: 16–17, 'The Lord called thy name, A green olive tree, fair, and of goodly fruit: with the noise of a great tumult he hath kindled fire upon it, and the branches of it are broken.'

l. 19. *the husbandman.* John 15: 1, 'I am the true vine, and my Father is the husbandman.'

l. 22. *the bright morning-star.* Christ. See Revelation 22: 16.

372   ll. 24–7. *blind ... Our fulness ... come in.* Romans 11: 25, 'that blindness in part is happened to Israel, until the fulness of the Gentiles be come in.'

l. 31. *Mamre.* Where Abraham dwelt: Genesis 13: 18. *Eschol's brook.* Place where the spies sent into Canaan cut down the 'cluster of grapes': Numbers 13: 23–4.

ll. 33–4. *Who loved ... only Son.* See John 3: 16.

l. 37. *From . . . veil remove.* II Corinthians 3: 15–16, 'But even unto this day, when Moses is read, the vail is upon their heart. Nevertheless when it shall turn to the Lord, the vail shall be taken away.'

l. 49. *the lost son by the newly found.* See the parable of the Prodigal Son, Luke 15: 11–32—especially verse 32: 'It was meet that we should make merry, and be glad: for this thy brother was dead, and is alive again; and was lost, and is found.'

Begging (II). First published in Vaughan's *Flores Solitudinis* (1654).

l. 1. *O.* The reading of 1654: *1655* reads *I* ('Aye').

373   l. 12. *the weeping lad.* Ishmael. See note on *The Timber*, ll. 45–8.

Palm Sunday. John 12: 12–13, 'On the next day much people that were come to the feast, when they heard that Jesus was coming to Jerusalem, Took branches of palm trees, and went forth to meet him, and cried, Hosanna: Blessed is the King of Israel that cometh in the name of the Lord.'

l. 3. *green and gay.* The phrase appears in Herbert's *The Search*, l. 10.

l. 4. *King of grief.* The phrase appears in Herbert's *The Thanksgiving*, l. 1. *man of sorrow.* See Isaiah 53: 3.

l. 12. *expect with groans.* Romans 8: 22, 'For we know that the whole creation groaneth.'

l. 13. *which all at ones. 1655* reads *which all at once,* a reading that does not appear to make sense. The printer of *1655* may have been misled by Vaughan's division of *atones,* reaching back toward the derivation and root-meaning of the word: to make one, bring into concord, reconcile. (*OED*, 'at one', 'atone'). This emendation was suggested by Sir Edward Marsh (*TLS*, 19 July 1947).

374   l. 21. *thrones and seraphins.* The titles of two of the nine orders of angels.

l. 28. *Seen long before this came to pass.* Vaughan's note at this point in *1655* cites Zechariah 9: 9, 'Rejoice greatly, O daughter of Zion; shout, O daughter of Jerusalem: behold, thy King cometh unto thee: he is just, and having salvation; lowly, and riding upon an ass, and upon a colt the foal of an ass.'

ll. 35–6. *I'll get me up . . . off many a tree.* See Herbert, *Easter*, ll. 19–20, 'I got me flowers to straw thy way; / I got me boughs off many a tree.'

l. 39. *wrong.* Probably in the old sense of 'bent', but also with modern meaning. See *The Palm-tree* and notes.

l. 46. *green branch . . . white robe.* Revelation 7: 9, 'a great multitude, which no man could number . . . clothed with white robes, and palms in their hands.'

375   *Jesus Weeping* (I). Luke 19: 41, 'And when he was come near, he beheld the city, and wept over it.'

ll. 5–6. *your fathers' breed ... not Abr'am's seed.* Offspring of those who worshipped the golden calf (Exodus 32: 3–4), not the descendants of Abraham. *stiff-neckèd.* See Exodus 32: 9.

l. 8. *The stones had spoke.* Luke 19: 39–40, 'And some of the Pharisees from among the multitude said unto him, Master, rebuke thy disciples. And he answered and said unto them, I tell you that, if these should hold their peace, the stones would immediately cry out.'

l. 10. *living water.* See John 4: 10.

l. 17. *This land.* England, as well as Jerusalem and Judea.

The Daughter of Herodias. For the story of Salome's dancing and asking for the head of John the Baptist, see Mark 6: 17–28 and Matthew 14: 6–11.

376   l. 9. *young sorceress; the ice.* Vaughan adds a note here in *1655*: 'Her name was Salome; in passing over a frozen river, the ice broke under her, and chopped off her head.'

l. 11. *his.* Vaughan adds a note here in *1655*: 'Herod Antipas.'

l. 20. *She tempts to incest.* Herod had thrown John the Baptist into prison because he denounced Herod's marriage to Herodias, the wife of Herod's brother: 'For John had said unto Herod, It is not lawful for thee to have thy brother's wife' (Mark 6: 18).

Jesus Weeping (II). John 11: 35, 'Jesus wept' (at the death of Lazarus).

l. 2. *groan and groan again.* John 11: 33, 38, 'When Jesus therefore saw her weeping, and the Jews also weeping which came with her, he groaned in the spirit, and was troubled ... Jesus therefore again groaning in himself cometh to the grave.'

l. 14. *refrain*: hold back.

l. 20. *tried*: known, experienced.

377   l. 32. *without leave*: without leaving off, without stopping.

l. 49. *Lilies and myrrh.* Song of Solomon 5: 13, 'his lips like lilies, dropping sweet smelling myrrh.'

l. 53. *swan-like.* Swans were supposed to sing as death approached.

378   *Providence.* ll. 3–6. *holy well ... Ishmael.* Another reference to the deliverance of Ishmael: Genesis 21: 14–19.

l. 15. *A fish shall all my tribute pay.* See the story of Peter and the tribute money, Matthew 17: 25–7: 'What thinkest thou, Simon? of whom do the kings of the earth take custom or tribute? of their own children or of strangers? Peter saith unto him, of strangers. Jesus saith unto him, Then are the children free. Notwithstanding, lest we should offend them, go thou to the sea, and cast an hook, and take up the fish that first cometh up; and when thou hast opened his mouth, thou shalt find a piece of money: that take, and give unto them for me and thee.'

l. 16. *The swift-winged raven . . . meat.* As the ravens brought food to Elijah: I Kings 17: 6.

l. 18. *I knew no month but May.* See Herbert, *Affliction* (I), l. 22: 'There was no month but May.'

l. 21. *Bags that wax old.* Luke 12: 33, 'provide yourselves bags which wax not old, a treasure in the heavens that faileth not.'

379   l. 46. *Pontic sheep.* Pliny in his *Natural History* (xxvii. 28) mentions Pontic wormwood because the cattle that are fattened on it are without gall. *Pontus* was the Roman name for the region around the Black Sea.

The Knot. Martin cites two Latin hymns that apply the word *vinculum* ('that with which anything is bound') to the Virgin Mary. It is bold of Vaughan to publish such defiant praise of the Virgin in 1655, when even moderate Protestants regarded such devotion with suspicion, as encroaching on the prerogative of Christ. See Herbert's *To All Angels and Saints.*

380   *The Ornament.* l. 14. *weeds*: clothing, garments.

l. 16. *the sheep-keeping Syrian maid.* Rachel. See Genesis 29: 9, 17, 'And while he yet spake with them, Rachel came with her father's sheep: for she kept them. . . . Leah was tender eyed; but Rachel was beautiful and well favoured.'

l. 20. *bravest*: the best dressed.

St. Mary Magdalen. Tradition identified the Mary of John 12: 3 with the unnamed 'sinner' (presumably a prostitute) of Luke 7: 36–50, 'And, behold, a woman in the city, which was a sinner, when she knew that Jesus sat at meat in the Pharisee's house, brought an alabaster box of ointment, and stood at his feet behind him weeping, and began to wash his feet with tears, and did wipe them with the hairs of her head, and kissed his feet, and anointed them with the ointment. Now when the Pharisee which had bidden him saw it, he spake within himself, saying, This man, if he were a prophet, would have known who and what manner of woman this is that toucheth him; for she is a sinner. . . . And he [Jesus] turned to the woman, and said unto Simon, seest thou this woman? I entered into thine house, thou gavest me no water for my feet: but she hath washed my feet with tears, and wiped them with the hairs of her head. Thou gavest me no kiss: but this woman, since the time I came in, hath not ceased to kiss my feet. . . . And he said to the woman, Thy faith hath saved thee; go in peace.'

381   l. 13. *Magdal-castle.* Tradition placed Mary's inheritance in the castle of Magdala, near Bethany.

l. 21. *pistic nard.* Translated as *spikenard* in John 12: 3, 'Then took

Mary a pound of ointment of spikenard, very costly, and anointed the feet of Jesus, and wiped his feet with her hair.' *pistic* is derived from a Greek word possibly meaning 'genuine' or 'pure' (*OED*).

ll. 21-4. *Why is this . . . waste?* See the associated incident in Matthew 26: 6-8, 'Now when Jesus was in Bethany, in the house of Simon the leper, There came unto him a woman having an alabaster box of very precious ointment, and poured it on his head, as he sat at meat. But when his disciples saw it, they had indignation, saying, To what purpose is this waste?'

l. 27. *Dear soul! thou knew'st.* See Herbert, *Mary Magdalene*, l. 13: 'Dear soul, she knew.'

ll. 27-8. *on earth / At their Lord's footstool.* Matthew 5: 35, 'the earth; for it is his footstool.'

l. 49. See Herbert, *The Thanksgiving*, l. 47 and note.

l. 50. *Who loved much and much more could move.* Luke 7: 47, 'Wherefore I say unto thee, Her sins, which are many, are forgiven; for she loved much: but to whom little is forgiven, the same loveth little.'

382 l. 51. *Her Art! whose memory must last.* Matthew 26: 13, 'Verily, I say unto you, Wheresoever this gospel shall be preached in the whole world, there shall also this, that this woman hath done, be told for a memorial of her.'

l. 69. *Go leper.* Vaughan takes Simon the Pharisee, in Luke's account, to be Simon the leper of Matthew 26: 6 and Mark 14: 3.

ll. 69-70. *till thy flesh / Comes like a child's.* See Naaman's cure from leprosy in II Kings 5: 14, 'then went he down, and dipped himself seven times in Jordan, according to the saying of the man of God: and his flesh came again like unto the flesh of a little child, and he was clean.'

l. 72. *Who saint themselves, they are no saints.* Since the epistles of St Paul and the book of Revelation constantly refer to the 'chosen' body of Christians as 'saints' (meaning 'holy ones'), some of the more radical religious groups of Vaughan's day had taken to referring to themselves as 'the saints'. This pious practice (often expressing a hope, not a conviction) was a cause of bitter protest and satire among Christians of more traditional leanings, such as Vaughan. It is especially bold of Vaughan to write a poem to this particular saint, the object of extravagant devotion among those of (or tending toward) Roman Catholic affiliation: see Richard Crashaw's *The Weeper* or Robert Southwell's prose meditation, *Mary Magdalen's Funeral Tears.*

The Rainbow. l. 3. *Shem's.* Genesis 9: 18, 'And the sons of Noah, that went forth of the ark, were Shem, and Ham, and Japheth.'

l. 5. *When . . . Lot.* Genesis 11: 27, 'Now these are the generations of Terah: Terah begat Abram, Nahor, and Haran, and Haran begat Lot.'

l. 11. *Rain gently spends his honey-drops.* See the similar wording in Herbert's *Providence*, ll. 117–18.

383   l. 14. *the object of his eye.* Vaughan's note at this point in *1655* refers to Genesis 9: 16, 'And the bow shall be in the cloud; and I will look upon it, that I may remember the everlasting covenant between God and every living creature, of all flesh that is upon the earth.'

l. 21. *the first sin was in blood.* Cain's shedding of his 'brother's blood': Genesis 4: 8–11.

l. 22. *drunkenness.* Of Noah: Genesis 9: 21.

ll. 27–8. *though both ... did weep.* The Flood: Genesis 7: 11–12.

ll. 31–2. *bad daughters ... their sire.* Lot's daughters: Genesis 19: 30–8. For the 'smoke' of Sodom, see Genesis 19: 24–8.

l. 37. *luctual:* mourning, sorrowful.

l. 42. *till rain turns fire.* II Thessalonians 1: 7–8, 'when the Lord Jesus shall be revealed from heaven with his mighty angels, In flaming fire taking vengeance on them that know not God, and that obey not the gospel of our Lord Jesus Christ.'

The Seed Growing Secretly. Mark 4: 26–7, 'So is the kingdom of God, as if a man should cast seed into the ground; And should sleep, and rise night and day, and the seed should spring and grow up, he knoweth not how.'

384   ll. 13–14. *O spread thy sacred wings ... drop.* Malachi 4: 2, 'But unto you that fear my name shall the Sun of righteousness arise with healing in his wings.'

l. 16. *O fill his bottle! Thy child weeps.* Another allusion to Ishmael: Genesis 21: 14–19.

l. 19. *blow:* bloom.

ll. 25–6. *greenness ... winter-nights.* Compare the second stanza of Herbert's *The Flower.*

l. 27. *Vex not:* be not disturbed.

l. 30. *in one crown.* Revelation 2: 10, 'be thou faithful unto death, and I will give thee a crown of life.'

l. 33. *bait:* food, along with modern sense.

385   ll. 45–6. *catch / At:* snatch at, attempt to lay hold of.

ll. 47–8. *bear fruit ... Reapers.* Matthew 13: 39, 'the harvest is the end of the world; and the reapers are the angels.' Mark 4: 29, 'But when the fruit is brought forth, immediately he putteth in the sickle, because the harvest is come.'

'As time one day by me did pass'. This and the next poem are probably written in memory of Vaughan's first wife.

l. 4. *curious:* carefully prepared.

l. 9. *kind*: sympathetic, well-disposed; also, related.

l. 13. *calendar*: a list or register of documents or events (along with modern meaning).

l. 16. *The Holy way*. Vaughan's typographical emphasis suggests the title of a book—a guide to holy life.

386 l. 19. *night-piece*: 'a painting or picture representing a night scene' (OED). *quails*: spoils, overpowers.

l. 25. *mark*: goal, target.

l. 29. *recruits*: provisions for renewal of strength.

ll. 35–6. *For whose . . . green branches . . . are bleached*. Revelation 7: 9, 'lo, a great multitude . . . stood before the throne and before the Lamb, clothed with white robes, and palms in their hands.'

l. 36. *in the Lamb's blood*. Revelation 7: 13–14, 'What are these which are arrayed in white robes? . . . These are they which came out of great tribulation, and have washed their robes, and made them white in the blood of the Lamb.'

387 'Fair and young light!' l. 10. *the surviving turtle*. The turtle-dove: a symbol of conjugal affection and constancy.

l. 37. *supplanters*: those who dispossess or cause the downfall of others.

l. 46. *For he . . . sin*. See Romans 6: 7.

388 l. 50. *spicy mountains*. Song of Solomon 8: 14, 'upon the mountains of spices'.

The Stone. Joshua 24: 27, 'And Joshua said unto all the people, Behold, this stone shall be a witness unto us; for it hath heard all the words of the Lord, which he spake unto us; it shall be therefore a witness unto you, lest ye deny your God.'

l. 24. *As loud as blood*. Genesis 4: 9–10, 'And the Lord said unto Cain, where is Abel thy brother? And he said, I know not: Am I my brother's keeper? And he said, What hast thou done? the voice of thy brother's blood crieth unto me from the ground.'

l. 28. *he that judgeth*. Vaughan's note at this point in *1655* cites John 5: 30, 45, 'I can of mine own self do nothing: as I hear, I judge: and my judgment is just; because I seek not mine own will, but the will of the Father which hath sent me. . . . Do not think that I will accuse you to the Father: there is one that accuseth you, even Moses, in whom ye trust.'

389 ll. 56–7. *his word / And not himself*. Vaughan's note at this point in *1655* cites John 12: 47–8, 'And if any man hear my words, and believe not, I judge him not: for I came not to judge the world, but to save the world. He that rejecteth me, and receiveth not my words, hath one that judgeth him: the word that I have spoken, the same shall judge him in the last day.'

The Dwelling-place. John 1: 38–9, 'Then Jesus turned, and saw them following, and saith unto them, What seek ye? They said unto him, Rabbi (which is to say, being interpreted, Master), where dwellest thou? He saith unto them, Come and see. They came and saw where he dwelt, and abode with him that day: for it was about the tenth hour.'

l. 4. *though not in story*: not told in any historical account.

390   l. 16. *My God, I mean.* See the last line of Herbert's *Misery*: 'My God, I mean myself.'

The Men of War. Luke 23: 11, 'And Herod with his men of war set him at nought, and mocked him, and arrayed him in a gorgeous robe, and sent him again to Pilate.'

l. 2. *saith holy John.* Vaughan's note at this point in *1655* cites Revelation 13: 10 (see also verse 9): 'If any man have an ear, let him hear. He that leadeth into captivity shall go into captivity: he that killeth with the sword must be killed with the sword. Here is the patience and the faith of the saints.'

l. 12. *Enact for saints.* See note on *St. Mary Magdalen*, l. 72.

l. 18. *conquerors.* Romans 8: 37, 'Nay, in all these things we are more than conquerors through him that loved us.'

ll. 21–2. *Armies thou hast . . . clothed in white.* Revelation 19: 14, 'And the armies which were in heaven followed him upon white horses, clothed in fine linen, white and clean.'

391   ll. 25–6. *The sword . . . in thy mouth.* Revelation 19: 15, 'And out of his mouth goeth a sharp sword that with it he should smite the nations.' Hebrews 4: 12, 'For the word of God is quick, and powerful, and sharper than any two-edged sword.'

ll. 27–8. *And all . . . martyrdom.* Revelation 12: 11, 'And they overcame him by the blood of the Lamb, and by the word of their testimony: and they loved not their lives unto the death.' See ll. 51–2.

ll. 29–31. *Soldiers . . . bowed the knee.* See Matthew 27: 29–30.

l. 42. *innoxious*: harmless, blameless.

l. 47. *thy throne is set.* Revelation 4: 2, 'behold, a throne was set in heaven, and one sat on the throne.'

392   *The Ass.* l. 6. *most kind.* (1) most akin, most like; (2) most favourable.

ll. 9–10. *no law . . . perfect liberty.* James 1: 25, 'But whoso looketh into the perfect law of liberty, and continueth therein, he being not a forgetful hearer, but a doer of the work, this man shall be blessed in his deed.'

l. 39–40. *though . . . not expedient.* I Corinthians 10: 23, 'All things are lawful for me, but all things are not expedient.'

393   l. 64. *And bones rejoice, which once were broken!* Psalm 51: 8, 'Make me

to hear joy and gladness; that the bones which thou hast broken may rejoice.'

The Hidden Treasure. Matthew 13: 44, 'Again, the kingdom of heaven is like unto treasure hid in a field; the which when a man hath found, he hideth, and for joy thereof goeth and selleth all that he hath, and buyeth that field.'

ll. 1–2. *the King . . . thing.* Vaughan's note at this point in *1655* cites Ecclesiastes 2: 12, 'And I turned myself to behold wisdom, and madness, and folly: for what can the man do that cometh after the king? even that which hath been already done.'

l. 4. *fire-drakes*: meteors, or will-o'-the-wisps.

l. 12. *Paths . . . the vulture's eyes.* Job 28: 7, 'There is a path which no fowl knoweth, and which the vulture's eye hath not seen.'

394   *Child-hood.* The hyphenated form of the title seems to stress the spiritual state which the speaker is striving to 'reach': to be one of the 'children of God,' as in Romans 8: 16 or the passage cited below, note to ll. 35–7.

l. 7. *make my path even.* Matthew 3: 3, 'Prepare ye the way of the Lord, make his paths straight.'

ll. 14–16. *But flowers . . . medicinal then.* See Herbert, *Life*, ll. 13–15.

395   l. 27. *practice*: (1) 'usual, customary, or constant action'; (2) 'exercise of a profession or occupation'; (3) trickery, underhanded plotting (see *OED*).

ll. 35–7. *which he . . . God's face see . . . angels guard.* Matthew 18: 2–3, 10, 'And Jesus called a little child unto him, and set him in the midst of them, And said, Verily I say unto you, Except ye be converted and become as little children, ye shall not enter into the kingdom of heaven. . . . Take heed that ye despise not one of these little ones; for I say unto you, that in heaven their angels do always behold the face of my Father which is in heaven.'

l. 44. *the narrow way.* See Matthew 7: 14.

The Night. John 3: 2 (*1655* reads 'John 2.3'), '[Nicodemus] came to Jesus by night, and said unto him, Rabbi, we know that thou art a teacher come from God: for no man can do these miracles that thou doest, except God be with him.'

ll. 1–2. *Virgin-shrine, / That sacred veil.* The body of Christ, 'the veil, that is to say, his flesh' (Hebrews 10: 20); the body derived from the Virgin Mary.

396   ll. 9–10. *healing wings . . . rise.* Malachi 4: 2, 'But unto you that fear my name shall the Sun of righteousness arise with healing in his wings.'

ll. 19–20. *No mercy-seat . . . nor carved stone.* Exodus 25: 17–22, 'And thou shalt make a mercy seat of pure gold . . . And thou shalt make two cherubims of gold ... And the cherubims shall stretch forth their wings on high, covering the mercy seat with their wings ... And there I will meet with thee, and I will commune with thee from above the mercy seat, from between the two cherubims which are upon the ark of the testimony.'

l. 29. *Christ's progress.* Vaughan's note at this point in *1655* cites Mark 1: 35, 'And in the morning, rising up a great while before day, he went out, and departed into a solitary place, and there prayed'; and Luke 21: 37, 'And in the day time he was teaching in the temple; and at night he went out, and abode in the mount that is called the mount of Olives.'

ll. 32–3. *When my Lord's head ... drops of night.* Song of Solomon 5:2, 'I sleep, but my heart waketh: it is the voice of my beloved that knocketh, saying, Open to me, my sister, my love, my dove, my undefiled: for my head is filled with dew, and my locks with the drops of the night.'

l. 34. *still, soft call.* Like the 'still small voice' heard by Elijah: I Kings 19: 12.

l. 35. *His knocking time.* See note on ll. 32–3; also Revelation 3: 20, 'Behold, I stand at the door, and knock.'

l. 36. *kinred*: old form of *kindred*.

397   l. 50. *A deep, but dazzling darkness.* A conception set forth by the writer of the fifth or sixth century (AD) known as Dionysius the Areopagite, or the 'pseudo-Dionysius'. His writings on the mystical approach to God had a great influence on medieval mystics and on the Spanish mystics of the sixteenth century.

Abel's Blood. l. 2. *first against a murth'rer cry.* Genesis 4: 10, 'the voice of thy brother's blood crieth unto me from the ground.'

l. 16. *deep still calleth upon deep.* See Psalm 42: 7.

l. 18. *many waters.* See Revelation 19: 6.

l. 22. *How long?* Revelation 6: 9–10, 'I saw under the altar the souls of them that were slain for the word of God, and for the testimony which they held: and they cried with a loud voice, saying, How long, O Lord, holy and true, dost thou not judge and avenge our blood on them that dwell on the earth?'

398   l. 33. *Aye. I* in *1655.*

ll. 40–1. *speak better ... Abel's doth.* Hebrews 12: 24, 'and to Jesus the mediator of the new covenant, and to the blood of sprinkling, that speaketh better things than that of Abel.'

l. 44. *Who prayed ... kill.* Luke 23: 34, 'Father, forgive them; for they know not what they do.'

Righteousness. The theme and manner resemble Psalm 15, 'Lord, who shall abide in thy tabernacle? who shall dwell in thy holy hill? He that walketh uprightly, and worketh righteousness, and speaketh the truth in his heart.' Compare also Herbert's *Constancy*.

l. 7. *turtles*: turtle-doves. *careless*: carefree.

l. 10. *meddled*: mixed with. See Ecclesiasticus 13: 1, 'He that toucheth pitch shall be defiled therewith.'

399   l. 19. *pretence*: expressed purpose.

l. 30. *pains*. An emendation: *1655* reads *prayers*.

l. 33. *his hope and Rock*. I Corinthians 10: 4, 'and that Rock was Christ.'

l. 48. *peculiar treasure*. Psalm 135: 4, 'For the Lord hath chosen Jacob unto himself, and Israel for his peculiar treasure.' Exodus 19: 5, 'If ye will obey my voice indeed, and keep my covenant, then ye shall be a peculiar treasure unto me above all people.'

401   *Tears*. l. 11. *thy poor Ass*. See *The Ass*, l. 21, 'me thy Ass'.

l. 14. *the lowest pitch*. The pitch of a falcon is the height of its flight before attacking its prey.

l. 15. *loves much*. See note on *St. Mary Magdalen*, l. 50.

Jacob's Pillow and Pillar. See Genesis 28: 11–22.

l. 1. *The Temple in thy Pillar reared*. Genesis 28: 18, 22, 'And Jacob rose up early in the morning, and took the stone that he had put for his pillows, and set it up for a pillar, and poured oil upon the top of it. . . . And [he said] this stone, which I have set for a pillar, shall be God's house.'

l. 3. *without a frown*. See Herbert, *To All Angels and Saints*, l. 2: 'the smooth face of God, without a frown'.

ll. 7–10. *This made him . . . lofty rocks*. Exodus 19: 16, 18, 'there were thunders and lightnings, and a thick cloud upon the mount . . . And mount Sinai was altogether on a smoke, because the Lord descended upon it in fire.' Also I Kings 19: 11–12, 'the Lord passed by, and a great and strong wind rent the mountains, and brake in pieces the rocks before the Lord; but the Lord was not in the wind: and after the wind an earthquake; but the Lord was not in the earthquake: And after the earthquake a fire; but the Lord was not in the fire: and after the fire a still small voice.'

ll. 22–3. An allusion to the 'darkness' that prevailed for the three hours preceding Christ's death: Matthew 27: 45–52.

402   ll. 23–6. *he foretold . . . nor at / Jerusalem*. John 4: 21, 23–4, 'the hour cometh, when ye shall neither in this mountain, nor yet at Jerusalem, worship the Father. . . . But the hour cometh, and now is, when the true worshippers shall worship the Father in spirit and in truth: for the Father seeketh such to worship him. God is a Spirit: and they that worship him must worship him in spirit and in truth.'

l. 26. *with blood of beasts and fat.* See Ezekiel 44: 15.

l. 29. *proud waters.* See Psalm 124: 5.

ll. 31–2. *This little Goshen . . . hath light.* Goshen was the land where the Israelites lived while they were in Egypt. See Exodus 10: 22–3, 'And Moses stretched forth his hand toward heaven; and there was a thick darkness in all the land of Egypt three days . . . but all the children of Israel had light in their dwellings.'

l. 33. *Bethel shall have tithes (saith Israel's stone).* Genesis 28: 19–22, 'And he [Jacob] called the name of that place Beth-el ['house of God'] . . . And Jacob vowed a vow, saying . . . this stone, which I have set for a pillar, shall be God's house: and of all that thou shalt give me I will surely give the tenth unto thee.'

l. 40. *turns our captivity.* See Psalm 126: 1, 4.

ll. 43–4. *thou a brother . . . Didst fly.* Esau. Vaughan's note at this point in *1655* cites Obadiah 1: 11, but verse 10 makes the allusion clearer: 'For thy violence against thy brother Jacob shame shall cover thee, and thou shalt be cut off for ever.' Vaughan also cites here Amos 1: 11, 'Thus saith the Lord; For three transgressions of Edom, and for four, I will not turn away the punishment thereof; because he did pursue his brother with the sword, and did cast off all pity, and his anger did tear perpetually, and he kept his wrath for ever.'

l. 53. *type*: something in the Old Testament which prefigures an event, object, person, or doctrine in the New Testament.

403   *The Agreement.* l. 10. *Like morning-stars did sing.* Job 38: 7, 'When the morning stars sang together.'

l. 15. *ascendents.* Those who ascend; with a play on the astrological meaning of *ascendent*: 'the point of the ecliptic, or degree of the Zodiac, which at any moment . . . is just rising above the eastern horizon' (*OED*).

l. 36. *healing wings.* See Malachi 4: 2.

404   ll. 51–2. *still infinite / Thy Covenant by Christ extends.* See Hebrews 13: 20, 'the blood of the everlasting covenant', and Psalm 105: 8, 'He hath remembered his covenant for ever, the word which he commanded to a thousand generations.'

l. 58. *cathartics*: purgative medicines.

l. 68. *For I . . . to thee.* Vaughan's note at this point in *1655* cites John 6: 44, 65, 'No man can come to me, except the Father which hath sent me draw him: and I will raise him up at the last day. . . . Therefore said I unto you, that no man can come unto me, except it were given unto him of my Father.'

405   *The Day of Judgement.* l. 13. *The fields are long since white.* John 4: 35, 'Lift up your eyes, and look on the fields; for they are white already to harvest.'

ll. 29–30. *thy old enemy . . . more raging grows.* Revelation 12: 12, 'Woe to the inhabiters of the earth and of the sea! for the devil is come down unto you, having great wrath, because he knoweth that he hath but a short time.'

406   l. 44. *Thy arm doth sleep.* Isaiah 51: 9, 'Awake, awake . . . O arm of the Lord.'

l. 46. *Make all things new.* Revelation 21: 5, 'And he that sat upon the throne said, Behold, I make all things new.'

Psalm 65. Another free paraphrase and expansion. Compare especially the third section with verses 9–13 of the KJ version.

407   l. 46. *purling*: rippling, undulating. *corn*: grain.

The Throne. Revelation 20: 11, 'And I saw a great white throne, and him that sat on it, from whose face the earth and the heaven fled away; and there was found no place for them.'

408   *Death.* l. 3. *six thousand years.* According to the widely-accepted chronology of Bishop Ussher.

ll. 12–13. *But there was One . . . to and fro.* I Peter 3: 18–20, 'For Christ also hath once suffered for sins, the just for the unjust, that he might bring us to God, being put to death in the flesh, but quickened by the Spirit: by which also he went and preached unto the spirits in prison; which sometime were disobedient.'

l. 15. *Discovered*: revealed.

l. 19. *fray*: disperse, frighten away.

l. 22. *virtues*: curative powers.

409   *The Feast.* ll. 1–2. *O come away, / Make no delay.* See the opening lines of Herbert's *Doomsday.*

l. 13. *true bread.* John 6: 32–3, 'Verily, verily, I say unto you, Moses gave you not that bread from heaven; but my Father giveth you the true bread from heaven. For the bread of God is he which cometh down from heaven, and giveth life unto the world.'

l. 19. *Aye. 1655* reads *I.*

410   l. 33. *The well, where living waters spring.* John 4: 14, 'but whosoever drinketh of the water that I shall give him shall never thirst; but the water that I shall give him shall be in him a well of water springing up into everlasting life.'

l. 50. *turtle's voice.* See Song of Solomon 2: 12.

411   *The Obsequies.* l. 19. *some wore white.* John 20: 12, 'two angels in white sitting, the one at the head, and the other at the feet, where the body of Jesus had lain.'

412   ll. 25–6. *Kerchiefs sometimes shed / To make me brave.* 'Those garments that were on one occasion shed to make me handsome.' Vaughan is using *kerchief* in the sense of 'a covering for the breast, neck, or

shoulders' (*OED*). *sometimes*: = *sometime*: 'at a certain time, on a particular occasion, in the past' (*OED*). The reference is to the grave-clothes left behind by Christ in his tomb: see Herbert, *The Dawning*, ll. 25–8 and note.

413   *The Waterfall*. l. 26. *Fountains of life, where the Lamb goes*. Revelation 7: 17, 'For the Lamb . . . shall feed them, and shall lead them unto living fountains of waters.'

ll. 30–2. *Unless that Spirit . . . quick'ning love*. See Genesis 1: 2.

l. 38. *My glorious liberty*. Romans 8: 21, 'the glorious liberty of the children of God'.

l. 40. *creeks*: inlets.

Quickness. The word means 'life, vitality'.

l. 1. *foil*. The word 'deception' (l. 3) indicates the meaning as a false or inferior gem, enhanced by foil to appear richer (see *OED*).

l. 5. *moon-like*: shifting, inconstant. *toil*: (1) labour, effort; (2) snare, trap.

l. 6. *self-posing*: self-puzzling.

l. 16. *without Eternity*. Even without the promise of immortality.

414   l. 20. *A quickness, which my God hath kissed*. The line (and indeed the whole poem) may evoke the two places where Herbert used the word *quickness*: *The Star*, l. 14: 'Touch it [my heart] with thy celestial quickness'; and *Dullness*, ll. 3–4, 'O give me quickness, that I may with mirth / Praise thee brim-full!'

The Wreath. Compare the similar repetitive technique of Herbert's *A Wreath*.

The Queer. Title: Vaughan is using an old, apparently colloquial form of *quaerè* (see *OED*), a term that indicates the formal proposing of a question. The index of *1655* gives the title as *The Quere*.

415   l. 12. *A wing with eyes*. Revelation 4: 8, 'And the four beasts had each of them six wings about him; and they were full of eyes within.'

The Book. l. 12. *since a cover made*. Refers to the thin boards (covered with leather) used in binding books in Vaughan's day.

416   *To the Holy Bible*. l. 2. *seized of*: in possession of.

l. 15. *Cried dross for gold*. Declared dross to be gold.

417   l. 26. *that pearl*. Matthew 13: 46, the 'pearl of great price'.

S. Luke chap. 2. ver. 14. Herbert closes *The Church* with this verse.

L'Envoy. Herbert closes *The Temple* with a shorter poem by this title, also in tetrameter couplets.

l. 4. *dressed in shining white*. Revelation 7: 9, 'lo, a great multitude, which no man could number . . . stood before the throne, and before the Lamb, clothed with white robes.'

l. 8. *like old clothes fold up these skies*. Hebrews 1: 10–12, 'the heavens are the works of thine hands: They shall perish; but thou remainest; and they all shall wax old as doth a garment; And as a vesture shalt thou fold them up.'

418   ll. 21–2. *A state for which ... and call*. See Romans 8: 19, 22.

l. 25. *Thy number*. The number of righteous souls saved: the 'train' (followers, retinue) of l. 27.

l. 30. *Thy seamless coat*. See John 19: 23.

l. 40. *solution*: dissolution.

419   l. 62. *turned our sad captivity*. See Psalm 126: 4.

Final motto. 'God lives, and the Lord Jesus Christ, and the Holy Spirit.' St Clement, quoted in *Liber de Spiritu Sancto* (chapter 29), by St Basil the Great.

POEMS, 1646

420   *To my Ingenuous Friend, R. W.* The friend has not been identified; perhaps the same person for whom Vaughan's *Elegy on the Death of Mr. R. W.* was written. *Ingenuous*: noble, generous, high-minded (frequently misused for *ingenious* in the seventeenth century).

l. 2. *score*: record of goods obtained by credit; tally of ale consumed.

l. 6. *drawers*: tapsters, drawers of liquor.

l. 8. *Moon, or Star*. Names of taverns, or of rooms in a tavern.

l. 11. *long bills*: lists of debts; also, halberds carried by law-officers.

l. 13. *Maze*. Rudrum's suggestion seems good: that the word 'refers to a network of little streets and alleys'. The capitalization in the text may suggest that it was the name for a section in London.

l. 15. *sergeants*: law-officers.

l. 22. *affect*: feel affection.

l. 29. *bays*: the laurel, both as a tree and as a wreath crowning the poet.

l. 30. *BEN*. Ben Jonson (1572–1637).

421   ll. 33–5. *Randolph ... Lovers ... Amyntas ... Nightingale*. Thomas Randolph (1605–35), author of *The Jealous Lovers*, a comedy, *Amyntas*, a pastoral drama, and a poem *On the Death of a Nightingale*.

l. 40. *virtue*: power (the water of Lethe has the power to cause forgetfulness).

l. 54. *They'll have of us*. Our souls (l. 51) will have of our mortal existence.

l. 57. *they that did of these discuss*. See l. 41: 'if what poets sing be true'.

422   *Les Amours.* l. 17. *influx*: influence (stellar). *quick'ning*: life-giving.

        l. 19. *inform*: animate.

423   *To Amoret.   The Sigh.* l. 14. *tried*: tested, afflicted.

        To His Friend, Being in Love. l. 7. *Witty to tyranny.* 'Clever to the
        point of tyranny' (?) 'Well-versed in the ways of tyranny' (?).

424   *To Amoret, Walking in a Starry Evening.* l. 1. *that glorious eye.* The eye
        of Amoret: subject of 'Had . . . Receivèd'.

        l. 7. *suspect*: conjecture, wonder.

        l. 9. *fiery stories.* The myths involved in the names of the stars; or the
        concentric rings of the Ptolemaic universe.

425   l. 18. *sympathy*: attraction, affinity (an astrological allusion).

        l. 19. *conspiring*: 'breathing together', acting in harmony.

        l. 23. *start*: disturb, displace. *decline*: deflect, cause to deviate.

        To Amoret Gone from Him. l. 1. *Fancy*: (1) love; (2) imagination,
        fantasy.

        l. 20. *influence.* From the stars.

        ll. 21–2. *Though fate . . . that element their love.* Compare Donne, *A
        Valediction: Forbidding Mourning*, ll. 13–16: 'Dull sublunary lovers'
        love / (Whose soul is sense) cannot admit / Absence, because it
        doth remove / Those things which elemented it.'

        l. 22. *element*: to compound, compose.

427   *An Elegy.* l. 6. *metempsychosis.* The transmigration of love from his
        dying 'sickly flames' to the living love of their 'warmer sighs'.

        l. 9. *Flora.* Goddess of flowers.

        l. 12. *quicker*: more keenly felt.

        l. 22. *Zephyrus.* The West Wind.

        l. 24. *inspirers*: those who breathe (i.e. the winds).

        l. 25. *Oh! jam satis.* 'Oh, now enough.' Martin cites Martial, *Epigrams*
        4. 91. 1, and Horace, *Satires* 2. 5. 96.

        A Rhapsody. Several meanings are involved in this title: (1) 'an ef-
        fusion (e.g. a speech, letter, poem) marked by extravagance of idea
        and expression, but without connected thought or sound argument'
        (*OED*); (2) 'a written composition having no fixed form or plan'
        (*OED*); (3) a mock-heroic glance at the basic meaning: an epic or
        part of an epic chosen for recitation by a bard. Heading: *Occasionally
        written upon a meeting.* That is, written on the occasion of a meeting.

        l. 5. *sack.* A white wine.

428   l. 17. *drawer's.* With a play on *drawer* as artist and tapster.

        l. 19. *clown*: peasant, rustic (shepherd).

        l. 29. *Endymion.* Loved by the moon (Diana).

ll. 33–4. *pencil ... churchwardens, and mortality.* The *pencil* is the painter's brush. Perhaps the lines express the speaker's wish to see no more paintings by this 'base painter' except those that are images of his death.

l. 36. *catchpoles*: officers who make arrests for debt.

l. 44. *From the Tower-wharf ... Lud.* The Tower wharf was at the south-east part of the city, and the statues of Lud and Cymbeline, legendary kings, were placed on the west wall of London, at Ludgate. The reference then is to all of London, from east to west.

ll. 47–8. *dish:* bowl of wine. *him ... senator.* Caligula.

429   ll. 52–3. *he ... Rubicon.* Julius Caesar.

ll. 55–6. *the dull grey beards ... Into Brundusium.* When Caesar took Rome, Pompey and some of the senators fled to Brundisium.

l. 57. *Sylla.* Lucius Cornelius Sulla (138–78 BC), dictator of Rome.

l. 67. *influx*: astrological influence.

430   *To Amoret, of the Difference 'Twixt Him and Other Lovers.* ll. 15–28. See Donne's *Valediction: Forbidding Mourning*, especially ll. 13–20: 'Dull sublunary lovers' love / (Whose soul is sense) cannot admit / Absence, because it doth remove / Those things which elemented it. / But we by a love, so much refined, / That our selves know not what it is, / Inter-assurèd of the mind, / Care less, eyes, lips, and hands to miss.'

ll. 29–30. *loadstones ... enamoured steel.* Magnetic oxide of iron attracts steel as a magnet.

l. 32. *affect*: (1) seek to obtain, aspire to; (2) love.

To Amoret Weeping. l. 1. *Leave*: leave off, stop.

431   l. 6. *clue*: ball of yarn or thread.

l. 9. *Fate cuts us all in marble.* 'Our fate is sealed.' *the Book.* Of life, as fate has decreed: see *flinty volume*, l. 12.

l. 13. *their triumphs.* That is, the triumphs of 'Fate' and 'the Book'.

l. 31. *patent it.* Have *patents* (exclusive rights) to sell soap and coal.

l. 33. *Geld*: tax—charge with 'geld'; or perhaps, weaken, dilute.

432   l. 57. *jointly vie*: match in competition.

Upon the Priory Grove. Part of the estate of Brecon Priory.

. l. 4. *My love's fair steps I first betrayed. betrayed* in the sense of 'revealed'. The reference appears to be to the writing of his love-poems to Amoret, which revealed the 'steps' or progress of his love, as well as her literal 'walking in a starry evening'.

l. 9. *laid*: quieted.

l. 10. *Philomel.* The nightingale.

APPENDIX I

Verses to the Queen of Bohemia by 'G.H.'

Two scholars have lately set forth impressive arguments indicating that George Herbert is indeed the 'G.H.' who wrote the following verses (see Kenneth Alan Hovey, *Renaissance Quarterly*, xxx (1977), 43–50; and the detailed account of the manuscripts, along with a new text, by Ted-Larry Pebworth, *English Literary Renaissance*, ix (1979), 108–20). The most impressive evidence for Herbert's authorship lies in the attribution to 'G.H.' in a Cambridge manuscript compiled during the years of Herbert's residence there, or shortly afterwards, along with the resemblance to the style of Herbert's *Church Militant*, with its Donneian management of the run-on pentameter couplet, and the use of an 'envoi' in tetrameter couplets.

The verses may be dated to 1621–2, when Elizabeth, Queen of Bohemia, was living in Holland, after her husband had suffered total defeat at the hands of the Austrian and Spanish forces, and had lost his rule over both Bohemia and the Rhineland Palatinate. For details of interpretation see the above articles. The following text is based upon Pebworth's transcription from Cambridge MS Add. 4138.

To the Lady Elizabeth Queen of Bohemia.

Bright soul, of whom if any country known
Had worthy been, thou had'st not lost thine own,
No earth can be thy jointure, for the sun
And stars alone unto thy pitch do run
And pace of thy sweet virtues; only they
Are thy dominions. Those that rule in clay
Stick fast therein; but thy transcendent soul
Doth for two clods of earth ten spheres control.
And though stars shot from Heaven lose their light,
Yet thy brave beams, excluded from their right,
Maintain their lustre still, and shining clear,
Turn wat'rish Holland to a crystal sphere.
Methinks in that Dutch optic I do see
Thy curious virtues much more visibly.
There is thy best throne, for afflictions are
A foil to set off worth, and make it rare.
Through that black tiffany, thy virtues shine
Fairer and rich[er], now we know what's thine
And what is fortune's. Thou hast singled out
Sorrows and griefs, to fight with them a bout

At their own weapons, without pomp or state
To second thee against their cunning hate.

O, what a poor thing 'tis to be a queen
When sceptres, state, attendants are the screen
Betwixt us and the people; whenas glory
Lies round about us, to help out the story;
When all things pull and hale, that they may bring
A slow behaviour to the style of king;
When sense is made by comments! But that face,
Whose native beauty needs not dress or lace
To set it forth, and being stripped of all,
Is self sufficient to be the self thrall
Of thousand hearts; that face doth figure thee
And show thy undivided majesty,
Which misery cannot untwist, but rather
Adds to the union, as lights, to gather
Splendours from darkness. So close sits the crown
About thy temples that the furious frown
Of opposition cannot place thee where
Thou should'st not be a queen, and conquer there.
Yet hast thou more dominions: God doth give
Children for kingdoms to thee. They shall live
To conquer new ones, and shall share the frame
Of th' universe, like as the winds, and name
The world anew. The sun shall never rise
But it shall spy some of thy victories.
Their hands shall clip the eagle's win[g]s and chase
Those ravening harpies, which peck at their face,
At once to Hell, without a baiting-while
At Purgatory, their Enchanted Isle
And Paris Garden. Then let their perfume
And Spanish saints, wisely laid up, presume
To deal with brimstone, that untimed stench
Whose fire, like their malice, nought can quench.

But joys are stored for thee, thou shalt return
Laden with comfort thence, where now to mourn
Is thy chief government, to manage woe,
To curb some rebel tears, which fain would flow,
Making a head and spring against thy reason.
This is thy empire yet, till better season
Call thee from out of that surrounded land,
That habitable sea and brinish strand,

Thy tears not needing. For that hand divine,
Which mingles water with thy Rhenish wine,
Will pour full joys to thee, but dregs to those
(And meet their taste) who are thy bitter foes.

[Envoi]

To the Same. Another.

Shine on, majestic soul, abide
Like David's tree planted beside
The Flemish rivers. In the end,
Thy fruit shall with their drops contend.
Our God will surely dry those tears
Which now that moist land to thee bears.
Then shall thy glory, fresh as flowers
In water kept, maugre the powers
Of Devil, Jesuit, and Spain,
From Holland sail into the main.
Thence, wheeling on, it compass shall
This, our great sublunary ball;
And with that ring, thy fame shall wed
Eternity into one bed.

APPENDIX II

A Note on The Collar

Away, Take Heed,
I will abroad,
Call in thy death's head there: tie up thy fears.

The above reading (p. 139, ll. 27–9) accepts the argument of Mario Di Cesare that the text of *B* here clarifies the meaning and is superior to the reading of *1633*, followed by Hutchinson and nearly all modern editions: 'Away; take heed: / I will abroad. / Call in thy death's head there: tie up thy fears.' As Di Cesare explains, the speaker is saying, 'Away with such advice as "Take Heed"'—the motto or 'legend associated with the skull as object of contemplation', and thus 'properly punctuated with a pair of commas, and linked by the firm rhythm and rapid movement' to the 'death's head' of line 29. (See 'The Bodleian Manuscript and the Text of Herbert's Poems,' *George Herbert Journal*, vi (1983), 15–35, esp. p. 31.) Beyond this, the words 'take heed' summon up dozens of passages of biblical advice, both in the Old Testament and the New, such as the words of Jesus: 'Take heed therefore that the light which is in thee be not darkness'; or 'Take heed, and beware of covetousness: for a man's life consisteth not in the abundance of the things which he possesseth' (Luke 11: 35; 12: 15). The speaker, then, is casting away all caution, denying the value of all biblical wisdom.

FURTHER READING

GEORGE HERBERT

Editions

The Works of George Herbert, ed. with introduction and commentary by F. E. Hutchinson (Oxford: Clarendon Press, 1941).

The English Poems of George Herbert, ed. with introduction, bibliography, and notes by C. A. Patrides (London: Dent, 1974).

The Williams Manuscript of George Herbert's Poems. A Facsimile Reproduction, with introduction by Amy B. Charles (Delmar, NY: Scholars' Facsimiles & Reprints, 1977). A facsimile of Jones MS B 62 in Dr Williams's Library, London.

The Bodleian Manuscript of George Herbert's Poems. A Facsimile of Tanner 307, with introduction by Amy B. Charles and Mario A. Di Cesare (Delmar, NY: Scholars' Facsimiles & Reprints, 1984).

Major Poets of the Earlier Seventeenth Century, ed. with introductions and notes by Barbara K. Lewalski and Andrew J. Sabol (New York: Odyssey Press, 1973). Contains *The Temple*, with text based upon the Bodleian MS, and *Silex Scintillans*.

The Latin Poetry of George Herbert. A Bilingual Edition, translated by Mark McCloskey and Paul R. Murphy (Ohio State University Press, 1965).

Guides to Study

George Herbert: An Annotated Bibliography of Modern Criticism, 1905–1974, compiled by John R. Roberts (University of Missouri Press, 1978).

Essential Articles for the Study of George Herbert's Poetry, ed. John R. Roberts (Hamden, Conn.: Archon Books, 1979). Includes 34 essays and a selective bibliography.

George Herbert: The Critical Heritage, ed. C. A. Patrides (London: Routledge & Kegan Paul, 1983). Selected commentary up to 1936.

George Herbert Journal, ed. Sidney Gottlieb, 1978–. See for current articles and reviews.

A Concordance to the Complete Writings of George Herbert, ed. Mario A. Di Cesare and Rigo Mignani (Ithaca, NY, and London: Cornell University Press, 1977).

Biographies

Charles, Amy M., *A Life of George Herbert* (Ithaca, NY, and London: Cornell University Press, 1977).

Walton, Isaak, *The Life of Mr. George Herbert* (1670), in Walton, *Lives*, World's Classics edn. (London: Oxford University Press, 1927). For the quality of Walton's *Life* see David Novarr, *The Making of Walton's Lives* (Ithaca, NY: Cornell University Press, 1958).

Studies

Asals, Heather A. R., *Equivocal Predication: George Herbert's Way to God* (University of Toronto Press, 1981).

Benet, Diana, *Secretary of Praise: The Poetic Vocation of George Herbert* (University of Missouri Press, 1984).

Bennett, Joan, *Five Metaphysical Poets* (Cambridge University Press, 1963). Essays on Herbert and Vaughan.

Bloch, Chana, *Spelling the Word: George Herbert and the Bible* (University of California Press, 1985).

Bottrall, Margaret, *George Herbert* (London: John Murray, 1954).

Clark, Ira, *Christ Revealed: The History of the Neotypological Lyric in the English Renaissance* (University Presses of Florida, 1982).

Colie, Rosalie L., *Paradoxia Epidemica: The Renaissance Tradition of Paradox* (Princeton University Press, 1966). See esp. chapter 6.

Denonain, Jean-Jacques, *Thèmes et formes de la poésie 'métaphysique'* (Paris: Presses universitaires, 1956).

Edgecombe, Rodney, *'Sweetnesse Readie Penn'd': Imagery, Syntax and Metrics in the Poetry of George Herbert* (Salzburg: Institut, 1980).

Eliot, T. S., *George Herbert*, Writers and their Work, no. 152 (London: Longmans, 1962). Also 'What is Minor Poetry?', in *On Poetry and Poets* (London: Faber & Faber; New York: Farrar, Straus & Giroux, 1957).

Ellrodt, Robert, *L'Inspiration personnelle et l'esprit du temps chez les poètes métaphysiques anglais*, 3 vols. (Paris: José Corti, 1960).

Festugière, A. J., *George Herbert, poète, saint, anglican* (Paris: J. Vrin, 1971).

Fish, Stanley, *The Living Temple. George Herbert and Catechizing* (University of California Press, 1978). Also chapter 3 in *Self-Consuming Artifacts* (University of California Press, 1972).

Freeman, Rosemary, *English Emblem Books* (London: Chatto & Windus, 1948). See chapter 6.

Freer, Coburn, *Music for a King: George Herbert's Style and the Metrical Psalms* (Baltimore and London: Johns Hopkins University Press, 1972).

Gardner, Dame Helen, Introduction to *The Poems of George Herbert*, World's Classics edn. (London: Oxford University Press, 1961). Also *Religion and Literature* (New York: Oxford University Press, 1971).

Grant, Patrick, *The Transformation of Sin: Studies in Donne, Herbert, Vaughan, and Traherne* (Montreal and London: McGill–Queen's University Press; University of Mass. Press, 1974).

Halewood, William H., *The Poetry of Grace: Reformation Themes and Structures in English Seventeenth-Century Poetry* (New Haven and London: Yale University Press, 1970).

Harman, Barbara Leah, *Costly Monuments: Representations of the Self in George Herbert's Poetry* (Cambridge, Mass., and London: Harvard University Press, 1982).

Hunter, Jeanne Clayton, '"With Winges of Faith": Herbert's Communion Poems', *Journal of Religion*, lxii (1982), 57–71.

Knights, L. C., 'George Herbert', in *Explorations* (London: Chatto & Windus, 1946).

Leishman, J. B., *The Metaphysical Poets* (Oxford: Clarendon Press, 1934).

Lewalski, Barbara Kiefer, *Protestant Poetics and the Seventeenth-Century Religious Lyric* (Princeton University Press, 1979). See esp. chapter 9 for Herbert, and chapter 10 for Vaughan.

Low, Anthony, *Love's Architecture: Devotional Modes in Seventeenth-Century English Poetry* (New York University Press, 1978). See esp. chapter 4 for Herbert, and chapter 6 for Vaughan.

Mahood, M. M., *Poetry and Humanism* (New Haven: Yale University Press, 1950). See chapter 2 for Herbert, chapter 8 for Vaughan. Also 'Something Understood: The Nature of Herbert's Wit', in *Metaphysical Poetry*, ed. Malcolm Bradbury and David Palmer, Stratford-upon-Avon Studies no. 11 (London: Edward Arnold, 1970).

Manley, Frank, 'Toward a Definition of Plain Style in the Poetry of George Herbert', in *Poetic Traditions of the English Renaissance*, ed. Maynard Mack and George deForest Lord (New Haven and London: Yale University Press, 1982).

Marcus, Leah Sinanoglu, *Childhood and Cultural Despair: A Theme and Variations in Seventeenth-Century Literature* (University of Pittsburgh Press, 1978). See esp. chapters 3 and 4 for Herbert and Vaughan.

Martz, Louis L., *The Poetry of Meditation* (New Haven: Yale University Press, 1954; second edn. with new preface and revised conclusion, 1962). See esp. chapters 7 and 8 for Herbert. Also comments on Herbert and Vaughan in 'The Action of the Self', *Metaphysical Poetry*, ed. Bradbury and Palmer (above, under Mahood).

Miller, Edmund, *Drudgerie Divine: The Rhetoric of God and Man in George Herbert* (Salzburg: Institut, 1979).

Miner, Earl, *The Metaphysical Mode from Donne to Cowley* (Princeton University Press, 1969).

Mulder, John R., *The Temple of the Mind: Education and Literary Taste in Seventeenth-Century England* (New York: Pegasus, 1969).

Nuttall, A. D., *Overheard by God: Fiction and Prayer in Herbert, Milton, Dante and St. John* (London and New York: Methuen, 1980).

Rickey, Mary Ellen, *Utmost Art: Complexity in the Verse of George Herbert* (University of Kentucky Press, 1966).

Ross, Malcolm Mackenzie, *Poetry and Dogma: The Transfiguration of Eucharistic Symbols in Seventeenth-Century English Poetry* (New Brunswick, NJ: Rutgers University Press, 1954). See chapters 6 and 7.

Seelig, Sharon Cadman, *The Shadow of Eternity: Belief and Structure in Herbert, Vaughan and Traherne* (University Press of Kentucky, 1981).

Shaw, Robert B., *The Call of God: The Theme of Vocation in the Poetry of Donne and Herbert* (Cambridge, Mass.: Cowley Publications, 1981).

Sherwood, Terry G., 'Tasting and Telling Sweetness in George Herbert's Poetry', *English Literary Renaissance*, xii (1982), 319–40.

Slights, Camille Wells, *The Casuistical Tradition in Shakespeare, Donne, Herbert, and Milton* (Princeton University Press, 1981).

Stein, Arnold, *George Herbert's Lyrics* (Baltimore: The Johns Hopkins Press, 1968).

Stewart, Stanley, *The Enclosed Garden: The Tradition and the Image in Seventeenth-Century Poetry* (University of Wisconsin Press, 1966). Also 'Herbert and the "Harmonies" of Little Gidding', *Cithara*, xxiv (1984), 3–26.

Strier, Richard, *Love Known: Theology and Experience in George Herbert's Poetry* (University of Chicago Press, 1983).

Summers, Claude J., and Pebworth, Ted-Larry, eds., *'Too Rich to Clothe the Sunne': Essays on George Herbert* (University of Pittsburgh Press, 1980).

Summers, Joseph H., *George Herbert: His Religion and Art* (London: Chatto & Windus; Cambridge, Mass.: Harvard University Press, 1954; reprinted Binghampton, NY: Medieval & Renaissance Texts & Studies, 1981). See also chapter 3 in Summers, *The Heirs of Donne and Jonson* (New York and London: Oxford University Press, 1970).

Taylor, Mark, *The Soul in Paraphrase: George Herbert's Poetics* (The Hague and Paris: Mouton, 1974).

Sister Thekla, *George Herbert, Idea and Image: A Study of The Temple* (The Greek Orthodox Monastery of the Assumption, Filgrave, Newport Pagnell [now Normanby, Whitby], 1974).

Tuve, Rosemond, *A Reading of George Herbert* (University of Chicago Press; London: Faber & Faber, 1952). Also 'George Herbert and *Caritas*' and 'Sacred "Parody" of Love Poetry', in *Essays by Rosemond Tuve*, ed. Thomas P. Roche, Jr. (Princeton University Press, 1970).

Van Wengen-Shute, Rosemary Margaret, *George Herbert and the Liturgy of the Church of England* (University of Leiden, 1981).

Vendler, Helen, *The Poetry of George Herbert* (Cambridge, Mass., and London: Harvard University Press, 1975).

Warnke, Frank J., *Versions of the Baroque* (New Haven and London: Yale University Press, 1972).

Warren, Austin, *Rage for Order: Essays in Criticism* (University of Chicago Press, 1948). Contains an essay on Herbert.

White, Helen C., *The Metaphysical Poets: A Study in Religious Experience* (New York: Macmillan, 1936). See chapters 6 and 7 for Herbert, chapters 10 and 11 for Vaughan.

HENRY VAUGHAN

Editions

The Works of Henry Vaughan, ed. with commentary by L. C. Martin, second edn., revised and enlarged (Oxford: Clarendon Press, 1957). (First edn., 2 vols., 1914.).

The Complete Poetry of Henry Vaughan, ed. with notes by French Fogle (New York: Doubleday, 1964).

Henry Vaughan: The Complete Poems, ed. with notes by Alan Rudrum. (Harmondsworth: Penguin Books, 1976; New Haven: Yale University Press, 1981).

The Secular Poems of Henry Vaughan, ed. with notes and commentary by E. L. Marilla (Uppsala: Lundequistka Bokhandeln, 1958).

The Works of Thomas Vaughan, ed. with introduction and commentary by Alan Rudrum, with the assistance of Jennifer Drake-Brockman (Oxford: Clarendon Press, 1984).

Guides to Study

Bourdette, Robert E., Jr., 'Recent Studies in Henry Vaughan', *English Literary Renaissance*, iv (1974), 299–310.

Tuttle, Imilda, *Concordance to Vaughan's Silex Scintillans* (Pennsylvania State University Press, 1969).

Biography

Hutchinson, F. E., *Henry Vaughan: A Life and Interpretation* (Oxford: Clarendon Press, 1947).

Studies

Bethell, S. L., *The Cultural Revolution of the Seventeenth Century* (London: Dobson, 1951). Includes an essay on Vaughan.

Calhoun, Thomas O., *Henry Vaughan: The Achievement of Silex Scintillans* (University of Delaware Press; London: Associated University Presses, 1981).

Durr, R. A., *On the Mystical Poetry of Henry Vaughan* (Cambridge, Mass.: Harvard University Press, 1962).

Friedenreich, Kenneth, *Henry Vaughan* (Boston: Twayne, 1978).

Garner, Ross, *Henry Vaughan: Experience and the Tradition* (University of Chicago Press, 1959). Also *The Unprofitable Servant in Henry Vaughan*, University of Nebraska Studies, new series, no. 29 (1963).

Hammond, Gerald, 'Henry Vaughan's Verbal Subtlety: Word-play in *Silex Scintillans*', *Modern Language Review*, lxxix (1984), 526–40.

Holmes, Elizabeth, *Henry Vaughan and the Hermetic Philosophy* (Oxford: Blackwell, 1932).

Martz, Louis L., *The Paradise Within: Studies in Vaughan, Traherne, and Milton* (New Haven and London: Yale University Press, 1964).

Pettet, E. C., *Of Paradise and Light: A Study of Vaughan's Silex Scintillans* (Cambridge University Press, 1960).

Post, Jonathan F. S., *Henry Vaughan: The Unfolding Vision* (Princeton University Press, 1982).

Post, Jonathan F. S., ed., 'Special Issue on Henry Vaughan', *George Herbert Journal*, vii, numbers 1 and 2 (1983–4).

Simmonds, James D., *Masques of God: Form and Theme in the Poetry of Henry Vaughan* (University of Pittsburgh Press, 1972). (Studies of Vaughan are also contained in many of the books listed above under Herbert.).

SELECTIVE GLOSSARY

(Words that occur frequently with meanings that differ from modern use.)

affect, aim at, seek to obtain; have liking for, be fond of.

affection, emotion or feeling; inclination, disposition towards.

brave *adj.*, with regard to dress or appearance: splendid, grand, fine, handsome; showy; more loosely, a general term expressing admiration.

centre, the earth.

commerce, relationship, interchange.

conceit, conception, thought, idea; clever turn of thought.

conversation, relationship in human society; behaviour in regard to others.

cordial, 'A medicine, food, or beverage which invigorates the heart and stimulates the circulation; a comforting or exhilarating drink' (*OED*).

cordial *adj.*, restorative, reviving.

cross *adj.*, contrary.

curious, of persons: particular, with high standards of excellence; also, ingenious, expert, skilful. Of things: 'Made with care or art; skilfully, elaborately, or beautifully wrought' (*OED*); exquisite, fine.

dress *vb.*, make ready, prepare, set in order; 'to treat or prepare (things) in some way proper to their nature or character' (*OED*).

expect, await.

fain *adj.*, glad; content under the circumstances; necessitated.

fain *adv.*, gladly, willingly.

frame *vb.*, construct, make, form, compose.

frame *n.*, construction, system, order (often applied to universe and to human body).

grief, bodily injury, physical suffering.

humour, 'one of the four chief fluids of the body (blood, phlegm, choler, and melancholy or black choler), by the relative proportions of which a person's physical and mental qualities and disposition were held to be determined' (*OED*).

kind *adj.*, akin to; also, 'having the natural (good) qualities well developed' (*OED*).

list *vb.*, wish, desire, choose.

meat, food in general.

mind *vb.*, intend, aim at, direct one's attention to; remember.

mirth, joy, happiness; something that gives pleasure.

motion, impulse, inclination; an emotion.

parcel *vb.*, divide, separate.

parcel *n.*, part, piece.

physic, medicine.

presently, immediately.

pretence, the act of putting forward.

pretend, put forward (a claim, assertion, or purpose).

prevent, come before, act before, anticipate.

quaint, ingeniously designed.

quick, living, lively, vital.

sad, serious.

score *n.*, innkeeper's bill; debt due to a tradesman.

several, separate, distinct.

still, constantly, always.

store *n.*, abundance.

straight, immediately (straightaway).

sweet, fragrant, melodious, delightful, beloved, pure (see notes on Herbert's *Church-music* and *Virtue*, pp. 448, 452–3).

tell, count.

temper *n.*, disposition, temperament (see note on Herbert's *The Temper* (I), p. 446).

turtle, turtle-dove.

virtue, 'a particular power, efficacy, or good quality inherent in, or pertaining to, something' (*OED*); e.g. in herbs, medicines, sacraments.

want *vb.*, lack.

weed *n.*, garment (usually plural, **weeds**).

wink *vb.*, close the eyes.

wit, mental capacity, intellect; sometimes, superior intellectual ability, remarkable quickness and liveliness of mind.

INDEX OF TITLES AND FIRST LINES

GEORGE HERBERT

HENRY VAUGHAN